INTERNATIONAL FINANCIAL MARKETS

INTERNATIONAL FINANCIAL MARKETS

J. Orlin Grabbe
The Wharton School of the University of Pennsylvania

Elsevier
New York · Amsterdam · London

Cover photograph courtesy of Salomon Brothers.

Elsevier Science Publishing Co., Inc.
52 Vanderbilt Avenue, New York, New York 10017

Sole distributors outside the United States and Canada:

Elsevier Science Publishers B.V.
P.O. Box 211, 1000 AE Amsterdam, The Netherlands

Library of Congress Cataloging in Publication Data

Grabbe, J. Orlin.
   International financial markets.

   Bibliography: p.
   Includes index.
   1. Foreign exchange. 2. Euro-bond market. 3. Euro-dollar
market. 4. Currency question—Europe. 5. International
finance. I. Title.
HG3851.G64 1986   332.4'5   85-32545
ISBN 0-444-01032-7

Current printing (last digit):
10 9 8 7 6 5 4

Manufactured in the United States of America

CONTENTS

PREFACE

This book, an introduction to international financial markets for students in an MBA program, should also be of interest to undergraduates and could serve as supplementary reading in doctoral courses. The subject matter—the international financial markets for foreign exchange, eurocurrencies, and international bonds—is a neglected topic. Standard economics courses, although labeled "international finance," are really courses in open-economy macroeconomics whose principal focus is optimal monetary and fiscal policy in an open economy. These courses seem to imply that government policy is the major issue of importance in international finance, a point of view that may not be convincing to someone envisioning a career in investment or commercial banking or international trade and investment. In addition, in these courses financial markets are often so stylized that an average student with a practical orientation may be tempted into mental segmentation: he or she comes to believe that there is economic theory and there is the real world, and never shall the twain meet. My own point of view is that optimal monetary and fiscal policy is appropriate subject matter for the standard *macroeconomics* course but does not need to be covered twice. There are no open and closed economies—only open and closed economists. If the macroeconomics instructor has never heard of imports, exports, or foreign exchange, that problem should be remedied at the source.

Many descriptive institutional accounts of the international financial markets are also available, but these sometimes suffer from too much institutional detail and not enough theory. The beginning student needs to grasp the basic dynamic structure of a market (which is what theory tries to get at) before he or she can easily stockpile a great many real-world facts. Without a proper organizing framework, the student is in much the same position as those international bureaucrats of the 1960s of whom it was said "They could not see the Bretton Woods for the Bretton trees."

In between these two extremes are standard financial management courses oriented toward multinational corporations or international banking. Such courses discuss international financial markets in connection with other management issues, but their scope is too broad for a proper treatment of financial markets *as markets*. For example, it would be desirable for a student already to have acquired an understanding of the interbank market in foreign exchange, an empirical feel for the nature or magnitude of FX risk, and an understanding of how to hedge with FX forwards, futures, and options before approaching the management question of how an operational FX risk-control system should or should not be organized.

This book attempts to delineate the basic rules of the game in each of the three major international financial markets and to convey to the student an intuitive feel for market dynamics. It is designed to logically precede courses devoted to the individual management issues faced, respectively, by multinational corporations, commercial banks, investment banks, and central banks or finance ministries. The material of this book should thus comprise an introductory course in international finance which can then be followed by standard courses in multinational corporate finance, open-economy macroeconomics, or international banking. The book will not only be of interest to international managers generally but also has immediate relevance for students desiring to participate in such market activities as FX trading, bond syndication, or eurodollar creation.

Since the text is a blend of theory and institutions, some sacrifice of detail in both areas has been necessary, and my guiding principle has been to select that which is of the greatest practical use. Of course, what is of most use is a matter for individual judgment; this book represents mine. For example, while I have included a discussion of risk-return tradeoffs in connection with international capital flows, I have not devoted space to the international capital-asset pricing model because I believe its extreme assumptions preclude its practical usefulness.

The student is assumed to have had, as academic prerequisites, an introductory course in economics (covering both macroeconomics and microeconomics) and an introductory course in statistics. No calculus is used in the text except for the integral of the normal distribution, and technical discussions are conducted at an intuitive level. The level of mathematical treatment varies from topic to topic. This is intentional and is based on value-added considerations. For example, the European Monetary System is treated in detail in Chapter 2 because it is a living institution that exerts a daily influence on European exchange rates. By contrast, no equations are used to describe the Bretton Woods system, which is primarily of historical interest. As another example, the mathematics of option pricing has proved to be of great practical importance, so Chapter 6 is somewhat more technical than other chapters. As an aid to the student, the more technical paragraphs that can be skipped without loss of continuity begin with an open square (□) and end with a solid square (■).

Most of the material in this book is based on multiple sources, with some of the most helpful published references listed in the bibliography. In addition, I am grateful for useful information provided by individuals at the following institutions: Bankers Trust Company; Chemical Bank; Credit Lyonnais; Drexel, Burnham, Lambert; European Inter-American Finance (Eurinam); Euroclear Clearance System, Ltd.; the Federal Reserve Board; Goldman Sachs; the International Monetary Fund; the International Money Market of the Chicago Mercantile Exchange; Irving Trust Co.; Merrill Lynch; the Ministry of Finance of Japan; the Ministry of Finance of Mexico; Morgan Guaranty Trust Co.; the Philadelphia Stock Exchange; Salomon Brothers; and the World Bank.

READER'S INTRODUCTION

International finance exists because individual sovereign states exist. Without different states that have different currencies and different policies governing financial assets denominated in those currencies there would only be domestic finance. For the immediate future, however, there seems little danger that the division of the world into domestic and foreign, Greek and barbarian, will disappear.

This book is concerned with the three major international financial markets — the foreign exchange market, the eurocurrency market, and the international bond market — and is oriented to those who may wish to participate in these markets. For market participants, the existence of diverse policy regimes is a fact of nature; devoting excessive amounts of time to the question of why different countries have different policies is comparable to extended preoccupation with the question of why different consumers have different tastes or why different investors have different risk preferences. The focus of attention here is thus on market action in an environment of which government is a part, an approach different from the widespread one that takes market behavior as given and concentrates on the manipulation of markets through government policy.

The foreign exchange, eurocurrency, and international bond markets are each treated in four aspects: historical, institutional, economic, and empirical. Each type of information has its place in understanding the operation of international financial markets. The existence of institutions such as the International Monetary Fund or currency arrangements like the European Monetary System is most easily understood in a historical context. While institutional features (what FX traders do, how eurobonds are cleared in the secondary market, where eurobanks are located) will change over time, they are not nearly so arbitrary as often thought, and at any rate represent the machine through which the ghost of theory operates. Clarification of the underlying economic principles governing international finance is the heart of this book and the basis on which it is organized. I have focused on the conceptual insights of theory as applied to markets — and avoided the methodological debates with which the academic literature is preoccupied — on the assumption that most readers are interested in achieving professional success in a market rather than an academic environment. An acquaintance with some empirical evidence—about purchasing-power parity, or transactions costs in the international bond market, or the performance of FX forecasters—is also important for understanding international financial markets.

Since the historical material is easier to grasp when told as a continuous story, it is collected and presented chronologically in Part I. Part I also serves as a general introduction to and overview of the rest of the book and should not, under any circumstances, be omitted. Chapter 1 covers the background of the Bretton Woods agreement, the rise of the eurocurrency markets, the gold politics of the 1960s, and the breakdown of Bretton Woods at the beginning of the 1970s. Chapter 2 looks at successor currency arrangements (including the European Monetary System), the background of the debt crisis, and the arrival of Japan on the international financial stage. In addition to illustrating the interaction between economics and politics, Part I also introduces a number of basic economic concepts in historical context. Chapter 1, for example, examines the effects of central bank intervention in the FX and gold markets, explains what eurocurrencies are, and illustrates the policy requirements of a fixed exchange rate system.

Part II covers the basic forms of foreign exchange contracts: spot, forward, futures, and option. Chapter 3 introduces the concept of the market-maker, surveys interbank currency trading in a free market, and looks at the effects of exchange controls. Chapter 4 explains forward and swap FX contracts and their relation to eurocurrency interest rates through the interest parity theorem. Chapter 5 looks at organized currency futures trading, compares futures and forward contracts, and explains futures hedging. Chapter 6 explains what FX option contracts are, how they may be used as FX insurance, and how to price them in relation to other financial assets.

After finishing Parts I and II, the reader may proceed directly to any one of Parts III, IV, or V, since these three sections are essentially independent of one another. The chapters within a part should, however, be read in the order presented.

Part III builds a framework for understanding why exchange rates change and how such changes relate to economic decision-making. Chapter 7 looks at foreign currency speculation in terms of a trader's expectations and information. Chapter 8 examines commodity arbitrage in international markets and examines the requirements for different versions of purchasing power parity to hold. Chapter 9 relates FX determination to a broader spectrum of economic forces, including not only trade in commodities but also consumption and savings and central bank intervention. It explains the basic structure of a "balance of payments" flow of funds statement and looks at some empirical evidence pertaining to central bank informational superiority. Chapter 10 interprets FX forecasting as the formal process of generating expectations and looks at the empirical evidence on forecasting performance in light of the Model Theorem introduced in Chapter 7. Chapter 11 then looks at risk-return tradeoffs in a portfolio context, given forecast-generated expectations and the associated uncertainty.

Part IV is devoted to the eurocurrency market. Chapter 12 describes the market in terms of the major features of a typical eurobank balance sheet and gives some additional material relevant to particular eurobanking centers. Chapter 13 covers the formation of eurocredit syndicates and relates the typical features of loan contracts to the economic risks involved in lending. The interbank market is the focus of Chapter 14. It points out the risks of maturity transformation, relates the term structure of eurocurrency interest rates to interest-rate expectations, and explains the use of eurodollar futures in hedging and arbitrage. Chapter 15 looks at the relation of eurobanks to the domestic banking system and analyzes the factors that determine the eurodollar market's size and growth.

The international bond markets are the subject of Part V. Chapter 16 distinguishes between the eurobond and foreign bond markets and describes the major features of the leading markets. Procedures followed by investment banks in bringing a new eurobond issue to market are explained in Chapter 17. Chapter 18 considers secondary eurobond trading and clearing, the valuation of eurobonds in relation to other assets, and eurobond futures. Interest rate and currency swaps often involve long-term debt contracts, so it was natural to include them in Part V as Chapter 19. Chapter 20 extends the analysis of Chapter 6 in that it examines the appearance of option features in international bond contracts.

Paragraphs set off by open (□) and solid (■) squares are fairly technical and may be skipped on the first reading without loss of continuity.

Numerical examples are dispersed throughout the book. Readers should make certain they understand each example as it is encountered before proceeding with the text. In most cases, this will involve working through the steps with pencil and paper. Further numerical problems are provided at the ends of chapters.

Readers are also encouraged to supplement the text with a steady diet of current news relating to international finance. Some useful sources in this regard include the daily newspapers *The Wall Street Journal* and the London *Financial Times,* the weekly newsmagazine *The Economist,* the monthly publications *Euromoney* and Morgan Guaranty's *World Financial Markets,* and the *Annual Report* of the Bank for International Settlements.

J. Orlin Grabbe

HISTORY OF THE INTERNATIONAL FINANCIAL SYSTEM, 1944-1984

1

THE RISE
AND FALL OF
BRETTON WOODS

BRETTON WOODS

The end of the Second World War can be taken as year zero for the current system of international finance. There wasn't much in the way of foreign exchange or international bond trading in 1945 and another decade would pass before eurocurrency markets were created. The depression of the 1930s, followed by the war, had vastly diminished commercial trade, the international exchange of currencies, and cross-border lending and borrowing. Left were only memories of what the system had once been, along with competing visions of what could and should be resurrected from the rubble. Revival, it was generally agreed, entailed new institutions and political agreements. Certainly not much thought was given to the enormous progress in information technology and telecommunications that had come about during the war and would later have a profound impact on international financial practice.

Reconstruction of the postwar financial system began with the Bretton Woods Agreement that emerged from the International Monetary and Financial Conference of the United and Associated Nations in July 1944 at Bretton Woods, New Hampshire. Bretton Woods is a tiny ski village in the White Mountains whose notable features are the world's longest cog railway and the mammoth Mount Washington Resort Hotel—which, situated at the foot of the Presidential range, is an ideal setting for a conference. The 1944 agreement, setting out the major parameters of the postwar system, represented an unusual degree of advance planning. The establishment of a beachhead on Normandy by Allied forces under General Dwight Eisenhower had taken place only the month before, and even the outcome of the war with Germany could not yet be predicted with total certainty.

But there was a deep-rooted reason for the timing of the Bretton Woods debate about postwar finances. Many at the conference were convinced that, by making advance preparations for the peace, they could avoid the mistakes associated with the aftermath of the "Great War" of 1914–1919. They had concluded that the primary reason they were at war—once again with Germany—was that, although the Allies had won the earlier war, they had mismanaged the peace. This mismanagement, they felt, had come about as a result of squabbling among the great powers, who had yielded to the political sentiments of the moment and had shown a lack of foresight in the economic provisions of the peace negotiations of 1919. Bretton Woods was part of an attempt to avoid a repetition of the same mistakes when the war with Hitler was over.

American and British rivalry was another factor that underlay the early planning. Although forty-four nations signed the Bretton Woods agreement, it was primarily the United States and Great Britain who negotiated the terms, each intent on persuading everyone else to adopt its particular vision of postwar monetary arrangements. The two principal individuals involved in the negotiations were Harry Dexter White, representing the United States, and John Maynard Keynes, representing Great Britain.

The chain of events leading to Bretton Woods had started in 1940. German propaganda broadcasts were describing a "New Order," the National Socialist vision of how the world would be organized financially and economically in the future, under German leadership. Such propaganda can be effective in two senses. By being first to propose a plan you get people thinking your way: you structure the debate. Second, such a plan implied Germany was so sure of winning the war that it could get on with planning the next stage. Such confidence invited neutral third parties to join a winning team. In November 1940, the British Ministry of Information asked John Maynard Keynes, the noted British economist, to prepare counterpropaganda broadcasts, which required Keynes to give some thought to financial organization after the war. Aside from the propaganda needs of the moment (Winston Churchill said that "in wartime, truth is so precious that she should always be attended by a bodyguard of lies"), both Keynes and British government officials were determined that, whatever plans were made, they could not afford to repeat the miscalculations associated with the Treaty of Versailles that had ended World War I.

In fact, Keynes had first become famous in 1919 with his international bestseller *The Economic Consequences of the Peace.* The official representative of the British Empire to the Supreme Economic Council that set out the terms of German reparations, Keynes had resigned in protest and had written a book explaining why. He had argued that the primary policy objective of the Allies should be the stabilization of central Europe, not the imposition of unpayable reparations on Germany. Europe was in a dangerously chaotic political condition following the collapse of the Austro-Hungarian Empire, he had said, and the terms of the Versailles treaty would aggravate the situation and play into the hands of extreme elements.

In warfare, the spoils traditionally go to the victor. The modern interpretation of this principle meant that the loser in the war reimbursed the victor for costs associated with conducting the war. This reimbursement was referred to as *reparations.* Germany had exacted reparations from France after the Franco-Prussian War of 1870–1871, for example. And in Article 231 of the Treaty of Versailles (signed on June 28, 1919) Germany and its allies were named the aggressors in the recent war and were held responsible for all loss and damage suffered by the Allies. But it seemed obvious, at least to Keynes, that the degree of international interdependence had now increased to the point that it was no longer necessarily in one's own self-interest to demand from the loser payment in gold and goods. He sounded the ominous warning that the "Carthaginian peace is not *practically* right or possible. . . . You cannot restore Central Europe to 1870 without setting up such strains in the European structure and letting loose human and spiritual forces as . . . will overwhelm not only you and your 'guarantees,' but your institutions and the existing order of your society."

Whether for the reasons Keynes set out or for others, events did not follow the course anticipated by most members of the Versailles Peace Conference in 1919, and by 1940 officials in both the British and the U.S. treasuries viewed Versailles as an administrative disaster. The treaty had been followed in Germany by the hyperinflation of 1920–1923 that had effectively undermined the power of the German middle class, with its moderating political influence, by destroying the real value of middle-class savings—which had been generally kept in the form of financial assets. The extent of the inflation can be seen in the exchange value of the mark, which was about 14 per U.S. dollar at the end of the war in 1919. When the inflation ended on November 20, 1923, the exchange rate was 4 *trillion* marks per U.S. dollar. (That same day the president of the Reichsbank—the German central bank—died of a heart attack, raising an interesting question of cause and effect.) Hitler's famous Munich beer-hall putsch occurred in November 1923, at the height of the inflation, and later the National Socialists were able effectively to exploit popular resentment over the terms of the treaty.

In 1941 Keynes was sent to Washington as a representative of Churchill and the Chancellor of the Exchequer to settle the terms of Lend-Lease aid that Britain would receive from the United States. As part of the conditions for receiving the ultimate $30 billion in aid, the British were pressured to commit themselves to postwar arrangements as foreseen by the United States. While not in much of a bargaining position, the British did press for their objectives. They did not want to surrender the reserve currency status of the pound sterling. They took it for granted (as did the United States) that exchange rates should be fixed. In this context, they assumed that Britain would have a persistent tendency to import more from the United States than it exported to the United States and thought that this factor, combined with the British goal of full employment, would require various types of import restrictions, barter arrangements, and capital controls. Keynes, in fact, approved of the methods practiced by Hjalmar Schacht—the German "financial wizard" who had brought about the termination of the German hyperinflation and later served as Hitler's economic minister—which involved economic units directly bartering (trading) one type of good for another without the use of currency.

On the U.S. side, Secretary of the Treasury Henry Morgenthau gave Harry Dexter White the task, in December 1941, of thinking about future international money arrangements. White's views were already on record in an earlier study he had done in 1934 for Jacob Viner at the Treasury. It had stressed the need for fixed exchange rates, international cooperation, and settlement in gold as the basis for the international financial system. White's report to Morgenthau, making similar proposals, formed the basis for the Bretton Woods agreement. The White report also proposed an Inter-Allied (later a United Nations) Stabilization Fund to stabilize exchange rates and remove exchange controls and an Inter-Allied (later United Nations) Bank to provide capital for economic reconstruction. These two proposals came to fruition as the present-day International Monetary

Fund (IMF) and the International Bank for Reconstruction and Development (World Bank).

The views of other U.S. officials were also important in setting the tone of the Bretton Woods negotiations. Secretary of State Cordell Hull believed that the fundamental causes of the two world wars lay in economic discrimination and trade warfare. Specifically he had in mind the trade and exchange controls (bilateral arrangements) of Nazi Germany and the imperial preference system practiced by Britain (by which members or former members of the British Empire were accorded special trade status). An internal State Department paper in 1939 had even proposed a trade agreement with Germany as a way to avoid war. Overall, the Americans wanted a postwar system in which trade could expand. William Clayton, the assistant secretary of state for economic affairs, said: "We need markets—big markets—around the world in which to buy and sell." The free trade concerns would finally lead in 1947 to the General Agreement on Trade and Tariffs (GATT), by which member nations would generally agree to accord no special trade status to any one member that was not accorded to all. The concern over exchange controls was incorporated in the articles of agreement of the International Monetary Fund. Members were pledged to work for the removal of all such controls.

In the State Department the view prevailed that the United States should remove itself from its historical isolation and play a leading role in a new world order in which it was thought power politics would be absent. According to Harry Dexter White, "it was expected that the early post-war world would witness a degree of unity and good-will in international political relationships among the victorious allies [including Russia] never before reached in peacetime. It was expected that the world would move rapidly . . . toward 'One World.' . . . No influential person, as far as I can remember, expressed the expectation or the fear that international relations would worsen during those years." International institutions like the International Monetary Fund and the World Bank, with willing U.S. participation, were a step in the direction of this one, united world.

Finally, a strong antibanking perspective led Secretary of the Treasury Morgenthau to throw his support to the new international financial institutions. At the Bretton Woods conference he predicted that the establishment of the IMF and the World Bank would "drive the usurious money lenders from the temple of international finance." Morgenthau's view contrasted with U.S. private-sector sentiment, which was not greatly exercised over usurious moneylenders but rather saw the proposed institutions as a covert scheme to subsidize debtor nations.

The main points of the Bretton Woods agreement that are important for our purposes, those regarding the establishment of the International Monetary Fund, can be summarized as follows:

1. A new institution, The International Monetary Fund (IMF), would be established in Washington, D.C. Its purpose would be to lend foreign exchange to any member whose supply of foreign exchange had become scarce. This lending would not be automatic, but would be conditional on the member's pursuit of economic policies consistent with the other points of the agreement, a determination that would be made by the IMF.

2. The U.S. dollar and the British pound would be designated as reserve currencies, and other nations would maintain their foreign exchange reserves principally in the form of dollars or pounds.

3. Each Fund member would establish a *par value* for its currency, and maintain the exchange rate for its currency within *1 percent* of par value. In practice, since the principal reserve currency would be the U.S. dollar, this meant that other countries would peg their currencies to the U.S. dollar, and — once convertibility was restored — would buy and sell U.S. dollars to keep market exchange rates within the 1-percent band around par value. The United States, meanwhile, separately agreed to buy gold from or sell gold to foreign official monetary authorities at $35 per ounce in settlement of international financial transactions. The U.S. dollar was thus pegged to gold, and any other currency pegged to the dollar was indirectly pegged to gold at a price determined by its par value.

4. A fund member could change its par value only with Fund approval and only if the country's balance of payments was in "fundamental disequilibrium." The meaning of fundamental disequilibrium was left unspecified, but everyone understood that par value changes were not to be used as a matter of course to adjust economic imbalances.

5. After a postwar transition period, currencies were to become convertible. That is, they could be freely bought and sold for other foreign currencies. Restrictions were to be removed, and hopefully eliminated. This meant that, in order to keep market exchange rates within 1 percent of par value, central banks and exchange authorities would have to build up a stock of dollar reserves with which to intervene in the foreign exchange market.

6. The Fund would get gold and currencies to lend through "subscription." That is, countries would have to make a payment (subscription) of gold and currency to the IMF in order to become a member. Subscription quotas were assigned according to a member's size and resources. Payment of the quota normally was 25 percent in gold and 75 percent in the member's own currency. Those with bigger quotas had to pay more but also got more voting rights regarding Fund decisions.

FIXING THE PRICE OF FOREIGN EXCHANGE AND GOLD

The Bretton Woods agreement committed member countries to peg exchange rates — or rather to keep them within a plus or minus 1 percent margin around a declared par value. What does it mean to fix the price (the exchange value) of something? If no trading other than with official authorities is allowed (as where a currency is "inconvertible"), then fixing the price is easy. The central bank or exchange authority simply says the price is S, say S = 4 German marks per 1 U.S. dollar, and no one can say differently. If you want to trade German marks for dollars, you have to deal with the central bank, and you have to trade at central bank prices. The central bank may in fact even refuse to trade with you, but it can still claim that the exchange rate is fixed. If, however, free trade is allowed, fixing the price requires a great deal more. The price can be fixed only by altering either the supply of or the demand for the asset. For example, if you wanted to fix the price of gold at $35 per ounce, you could only do so by being willing and able to supply unlimited amounts of gold to the market to drive the price back down to

$35 per ounce whenever there would otherwise be excess demand at that price, or to purchase unlimited amounts of gold from the market to drive the price back up to $35 per ounce whenever there would otherwise be excess supply at that price.

In order to peg the price of gold you would thus need two things: a large stock of gold to supply to the market whenever there is a tendency for the market price of gold to go up, and a large stock of dollars with which to purchase gold whenever there is a tendency for the market price of gold to go down. The same is true if the central bank wants to peg the exchange value of the domestic currency with respect to a foreign currency. If the German central bank wants to peg the exchange rate at DM 4 = U.S. $1, it has to have a stock of deutschemarks and a stock of dollars. The deutschemarks are no problem—the central bank can always create more of them at will. But dollars are a problem to the German central bank. If there is excess demand for dollars, perhaps because at the pegged exchange rate dollars are too cheap (the central bank is selling them for 4 DM when it should be selling them for, say, 5 DM), the central bank may run out of dollars and will no longer be able to maintain the peg. Dollars in this case are the German central bank's reserves, so we may summarize by saying: *if the central bank or exchange authority sets an exchange rate that undervalues foreign currency—that is, overvalues domestic currency—the central bank will lose reserves. Conversely, if the pegged rate undervalues domestic currency and over-values foreign currency, the central bank will gain reserves.*

If a central bank is *losing* reserves, there is an excess demand for foreign currency (an excess supply of domestic currency) at the rate at which the central bank is pegging. In this case, the country is said to be running a *balance of payments deficit.* If a central bank (or exchange authority) is *gaining* reserves, there is an excess supply of foreign currency (an excess demand for domestic currency) at the rate at which the central bank is pegging. In the second case, the country is said to be running a *balance of payments surplus.*

We will explore the concept of balance of payments in Chapter 9. It should be obvious from the preceding paragraph, however, that if the central bank is not pegging or otherwise making any attempt to influence the market value of its currency, it will not have either a surplus or deficit on the balance of payments except as an accounting artifice. This qualification is used because creative accountants can always jerry-rig a "deficit" or a "surplus" by calculating the balance in an arbitrary way. Such engineered deficits or surpluses may have no importance, however, except as political entertainment.

As an additional part of the Bretton Woods agreement, the United States committed itself to trade gold with foreign officials at a fixed price of $35 per ounce. In a sense, this was a commitment to peg the market price of gold, because if the private market price of gold differed from the official price—if, for example, the private market price were $37 per ounce—a foreign central bank would have an incentive to buy from the United States at $35 per ounce and sell on the private market at $37 per ounce. So the U.S. commitment meant that the United States needed, in principle, a large stock of gold to sell whenever the private market price rose above $35. Gold the United States had aplenty: by war's end in 1945 the United States had about 60 percent of the total world stock.

The U.S. commitment to peg the price of gold had other implications. Suppose that gold would always at any time trade for the same amount of other real goods — wheat, steel, bananas. In such a situation, the price of gold would be synonymous with *purchasing power*. You could always trade an ounce of gold for a predetermined bundle of other commodities. The U.S. commitment to buy and sell gold for $35 per ounce would then mean that the purchasing power of the dollar would have to be maintained at a constant level; there could be no inflation in the United States. In addition, if other countries did not alter the par value of their currencies in terms of the U.S. dollar, their currencies would also have fixed purchasing power, and there could be no inflation in these countries either.

It will, of course, not work exactly that way in practice. The relative price of gold in terms of wheat, steel, and bananas will change over time depending on relative supply and demand in each of those commodity markets. Thus the price of gold will at best only roughly approximate purchasing power. In addition, the 1 percent margins around par value for exchange rates will allow some additional variation in the gold value of other countries' currencies. Finally, in case of "fundamental disequilibrium," a country might be allowed to change its par value from time to time, which would also alter its currency's gold value.

But even when we grant all these modifications, it is still safe to summarize: *the Bretton Woods agreement, if adhered to, precluded sustained inflation on the part of member nations.* The values of other currencies were pegged to the dollar, which was pegged to gold. On the other hand, if the requirement that the dollar be pegged to gold were dropped and only the requirement that the par values of other currencies be maintained with respect to the dollar kept, a different implication would emerge. The implication, without the dollar-gold peg, would be that the United States and other countries would in the long run have to have the same rate of inflation or deflation. (For further details see Chapter 8.)

THE COLD WAR, THE MARSHALL PLAN, AND EUROPEAN INTEGRATION

The Bretton Woods agreement committed member nations to restore the convertibility of their currencies as soon as possible, and there was no reason free trade in foreign exchange could not have begun immediately. Without government controls or threats of punishment, a foreign exchange market would automatically emerge through the voluntary association of buyers and sellers. (Some trade in foreign exchange would take place anyway, despite controls. Such trading, defined as illegal by the government, is referred to as the black market or parallel market. Parallel markets exist wherever government exchange or other restrictions create a divergence between the market value of a currency and the government's declared official value. Today, for example, parallel markets are widespread throughout Latin America, Eastern Europe, and certain countries of the Middle East.)

Most governments at the end of the war, however, were not inclined to allow free trading in their currencies. If private citizens were allowed free access to foreign exchange, they would use it as they desired. Governments, however, wanted prior access to foreign exchange so they could spend it on what *they* wanted: to import food, to import materials considered essential for reconstruction, to buy military equipment, or to reward companies who politically supported the current regime. In addition, many governments had preconceived ideas of what exchange rates ought to be. Back in 1925 Great Britain had set the exchange rate for the pound sterling at £1 = $4.86, the pre-Great War rate, "so the pound could look the dollar in the face" (meaning that British government officials could look American government officials in the face and pretend that the world of 1925 was not different from the world of 1910.) And, in the new postwar years of the late 1940s, if free trading were allowed in its currency, a government would either have to set a par value that represented market equilibrium or find itself continuously intervening in order to maintain an artificial price.

When governments got around to restoring convertibility as planned under the Bretton Woods agreement they would need a supply of dollars with which to do exchange intervention. And that, they felt, was the key missing ingredient: *there was a shortage of dollar reserves with which to intervene in the exchange market.* As Hendrik Houthakker, a later member of the U.S. Council of Economic Advisors, was to say: "You can't play poker unless all the participants have at least some chips." The Cold War would eventually assure European nations enough dollar chips to play the intervention game.

The U.S. Congress had agreed only reluctantly to fund the American contribution to the new IMF, and there was a great deal of skepticism in the private sector concerning an increased international role for the United States. Domestic support for a traditional U.S. isolationist stance began to erode, however, as tensions between the Soviet Union and the other nations allied against Nazi Germany—the United States, Britain, and France—increased following the war. In the United States, the overriding foreign policy concern became that of stopping the spread of communism internationally. An early expression of this policy was the European Recovery Program (Marshall Plan) proposed by Secretary of State Marshall at the Harvard commencement in 1947. The idea was to supply capital to European economies to enable them to rebuild and to become capable military allies of the United States against the Soviet Union. The Organization for European Economic Cooperation (OEEC), later reorganized as the organization for Economic Cooperation and Development (OECD), was set up to administer Marshall Plan aid. The Soviet Union responded by forming an Eastern European equivalent, the Council for Mutual Economic Assistance (COMECON).

The opening rounds of the Cold War arrived in connection with currency reform in occupied Germany. In 1945 the American army had brought with it to Germany occupation reichsmarks printed in the United States. The Soviets had also been given printing plates for the currency, and the millions of reichsmarks printed in Russia were used to extract, in a matter of weeks, several hundred million dollars worth of goods from the American and British occupation zones. The Soviet paper was then declared unacceptable in the Western zones. The payment of troops in reichsmarks was discontinued, and cigarettes became the de facto medium of exchange and store of value in Germany, Lucky Strikes reaching at one point a price of $2300 a carton. Currency reform, planned under the name Operation Bird Dog, involved the replacement of the old reichsmarks with new deutschemarks (DM) printed in Washington at an exchange ratio of 1000 reichsmarks = 65 DM. The new currency would be legal tender in the

Western zones, and its supply would be outside Soviet control. The Soviet Union viewed this as part of an overall American plan to set up a separate West German government that would be ideologically opposed to the Soviets. On the day the new currency was to go into circulation in Berlin's Western zones the Soviet military blockaded the city.

With the Berlin blockade of 1948, the successful communist revolution under Mao Tse-tung in China in 1949, and the outbreak of the Korean War in 1950, the mood of the U.S. Congress and the country changed to one of support for effecting a real financial transfer from the United States to Western Europe.

Initially, foreign trade was carried out in Europe through a set of clearing accounts. Under an arrangement called the European Payments Union, member countries kept track of all their payments deficits and surpluses with other member countries. The monthly net deficit or surplus of a particular country with all other member countries combined was considered a deficit or surplus of the union. At the end of each month, each country settled its net position with respect to the union in terms of U.S. dollars, gold, or credits. Credits were any amounts not settled in dollars or gold and could be accumulated only up to a specified limit. Calculation of the monthly surplus or deficit among countries took place at fixed exchange rates. Thus member countries could maintain the fiction that they were adhering to the Bretton Woods system of par values.

Throughout the 1950s European governments, who never felt they had enough dollar reserves, made frequent reference to a "dollar shortage." In one sense, there actually was not a dollar shortage, since dollars would have always been available at *some* exchange rate, though not necessarily at the rate countries were willing to pay. A better phrase would have been "capital shortage," since capital goods were really the issue. The demand for dollars was equivalent to a demand for imports and raw materials to rebuild the European industrial base. "Hard currencies," such as the U.S. and Canadian dollars, could be spent anywhere in the world for such goods, while (because of exchange controls and other restrictions) so-called soft currencies had to be spent in the country in which they were earned. The reduction of the European capital shortage through Marshall Plan aid made it possible for European nations to build up foreign exchange reserves. While the total amount of Marshall Plan aid constituted only about 4 percent of European gross national product (GNP), it made up about 40 percent of European receipts of hard currency.

In addition to receiving aid, European countries were encouraged by the United States to liberalize trade among themselves. Official support was given to the ideas of individuals like Jean Monnet and Robert Shuman, who wanted to bring about a united Europe and to so integrate the economies of Germany and France that the two countries could never go to war again. "There will be no peace in Europe if States re-establish themselves on the basis of national sovereignty, with all that this implies by way of prestige politics and economic protectionism," Monnet had written in 1943. The European Coal and Steel Community, with Jean Monnet as its head, was formed in 1952, and in 1958 the European Economic Community (abbreviated EEC but frequently referred to as the Common Market) went into operation. The goal of the Common Market was to create a free trade area among member nations with free movement of labor and capital. It also entailed, however, the erection of common tariff barriers

against the rest of the world. The political motivation for this economic organization was emphasized by a president of the EEC commission: "We are not in
business at all; we are in politics."

European nations were officially encouraged by the United States to expand
their exports to the dollar area even while maintaining restrictions on U.S. goods,
and to use part of the earnings to build up dollar exchange reserves. As a consequence, between the end of 1949 and the end of 1959, U.S. liabilities to foreign
monetary authorities rose from $3.1 billion to $10.1 billion. Toward the end of
the 1950s European authorities felt they had enough dollar reserves both to allow
trade in their currencies and to defend their chosen par values, and at the end of
1958 current account convertibility was restored for the major European currencies. Current account convertibility meant that foreign exchange could be
freely bought and sold provided its use was associated with international trade in
goods and services. But there were still restrictions that applied when the intended use of the foreign exchange was to purchase foreign bonds or stock. (Free
trade in currencies for the latter purpose is called capital account convertibility.)
Current acount convertibility for the Japanese yen was not restored until 1964.
(Japan is discussed in Chapter 2.)

Thus, almost fifteen years after the Bretton Woods agreement, foreign exchange markets were once again in operation in the Western world.

DOLLAR RESTRICTIONS AND THE ORIGINS OF THE
EURODOLLAR MARKET

After the return to European convertibility, it was discovered that there was no
longer any dollar shortage. Par values of roughly the market equilibrium values
had been chosen. The deutschemark price of dollars had been set too high,
however. The dollar was overvalued and the deutschemark undervalued, so the
Bundesbank, the German central bank, continued to accumulate dollars (Germany continued to run a balance of payments surplus).

With a dollar shortage no longer a problem, European countries began to add
up the total stock of U.S. dollars in foreign official hands and compare them to
the total U.S. gold supply. They began to realize that the United States could no
longer keep its part of the Bretton Woods agreement to convert dollars into gold
at $35 per ounce. By 1960 total foreign dollar claims on the United States were
greater than the total value of the U.S. gold stock when gold was valued at $35 per
ounce. If all foreign official dollars were turned in for gold at the same time, U.S.
gold would run short. The United States would either have to turn away dollar-
holders or increase the dollar price of gold. (An increase in the dollar price of gold
was referred to as a devaluation of the dollar.)

The right to exchange dollars for gold had become roughly equivalent to the
right to exchange the money in a checking account for cash. Anyone has the right
to convert his or her checking account into cash. But if everyone tries to exercise
this right at once, the bank will eventually run out of cash, since a bank's vault
cash amount is much smaller than its checking-account liabilities. Now, in one
sense, it did not make a material economic difference whether the United States
could convert dollars to gold or not. As long as the purchasing power of the dollar
remained constant, dollar-holders would suffer no economic loss, and if they
really wanted gold they could always buy it in the private market. Moreover, even

if there were dollar inflation, as long as official reserve holders were paid an interest rate sufficient to compensate them for inflation and in addition pay them a competitive real return, they had no basis to complain that holding dollars involved an opportunity cost on their part.

There were, however, problems of perception. First, suppose that the price of gold had a tendency to rise above $35 per ounce in the private market. This could happen because there was dollar inflation, so that prices in general – including the price of gold — would rise. Or there could be an increase in the value of gold relative to other goods. If the increase were due to inflation, then Germany, for example, might not be happy, because Germany could argue that the Bretton Woods agreement was implicitly an agreement by the United States to maintain a stable price level. (Memories of the 1920s hyperinflation have since given Germany a strong noninflationary stance.) If there was inflation in the United States, then — since the mark was pegged to the dollar — there would be inflation in Germany. Secondly, if the market price of gold rose above $35 per ounce, whether due to inflation or to an increase in the relative price of gold, even official dollar-holders might be tempted to switch from dollars to gold in order to enjoy a capital gain if the official U.S. dollar price of gold were later altered also. Finally, as we shall see, the French president de Gaulle made an issue out of gold purely on principle.

The inability to convert dollars into gold at $35 per ounce was therefore treated as a political problem by the U.S. administration. It became concerned about the private market price of gold (discussed further in the following section) and about the statistical measure of the U.S. balance of payments. The growing U.S. liabilities to foreign official agencies — obligations that could be converted into gold — reflected the deficit on the U.S. balance of payments, which was matched by a European surplus. American President Kennedy said he feared only two things: nuclear war and a deficit in the balance of payments. Nuclear war could wipe out all of one's assets. A deficit in the balance of payments could — in the context of German and French complaints — be used as a basis for domestic politicians to charge the administration with economic mismanagement and could act as an impediment to the Kennedy administration's plan to construct an Atlantic Alliance against the Soviet Union.

One solution to the "problem" of the U.S. balance of payments deficit would have been to allow the price of major foreign currencies with respect to the U.S. dollar to rise. This action would have decreased the demand for those currencies: equivalently, it would have decreased the supply of dollars to foreigners. However, many felt that the dollar, as the central reserve currency, should not be allowed to devalue generally with respect to other currencies (and thus to devalue with respect to gold). They felt that the dollar ought to be a riskless asset. Another solution might have been to take no action at all, since it was not clear there was a problem. The accumulation of dollars by foreign official agencies was, after all, voluntary, and if they desired to continue to add dollars to their reserves, the United States would have to run a deficit to supply those reserves. But this fact was also ignored. Instead, the concern over the deficit led to a series of credit restrictions and capital controls under Presidents John Kennedy and Lyndon Johnson.

On July 18, 1963, Kennedy proposed an **Interest Equalization Tax (IET)** on American purchases of foreign securities. This tax raised the cost to foreign borrowers who came to New York to issue bonds in the Yankee bond market. Bond coupons would have to be raised to compensate bond-buyers for the withholding tax they would have to pay the U.S. government. The naive idea of the tax was to keep dollars out of foreign hands, so outsiders would not have any dollars with which to demand gold. (This tax created a reason for issuing euro-bonds denominated in dollars. Such bonds would be issued internationally, in foreign capital markets, and would be free of the tax; see Chapter 16.) In February 1964 the IET was extended to apply to loans with a maturity of one to three years when these loans were made by U.S. banks and other financial institutions to designated foreign borrowers.

In February 1965 the U.S. voluntary Foreign Credit Restraint Program (FCRP) was instituted. (It was "voluntary" in the sense that the government would not interfere in bank lending activity as long as the banks obeyed the general guidelines of the FCRP anyway.) This program involved the setting of quotas — maximal amounts — on lending by U.S. banks to U.S. multinationals involved in foreign direct investment. On January 1, 1968, these controls were made legally mandatory. This set of controls gave companies an incentive to borrow dollars from sources not subject to these quotas.

The effect of the IET and FCRP was to give a strong impetus to the rate of growth of a new international money market that had slowly begun to emerge: the eurodollar market. In order to make clear what was involved, a slight digression from the historical sequence will be useful. An up-to-date definition of a eurodollar is "a dollar-denominated deposit in a bank outside the United States or in International Banking Facilities in the United States." (International Banking Facilities did not yet exist in the 1960s but were created beginning December 1981 and will be discussed in Chapter 12.) The typical eurodollar deposit is a 30- or 90-day time deposit. The principal characteristic that makes it a "euro" deposit is the location of the bank giving the deposit, not the ownership of the bank or the funds. For example, if a U.S. corporation owns a dollar deposit at the Cayman Islands branch of a U.S. bank, the deposit is a eurodollar deposit because it is a deposit in a bank outside the United States. It is irrelevant whether the Cayman Islands bank is or is not a U.S. bank, and it is irrelevant whether the deposit is owned by a foreigner or a U.S. citizen. If a German corporation owns a deposit in a New York bank, the deposit is *not* a eurodollar deposit, because the bank is not located outside the United States.

Similarly, a eurocurrency is a foreign-currency-denominated deposit in a bank outside the country where the currency is issued as legal tender. For example, a deutschemark-denominated deposit in a bank in Luxembourg is a euro-deutschemark deposit. As of the early 1980s, there were fifteen eurocurrencies regularly traded in London. The dollar usually accounts for 75 percent of the total euromarket's gross assets and the deutschemark for another 15 percent.

A eurodollar is created this way. Suppose a U.S. company transfers $1 million from a U.S. domestic bank to a eurobank. This eurobank may, for example, be a branch of the U.S. bank in London or Nassau, or it may be a foreign bank. The company writes a check on its account at the U.S. bank and gives the check to the eurobank. The eurobank now owns a deposit at the U.S. bank. In return for the check, the company is issued a time deposit at the eurobank. The $1-million transfer would show up on the books of the two banks as follows:

U.S. Domestic Bank		Eurobank	
Assets	Liabilities −$1 million deposit of U.S. company +$1 million deposit of Eurobank	Assets +$1 million deposit at U.S. domestic bank	Liabilities +$1 million deposit of U.S. company

Dollar liabilities of U.S. domestic banks have not altered in the slightest by this transaction. All that has changed at this point is that *ownership* of the $1-million deposit has been transferred from the U.S. company to the eurobank. The company may have been moved to transfer its deposit to the eurobank by the offer of a higher interest rate on deposits. The eurobank in turn can afford to pay higher interest only if it can loan out the deposit acquired at the U.S. domestic bank at an interest rate sufficiently higher than its deposit rate to obtain an acceptable profit margin. The U.S. domestic bank, meanwhile, is indifferent as to whether its liability is to a U.S. company or to a eurobank, except in the sense that there are legal distinctions (such as reserve requirement differences) among deposit-holders. Prior to May 1969, for example, there was no reserve requirement if the deposit-holder was a foreign branch of the U.S. domestic bank.

If the eurobank now makes a $1 million loan to Party Z, where Party Z may be another eurobank or a corporate customer, the accounting changes that take place are:

U.S. Domestic Bank		Eurobank		Party Z	
Assets	Liabilities −$1 million deposit of Eurobank +$1 million deposit of Party Z	Assets −$1 million deposit at U.S. domestic bank +$1 million loan to Party Z	Liabilities	Assets +$1 million deposit at U.S. domestic bank	Liabilities +$1 million debt to Eurobank

The Eurobank makes the loan, in effect, by writing a check on its account at the U.S. domestic bank. The net result is that the $1-million deposit at the U.S. domestic bank again undergoes a transfer of ownership. But there has been no change in U.S. domestic bank liabilities.

Several points concerning the above process should be noted:

1. The eurobank is playing the role of a thrift institution in the U.S. financial system. Thrift institutions (like savings and loans and mutual savings banks) acquire ownership of demand deposits at commercial banks and loan out these same demand deposits; exactly what the eurobank is doing. *Hence the eurobank can be viewed as an essentially unregulated international thrift institution.*

2. Whether U.S. domestic bank liabilities are affected by eurobank activity depends on the structure of **reserve requirements**. If all deposit (or similar) liabilities of U.S. domestic banks are treated uniformly according to reserve requirements, eurobank activity cannot affect the quantity of total U.S. domestic bank liabilities. But if, for example, foreign branch banks have a smaller reserve requirement, an increase in the ownership share of U.S. domestic bank liabilities by foreign branch banks will free up reserves and will — under certain conditions — expand total U.S. domestic bank liabilities.

3. If Party Z is a eurobank, then total eurobank liabilities will stand at $2 million as a result of the $1 million transferred initially to the first eurobank and the same $1 million transferred again to Party Z. While $2 million is a bigger amount than $1 million, it is not clear that there is any economic significance to be attached to the difference in the two numbers. If we subtract out intereurobank deposits ($1 million liability of Party Z to the first eurobank) from the $2 million, we get back the original $1-million eurodollar deposit. Even so, this original $1-million eurodeposit represents a double-counting of a $1-million deposit at a U.S. domestic bank. All economic transactions will have to involve the original demand deposit at a U.S. domestic bank. So is there any way in which the eurodeposit has *independent* importance? One possibility that suggests the answer might be yes is that the original eurobank deposit could lead to a marginal increase in the *velocity* of turnover of demand deposits, because the eurobank deposit is a time deposit. A company that takes out a time deposit is not planning to spend its money immediately. But the eurobank will loan out the demand deposit it acquires from the company to someone who will employ it right away. This conversion of $1 million from a deposit of longer maturity (the company's time deposit) into a deposit of shorter maturity (into a loan in the form of a demand deposit, in this case) is referred to as **maturity transformation**. Maturity transformation could result in a change in aggregate demand for goods and services. (These issues are explored in Chapter 15.)

Returning now to our main story, the eurodollar market had emerged shortly before the general return to European currency convertibility and had come about this way. The Bretton Woods agreement had established the British pound sterling as an international reserve currency along with the dollar. During the 1950s this par value was set as £1 = $2.80. As a result of the Suez crisis in 1956, during which Egyptian president Gamal Abdel Nasser's nationalization of the Canal was followed by a joint British-French-Israeli attack on Egypt, there was a run on the British pound as pound-holders switched from pounds to dollars. The Bank of England had difficulty maintaining the market price at the lower range of the 1-percent band, $2.7720/£. The U.S. Federal Reserve was itself a seller of pounds, and as a way of pressuring Britain to withdraw from Egypt the United States blocked British attempts to borrow from the IMF. One consequence of the sterling crisis was the Bank of England's prohibition of external sterling loans, the notion being that if foreigners did not have sterling they could not put pressure on the exchange rate by trading sterling for dollars.

However, one group of financial institutions, London overseas and merchant banks, made their living in part by arranging sterling financing for international trade. Trade between India and Nigeria, for example, was usually denominated in sterling, as opposed to the currencies of either of these two countries. These London institutions had the choice of closing shop or finding some other way to provide international trade financing. Their solution was to open a market in U.S. dollars. By offering to take in dollar deposits at competitive interest rates, they would have dollars to loan. (Bank of England prohibitions said nothing about dollars.) The idea that financial institutions in one country would open up a deposit market denominated in the currency of another country was considered a practice so strange that only merchant bankers would engage in it and in its early years was referred to as the Merchant Bank's Market. When a journalist for the *Financial Times,* Paul Einzig, discovered the market's existence, he was asked not to write about it.

The eurodollar market turned out to be a spectacular financial innovation, and as with any successful invention, all sorts of people later claimed to have thought of it first. What was *new* about the new market was that it was a market for *both deposits and loans* denominated in a foreign currency. The simple fact that these banks offered foreign-currency deposits was not new: banks in Vienna and Berlin had commonly done this prior to World War II. Later, in the early 1950s, when currencies in Europe were generally inconvertible, Italian banks took in dollars in a small way to make loans to local businessmen. But this was viewed as a temporary expedient and did not endure. During the early years of the Cold War, the Soviet Union began to fear expropriation of its dollar deposits in New York and so switched ownership of these deposits to Soviet-controlled banks like the Moscow Narodny in London and the Banque Commerciale pour l'Europe du Nord in Paris. It was felt that the United States would not expropriate deposits owned by a British or a French bank. These banks in turn issued dollar deposits to the Soviet Union. Though this practice would later give rise to the rumor that the Russians created the eurodollar market, the two banks were simply holding dollars in trust and did not get involved in dollar-lending until the later emergence of the Merchant Bank's Market in 1957. Thus the eurodollar market really began as the Merchant Bank's Market. With respect to merchant bankers, Kleinwort Benson and Brown Shipley claim to have created the market.

There is no reason a specialty market in dollars could not have arisen in London without the artificial help of official regulatory restrictions. British banks might, for example, have specialized knowledge of financing trade in former parts of the British empire that New York did not and might enjoy a comparative advantage in financing in dollars even given the fact that British banks would, in turn, have to hold and lend deposits in New York. Nevertheless, it is historically clear that regulatory restrictions were enormously important in inspiring the rapid growth of the market.

First of all, there were supply restrictions that hindered the ability of some to borrow dollars in New York. The Interest Equalization Tax and the Foreign Credit Restraint Program increased the interest cost, and placed limits on the amount, of bank loans available to foreigners and to U.S. companies investing abroad. Thus, for dollar loans many had little choice but to turn to the eurodollar market.

Second, there were demand restrictions that reduced the attractiveness of New York as a place to lend dollars by placing deposits with New York banks. In particular, the Federal Reserve's Regulation Q placed an interest ceiling on the

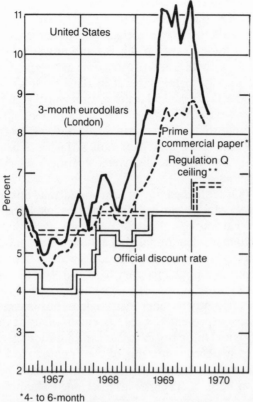

FIGURE 1.1
Short-term interest rates compared to Regulation Q ceiling rate. [*Source:* Bank for International Settlements, *Annual Report* (1970).]

amount U.S. banks could pay on bank deposits. Of course, such a ceiling is irrelevant if it is not binding—if market interest rates are lower than the ceiling. But, as seen in Figure 1.1, in 1966 and again in 1968–1969 market interest rates rose above Regulation Q ceiling rates—eurodollar deposits in the latter case paying as much as 500 basis points more.

As market interest rates rose above Regulation Q ceilings in 1966, money center banks experienced **disintermediation**: funds were switched out of time deposits and into Treasury bills and commercial paper, assets for which there were no interest ceilings. Banks with eurobank branches were better able to maintain their deposit base, since eurobank branches could pay market interest rates and relend the funds to headquarters. With a repetition of disintermediation in 1968–1969, many banks looked to open up eurobranches as a temporary solution to their funding problem but were hindered by the $500,000 minimum capital investment required to open a branch in London. A change in Federal Reserve regulations enabled them to open so-called shell branches in the Caribbean. Though such branches were legally established in a foreign country, a branch was really operated as a separate set of books in New York. The Cayman Islands branch of a major New York bank might, for example, be nothing more than a fellow named Bill with a desk and a telephone next to the foreign exchange traders in the New York bank's trading room. During the year 1969, forty U.S.

banks opened branches, referred to as "Nassau shells," in the Bahamas. For a small investment of capital, U.S. banks could offer competitive rates of interest on deposits through eurobank branches in Nassau.

THE POLITICS OF GOLD AND THE SDR

In addition to the various restrictions referred to above, the United States joined with the central banks of the Common Market countries as well as with Great Britain and Switzerland to intervene in the private market for gold in the fall of 1960. If the private market price did not rise above $35 per ounce, it was felt, the Bretton Woods price was de facto the correct price, and in addition no one could complain if dollars were not exchangeable for gold. This coordinated intervention, which involved maintaining the gold price within a narrow range around $35 per ounce, became formalized a year later as the *gold pool*. Since London was the center of world gold trading, the pool was managed by the Bank of England, which intervened in the private market via the daily gold price fixing at N. M. Rothschild. In order to see how this worked, we now turn to a brief description of the gold market and once again depart slightly from a strictly chronological sequence.

In its current form, the London gold price fixing takes place twice each business day, at 10:30 A.M. and 3:00 P.M. in the "fixing room" of the merchant banking firm of N. M. Rothschild. Five individuals, one each from one of five major gold-trading firms, are involved in the fixing. The firms represented are Mocatta & Goldsmid, a trading arm of Standard Chartered Bank; Sharps, Pixley, a broker owned by the merchant bank Kleinwort Benson; N. M. Rothschild & Sons, whose representative acts as the auctioneer; Johnson Matthey, a metallurgical firm; and Samuel Montagu, a merchant banking subsidiary of Midland Bank. Each representative at the fixing keeps an open phone line to his firm's trading room. Each trading room in turn has buy and sell orders, at various prices, from customers located all over the world. In addition, there are customers with no existing buy or sell orders who keep an open line to a trading room in touch with the fixing and who may decide to buy or sell depending on what price is announced. The N. M. Rothschild representative announces a price at which trading will begin. Each of the five individuals then confers with his trading room, and the trading room tallies up supply and demand — in terms of 400-ounce bars — from orders originating around the world. In a few minutes, each firm has determined if it is a net buyer or seller of gold. If there is excess supply or demand a new price is announced, but no orders are filled until an equilibrium price is determined. The equilibrium price, at which supply equals demand, is referred to as the "fixing price." The A.M. and P.M. fixing prices are published daily in major newspapers.

Even though immediately before and after a fixing gold trading will continue at prices that may vary from the fixing price, the fixing price is an important benchmark in the gold market because much of the daily trading volume goes through at the fixing price. Hence some central banks value their gold at an average of daily fixing prices, and industrial customers often have contracts with their suppliers written in terms of the fixing price. Since a fixing price represents temporary equilibrium for a large volume of trading, it is subject to less "noise" than are trading prices at other times of the day. Usually the equilibrium fixing price is found rapidly, but sometimes it takes twenty to thirty tries. Once in October 1979, with supply and demand fluctuating rapidly from moment to moment, the afternoon fixing in London lasted an hour and thirty-nine minutes.

The practice of fixing the gold price began in 1919. It continued until 1939, when the London gold market was closed as a result of war. The market was reopened in 1954. When the central bank gold pool began officially in 1961, the Bank of England — as agent for the pool — maintained an open phone line with N. M. Rothschild during the morning fixing (there was as yet no afternoon fixing). If it appeared that a fixing price would be established that was above $35.20 or below $34.80, the Bank of England (as agent) became a seller or buyer of gold in an amount sufficient to ensure that the fixing price remained within the prescribed bands.

While the gold pool held down the private market price of gold, gold politics took a new turn in the international arena. While it was actually Germany that was running the greatest surplus and accumulating dollar reserves in the early 1960s, it was France under the leadership of Charles de Gaulle that made the most noise about it. During World War II, in conversations with Jean Monnet, de Gaulle had supported the notion of a united Europe — but a Europe, he insisted, under the leadership of France. After the war, France had opposed the American plan for German rearmament even in the context of European defense. France had been induced to agree, however, through Marshall Plan aid, which France was not inclined to refuse after it became embroiled in the Indo-China War. But now, in the 1960s, de Gaulle's vision of France as a leading world power led him to withdraw from NATO because NATO was a U.S.-dominated military alliance. It also led him to oppose Bretton Woods, because the international monetary system was organized with the U.S. dollar as a reserve currency.

In the early 1960s there was, however, no realistic alternative to the dollar as a reserve asset, if one wanted to keep reserves in a form that would both bear interest and could be traded internationally. Official dollar-reserve holders were not only made exempt from the interest ceilings of Regulation Q for their deposits in New York but also began as a regular practice to hold dollars in the eurodollar market. Prior to 1965, central banks were the largest suppliers of dollars to the euromarket. Thus reserve holders received a competitive return on their dollar assets, and the United States gained no special benefit from the use of the dollar as a reserve asset.

Nevertheless, de Gaulle's stance on gold made domestic political sense, and in February 1965 in a well-publicized speech, he said: "We hold as necessary that international exchange be established . . . on an indisputable monetary base that does not carry the mark of any particular country. What base? In truth, one does not see how in this respect it can have any criterion, any standard, other than gold. Eh! Yes, gold, which does not change in nature, which is made indifferently into bars, ingots and coins, which does not have any nationality, which is held eternally and universally. . . ." By the "mark of any particular country" he had in mind the United States, which announced the Foreign Credit Restraint Program about a week later, in part as a direct response to de Gaulle's speech. France stepped up its purchases of gold from the U.S. Treasury and in June 1967, when the Arab–Israeli Six-Day War led to a large increase in the demand for gold, withdrew from the gold pool.

Then in November 1967 the British pound sterling was devalued from $2.80 to $2.40. Those holding sterling reserves took a 14.3 percent capital loss in dollar terms. This raised the question of the exchange rate of the other reserve assets: if the dollar was devalued with respect to gold, a capital gain in dollar terms could be made by holding gold. Therefore demand for gold rose and, as it did, gold pool sales in the private market to hold down the price were so large that month that the U.S. Air Force made an emergency airlift of gold from Fort Knox to London, and the floor of the weighing room at the Bank of England collapsed from the accumulated tonnage of gold bars.

In March 1968 the effort to control the private market price of gold was abandoned. A *two-tier* system began: official transactions in gold were insulated from the free market price. Central banks would trade gold among themselves at $35 per ounce but would not trade with the private market. The private market could trade at the equilibrium market price and there would be no official intervention. The price immediately jumped to $43 per ounce, but by the end of 1969 it was back at $35. The two-tier system would be abandoned in November 1973, after the emergence of floating exchange rates and the de facto dissolution of the Bretton Woods agreement. By then the price had reached $100 per ounce.

When the gold pool was disbanded and the two-tier system began in March 1968, there was a two-week period during which the London gold market was forceably closed by British authorities. A number of important changes took place during those two weeks. South Africa as a country is the single largest supplier of gold and had for years marketed the sale of its gold through London, with the Bank of England acting as agent for the South African Reserve Bank. With the breakdown of the gold pool, South Africa was no longer assured of steady central bank demand, and — with the London market temporarily closed — the three major Swiss banks (Swiss Bank Corporation, Swiss Credit Bank, and Union Bank of Switzerland) formed their own gold pool and persuaded South Africa to market through Zurich. In 1972, the second major country supplier of gold, the Soviet Union, also began to market through Zurich. In 1921 V. I. Lenin had written "sell [gold] at the highest price, buy goods with it at the lowest price." Since the Soviet ruble is not convertible, the Soviet Union uses gold sales as one major source of its earnings of Western currencies, and in the 1950s and 1960s sold gold through the Moscow Narodny in London (the same bank that provided dollar cover for the Soviets during the early days of the Cold War). In Zurich, the Soviet Union dealt gold via the Wozchod Handelsbank, a subsidiary of the Soviet Foreign Trade Bank, the Vneshtorgbank. (In March 1985 the Soviet Union announced that the Wozchod would be closed because of gold trading losses and would be replaced with a branch office of the Vneshtorgbank. The branch office, unlike the Wozchod, would not be required to publish information concerning operations.)

London, in order to stay competitive, has since become more of a gold trading center than a distribution center. When the London market reopened in March 1968 after the two-week "holiday," a second daily fixing (the 3:00 P.M. fixing) was added in order to overlap with U.S. trading hours, and the fixing price was switched to U.S. dollar terms from pound sterling terms. In more recent years, London's role as a trading center has also been challenged by the Comex gold futures market in New York.

During the early years of the gold pool, it came to be believed that there was a deficiency of international reserves and that more reserves had to be created by legal fiat to enable reserve-holders to diversify out of the U.S. dollar and gold. In retrospect, this was a curious view of the world. The form in which reserves are held will ultimately always be determined on the basis of international competition. People will hold their wealth in the form of a particular asset only if they want to. If they do not have an economic incentive to desire a particular asset, no legal document will alter that fact. A particular currency will be attractive as a reserve asset if these four criteria exist: (1) An absence of exchange controls so people can spend, transfer, or exchange their reserves denominated in that currency when and where they want them. (2) An absence of applicable credit controls and taxes that would prevent assets denominated in the currency from bearing a competitive rate of return relative to other available assets. (3) Political stability, in the sense that there is a lack of substantial risk that points (1) and (2) will change within or between government regimes. (4) The currency is in sufficient use internationally for the costs of making transactions in the currency not to be prohibitive. This latter point is partly a function of the first three points and partly of the relevant country's importance in world trade. These four points explain why, for example, the Swiss but not the French franc is widely used as an international reserve asset.

Many felt that formal agreement on a new international reserve asset was nevertheless needed, if only to reduce political tension. And while France wanted to replace the dollar as a reserve asset, other nations were looking instead for a replacement for gold. The decision was made by the Group of Ten (ten OECD nations with most of the voting rights in the IMF) to create an artificial reserve asset that would be traded among central banks in settlement of reserves. The asset would be kept on the books of the IMF and would be called a **Special Drawing Right (SDR)**. In fact it was a new reserve asset, a type of artificial or "paper gold," but it was called a drawing right by concession to the French, who did not want it called a reserve asset.

The SDR was approved in July 1969, and the first "allocation" (creation) of SDRs was made in January 1970. Overnight countries gained more reserves at the IMF, because the IMF added new numbers to its accounts and called these numbers SDRs. The timing of the allocation was especially maladroit. In the previous four years the United States had been in the process of financing the Great Society domestic social programs of the Johnson administration as well as a war in Vietnam, and the world was being flooded with more reserves than it wanted at the going price of dollars for deutschemarks, yen, or gold. In the 1965 Economic Report of the President, Johnson wrote, in reference to his Great Society Program and the Vietnam War: "The Federal Reserve must be free to accommodate the expansion in 1965 and the years beyond 1965." U.S. money supply (M1) growth, which had averaged 2.2 percent per year during the 1950s, inched upward slightly during the Kennedy years (2.9 percent per year for 1961–1963) but changed materially under the Johnson administration. The growth rate of M1 averaged 4.6 percent per year over 1964–1967, then rose to 7.7 percent in 1968. Under the Nixon administration that followed, money growth initially slowed to 3.2 percent in 1969 and 5.2 percent in 1970, then accelerated to 7.1 percent for 1971–1973. The latter three years would encompass the breakdown of Bretton Woods.

THE BREAKDOWN OF BRETTON WOODS

In order to succeed, a regime of fixed exchange rates (and under Bretton Woods rates for the major currencies were fixed in terms of their par values, which could not be casually altered) requires coordinated economic policies, particularly monetary policies. If two different currencies trade at a fixed exchange rate and one currency is undervalued with respect to the other, the undervalued currency will be in excess demand. By the end of the 1960s both the deutschemark and the yen had become undervalued with respect to the U.S. dollar. Therefore the countries concerned (Germany and Japan) had two choices: either increase the supplies of their currencies to meet the excess demand or adjust the exchange values of their currencies upward enough for there to be no longer any excess demand.

As long as either country intervened in the market to maintain the par value of its currency with respect to the U.S. dollar, an increased supply of the domestic currency would take place automatically. To see why this is so, take the case of Germany. In order to keep the DM from increasing in value with respect to the U.S. dollar, the Bundesbank would have to intervene in the foreign exchange market to buy dollars. It would buy dollars by selling DM. The operation would increase the supply of DM in the market, driving down DM's relative value, and increase the demand for the dollar, driving up the dollar's relative value.

Any time the central bank intervenes in any market to buy or sell something, it changes the domestic money supply. If the central bank buys assets such as government bonds or foreign exchange, it does so by writing a check on itself. Central bank assets go up: the central bank now owns the bonds or the foreign exchange. But central bank liabilities go up also, since the check represents a central bank liability. The seller of the bonds or foreign exchange or other asset will deposit the central bank's check, in payment for the value of the assets, in an account at a commercial bank. The commercial bank will in turn deposit the check in its account at the central bank. The commercial bank will now have more reserves, in the form of a deposit at the central bank. The bank can use the reserves to make more loans, and the money supply will expand by a multiple of the initial reserve increase.

Below is a typical central bank balance sheet. Central banks have two general types of assets: domestic and foreign. Domestic assets are things like government bonds and direct loans to the commercial banking system. In some countries they have included corporate stock and direct loans to private industry. Foreign assets are things like gold, SDRs, and foreign exchange.

Central Bank

Assets	Liabilities
Domestic assets	High-powered money
Foreign assets	

Central bank liabilities make up the **monetary base,** or "high-powered money." In the case of the Federal Reserve in the United States, the two principal components of this liability are currency in circulation (printed money and coins) and commercial bank checking accounts (federal funds). Either component can serve as reserves of commercial banks. Checking accounts at the Federal Reserve are automatically reserves, and currency can serve as bank reserves if it is held in a bank's vault ("cash in the vault").

Different banking systems differ in detail but generally have a similar structure. Consider now the Bundesbank, the German central bank, intervening in the foreign exchange market to buy up $1 billion, at a fixed exchange rate of 4 DM = $1. The transaction would show up on the books of the Bundesbank as follows:

Bundesbank	
Assets	Liabilities
+DM 4 billion in foreign assets	+DM 4 billion in reserves of banking system

The foreign exchange intervention automatically increases the monetary base in Germany by DM 4 billion. Eventually the money supply in Germany will increase by a multiple of this amount. The total increase in the German money supply will depend on the size of the **money multiplier** in Germany. If the money (M1) multiplier were 2.5, then the M1 money supply in Germany would eventually rise by (DM 4 billion)(2.5) = DM 10 billion.

Is there anything the German authorities can do to prevent the money-supply increase? Essentially not as long as they attempt to maintain the fixed exchange rate. There is, however, an operation referred to as **sterilization.** Sterilization refers to the practice of offsetting any impact on the monetary base caused by foreign exchange intervention, by making reverse transactions in terms of domestic assets. For example, if the money base went up by DM 4 billion because the central bank bought dollars in the foreign exchange market, a sterilization operation would involve selling DM 4-billion worth of domestic assets to reduce central bank liabilities by an equal and offsetting amount. If the Bundesbank sold domestic assets, these would be paid for by checks drawn on the commercial banking system and reserves would disappear as the commercial banks' checking accounts were debited at the central bank.

However, the Bundesbank could not simultaneously engage in complete sterilization (a complete offset) and also maintain the fixed exchange rate. If there was no change in the supply of DM the DM would continue to be undervalued with respect to the dollar, and foreign exchange traders would continue to exchange dollars for DM. During the course of 1971 the Bundesbank intervened so much that the German high-powered money base would have increased by 42 percent from foreign exchange intervention alone. About half this increase was offset by sterilization, but even so the increase in the money base — and eventually the money supply — by more than 20 percent in one year was enormous by German standards. The breakdown of the Bretton Woods system began that year.

It came about this way. From the end of World War II to about 1965, U.S. domestic monetary and fiscal policies were conducted in such a way as to be noninflationary. As world trade expanded during this period, the relative importance of Germany and Japan grew, so that by the end of the 1960s it was unreasonable to expect any system of international finance to endure without a consensus at least among the United States, Germany, and Japan. But after 1965, U.S. economic policy began to conflict with policies desired by Germany and Japan. In particular, the United States began a strong expansion, and moderate inflation, as a result of the Vietnam War and the Great Society program.

When it became obvious that the DM and yen were undervalued with respect to the dollar, the United States urged these two nations to revalue their currencies upward. Germany and Japan argued that the United States should revise its economic policy to be consistent with those in Germany and Japan as well as with previous U.S. policy. They wanted the United States to curb money-supply growth, tighten credit, and cut government spending. In the ensuing stalemate, the U.S. policy essentially followed the recommendations of a task force chaired by Gottfried Haberler. This was a policy of officially doing nothing and was commonly referred to as a policy of "benign neglect." If Germany and Japan chose to intervene to maintain their chosen par values, so be it. They would be allowed to accumulate dollar reserves until such time as they decided to change the par values of their currencies. That was the only alternative, given that the United States would not willingly change its policy. It was clearly understood at the time that a unilateral action on the part of the United States to devalue the dollar by increasing the dollar price of gold would be matched by similar European devaluations.

In April 1971 the Bundesbank took in $3 billion through foreign exchange intervention. On May 4 it took in $1 billion in the course of the day. On May 5 the Bundesbank took in $1 billion during the first hour of trading, then suspended intervention in the foreign exchange market. The DM was allowed to float upward. On August 15 the U.S. president, Nixon, suspended the convertibility of the dollar into gold and announced a 10 percent tax on imports. The tax was temporary and was intended to signal the magnitude by which the United States thought the par values of the major European and Japanese currencies should be changed.

An attempt was made to keep the Bretton Woods system going by a revised agreement, the **Smithsonian Agreement**, reached at the Smithsonian Institution in Washington on December 17–18, 1971. Called by President Nixon "the most important monetary agreement in the history of the world," it lasted only slightly more than a year, but beyond the 1972 U.S. presidential election. At the Smithsonian Institution the Group of Ten agreed on a realignment of currencies, an increase in the official price of gold to $38 per ounce, and expanded exchange-rate bands of 2¼ percent around their new par values.

Over the period February 5–9, 1973, history repeated itself, with the Bundesbank taking in $5 billion in foreign exchange intervention. On February 12, exchange markets were closed in Europe and Japan, and the United States announced a 10 percent devaluation of the dollar. European countries and Japan allowed their currencies to float and, over the next month, a de facto regime of floating exchange rates began. The floating rate system has persisted to the present, with none of the five most widely traded currencies (the dollar, the DM, the British pound, the Japanese yen, the Swiss franc) in any way officially fixed in exchange value with respect to the others. With the breakdown of Bretton Woods there began a slow dismantling of the array of controls that had been erected in its name. Over 1973–1974, for example, the Interest Equalization Tax, the Foreign Credit Restraint Program, and the two-tier system for gold were all discarded.

The U.S. inflationary process, mild as it was by later standards, had a profound impact, via the Bretton Woods regime of par values, on other industrial countries. Economist Ronald McKinnon notes "the remarkable loss of monetary control among the major industrial economies concurrently in the last years of the fixed exchange-rate regime. Taking ten industrial countries combined, their aggregate money supply grew about 12 percent per annum in the 1971–1973 period as compared to a little over 7 percent per annum in the preceding ten years." The stage was set for the inflationary seventies.

PROBLEMS FOR CHAPTER 1

1. Suppose that free trading is allowed in both the Belgian franc and the French franc, but that the French and Belgian central banks peg their currencies with respect to each other at an exchange rate that undervalues the French franc relative to the Belgian franc. Which central bank will gain foreign exchange reserves? Which central bank will lose foreign exchange reserves?

2. The central bank of Surlandia pegs the peso to the U.S dollar at a price of Ps. 150/$. The market exchange rate is Ps. 180/$. Will the central bank of Surlandia gain or lose dollar reserves?

3. Which of the following items would be defined as eurodollars: German-owned dollar deposits in a New York bank; any deposit in a branch of a U.S. bank located in Zurich; a dollar deposit in the Los Angeles branch of the Bank of Tokyo; U.S. treasury bills owned by the Saudi Arabian Monetary Authority; dollar deposits in London banks owned by French exporters?

4. A company in Houston transfers $10 million to a eurobank in Panama, writing a check on Texas Commerce Bank. The bank in Panama deposits the check in Chemical Bank, New York, and subsequently loans $8 million to a eurobank in Nassau. Show the accounting changes that take place on the balance sheets of Texas Commerce Bank and the Panamanian eurobank.

5. Suppose the Bundesbank intervenes in the foreign exchange market and sells dollars. How does this affect the German monetary base?

6. The Federal Reserve sells 24 million ounces of gold at $35 an ounce, buys $2.38 billion worth of Treasury bills, and sells DM 2.2 billion at an average exchange rate of DM 3.90/$. What is the net change in the U.S. monetary base from these operations? If the U.S. money (M1) multiplier is 2.58, what will be the net change in the U.S. money supply?

7. Suppose the Federal Reserve were required to buy gold from, or sell gold to, *anyone* at a fixed price of $35 per ounce. Assume that the gold market is currently in equilibrium at that level. Explain why inflation in the United States would then automatically lead to a decrease in the U.S. money supply, assuming that changes in the price of gold accurately reflected changes in the purchasing power of the dollar.

2

CURRENCY COMPETITION AND THE DEBT GAME

FURTHER DEVELOPMENTS IN FINANCIAL MARKETS

The final breakdown of Bretton Woods in 1973 appeared to usher in a new era. The next ten years would see the fall and rise of the U.S. dollar in exchange markets, industrial country inflation followed by deflation, worldwide "crises" in energy and debt, and a remarkable growth in international financial markets as the flow of resources from savers to borrowers increasingly took international channels. Net new eurocurrency loans grew from a yearly flow of $6.8 billion in 1972 to a peak of $133.4 billion in 1981 before retreating somewhat as an international "debt crisis" unfolded. New international bond issues increased from a yearly flow of $9.7 billion in 1972 to $107.4 billion in 1984. (See Table 2.1.)

There were new risks in the world of currency trading, whose daily volume had grown by 1980 to exceed $100 billion each business day. In the final years of Bretton Woods, foreign exchange traders had become accustomed to taking large speculative positions against central banks at times when central banks intervened to maintain exchange rates at levels traders did not see as representing market equilibrium. If central banks stopped their intervention and rates were allowed to adjust, then traders made a speculative profit. If central banks continued to intervene and were able to maintain the fixed rate, traders did not make a profit, but there was little risk at such times of rates going in the other direction with a resulting loss. After March 1973, however, with the central banks of Europe and Japan committed to no specific prices for their currencies with respect to the U.S. dollar, it had become more risky to take speculative exchange positions. Traders who took such positions did so against other traders, and it was a sure thing that someone would prove to be wrong. This was dramatized in 1974 when two large banks—Bankhaus I. D. Herstatt in Cologne and Franklin National in New York—failed as a result of foreign exchange losses.

Central banks of industrial countries did, however, continue to intervene in currency markets in a discretionary fashion whenever officials felt exchange rates

TABLE 2.1
Financial Markets in the New Era

Year	Eurocurrency bank credits (U.S.$, billions)	International bond issues (U.S.$, billions)	DM per U.S.$ (average)	¥ per U.S.$ (average)	6-mo. rate on eurodollar deposits (%)
1972	6.796	9.748	3.19	303	
1973	21.851	7.838	2.64	271	
1974	29.263	6.857	2.58	292	
1975	20.992	19.911	2.46	297	
1976	28.849	32.669	2.52	296	6.13
1977	41.766	33.976	2.32	268	6.17
1978	70.179	34.279	2.01	208	9.36
1979	82.812	40.990	1.83	218	11.99
1980	77.392	41.920	1.82	226	14.12
1981	133.379	52.985	2.25	220	16.52
1982	85.015	78.042	2.43	249	13.24
1983	74.222	76.329	2.55	238	9.79
1984	112.605	107.411	2.84	237	11.03

Sources: Morgan Guaranty, World Financial Markets; Economic Report of the President.

ought to be different from their prevailing market levels. This was called "managed" or "dirty" floating. (Such intervention, as we will see in Chapter 9, has remained an important source of profit for traders.) Not only has central bank intervention remained widespread, but capital controls have also been temporarily imposed from time to time to influence the direction taken by rates in the foreign exchange market. In early 1978, for example, during a period when there were large shifts out of dollar assets and into assets denominated in DM, Swiss francs, and Japanese yen, the Swiss National Bank imposed negative interest rates on deposits held by foreigners and also prohibited foreign purchase of stocks and bonds. The Bundesbank placed a 100-percent reserve requirement on foreign deposits at German commercial banks. Japan took similar measures.

One of the more dramatic examples of exchange manipulation was the Carter package of November 1, 1978, under the administration of U.S. President Jimmy Carter. Thirty billion dollars' worth of foreign currencies were gathered for potential foreign exchange intervention in support of the U.S. dollar: $15 billion in new Federal Reserve swap lines with other central banks, $10 billion through the issue of foreign-currency-denominated bonds in foreign markets ("Carter bonds"), $3 billion from IMF borrowing, and $2 billion through the sale of SDRs. In addition, increased reserve requirements were placed on large-denomination time deposits at U.S. commercial banks, and the U.S. Treasury (which had begun to sell off its holdings of gold) announced that sales would rise to 1.5 million ounces annually. This package, however, had only little effect on the value of the dollar as measured by Morgan Guaranty's trade-weighted average of the dollar's nominal exchange rate with respect to fifteen other currencies. Based on an index of 100 in October 1978, the index stood at 101.7 in October 1980.

By contrast, exchange intervention operations were essentially suspended altogether under the following U.S. administration of Ronald Reagan. But the dollar rose sharply against foreign currencies beginning in 1981. The index rose to 116.9 by October 1981. In March 1985 it stood at 156.6. The 1984 Economic

Report of the President attributed the rise of the dollar to portfolio shifts from other foreign-currency assets into the dollar—a result of decreased expectations of U.S. inflation, an increase in U.S. real interest rates relative to real interest rates elsewhere, and increased political risk in Latin America and Europe. Even though the U.S. current account deficit in 1984 supplied foreigners with a net total of about $100 billion in U.S. assets, demand for dollar assets remained greater than the supply at exchange rates prevailing in early 1985. Consequently, the price of the dollar continued to be driven up, hitting a thirteen-year high of DM 3.47 per dollar in late February.

The mood in Europe for further European integration alternated between mild enthusiasm and disinterest throughout the 1970s. United States support was decidedly cooler, for reasons such as those listed in a report prepared for the U.S. national security advisor, Henry Kissinger: "In the long run we could be confronted by an 'expanded Europe' comprising a Common Market of at least ten full members, associated memberships for the EFTA [European Free Trade Area] neutrals, and preferential trade arrangements with at least the Mediterranean and most of Africa. This bloc will account for about half of world trade, compared with our 15%; it will hold monetary reserves approaching twice our own; and it will even be able to outvote us in the international economic organizations." In addition to energy and defense issues, the United States and Europe squabbled over financial issues, such as the weakness of the U.S. dollar during the Carter administration and the strength of the U.S. dollar and high U.S. interest rates during the Reagan administration. Meanwhile, in March 1979, the member nations of the European Economic Community began operation of the European Monetary System (EMS), a cooperative arrangement linking together EEC member currencies and discussed below.

When the principal industrial countries allowed their currencies to float beginning in March 1973 the International Monetary Fund took the position that such floating was illegal, since it was in violation of the Bretton Woods agreement as amended in the Smithsonian agreement. The currencies and countries involved were, however, those playing a major role in international finance. As a consequence, the IMF came to be increasingly viewed as an irrelevant institution, having little to do with daily international financial practice. Then, in a meeting in Jamaica in 1976, the IMF articles were formally amended to say that countries could choose their own exchange regimes. The Jamaica agreement canonized what was already fact and was of little help in restoring the primary relic of Bretton Woods—the IMF itself—as a forum for international financial coordination. More recently, however, following the second oil shock in 1979, the IMF has re-entered the financial scene in a major way as a dispenser of macroeconomic advice to international debtor nations. Since most countries of the world—particularly developing countries—still maintain fixed exchange rates, the IMF continues to supply balance-of-payments loans. In recent years, the IMF has concentrated its balance-of-payments lending to the same group of countries dealt with by the World Bank. (The World Bank had fulfilled its role in reconstruction finance by 1960 but continued to make development and project loans to countries with low per capita incomes.) IMF lending is conditional on countries following macroeconomic policies the IMF deems suitable (referred to as conditionality), a fact that has been used by private international banks as a basis for their own lending. Commercial banks with large loans outstanding to developing countries have usually been willing to reschedule existing debt only if a country first accepts an IMF program of macroeconomic adjustment. The acceptance of an IMF program is viewed by the banks as increasing the probability the loans will eventually be repaid.

Even though the most widely traded currencies — the U.S. dollar, the DM, the British pound, the Japanese yen, and the Swiss franc — do not now trade within a range of any agreed par values, a majority of countries worldwide still set par values for their currencies in one form or another. A classification of recent practices is given in Table 2.2. As of 1984, many countries pegged value of their currencies with respect to either the U.S. dollar (Venezuela), the French franc (Chad), or the SDR (Iran). A number of Latin American countries maintained exchange rates fixed in terms of the U.S. dollar but devalued their currencies at regular intervals by fixed amounts (Mexico, for instance) or according to a set of economic indicators (Brazil). These scheduled monthly or daily devaluations are referred to as **minidevaluations**. When an unscheduled devaluation takes place,

TABLE 2.2
Currency Arrangements as of March 31, 1984

Countries pegging their currencies to U.S. dollar:			
Antigua and Barbuda	Egypt	Liberia	Sudan
Bahamas	El Salvador	Libya	Suriname
Barbados	Ethiopia	Nicaragua	Syrian Arab Republic
Belize	Grenada	Oman	Trinidad and Tobago
Bolivia	Guatemala	Panama	Venezuela
Djibouti	Haiti	Paraguay	Yemen Arab Republic
Dominica	Honduras	St. Lucia	Yemen
Dominican Republic	Iraq	St. Vincent and the Grenadines	
	Lao People's Democratic Republic	Sierra Leone	

Countries pegging their currencies to the French franc:			
Benin	Chad	Ivory Coast	Togo
Cameroon	Comoros	Mali	Upper Volta
Central African Republic	Congo	Niger	
	Gabon	Senegal	

Countries pegging their currencies to the SDR:			
Burma	Iran	Rwanda	Seychelles
Burundi	Jordan	Sao Tome and Principe	Vanuatu
Guinea	Kenya		Viet Nam

Countries pegging to a currency basket:			
Algeria	Fiji	Mauritania	Solomon Islands
Austria	Finland	Mauritius	Sweden
Bangladesh	Hungary	Nepal	Tanzania
Botswana	Kuwait	Norway	Tunisia
Cape Verde	Madagascar	Papua New Guinea	Zambia
China, People's Republic of	Malawi	Romania	Zimbabwe
Cyprus	Malaysia	Singapore	
	Malta		

Country with currency pegged to Indian rupee: Bhutan
Country with currency pegged to Spanish peseta: Equatorial Guinea
Country with currency pegged to pound sterling: The Gambia
Countries with currencies pegged to South African rand: Lesotho, Swaziland

TABLE 2.2 (Continued)

	The European Monetary System:	
Belgium	Germany, Federal	Italy
Denmark	Republic of	Luxembourg
France	Ireland	Netherlands

Countries whose currencies have limited flexibility
with respect to a single other currency:

Afghanistan	Guyana	Saudi Arabia	United Arab
Bahrain	Maldives	Thailand	Emirates
Ghana	Qatar		

Countries whose currencies are adjusted
to a set of economic indicators

Brazil	Colombia	Portugal
Chile	Peru	Somalia

Countries with other managed floating arrangements

Argentina	India	Morocco	Sri Lanka
Costa Rica	Indonesia	New Zealand	Turkey
Ecuador	Israel	Nigeria	Uganda
Greece	Jamaica	Pakistan	Western Samoa
Guinea-Bissau	Korea	Philippines	Yugoslavia
Iceland	Mexico	Spain	Zaire

Countries whose currencies are floating independently

Australia	Japan	South Africa	United States
Canada	Lebanon	United Kingdom	Uruguay

Source: International Monetary Fund, *Annual Report on Exchange Arrangements and Exchange Restrictions, 1984.*

it is termed a **maxidevaluation.** Other countries (such as Kuwait) peg to a portfolio of foreign currencies. The currencies of the European Monetary System are pegged with respect to each other. The currencies of the Soviet Union and much of Eastern Europe are not classified in Table 2.2, but these currencies are generally not convertible.

The demise of fixed exchange rates for the widely traded currencies brought a change in the IMF's definition of its artificial reserve asset, the SDR. In 1974 the SDR was redefined in terms of a basket of sixteen currencies. The composition of the sixteen currencies was altered slightly in 1978. Finally, in 1981, the SDR was defined as a basket of five currencies: the U.S. dollar, the German mark, the French franc, the British pound sterling, and the Japanese yen:

$$1 \text{ SDR} = .54 \, \$ + .46 \text{ DM} + .74 \text{ FF} + 34 \, ¥ + .071 \, £ \,.$$

The redefinition was intended to promote the use of the SDR in the private sector, but thus far little enthusiasm has been shown outside the offices of the IMF. A number of regional organizations, however, now use the SDR as their unit of account, and a small market in SDR bank deposits has developed. In connection with the SDR, the IMF has recently promoted the idea of a "substitution account." This involves a scheme by which the IMF would issue SDR claims to member nations in return for their voluntary deposit of U.S. dollars with the IMF. The purpose of the scheme is to promote the role of the SDR as a reserve asset and, allegedly, to allow central banks to shift out of dollars without affecting exchange rates. Support for this scheme on the part of members holding dollar reserves dwindled in 1981 and afterward as the dollar's value rose in foreign exchange markets.

Gold, the principal international reserve asset outside the dollar, was another issue. As part of the Jamaica agreement in 1976 IMF members agreed to demote the role of gold, but few central banks have subsequently followed up this agreement in practice (see Chapter 11 for a further discussion of the changing pattern of international reserve assets). One associated change that did come about, however, affected the private gold market in the United States. On January 2, 1975, after forty years of prohibition, U.S. citizens were allowed to purchase gold bullion legally. The Comex in New York subsequently became an important center for the trading of gold futures.

FROM THE SNAKE TO THE EUROPEAN MONETARY SYSTEM

In the Smithsonian agreement, signed in December 1971, it had been decided to widen the plus-or-minus-1-percent bands of the Bretton Woods agreement to plus or minus $2\frac{1}{4}$ percent. However, the members of the European Economic Community decided to keep their currencies within narower margins with respect to each other. Recall that at the time of the formation of the European Economic Community (the Common Market) in 1958, the eventual goal had been economic unification as a prelude to political unification. By 1970 many trade restrictions between community members had been removed, and a new goal of monetary unification by 1980 was set. The Werner Plan, developed by a group of experts headed by Pierre Werner of Luxembourg, called for smaller margins of fluctuation between European currencies and exchange market intervention in local currencies rather than the dollar as steps toward eventual monetary unification. To maintain these narrow margins, community members would have to coordinate monetary policies. The ultimate stage of coordination would be a single policy with a single EEC currency.

Thus, following the Smithsonian agreement, the EEC decided on narrower bands of plus or minus $1\frac{1}{8}$ percent for community members. Because of the visual appearance of a time graph giving changes in the value of EEC currencies with respect to the U.S. dollar, the arrangement was referred to as the "snake in the tunnel." The snake was the EEC currencies, which moved closely together with respect to third currencies such as the dollar, while the tunnel was formed by non-EEC currencies which moved in the larger Smithsonian band of plus or minus $2\frac{1}{4}$ percent. The snake arrangement commenced in April 1972.

With the beginning of floating exchange rates in March 1973, European countries continued the joint float of their respective currencies. Since non-EEC currencies no longer traded in any fixed range with respect to each other, the joint EEC float was referred to as the "snake in the lake." The snake arrangement was not terribly successful after the movement to floating rates, however, because there was no strong commitment on the part of member countries to undertake the coordination of monetary and other economic policies necessary to make the arrangement work. France, for example, dropped out of the snake in January 1974, joined again in July 1975, and dropped out again in March 1976. Nevertheless a small core of currencies remained in a joint float around the DM up to 1979, when the European Monetary System (EMS) was formed.

The EMS was proposed by Helmut Schmidt at the European Community summit meeting in Copenhagen in April 1978. Though some sentiment was expressed that the United States and Japan did not worry sufficiently about currency fluctuations, the primary motive for the formation of the EMS was really political: the proposal represented a joint effort by Germany and France to revive the movement toward European unification. The unification movement had fizzled out, and working on monetary union appeared to be a good way to get it going again. So, on March 13, 1979, a new "zone of monetary stability" in Europe was born. Seven of the community members had jointly floated their six currencies from January to March, and the EMS began officially when France joined in March. Following are the main points of the original EMS agreement.

1. Under the terms of the original agreement in 1979, the snake was to be enlarged to include all European Community member currencies. Great Britain, however, decided not to participate. It did not become a member of the parity grid system (2, below), even though the pound was included in the definition of the ECU (3, below). That left eight countries and seven currencies (since the Luxembourg franc is equivalent to the Belgian franc by a longstanding agreement between the central banks of those two countries). Greece subsequently became a member of the European Economic Community, but—like Britain — did not become a member of the European Monetary System. The Greek drachma was, however, included in the definition of the ECU beginning September 1984.

2. A **parity grid** system would be established. The parity grid would be a system of fixed par values, much like the Bretton Woods system although with fewer currencies and bigger bands around par. Each currency within the European Monetary System would have a declared par value with respect to each other currency in the system. A given currency would be allowed to deviate a maximum of plus or minus $2\frac{1}{4}$ percent from its par value with respect to any other currency, except for Italian lira, which would be allowed a range of plus or minus 6 percent. The parity grid as it originally existed on March 13, 1979, is illustrated in Table 2.3. The middle number in a cell is the par value, and the upper and lower numbers present the allowable range for market exchange rates. For example, the par value for the DM and French franc (FF) was originally set at DM 1 = FF 2.3095 (equivalently, FF 1 = DM .432995). The upper limit for the DM was DM 1 = FF 2.3621 (equivalently, the lower limit for the FF was FF 1 = DM .42335). The lower limit for the DM was DM 1 = FF 2.2581 (equivalently, the upper limit for the FF was FF 1 = DM .44285).

When a currency is at its upper or lower intervention point with respect to the parity grid, the central banks of *both* countries are obligated to intervene in the foreign exchange market to keep market exchange rates within the range allowed by the upper and lower bands. The intervention is "no-fault" under the parity grid system: each country is required to intervene to keep market exchange rates within the upper and lower grid values, irrespective of how it may feel about the other country's economic policies.

Technically, the par values in the parity grid are calculated by first defining a par value for each currency with respect to the ECU. (The ECU will be explained below. For now just think of it as another currency.) These par values defined in terms of the ECU are called ECU *central rates*. The ECU central rates are used to calculate the bilateral par values. For example, if the ECU central rates for the DM and the FF are ECU 1 = DM 4 and ECU 1 = FF 12, this implies a bilateral par value of DM 1 = FF 3. The ECU central rates used to calculate the parity grid are published daily in the *Financial Times* of London. When there is a "devaluation" or a "revaluation" in the EMS, a new set of ECU central rates is picked. The new ECU central rates then give rise to a new parity grid.

The device used to calculate the par values in the parity grid is irrelevant, however, since par values could just as easily be defined from scratch. In particular, the operation of the parity grid does not depend in any way on the ECU.

EXAMPLE 2.1

Here are the ECU central rates giving rise to the par values in the parity grid of Table 2.3:

ECU 1 = DM 2.51064
ECU 1 = FF 5.79831
ECU 1 = DG 2.72077
ECU 1 = BF 39.4582
ECU 1 = IL 1148.15
ECU 1 = DK 7.08592
ECU 1 = IP .662638

For example, since ECU 1 = DK 7.08592 and ECU 1 = IP .662638, we obtain IP 1 = DK (7.08592/.662638) = DK 10.6935. Alternatively, DK 1 = IP 1/(10.6938) = IP .0935147. And so on. As an example of a devaluation of the French franc in the EMS, we might reassign the ECU central rate for the French franc to be ECU 1 = FF 5.92884 instead of ECU 1 = 5.79831. This reassignment would give rise to a new set of bilateral par values in the parity grid, and —at these new par values— the French franc would buy smaller amounts of all other EMS currencies. Notice that "devaluation" in this case would refer to a change in the ECU central rate: a change in a number written down on paper. The market exchange rate for the French franc might or might not depreciate, depending on whether the new upper and lower bands implied central bank intervention to alter the market rate or whether the change in the ECU central rate caused market participants to change their demand for, or supply of, French francs.

After par values are determined, the next task is to calculate upper and lower intervention points around each parity grid par value. The allowable market exchange rate ranges above and below par are usually referred to as "$2\frac{1}{4}$ percent" bands (or "6 percent" bands in the case of lira). However, because of a mathematical relationship known as Jensen's inequality, the upper and lower intervention points cannot be calculated literally by adding or subtracting $2\frac{1}{4}$ percent (or 6 percent). Instead, the upper (lower) intervention points are obtained by multiplying (dividing) the par values by 1.022753 except for Italian lira, where the par value is multiplied (divided) by 1.061798.

□

To see why, consider the exchange rate of DM for FF. Suppose a par value of FF 4 = DM 1 is chosen. Rewriting this exchange rate in terms of the FF, we have FF 1 = DM .2500. If we then calculate plus or minus $2\frac{1}{4}$ percent upper and lower limit points, we get that (.0225) (4) = .0900 is to be added to, and subtracted

TABLE 2.3
The Original Parity Grid, March 13, 1979

	DM	FF	BF	IL	DK	DG	IP
DM		2.3621	16.074	485.576	2.8866	1.10835	.269937
		2.3095	15.7164	457.314	2.82237	1.0837	.263932
		2.2581	15.3665	430.698	2.7596	1.0596	.25806
FF	.44285		6.96	210.252	1.24985	.4799	.116881
	.432995		6.80512	198.015	1.22207	.469235	.114281
	.42335		6.65375	186.49	1.1949	.4588	.111739
BF	.06508	.15029		30.8961	.183665	.07052	.0171755
	.0636227	.146948		29.0979	.179581	.0689531	.0167934
	.06221	.14368		27.4044	.175585	.06742	.0164198
IL	.002322	.005362	.03649		.006553	.002516	.000612801
	.00218668	.00505013	.0343668		.0061716	.0023697	.000577135
	.002059	.004756	.032365		.005813	.00223175	.000543545
DK	.36235	.8369	5.695	172.045		.3927	.0956424
	.354313	.818286	5.56852	162.033		.383967	.0935147
	.34645	.8001	5.4445	152.605		.375425	.0914343
DG	.94375	2.1796	14.8325	448.074	2.66365		.249089
	.922767	2.13113	14.5026	421.995	2.60439		.243548
	.90225	2.0838	14.18	397.434	2.54645		.23813
IP	3.875	8.9495	60.9020	1839.78	10.9365	4.1995	
	3.78886	8.75034	59.5471	1732.7	10.6935	4.10597	
	3.705	8.5555	58.2225	1631.85	10.4555	4.0145	

DM = Deutschemark; FF = French franc; BF = Belgian franc; IL = Italian lira; DK = Danish krone; DG = Dutch guilder; IP = Irish pound.

from, the par value of 4, while $(.0225)(.2500) = .005625$ is to be added to, and subtracted from, the par value of .2500:

	FF per DM	DM per FF
Upper	4.0900	.255625
Par	4	.2500
Lower	3.9100	.244375

Examination of these numbers shows that even though 4 is the reciprocal of .2500, it is *not* true that 4.0900 is the reciprocal of .244375, nor is 3.9100 the reciprocal of .255625. Therefore, whether central banks are obligated to intervene may depend on which of the two currencies they use to calculate the upper or lower intervention points. This is obviously absurd: the same answer should be obtained independently of whether calculation is done in terms of DM or in terms of FF. ∎

☐
To get around this paradox, suppose we choose a number X by which we will first multiply, then divide, the par value P to get the upper and lower bands. If we do

the calculation this way, the paradox goes away: the upper and lower bands in terms of one currency are the reciprocals of the lower and upper bands of the other currency. If P represents the number of FF per DM at par, our table would read, after multiplying and dividing the par values by X:

	FF per DM	DM per FF
Upper	XP	X/P
Par	P	$1/P$
Lower	P/X	$1/XP$

As we see, XP is the reciprocal of $1/XP$, and P/X is the reciprocal of X/P. The next step then is to calculate the value of X in such a way that we get a total range of $4\frac{1}{2}$ percent around the par value (just as we would get by taking plus or minus $2\frac{1}{4}$ percent of par). That is, we want

$$XP - P/X = .045\ P,$$

which implies

$$X^2 - .045X - 1 = 0.$$

Solving for X, we get $X = 1.022753$. Therefore the par value is alternatively multiplied and divided by 1.022753 to get the upper and lower intervention points. For Italian lira, the total range is 12 percent or .12. Substituting .12 for .045 in the above equation and solving again for X, we get $X = 1.061798$ in the case of Italian lira. There are special rules as to whether a fraction is to be rounded up or down after the multiplication or division. These need not concern us here. ∎

EXAMPLE 2.2

Referring again to Table 2.3, we see that the par value for the DM with respect to the FF is DM 1 = FF 2.3095. If we multiply and divide the par value of FF 2.3095 by 1.022753, we get the upper and lower limits of DM 1 = FF 2.3621 and DM 1 = FF 2.2581. Similarly, the par value for the DM against the Italian lira is DM 1 = IL 457.314. If we multiply and divide IL 457.314 by 1.061798, we get the upper and lower limits of DM 1 = IL 485.576 and DM 1 = IL 430.698.

---

3. Germany had insisted on the parity grid system because it had viewed the purpose of the EMS as a way of imposing monetary discipline on member countries. However, other nations, in particular the United Kingdom and France, wanted a system organized according to the concept of community average, where average behavior would be considered good and "divergent" behavior bad. Either too little or too much inflation could be divergent behavior, for example, if the European Community average was moderate inflation.

The concept of average behavior was used as the basis for the divergence indicator system. The divergence indicator system differs in purpose and in practice from the parity grid system. The divergence indicator system is intended to deal with the old Bretton Woods question of who has to alter economic policies in order to maintain a fixed exchange rate. Bretton Woods broke down when the United States, on one hand, and Germany and Japan, on the other, disagreed on whose economic policy should be altered to conform to the other's. So the EMS set up a finger-pointing system, the divergence indicator system, which is supposed to answer the question of who is conducting economic policy that conflicts with everyone else's. For example, if both France and Germany are intervening in the foreign exchange market under the parity grid system to keep the French franc from falling in market value with respect to the DM, this could happen because French monetary policy is too expansionary or because German monetary policy is not expansionary enough. Hopefully, in such a case, the divergence indicator will pick out one of the two countries as having a divergent policy. If a country is divergent, then it is expected to adjust such things as money supply growth and the size of its government deficit to bring its macroeconomic policies in line with other EEC member countries.

Here is how the divergence indicator system works. First, an artificial currency, the European Currency Unit (ECU) was defined as a basket, or portfolio, of member currencies. The composition of the ECU as set in 1979 was:

$$1 \text{ ECU} = .828 \text{ DM} + 1.15 \text{ FF} + .0885 \text{ £} + .286 \text{ DG} + 109 \text{ IL}$$
$$+ 3.66 \text{ BF} + .14 \text{ LF} + .217 \text{ DK} + .00759 \text{ IP}$$

where LF = Luxembourg franc (equivalent to the Belgian franc), and the other currencies are those listed in Table 2.3. In September 1984, the composition of the basket was altered to include the Greek drachma (GD):

$$1 \text{ ECU} = .719 \text{ DM} + 1.31 \text{ FF} + .0878 \text{ £} + .256 \text{ DG} + 140 \text{ IL}$$
$$+ 3.71 \text{ BF} + .14 \text{ LF} + .219 \text{ DK} + .00871 \text{ IP} + 1.15 \text{ GD}.$$

Since the portfolio composition of the ECU is used as a measuring rod to determine "divergence," its composition will be altered infrequently. If, however, the Spanish peseta and Portuguese escudo were added to the EMS, the definition of the ECU would be changed to include these currencies. The economic policies of Spain and Portugal would then form part of the "community average."

Given the portfolio definition of the ECU, the *market* value of the ECU in terms of, say, the U.S. dollar would depend on the U.S. dollar price of each of the component currencies in the ECU. Suppose market exchange rates were these:

Foreign currency	U.S. dollar price of foreign currency
DM	.3998
FF	.1415
£	1.7125
DG	.3663
IL	.00071
BF,LF	.02
DK	.1134
IP	1.3650
GD	.0095

Then the current market value of the ECU, using the September 1984 definition, would be (adding together the weights for the BF and LF):

$$
\begin{aligned}
1 \text{ ECU} = &\ .719 \text{ DM } (\$.3998/\text{DM}) + 1.31 \text{ FF } (\$.1415/\text{FF}) \\
&+ .0878 \text{ £ } (\$1.7125/\text{£}) + .256 \text{ DG } (\$.3663/\text{DG}) \\
&+ 140 \text{ IL } (\$.00071/\text{IL}) + 3.85 \text{ BF } (\$.02/\text{BF}) \\
&+ .219 \text{ DK } (\$.1134/\text{DK}) + .00871 \text{ IP } (\$1.3650/\text{IP}) \\
&+ 1.15 \text{ GD } (\$.0095/\text{GD}) \\
= &\ \$.9410.
\end{aligned}
$$

In this example, the market value of the ECU in terms of a common measuring unit, the U.S. dollar, is ECU 1 = $.9410. If we compare this value to the market value of a member currency in terms of the U.S. dollar, we get the ECU market exchange rate for that currency. For example, since DM 1 = $.3998 in the foreign exchange market, and ECU 1 = $.9410 in the foreign exchange market, we get that the number of DM per ECU is ECU 1 = DM (.9410/.3998) = DM 2.3537. In the divergence indicator system, this ECU *market* value is compared to the ECU central rate (the rate written down on paper that is used to calculate the parity grid values). For example, suppose the ECU central rate were ECU 1 = DM 2.3324:

ECU central rate: ECU 1 = DM 2.3324
ECU market rate: ECU 1 = DM 2.3537.

Clearly, for the hypothetical market exchange rates above the DM would have diverged somewhat from its central value. The percentage movement in the DM from the central rate would be (DM 2.3537/DM 2.3324 − 1) × 100 = 1.009 percent. The DM would have depreciated in the foreign exchange market with respect to the ECU. The DM would have become less valuable.

EXAMPLE 2.3

In Table 2.4 we see the European monetary system as reported in the *Financial Times* for a particular date: January 23, 1984. The first column lists the ECU central rates used to determine the parity grid par values. These central rates were the ones in force in January 1984. The second column (Currency amounts against ECU January 20) gives the ECU *market* value of each currency as calculated using market exchange rates on January 20, 1984. The third column (Percent change from central rate) is calculated from the first two columns. For example, for the Belgian franc we have (46.0672/44.9008 − 1) × 100 = 2.60 percent.

How much movement of a currency's ECU market value away from the currency's ECU central value is too much under the divergence indicator? Two further steps are required to answer this question. First, an adjustment to the calculated amount of divergence is made in order to strip out the effects of the British pound and the Greek drachma (which are not in the grid, but are in the ECU), and to deal with the fact that the Italian lira has a wider band around par than do other currencies. In Table 2.4 this adjustment yields column 4 (Percent change adjusted for divergence), which is derived from column 3. Second, this

TABLE 2.4
The European Monetary System as Reported in the Financial Press

		EMS European Currency Unit Rates			
	ECU central rates	Currency amounts against ECU January 20	Percent change from central rate*	Percent change adjusted for divergence*	Divergence limit percentage
Belgian franc	44.9008	46.0672	+2.60	+1.89	±1.5447
Danish krona	8.14104	8.17828	+0.46	−0.25	±1.6425
German DM	2.24184	2.25708	+0.68	−0.03	±1.0642
French franc	6.87456	6.90646	+0.46	−0.25	±1.4052
Dutch guilder	2.52596	2.53921	+0.52	−0.19	±1.4964
Irish punt	0.72569	0.729121	+0.47	−0.24	±1.6699
Italian lira	1403.49	1374.85	−2.04	−2.04	±4.1505

* Changes are for ECU, therefore positive change denotes a weak currency. Adjustment calculated by *Financial Times.*
Source: Financial Times, January 23, 1984

adjusted percentage market divergence of a currency is compared to another number, the "threshold of divergence." If the adjusted divergence is greater than the threshold of divergence, the country is supposed to take action to bring its economic policy into conformity with the European Economic Community average. In Table 2.4, column 5 (Divergence limit percentage) gives the threshold of divergence for each currency. Comparing column 5 to column 4, we see that the Belgian franc is outside its threshold of divergence but that the other currencies are not. Thus Belgium was obligated at that time to bring its economic policies in line with the EEC average.

☐

Calculation of the threshold of divergence (column 5) as well as the adjusted market divergence (column 4) is somewhat complicated. To calculate the threshold of divergence, we first have to calculate the *weight* of each of the component currencies in the ECU, *using ECU central rates.* To get a currency's weight, simply divide the amount of a currency in the formal definition of the ECU by the ECU central rate for the currency. For example, the amount of the DM in the ECU in the 1979 portfolio definition was .828 DM. Table 2.4 shows that the ECU central rate on January 20, 1984, for the DM was ECU 1 = DM 2.24184. This implies a weight (w) for the DM of $w = (.828/2.24184) = .3693$. The DM, at the ECU central rates prevailing on January 20, 1984, made up 36.93 percent of the value of the ECU.

Each of the currencies in the ECU has its own weight, and the sum of the weights of the component currencies is 1. Since the British pound sterling and the Greek drachma are two of the ECU's component currencies, they too have a weight. Even though neither currency is part of the parity grid, they are assigned an ECU central value like other currencies, and these ECU central values are used to calculate the weights for the pound and the drachma. The presence of the pound and the drachma in the portfolio definition of the ECU introduces a complication in making the final calculation of the divergence indicator.

Under the parity grid, a currency can diverge approximately (but not exactly, as we saw above) 2.25 percent against other currencies, except for lira (approximately 6 percent) and the pound and the drachma (which are not in the grid). But in the divergence indicator calculations, it is initially pretended that all currencies, including lira, pound, and drachma, are only allowed an exact 2.25 percent divergence. Thus a currency can diverge 2.25 percent (.0225) against all other currencies, but even so a currency cannot diverge against itself. Since its divergence against itself is zero, the maximum possible divergence against the ECU is .0225 $[1 - w(i)]$, where $w(i)$ is the weight of the currency in the ECU. This is the idea behind the following definition.

Define a *maximum divergence M(i)* for each currency i, using the weight $w(i)$ of the currency in the ECU, where the weight is calculated using ECU central rates:

$M(i) = .0225 \, [1 - w(i)]$, currency i not Italian lira
$M(i) = .0600 \, [1 - w(i)]$, if i is Italian lira.

After the influence of a currency's own weight is eliminated (by multiplying by $1 - w(i)$), and if we ignore complications rising from lira, pound, and drachma, a maximum percentage divergence of 2.25 is possible if the currency is not Italian lira, or 6 percent for lira.

EXAMPLE 2.4

Referring to Table 2.4, we can calculate the maximum divergence for the DM against the ECU for January 20, 1984. Since the amount of the DM in the 1979 portfolio definition of the ECU was .828 DM, we calculate the weight of the DM as $w = (.828/2.24184) = .3693$. The maximum divergence M is then $M = (.0225) (1 - .3693) = .0142 = 1.42$ percent. For Italian lira, the weight is $w = (109/1403.49) = .0777 = 7.77$ percent. The maximum divergence for Italian lira is then $M = (.0600) (1 - .0777) = .0553 = 5.53$ percent.

A good "divergence" indicator should sound a warning before the maximum is reached, so finally, a *threshold of divergence T(i)* is calculated as 75 percent of the maximum divergence:

$T(i) = .75 \, (.0225) \, [1 - w(i)]$, i not lira
$T(i) = .75 \, (.0600) \, [1 - w(i)]$, for lira.

EXAMPLE 2.5

The threshold of divergence for the DM on January 20, 1984, was

$T = .75 \, (.0225) \, (1 - .3693) = .01064 = 1.064\%.$

This value is recorded in the *Financial Times* column labeled "Divergence limit percentage" in Table 2.4. What this number indicates is that if the DM goes up or down more than 1.064 percent from its ECU central rate, the threshold of divergence has been reached, and the German authorities are supposed to alter economic policy in such a way that the market exchange value of the DM will move back in the other direction. The threshold of divergence for the Italian lira is $T = .75\ (.0600)\ (1 - .0777) = .04150 = 4.150$ percent. And so on for the other values in the column.

The values for the threshold of divergence remain the same as long as the ECU central values (and definition of the ECU) remain the same. At times when there has been a devaluation or revaluation in the EMS and new ECU central values assigned, the values for the threshold of divergence have changed correspondingly.

The .75 used in the definition of threshold of divergence is a number that was assigned arbitrarily. One problem the EMS wished to avoid, however, was that of having two countries reach a divergence limit in the parity grid and also have both countries "divergent" according to the threshold of divergence indicator. It was calculated that if the assigned number was as low as .68, it was possible for the DM/FF to hit the upper or lower band of the parity grid and also to have both France and Germany divergent according to the divergence indicator system. Thus a number larger than .68 but smaller than 1.0 was picked.

Now, it may seem at this point that all that is left to do is compare the ECU central rate for each currency with the ECU market rate for that currency and see if they differ by more than the threshold of divergence. That is, we would just compare column 3 and column 5. However, one more necessary calculation involves an adjustment to column 3. Remember that when we defined the threshold of divergence we pretended that the lira, pound, and drachma were only allowed a 2.25 percent margin around par in the parity grid. But since the United Kingdom and Greece do not participate in the parity grid, and since the lira's margin is really 6.0 percent, in the foreign exchange market these currencies can move freely outside the pretended range. So the final adjustment is to strip out the effects of market movements of these currencies that are greater than 2.25 percent from par. We start by finding the weakest currency in the system. Suppose it is the Belgian franc. If the Belgian franc has moved more than 2.25 percent against either the lira, the pound, or the drachma, adjustments are calculated. Let (BF/£)market denote the current market exchange rate of the BF against the £, and let (BF/£)central denote the BF/£ exchange rate calculated from their ECU central rates. An adjustment factor for the £, Adj(£), is then calculated (for a movement greater than 2.25 percent) as:

$$\text{Adj(£)} = (100\ [(\text{BF/£})\text{market}/(\text{BF/£})\text{central}] - 102.25) \times \\ (\text{weight of £ in the ECU}).$$

A similar adjustment for the Italian lira is calculated (if the movement has been greater than 2.25 percent):

$$\text{Adj(IL)} = (100\ [(\text{BF/IL})\text{market}/(\text{BF/IL})\text{central}] - 102.25) \times \\ (\text{weight of IL in the ECU}).$$

In the same way, an adjustment—Adj(GD)—is also calculated for the Greek drachma. The measure of current market divergence for currency i, before the adjustments for the lira and pound have been taken into account, is

$$\text{Div}(i) = 100\ (\text{ECU market rate for currency } i/ \\ \text{ECU central rate for currency } i) - 100.$$

In Table 2.4, the column giving values for Div(i) is labeled "Percent change from central rate" (column 3). Finally, if

$$|\text{Div}(i) - \text{Adj}(\pounds) - \text{Adj}(IL) - \text{Adj}(GD)| > T(i),$$

then currency i has crossed its threshold of technical divergence, and the country is signaled that it must take measures to bring its economic policy into conformity with that of other countries. The expression $|\text{Div}(i) - \text{Adj}(\pounds) - \text{Adj}(IL) - \text{Adj}(GD)|$ is called "Percentage change adjusted for divergence" in Table 2.4, column 4.

EXAMPLE 2.6

On January 20, 1984, the British pound was outside the $2\frac{1}{4}$ percent range from its assigned ECU central rate. Simultaneously, the weakest currency in the EMS system was the Belgian franc. A calculation, using the weight of the £ in the ECU and the Belgian franc/£ pound exchange rate, determined that Adj(£) = −.71%. The Italian lira was not outside the $2\frac{1}{4}$ percent range, so Adj(IL) = 0. Hence Adj(£) + Adj(IL) = −.71% + 0% = −.71%. A total adjustment factor of −.71 percent was then added to column 3 in Table 2.4 to determine the values in column 4 (" Percent change adjusted for divergence"). For example, the percentage change from the central rate for the Belgian franc was 2.60 percent. Adding the adjustment factor, we get 2.60% + (−.71%) = 1.89%. Comparing this value with the divergence limit of 1.5447 percent, we see that the Belgian franc was outside the allowable range. This implied that it was the responsibility of the relevant authorities in Belgium to change economic policy to conform to EMS standards. All other EMS currencies, by contrast, were well within their divergence limits.

■

4. A final provision of the EMS agreement was that member countries would buy into a credit fund with 20 percent of their dollars, gold, and other reserves. In return they would be issued ECUs to be used for central bank settlement and would also have borrowing privileges to obtain foreign exchange for intervention. This "fund" was really just a set of books kept at the Bank for International Settlements (BIS) in Basel, Switzerland. The portion of a central bank's gold and other reserves which has been "turned over" to the fund through book entry transfers really remains safe and sound in the central bank's own vault.

This, then, is the cumbersome system of the EMS. Has it been a success? The answer depends on what one means by success. In terms of the original goal to revive the movement toward political unification by working for monetary union, little has been accomplished. Countries such as Germany and France have done little to coordinate economic policies, even though their central banks have generally maintained exchange rates within the ranges permitted by the parity grid. A combination of relatively fixed exchange rates with divergent inflation rates in the early 1980s may have resulted in distortions in international trade through unnecessary changes in real exchange rates (discussed in Chapter 8). As a result of this lack of policy coordination, the ECU central rate for the DM was changed by 5.5 percent on October 5, 1981, by 4.25 percent on June 14,

1982, and by 5.5 percent on March 21, 1983, the changes reflecting an increase in the value of the DM. The corresponding ECU percentage changes for the French franc on those dates were − 3 percent, − 5.75 percent, − 2.5 percent. For example, the combination of a 5.5 percent increase in the ECU value of the DM on March 21, 1983, along with a − 2.5 percent change in the ECU value of the French franc resulted in a net change of roughly 8 percent in the bilateral par value of the DM against the FF in the parity grid. On paper, at the par value, the DM bought 8 percent more FF after the realignment. In all, ECU central rates were realigned eight times from 1979 to July 1985. In the last realignment, the Italian lira was devalued by 6 percent, while the other participating EMS currencies were revalued upward by 2 percent, following a fall in the lira from IL 1840/U.S. dollar to IL 2200/U.S. dollar on July 19, 1985. (See problem 11 at the end of this chapter.)

The ECU, however, has become an important unit used to denominate trade between Common Market countries. ECU-denominated bond issues and syndicated loans are common, and there has developed a liquid ECU interbank deposit market formed by more than a thousand banks in thirty countries. By 1985, ECU traveler's checks and credit cards were available, and more than 200 European banks offered ECU-denominated checking accounts. The market's further development, however, was hindered somewhat by Bundesbank opposition to the use of the ECU in Germany. As of 1985, it was not clear that business contracts stated in terms of the ECU were legally binding under German commercial law.

THE INTERNATIONAL DEBT CRISIS

In the mid-1970s and again in the early 1980s, the "debt crisis" was a prominent financial market preoccupation, particularly in the eurocurrency markets, but eventually spilling over into domestic markets as well. Of particular relevance was debt owed by borrowers in developing countries to commercial banks in industrial countries. During the period extending from the end of 1973 to the end of 1982, debt of non-OPEC developing countries owed to banks in the United States, Canada, Western Europe, and Japan (BIS reporting banks) increased by $215 billion, according to BIS data. This total growth in bank debt was approximately twice the growth in nominal GNP of non-OPEC LDCs and more than two times the growth in their exports. Bank debt as a proportion of exports rose from 60 percent to 130 percent. This dramatic increase in non-OPEC LDC bank debt (accompanied also by an increase in other types of debt) was only in part associated with an increase in the price of energy. More importantly, bank debt growth represented a significant expansion in non-energy-related public sector deficits financed by foreign borrowing and a major shift from equity to debt financing in the non-OPEC LDC private and state enterprise sectors.

We can divide up this time period into OPEC I (1973–1978) and OPEC II (1979–1982). The embargo by the Organization of Petroleum Exporting Countries (OPEC) that followed the Egyptian attack on Israel in October 1973 saw the price of Saudi Arabian light crude rise from $1.73 per barrel to $10. Over the next year, the nominal price increased to $12. Afterward, however, while the nominal price continued to rise, the real price (the price adjusted for purchasing power) fell and continued to fall until 1979. With the Iranian revolution in 1979 (OPEC

II), the real price of oil rose again, the nominal price going to $30 a barrel, then higher. Only in 1982 did the nominal price begin a significant drift downward.

Prior to the first round of oil price increases, non-OPEC LDCs had run modest current account deficits financed mostly through official capital transfers, direct investment, and import finance. With a rise in oil costs, many nations (such as Brazil) decided as a matter of deliberate policy to continue their pace of energy consumption through international borrowing. Others, such as Mexico and Nigeria, used the presence of oil reserves as the basis for new social and "development" programs. Since there was neither a large domestic savings base nor a significant capital market in any of these countries, government deficits were financed either by borrowing in foreign capital markets, thus increasing foreign debt, or by selling bonds to the central bank, which vastly increased the high-powered monetary base. Large money supply increases were accompanied by significant inflation and — because exchange rates were fixed and only adjusted at government discretion — the domestic currency in many cases became significantly overvalued. As a result, export sectors became increasingly noncompetitive while import sectors were subsidized by access to artificially cheap foreign exchange. Deterioration in the balance of trade from currency overvaluation made it increasingly difficult to generate foreign exchange to repay foreign debts independently of other factors mentioned below.

Over the 1974–1978 period the OPEC countries ran an accumulated current account surplus of $179.1 billion, according to IMF data. That means that, in terms of goods and services, OPEC countries sold more than they purchased by $179.1 billion. When a country runs a current account surplus, it accumulates wealth in the form of financial assets: bank deposits, treasury bills, and other types of IOUs. The mirror image of OPEC's surplus is the rest of the world, which — if the numbers are measured correctly (and they usually are not) — had an equivalent deficit. If the numbers are to be believed, the non-OPEC LDCs had an accumulated deficit over the 1974–1978 period of $187.4 billion (see Table 2.5). That is, much of the OPEC surplus translated directly into a non-OPEC LDC deficit. Thus the accumulation of financial assets by OPEC countries was mirrored by an accumulation of foreign debt by non-OPEC developing countries.

The largest single category of asset accumulation by OPEC countries was in the form of eurocurrency deposits. According to Bank of England estimates, net OPEC eurodeposits over the 1974–1978 period were about $64 billion. Eurobanks accumulated OPEC assets and made loans on the basis of these assets. Now, there is no reason these loans necessarily had to go to any particular category of borrower. It is conceivable, for example, that eurobank lending could have gone exclusively to U.S. or French companies. However, as it turned out, eurobanks played a direct role in the "recycling" process. Gross medium-term euroborrowing by non-OPEC LDCs was about $63 billion over the 1974–1978 period. Thus eurobanks acted to channel the financial savings of OPEC directly to non-OPEC LDCs, during the OPEC I period.

The "Erdman scenario" presented by Paul Erdman in his novel *The Crash of '79,* a book that appeared in 1976 and was widely read by policy-makers, went like this: OPEC accumulates a lot of short-term deposits in eurobanks. Banks turn these short-term deposits into longer-term loans to developing countries on a rollover basis. Then one day there is a run on eurobanks when OPEC funds are

TABLE 2.5
Current Account Balances of OPEC and Non-OPEC LDCs During the First and Second Oil Shocks

	1973	1974	1975	1976	1977	1978	1979	1980	1981	1982	1983
Current account (billions of U.S.$)											
OPEC:	6.7	68.3	35.4	40.3	29.4	5.7	62.3	110.3	52.0	−13.5	−18.4
Non-OPEC LDCs:	−11.3	−37.0	−46.3	−32.6	−29.6	−41.9	−62.1	−87.7	−108.3	−86.1	−52.1
Increase in official reserves by non-OPEC LDCS (billions of U.S.$)	10.4	2.7	−1.7	13.0	11.2	16.5	11.7	6.7	3.7	−4.1	10.1
Price index of non-oil primary commodities exported by non-OPEC LDCs (percentage change per year)	51.2	30.3	−17.8	17.0	25.4	−7.2	14.4	9.7	−15.2	−13.4	9.1

Source: IMF, *World Economic Outlook* (data prior to 1977 are taken from 1983 volume; subsequent data are taken from 1985 volume).

switched from eurodeposits to other types of assets. Banks try to call in their loans, but the developing countries cannot pay. The international financial system collapses. "Do you really think it could happen?" U.S. Vice-President Nelson Rockefeller reportedly asked Erdman. The Erdman scenario never came about. An OPEC run on eurodollar assets was fairly implausible, because OPEC assets were being managed by people trained in the top U.S. and U.K. business schools. A massive switch into other currencies would drive down the exchange value of the dollar, with a resulting capital loss of OPEC assets. In addition, a run on particular banks conducted in such a way as to lead to widespread bank failures would also threaten OPEC's accumulated financial wealth. Finally, as the most important factor, non-OPEC LDCs were able to repay their debts without any great difficulty during the OPEC I period.

The real burden of non-OPEC LDC debt was steadily eroded over the 1974–1978 period because nominal interest rates on borrowing failed to keep pace with the rise in inflation. As a result, the great "recycling problem" was solved under OPEC I without protracted adjustments in economic policy in developing countries. The average dollar borrowing rate over the 1974–1978 period was roughly zero in real terms. Much of the lending had been made at a margin above the six-month London Interbank Offer Rate (LIBOR), the market rate at which banks lend eurodollars to each other in London. Interest rates would be fixed at the beginning of each six-month period, then changed at the beginning of the next period, according to the prevailing LIBOR rate. Average six-month LIBOR for the U.S. dollar during 1974–1978 was 8.3 percent. The average dollar inflation rate was about 8.0 percent, giving an ex-post real interest rate of .3 percent (see Table 2.6). The existence of low real borrowing rates is further seen when the

TABLE 2.6
Real Borrowing Rates and Real Growth Rates for Selected Borrowing Countries

	1974–1978 (%)	1979 (%)	1980 (%)	1981 (%)	1982 (%)
Average 6-months LIBOR (U.S.$)	8.3	12.1	14.3	17.2	13.0
U.S.$ inflation (CPI)	8.0	13.2	12.4	8.9	6.0
Real dollar rate of interest	.3	−1.1	1.9	8.3	7.0
Real growth in GNP					
Mexico	5.5	8.7		4.5	
Brazil	7.0	7.4		−1.7	
Argentina	1.4	4.3		−6.0	
Chile	3.3	7.9		−2.6	
Colombia	5.6	4.5		3.0	
Ecuador	6.8	4.9		2.9	
Peru	2.0	3.5		2.3	
Venezuela*	6.1	−0.2		0	
Indonesia*	7.0	7.5		6.3	
Korea	10.4	0.1		6.0	
Malaysia	7.1	8.6		5.2	
Phillipines	6.3	5.9		3.2	
Taiwan	9.0	7.3		4.7	
Thailand	10.3	5.9		6.3	

* OPEC member.

Source: Morgan Guaranty, World Financial Markets.

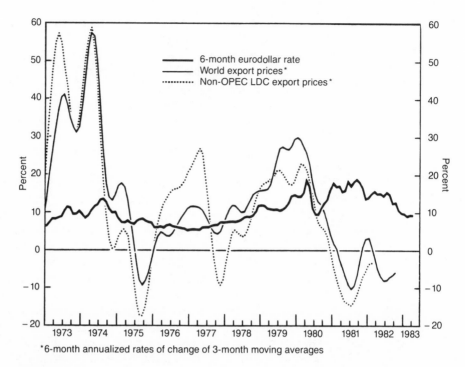

FIGURE 2.1
Growth in non-OPEC LDC export prices compared to eurodollar borrowing rate, 1973 – 1983. [*Source:* BIS, *Fifty-Third Annual Report.*]

nominal eurodollar borrowing rate is compared, not with inflation, but with the rate of growth of non-OPEC LDC export prices (see Figure 2.1 and Table 2.5). The rapid growth in export prices meant that the burden of foreign interest payments on debt used to finance exports was falling continuously over this period. (A similar situation existed in the U.S. domestic market, where the appreciation in real estate, energy, and farm product prices outran interest payments on mortgages, and energy and farm loans.) This propitious state of affairs, from a borrower's standpoint, allowed non-OPEC LDCs to accumulate a considerable proportion of borrowings in the form of foreign exchange reserves. (See Table 2.5 for the years 1976–1978.)

Some significant changes in the outlook for further debt increases had taken place by 1979, however. The variable interest rate portion of the debt (such as that based on LIBOR) had gone up, leaving debtors more vulnerable to a sudden increase in short-term real interest rates. And by the end of 1979, 52 percent of non-OPEC LDC debt to BIS-reporting banks was concentrated in the MBA countries (Mexico, Brazil, and Argentina), leaving lending banks with a relatively nondiversified international loan portfolio. With the second major round of oil-price increases in 1979, apparently remembering the relative ease in which the first oil shock had been endured, major developing countries like Brazil and Mexico not only continued the previous pace of borrowing but expanded it considerably — Mexico expecting ever-increasing oil revenues, while Brazil faced increased payments for imported oil. Greater borrowing implied, of course, greater lending, showing that borrowers' repayment assumptions were shared also by the headquarters offices of lending banks. (A clear shift in bank lending assumptions did not emerge until the announcement of a ninety-day debt moratorium by Mexico on August 20, 1982.) The role of the euromarkets continued to be important under OPEC II, as under OPEC I, with eurocurrency bank credits to non-OPEC LDCs totaling $113 billion from the beginning of 1979 to mid-1982, according to Morgan Guaranty data. Branches and subsidiaries, as well as head offices, of U.S. banks played a particularly important role. By 1982, total outstanding loans made by the nine largest U.S. banks to borrowers in the three MBA countries alone exceeded 100 percent of the aggregate paid-in capital and reserves of those nine banks.

Not only was the pace of borrowing initially much greater than before, it coincided with a major shift in the pattern of real interest rates. In the first two years of OPEC II, 1979–1980, real dollar borrowing rates remained at zero but rose dramatically afterward, as seen in Table 2.6. The worldwide economic slump among industrial countries over the period (real GNP growth fell from about 4 percent in 1978 to 0 in 1982) resulted also in a sharp drop in demand for non-OPEC LDC exports, with a consequent drop in non-OPEC LDC export revenues and real growth rates. Standard development models suggest that if a country's foreign borrowing is used for productive investment, then the country's foreign debt will stabilize at some fraction of GNP as long as the country's real growth rate exceeds its real borrowing rate. But Table 2.6 shows that after 1980 real dollar borrowing rates had come to exceed real growth rates in many developing countries. Complicating the picture was the fact that borrowing was sometimes used to finance consumption or nonproductive prestige investment projects or was funneled into inefficient state enterprises, and thus had little potential to generate a sufficient return to repay the debt. Further complications were introduced by bizarre political developments, such as the decision of Argentina's military government to go to war over the Falklands/Malvinas Islands in April 1982 during a period of negative real GNP growth, and Lopez-Portillo's compounding of a crisis of confidence in the Mexican financial system by nationalizing Mexican banks following the debt moratorium announced in August 1982.

Thus, not only were developing countries not aided by an inflationary erosion of their debt burden accompanied by rapidly increasing export prices, as happened in the mid-1970s, but in the early 1980s they faced real interest rates that were as much above the historical norm as the 1970s' real interest rates had been below the norm. In the year following the Mexican crisis of August 1982, some thirty countries entered rescheduling agreements with commercial banks, and policy-makers in the United States and other major lending countries worried greatly about the possible consequences of widespread defaults on both the international and domestic financial systems. Relations among debtor countries, international banks, the IMF, and industrial country governments took on the characteristics of a complex game of strategy. We can briefly summarize the players and their roles as follows.

Lending Banks

By 1983 most lending banks viewed the amount and pace of lending from 1979 to mid-1982 as excessive and a mistake of judgment on their part, regardless of the amount of time they spent justifying themselves in public. But now they had to make the best of the situation. To cut off all lending immediately would ensure that bank lending exposure did not increase and also promised to bring about an economic and political crisis in borrowing countries of sufficient magnitude to ensure that little of the debt already outstanding would ever be repaid. That would leave the major banks technically bankrupt, which was not a possibility they could contentedly contemplate, and at any rate appeared to be a suboptimal solution. Therefore, they were willing to lend even more, because they calculated that to do so would increase the total risk-adjusted expected return on lending. The probability of the lending banks being repaid was not independent of the lending behavior of the banks themselves. However, the probability of banks being repaid was not independent of the behavior of borrowing countries either. To ensure that borrowing countries adjusted their economic policies in ways the banks considered appropriate, they made both new lending and rescheduling of existing debt contingent on borrowing countries' acceptance of an IMF program of macroeconomic adjustment.

Borrowing Country Governments

The governments of borrowing countries did not want IMF programs. In the first place, they didn't like other people telling them what to do. IMF lending was based on conditionality, and the IMF would not lend unless the country agreed to certain criteria with respect to government deficits, growth of the money supply, wage increases, price inflation, and exchange rates. In the second place, to admit the need for an IMF program could suggest that the current government was economically incompetent. This meant that, at best, IMF programs could only be accepted after — and not immediately before — governmental elections. But the amount of funds the IMF itself had to lend was puny. Borrowing country governments did not consider the magnitude of IMF loans worth the IMF hassle. Rather, they would only countenance an IMF program because that was the only way they could get money from commercial banks.

As an alternative, borrowing country governments could simply refuse to pay their debts. That way they wouldn't need to deal with the IMF or the banks, and they could keep the foreign exchange that would otherwise be spent on debt payments. This, however, was not an attractive option. Foreign banks would no longer lend, and foreign countries would embargo trade in the goods of the debt-repudiating country. Repudiation might prove politically popular at home for a time. But sentiment would change when import credits and imports dried up and export markets were closed. A few countries (including Argentina, which Walter Wriston, the Citibank chairman, suggested *was* the debt crisis) were essentially self-sufficient, but there would be little joy in having all of one's foreign assets seized by banks in the industrial countries. In addition, in the absence of borrowing, the curtailment of certain domestic programs would be much more severe than would be the case if an IMF program were accepted along with additional credit. So the best policy appeared to be to negotiate with the banks and the IMF but to try to arrange things so that the banks and the IMF took as much of local dissatisfaction as possible while the government took as little as possible. The government strategy would be to nurture the image that it was "standing firm" against the banks and the IMF and getting as many "concessions" as possible. Of course, changes would still have to be made. But if, for example, the IMF insisted that the government deficit be cut and the government elected to remove food subsidies in place of a reduction in military expenditures as a way of meeting the IMF requirement, the reduction in food subsidies could be announced as part of the IMF program. The IMF was responsible — not the government, which had done its best. But this strategy, too, was dangerous. It ran the risk of making any negotiation appear government collaboration with the enemy. A graffito on a wall in Brazil alleged that IMF (abbreviated FMI, in Portuguese) stood for *fome* (hunger), *morte* (death), and *imperialismo*. Was not a government that accepted an IMF program guilty of the same things?

The IMF

The IMF was subject to the normal bureaucratic imperative to increase its role in world affairs. With the breakdown of Bretton Woods, no one was certain what the function of the IMF was, and no one seemed to care. Henry Morgenthau had thought the IMF would "drive the usurious money-lenders from the temple of international finance," but in the mid-1970s the IMF found itself very much on the outside, looking in, while the international banks recycled the OPEC surplus. The new offices on 19th Street in Washington were filled with people, but not — apparently — with purpose. Then came OPEC II. The desire of the commercial banks to involve the IMF in rescheduling gave the IMF new leverage in the affairs of member nations. And it exercised this leverage in accordance with its charter. The banks and the public often seemed to view the IMF as an international aid agency. It was not. It was set up to make balance of payments loans, and its programs were designed to improve the current account balance.

In pursuing its policies, the IMF faced criticism beyond simple developing country resentment. The focus of IMF programs did not appear to meet the objective of a long-run solution to the borrowing countries' debt problem. It seemed to be clear that repayment of non-OPEC LDC debt could only be brought about in the long run by the pursuit of policies that promoted real growth in those countries. IMF programs had certainly led to dramatic improvement in the trade balances of, for example, the MBA countries during 1982 and 1983. The current account deficit of $30.4 billion in 1981 fell to $5.9 billion in 1983. But this improvement had come largely by cutting imports. Such a policy was not sustainable, because the reduction in raw material stocks and spare parts had brought investment to a standstill in certain sectors. In addition, since many borrowing countries traded with each other, a reduction in imports automatically entailed a reduction in the exports of their trading partners. An IMF program that might be good for one country did not appear to make much sense when simultaneously applied to thirty.

Industrial Countries

United States policy was of particular relevance. Even though commercial banks would be the major lenders to non-OPEC LDCs, by 1983 the IMF needed more funds even to do the limited lending associated with the acceptance of its programs. That meant more funds for the IMF had to be supplied by member countries, and the United States was to make the largest contribution ($8.4

billion). While an increased contribution was supported by the administration of Ronald Reagan, the funds had to be approved by Congress, which in turn was simultaneously concerned with the interests of U.S. banks and with U.S. voter preferences. The mood of Congress was to punish the banks, for they had sinned. Congress might be willing to vote more funds for the IMF, but not without a bit of bank-bashing first. Did not banks, who had used the hard-earned savings of American workers to fund jungle boondoggles, need more oversight? The IMF was not popular either. The Black Caucus did not like the IMF because it had made balance of payments loans to South Africa. Conservatives did not like the IMF because it had made loans to communist countries in Eastern Europe. Libertarians viewed the IMF quota increase as a scheme to bail out bank stockholders. And those who disliked financial market deregulation said "Look, we loosened up on bank regulation, and now see what a fine mess we have." While the U.S. contribution to the IMF was eventually approved in early 1984, the various domestic political approaches continued to be important influences in international negotiations. Meanwhile, until mid-1985, the banks and bank regulators coordinated in bending reporting rules on performing and nonperforming loans. They appeared to think that the debt crisis was a big secret. They were convinced that there would be a public financial panic if banks' financial disclosure forms accurately reported what everyone already knew to be the case.

By mid-1985, three years after the Mexican "shock" of August 1982, the question of debt repayment appeared to have been postponed rather than resolved. New scheduling arrangements had shifted the burden of principal repayment to the latter half of the 1980s, suggesting the probability that any downturn in the world business cycle in that period would bring with it renewed problems. In the meantime, the crisis atmosphere had disappeared. Largely responsible for this was a pickup in LDC exports due to renewed growth in the United States, which by 1985 was buying about 45 percent of the exports of the seventeen largest debtors. According to IMF data, the combined current account deficit of the non-OPEC LDCs fell from $108 billion in 1981 to $38 billion in 1984. Other significant changes, in addition to the renewed growth in world trade, were increases in non-oil commodity prices and a falling level of nominal interest rates. But even in this improved environment, some countries—such as Argentina—were failing to make timely payments of interest, much less principal.

THE OPENING OF JAPANESE FINANCIAL MARKETS

Outside the United States, the country with the largest bond and stock markets and banking and thrift sectors is Japan. One of the most significant international financial developments of the 1980s has been the gradual opening of these markets to the outside world. Some background history will give perspective to this trend.

U.S. occupation policy after World War II in Japan followed a course similar to that in Europe. The initial emphasis under General Douglas MacArthur in Japan was with demilitarization and political reform. But after 1948 the focus shifted to the economy, both because economic stability and prosperity were considered a necessary prerequisite to make the Japanese reforms work and because economic growth promised to reduce the costs of U.S. occupation. In

Germany, the original occupation plan had been for deindustrialization and the breaking up of "dangerous concentrations of economic power" (JCS 1067), but this plan was soon replaced with the operating assumption that an "orderly and prosperous Europe requires the economic contribution of a stable and productive Germany" (JCS 1779). Similarly in Japan, MacArthur's preoccupation with breaking up the *zaibatsu* (major industrial or financial groupings characterized by joint decision-making) was de-emphasized, and rein was given to those who could make the economy work. Versailles formed a backdrop in Japan as it had in Europe. The Japanese peace treaty was negotiated by John Foster Dulles from the U.S. side and Shigeru Yoshida from the Japanese. Both had served in a diplomatic capacity at Versailles in 1919, and both were convinced that the vindictive terms of the 1919 peace treaty with Germany had been partly responsible for the later war of Adolf Hitler and General Tojo Hideki.

The financial legacy of the occupation was a semimarket economy involving heavy government regulation. Foreign exchange transactions were strictly controlled. Interest rates on bank deposits were fixed by law in an attempt to channel the flow of private savings, and hence bank credit, into those economic sectors favored by government policy. Special long-term credit banks, which made loans to industry, were given the exclusive banking right to finance themselves by issuing long-maturity bonds. Although private nonfinancial corporations also had the right to issue bonds, the latter companies were effectively denied access to the bond market by the requirement that bond issues be collaterized with company assets. As a result, a significant corporate bond market in Japan did not develop. A further and much later consequence was that Japanese companies would begin to make increasing use of the eurobond and foreign bond markets in the 1970s.

Article 65 of the Securities and Exchange Law erected a division between commercial and investment banking. It prohibited banks from underwriting bond issues or trading corporate stock. This article was patterned after the Glass-Steagall Act (1933) in the United States.

Despite these and other impediments to the development of financial markets, the *potential* importance of Japan as an international financial center grew because of the expanding economy and domestic savings base. American involvement was important to Japanese growth in the beginning. U.S. assistance to Japan over the 1945–1952 period amounted to about 4 percent of Japan's GNP and 15 percent of Japan's imports. The Korean War (1950–1953) that followed brought an economic boom to the country, with U.S. military procurements from Japan reaching 7 percent of Japan's GNP in 1953. Real gross domestic product growth of over 9 percent per year continued to 1965, when the Vietnam War (1965–1972) brought another economic boom. Japan became a member of GATT in 1955 and the IMF in 1964. By 1980 Japan was not only the world's third largest economy (after the United States and the Soviet Union) as measured by GNP, but also the third largest trading nation (after the United States and West Germany) as measured by the dollar value of exports. As in the United States, however, the export sector was a smaller fraction of the overall domestic economy than in other trading nations. Exports as a percentage of GNP were 10 percent for the United States and 15 percent for Japan, as compared to 20 percent for France, 28 percent for the United Kingdom and West Germany, and 57 percent for the Netherlands.

Nevertheless, Japan treated trade with special importance, not only because exports formed a major share of certain industries (like automobiles, electronic goods) but also because Japan imported most of its raw materials. This included most of its oil and about half the caloric value of its food. This export/import dependence focused attention on the U.S. dollar/Japanese yen exchange rate, since on the one hand the United States was Japan's most important export destination (so that a rise in the real value of the yen against the dollar was considered by Japanese exporters to be threatening) and, on the other hand, crucial imports such as oil were also priced in dollars (so that a fall in the exchange value of the yen against the dollar raised the price of oil in domestic currency terms). Major shocks to the Japanese economy in the 1970s revolved around these simple relationships. Of particular note were the "Nixon shock" of 1971 (the revaluation of the yen upward by 16.9 percent against the U.S. dollar), the U.S. embargo on soybean exports in 1973, and the unanticipated oil price increases in 1973 and 1979. The initial Japanese policy reaction to the supply-related increases in the prices of food and energy in 1973 was strongly to expand aggregate demand. Significant additional price inflation was the principal result. The rate of growth of the GNP deflator, which had averaged 4.7 percent in the previous ten years (1963–1972) rose to 11.7 percent in 1973 and 20.6 percent in 1974. Overall, the yearly inflation rate during the OPEC I period (1974–1978) was 8.9 percent. The same type of expansionary policy was not repeated during the OPEC II period (1979–1982), and the yearly rate of Japanese inflation only averaged 2.5 percent.

In the late 1960s, as the DM and the yen became undervalued with respect to the U.S. dollar, official Japanese policy seemed to prefer the situation, since at that time the price of imported oil was low anyway, and the undervalued yen gave a stimulus to exports. According to Hendrik Houthakker, the Japanese "were happy with their undervalued currency which gave them a tremendous volume of exports. The Japanese were (and perhaps are) great believers in 'export-led growth'; the large growth in their exports meant a high rate of growth for the country as a whole. It was a dubious proposition because they were in effect giving some of their exports away. The imports they got in return were not commensurate with the value of those exports." After the breakdown of Bretton Woods, on the other hand, there was no official Japanese attempt to undervalue the yen, though some company executives in inefficient U.S. industries such as automobiles and steel would sometimes suggest otherwise. Rather, the Bank of Japan pursued a policy of " leaning against the wind" — intervening to slow the pace of yen appreciation against the dollar in years like 1978, while intervening to slow the pace of yen depreciation against the dollar in years like 1982.

The feeling of yen undervaluation became particularly strong after 1980, when an increasing Japanese current account surplus was accompanied by an increasing U.S. current account deficit. This feeling was based in part on a misconception, since a Japanese current account surplus was not of itself evidence of an undervalued yen. Rather, the current account surplus was partly the simple consequence of the high Japanese savings rate. In a world of capital (savings) mobility, the Japanese would save in part through a net acquisition of foreign financial assets. This would require Japan to run a current account surplus (sell more than it purchased) as a way of generating a net yearly flow of savings in the form of foreign IOUs.

Nevertheless, it was not clear how much the high Japanese savings rate represented a genuine difference in preferences and how much was inspired by policy. Some of the factors contributing to the high savings rate included tax-exempt savings deposits available from the postal savings system, minimal provisions for social security, and limited availability of mortgages and consumer credit.

Capital controls were another issue. With the demise of Bretton Woods, the United States, Germany, and the United Kingdom worked gradually to relax constraints on the movements of capital. But Japan maintained strict controls both on the inflow of capital (direct or portfolio investment in Japanese assets by foreigners) and on the outflow of capital (the acquisition of foreign assets by Japanese citizens). An exception to the inflow prohibition was that Japanese companies were allowed to issue foreign-currency-denominated bonds (such as U.S. dollar eurobonds) after December 1973. However, foreigners were barred from membership in the Tokyo Stock Exchange, and foreign securities and insurance companies were not allowed to compete with domestic firms. Foreign banks could make foreign currency loans to Japanese business but faced restrictions on conducting local currency (yen) business, as they were restricted in their ability to borrow in the domestic (yen) money market or to engage in currency swaps to hedge their exchange risk if they borrowed in external money markets (currency swaps are explained in Chapter 4). Japanese citizens had only a limited right to exchange the yen or to borrow and lend foreign currencies. The maintenance of capital controls overall impeded the growth of Tokyo as an international financial center and gave an artificial advantage to regional financial centers such as Singapore and Hong Kong.

In recent years, a number of factors have worked toward financial market deregulation. The structure of interest rate ceilings has been undermined since 1975 by Japanese budget deficits and a growing supply of government debt that is traded in a secondary market. The increased supply of government debt has tended to drive up market interest rates on the debt, which in turn has competed with bank deposits and put pressure on banks to raise deposit interest rates above government-imposed ceilings. Restrictions on capital inflows began to be loosened in 1979, as the dollar price of oil rose and the dollar also appreciated slightly against the yen. In May of that year foreigners were given access to the *gensaki* market. (This is a market similar to the U.S. repo market, which involves the sale and subsequent repurchase of government securities. The interest rate on a transaction is determined by the difference between the purchase price and the resale price of the securities. If the borrower turns the securities over to the lender for the short-term life of the loan, the loan is virtually risk-free.) Later in the year a market in bank CDs was created and foreigners were allowed to participate.

The admission of foreign capital inflows was initially justified by the authorities as a move to strengthen the value of the yen by allowing foreigners to diversify their portfolios into yen-denominated assets. Increased foreign demand for the yen would bring about a yen appreciation until a new exchange rate level representing portfolio equilibrium was reached. However, with the Foreign Exchange and Foreign Trade Control Law of 1980, Japanese official restrictions on capital outflows began to be relaxed also. And as a result of the rise in U.S. real interest rates after 1980, the outflow of Japanese capital into dollar-denominated assets was larger than inflows into yen-denominated assets. The net shift into dollar assets acted to strengthen the dollar against the yen.

In 1981 a new banking law allowed Japanese banks to sell government bonds to the public for the first time. In response to the entry into securities dealing by the banks, the brokerage firms eventually acquired the right to set up money market funds. Since money market funds allowed small savers to obtain market interest rates, ceilings on bank deposit rates became increasingly ineffective.

In May 1984, the U.S. Treasury and the Japanese Ministry of Finance concluded negotiations on a program to "internationalize the yen." Even though Japan had the second largest economy in the noncommunist world, as a result of years of capital controls the yen was little used in international transactions or as a reserve asset. (At the end of 1983, according to IMF data, 69.1 percent of world official foreign exchange reserves were denominated in the U.S. dollar, 11.9 percent in the DM, and only 4.2 percent in the Japanese yen.) The points agreed to between Japan and the United States included further measures to liberalize capital movements, promote Japanese domestic deregulation, and improve foreign access to Japanese domestic markets. The agreement also sought to promote increased international use of the yen by encouraging the growth of the euroyen market and greater use of the yen in trade finance. (As of 1982, 40 percent of Japanese exports were yen-denominated, but only 3 percent of Japanese imports.)

The pace of opening of Japanese financial markets since the 1984 agreement has been slow, but nevertheless real. The newly created euroyen market has continued to exert competitive pressure to further deregulate the domestic market, just as the eurodollar market once acted to make obsolete U.S. deposit ceilings and capital controls. The parallel existence of free and regulated markets for yen implies that financial wealth will increasingly flow through the more efficient channel. The less efficient channel will have to change to survive.

PROBLEMS FOR CHAPTER 2

1. Using the information given in the table below, calculate the bilateral par values among the DM, the French franc, and the Italian lira, as well as the upper and lower intervention points in the parity grid. What do these points imply about central bank behavior?

EMS European Currency Unit Rates

	ECU central rates	Currency amounts against ECU August 7	Percent change from central rate*	Percent change adjusted for divergence*	Divergence limit percentage
Belgian franc	44.8320	44.8613	+0.07	+0.63	±1.5425
Danish krone	8.12857	8.02794	−1.24	−0.68	±1.6421
German DM	2.23840	2.22646	−0.53	+0.03	±1.1455
French franc	6.86402	6.78807	−1.11	−0.55	±1.3654
Dutch guilder	2.52208	2.50506	−0.67	−0.11	±1.5162
Irish punt	0.724578	0.713114	−1.58	−1.02	±1.6673
Italian lira	1520.60	1483.16	−2.46	−2.38	±4.0856

* Changes are for ECU, therefore positive change denotes a weak currency. Adjustment calculated by *Financial Times*.

2. How is column 2 ("Currency amounts against ECU") derived? In what sense is it a measure of a currency's "average" value?

3. Show how column 3 ("Percent change from central rate") is derived from columns 1 and 2. In what sense does column 3 measure a country's departure from the "community average"?

4. Why does column 4 differ from column 3?

5. Explain the significance of column 4 for the operation of the divergence indicator. When does column 4 indicate the need for a change in a country's economic policy?

6. Derive the weight of the Dutch guilder in the ECU (measured at ECU central rates) using *only the information given in the table*. [*Hint:* use the number in the last column.] Independently derive the weight of the Dutch guilder in the ECU using the September 1984 definition of the ECU and the information in column 1. Verify that the numbers are the same.

7. What is the relation between a currency's weight and the size of its divergence limit?

8. Using information given in the table, determine the following *market* exchange rates for the date given: French franc/DM and Italian lira/Belgium franc.

9. Suppose the French franc price of the ECU (the FF "ECU central rate") is increased by 5 percent (i.e., the FF is "devalued" by 5 percent). What are the new par values for the currencies given in Problem 1?

10. Suppose that it were desired to change the upper and lower bands to plus or minus 5 percent for all currencies. Solve for the number that would then be used to determine the upper and lower intervention points around par in the parity grid.

11. On July 20, 1985, financial newspapers announced that the Italian lira was "devalued by 6 percent" in the EMS, while other participating currencies were "revalued upward by 2 percent." Below are the EMS central rates before and after this realignment:

Currency	Currency/ECU before	Currency/ECU after
Irish punt	.72569	.724578
French franc	6.87456	6.86402
Danish krone	8.14104	8.12857
Dutch guilder	2.52595	2.52208
DM	2.24184	2.2384
Belgian franc	44.9008	44.832
Luxembourg franc	44.9008	44.832
Italian lira	1403.49	1520.6
British pound	.585992	.555312
Greek drachma	87.4813	100.719

Verify that the Italian lira/DM par value has changed by approximately 8 percent. Compare the percentage change in the DM/Italian lira par value. How do these percentage changes compare to the actual percentage changes in the ECU central rates?

FOREIGN
EXCHANGE
MARKETS

INTRODUCTION TO THE FOREIGN EXCHANGE MARKET

The foreign exchange market is the world's largest market. The exact size of the market is difficult to pin down, but rough estimates indicate that in the early 1980s the dollar value of daily turnover was fifty times daily turnover on the New York Stock Exchange, and ten times daily turnover in the U.S. government securities market. Most of this trading takes place in just a few currencies—the U.S. dollar ($), West German mark (DM), British pound sterling (£), Swiss franc (SF), Japanese yen (¥), Canadian dollar (Can$), French franc (FF), Netherlands (Dutch) guilder (DG), Belgian franc (BF), and the Italian lira (IL). Participants in the market include importers, who may pay for goods invoiced in foreign currencies; exporters, who may have foreign currency sales; portfolio managers, who may buy or sell foreign currency assets and receive foreign currency dividends or interest payments; central banks, who may conduct exchange intervention; foreign currency brokers, who earn a profit by matching buy and sell orders; and commercial banks, who may be borrowing in multiple currencies, servicing their own or their customers' needs, and whose traders make the foreign exchange market through continual interbank trading.

The foreign exchange market is an over-the-counter market. That is, there is no one physical location where traders get together to exchange currencies. Rather, traders are located in the offices of major commercial banks around the world and communicate using computer terminals, telephones, telexes, and other information channels. If a foreign exchange (FX) trader in a bank in New York deals dollars for pounds with an FX trader in London, the traders will, over the phone, agree on a price. Each trader will then enter the trade in the bank's computer or other record system, and then get on with the business of trading. The mechanics of actually transferring the currencies are not the traders' concern, so a trade takes a few seconds at most. Later, however, the two banks will send each other confirmation messages concerning the details of the trade, and will make arrangements for *settlement* of the traders' contract. The bank in New York will turn over a dollar deposit (at some New York bank) to the bank in London, and the bank in London will turn over a pound deposit (at some

London bank) to the bank in New York. This exchange of currencies will take place entirely in the form of an exchange of electronic messages. The messages will be sent through established communications networks.

The most important communications network for international financial market transactions is the Society for Worldwide Interbank Financial Telecommunication (SWIFT), a Belgian not-for-profit cooperative. This system for transferring foreign exchange deposits and loans began actual operation in May 1977 and by 1983 connected over a thousand banks in various countries and carried an average of 400,000 messages per day. SWIFT messages are transmitted from country to country via central, interconnected operating centers located in Brussels, Amsterdam, and Culpeper, Virginia. These three operating centers are in turn connected by international data-transmission lines to regional processors in most member countries. Banks in an individual country use the available national communication facilities to send messages to the regional processor. A bank in London, for example, will access SWIFT by sending messages to a regional processing center in the north of London. The message will be received by a bank in New York via the SWIFT operating center in Culpeper, Virginia.

The FX market is almost a twenty-four hour market, since as one center closes another is still trading. Business hours overlap around the world. When it is 3:00 P.M. in Tokoyo it is 2:00 P.M. in Hong Kong. When it is 3:00 P.M. in Hong Kong, it is 1:00 P.M. in Singapore. When it is 3:00 P.M. in Singapore, it is noon in Bahrain. When it is 3:00 P.M. in Bahrain, it is noon in Frankfurt and Zurich and 11:00 A.M. in London. When it is 3:00 P.M. in London, it is 10:00 A.M. in New York. When it is 3:00 P.M. in New York, it is noon in Los Angeles. When it is 3:00 P.M. in Los Angeles, it is 9:00 A.M. the next day in Sydney, Australia. The major foreign exchange trading centers are London, New York, Frankfurt, and Zurich, and the market is busiest in the early morning, New York time, when banks in these four centers are simultaneously open and trading. The working life of a trader is not necessarily limited to banking hours, however. Senior traders may have Reuters and Telerate monitors installed at home so they can keep track of foreign exchange and news developments around the clock and adjust their foreign exchange positions accordingly. They may expect phone calls from foreign offices of their bank at midnight or 4 A.M.

MARKETMAKERS VERSUS WALRASIAN AUCTIONEERS

What do FX traders do? Of course they buy and sell currencies. But, more important, they create prices. The creation of prices is no trivial feat, and before explaining how it takes place in the FX market it will be helpful to simplify by describing the simplest case of price creation. It involves a one-room market with a Walrasian auctioneer.

In the nineteenth century the French economist Léon Walras told the following story about how market equilibrium prices are determined. Suppose you get all the buyers and sellers of a particular commodity — wheat, for example — in a single room. One individual will serve as an auctioneer. The auctioneer will start off by announcing an arbitrary price, say $3.00 per bushel. At that price, each trader will decide whether he wants to be a buyer of wheat or a seller of wheat. If he views wheat as cheap at the $3.00 price, he will want to buy. If he views $3-a-bushel wheat as expensive, he will want to sell. Each trader writes down on a slip of paper the amount he wishes to buy or to sell at $3.00, and gives the slip to the auctioneer. The auctioneer will tally the total amount of wheat supplied at that price and the total amount demanded. If the two amounts are equal, the market is in equilibrium, and suppliers deliver wheat to the buyers, who pay them $3.00 per bushel. If, however, the two amounts are not equal at $3.00, the rules of the game say that no trading takes place. Instead, a new price is announced. If there is more wheat supplied than demanded ("excess supply") at $3.00, the price is too high, so a new price less than $3.00 is announced. If there is excess demand at $3.00, the price is too low, so a new price greater than $3.00 is announced. Eventually, through this process, a price at which supply exactly equals demand will be found. To summarize the story: The Walrasian auctioneer announces prices, excess (positive or negative) demand is tabulated, and trading takes place when and only when the equilibrium price has been established. We have already seen one real-world example of a Walrasian market in Chapter 1: the twice-daily fixing of the price of gold at the London merchant banking firm of N. M. Rothschild.

Let's now contrast this simple process by which a single market equilibrium price is determined in a Walrasian market with the more complex system of price creation in an over-the-counter speculative market such as the foreign exchange market. This more complex process makes the job of an FX trader correspondingly more difficult. There are at least three important aspects that distinguish the foreign exchange market from a simple Walrasian market.

1. There are two prices, not one, that are announced: a **bid price** at which a trader is willing to buy, and an **offer** or **asked price** at which a trader is willing to sell. The difference between the two prices is referred to as the *bid/asked (or bid/offer) spread.* Traders in the major money center banks around the world who deal in two-way prices, for both buying and selling, are referred to as **marketmakers.** Whether you want to buy or to sell, they will quote a price at which they are willing to take the other side of your transaction. They create the market by creating bid and asked prices and dealing at those prices.

    Marketmakers differ conceptually from **brokers,** who are individuals who simply match up buy and sell orders from two different parties. If every time a corporation wanted to sell U.S. dollars and buy Dutch guilders, there would be simultaneously available a corporation that wanted to buy U.S. dollars and sell Dutch guilders, the market could easily be handled by foreign exchange brokers. There would be no need for marketmakers. But in a real-world continuous auction market, buy and sell orders do not match at all points in time. Marketmakers make possible the immediate execution of orders from ultimate buyers and sellers of foreign exchange because marketmakers are willing to take the other side of the transaction themselves.

2. By contrast to the single Walrasian auctioneer, there are dozens of marketmakers, all of whom simultaneously announce bid and offer prices at which they will exchange two currencies. And since any particular trader in a particular bank will have difficulty keeping track of all the bid and asked prices concurrently announced by all other traders, there will normally be a dispersion of bid and asked prices throughout the foreign exchange market, and even simultaneous trades may take place at different exchange rates.

3. The concept of a single overall "equilibrium" market price is only a conve-

nient simplifying fiction. A particular marketmaker is usually concerned only with equilibrium as viewed from his or her own vantage point. To see what is involved, suppose a trader buys deutschemarks for $.3550/DM and sells them for $.3560/DM. The difference in the prices (the bid/asked spread) is $.001/DM. If (a) the trader is able to buy and sell equal amounts of DM at these prices, and (b) has a large volume of trade, then the trader will make a large profit and go home that night a happy person. The trader will earn an amount equal to the size of the bid/asked spread multiplied by the day's volume measured as the number of units of DM that have been both bought and sold. In this example, if the trader both buys and sells DM 50,000,000 with a spread of $.001/DM, then the profit would be ($.001/DM)(DM 50,000,000) = $50,000.

But here is the trader's problem. At any moment the trader may find that the number of times he is "hit" on the bid side is different from the number of times he is hit on the offer side. He is selling more of a particular currency than he is buying, or buying more than he is selling. The trader is then no longer living off the bid/asked spread: he is acquiring a long or short position in a foreign currency and becomes subject to the risk of exchange-rate movements. He becomes a net speculator. If he wishes to avoid a speculative position, he has to keep moving his bid and asked prices up and down in response to the relative frequency at which he gets hit on either side. Moreover, even if the relative frequency of hits is the same, the volume may be too low if his bid/asked spread is being undercut by other marketmakers. The size of the spread is then another variable that must be adjusted. The marketmaker's profit on the bid/asked spread is thus compensation for the opportunity cost of the marketmaker's time as well as for the exposure of the bank's capital to the risk of equilibrium price fluctuations (Stigler, 1961).

Now, some countries do have a daily "fixing" for their currencies, where a price will be fixed once a day by representatives of commercial banks and the central bank. They meet at a central location such as a stock exchange and follow a process similar to the gold-price fixing. These fixings do represent Walrasian auctions. But the volume of trade is small, so that the fixing price has limited relevance to the overall market, except as a benchmark price for certain small dealers. There are daily fixings in Japan, Germany, France, Italy, the Scandinavian countries, and Belgium.

It has been estimated that there are two hundred marketmaking banks worldwide (Bodner, 1983). Much of their trading takes place by *direct dealing*, in which marketmakers call each other to ask for two-way prices, while the rest takes place through *brokers*. A survey of New York banks in 1983 showed 42 percent direct dealing, while 58 percent went through brokers (Andrews, 1984). Brokers charge a fee for matching up buyers and sellers. A bank dealing through a broker typically quotes only a bid or an asked price, and the broker — who may have open phone lines to one or two hundred banks — will see if anyone wants to take the other side of the transaction. The broker will facilitate the process by quoting at the outset indicative bid/asked prices that he will attempt to make firm by finding a matching party to a dealer's bid or offer (Riley, 1983). In contrast to direct dealing, a bank dealing through a broker keeps its identity confidential until just prior to the consummation of the transaction.

In the major trading centers like London and New York, about 95 percent of all FX trading is between marketmakers (Giddy, 1979; Bodner, 1983; Walmsley, 1983). Less than 5 percent is commercial business: FX purchases and sales by companies engaged in trade, by tourists, and so on. (Tokyo is an exception, with perhaps one-third of trading involving customer orders.) That most trading involves marketmakers is a crucial detail when we come to the question of exchange rate determination (in Part III). Factors such as trade balances, relative prices, and so on are irrelevant to exchange rate movements in the short run, except to the extent they influence the actions of interbank traders. Suppose, for example, that all traders simultaneously come to the conclusion that the DM will drop in value with respect to the dollar and consequently began selling DM for dollars. If 95 percent of the market is selling DM, the value of the DM will fall relative to the dollar. Similarly, if 95 percent of the market is ignoring relative price levels, it will be difficult to prove them wrong in the short run, because the 5 percent of commercial-trade-related business is small compared to the interbank market. To summarize: *Day-to-day exchange rate movements hinge on the activity of interbank traders. Their actions and expectations are decisive. Any variable used as a basis for decision-making by traders is important in the short run, while other variables may be irrelevant.*

The fact that most trading takes place between marketmakers also has important implications for speculative gains and losses. Foreign exchange traders as a whole are able to make a profit because they provide a basic service to the final users of the market: exporters, importers, portfolio managers, and tourists. The fact that marketmakers deal with each other keeps the market liquid and helps keep the prices announced by various marketmakers from diverging greatly from marketmaker to marketmaker. But if marketmakers, in addition, accumulate long or short positions in a currency and make speculative gains or losses, they do so principally with respect to other marketmakers. That is, speculation in the FX market is essentially a zero-sum game: one trader's speculative gain will be another trader's speculative loss. This is *essentially* true but not entirely true, because of central bank intervention. If central banks intervene, speculation will become a positive-sum game to FX traders viewed as a group if central banks make net speculative losses. (That is, FX traders *as a group* can earn a net speculative profit.) Similarly, speculation will become a negative-sum game to FX traders as a group if central banks make net exchange gains from intervention, while speculation will remain a zero-sum game if central banks make no net profit or loss.

THE MECHANICS OF CURRENCY TRADING

Almost all trading of convertible currencies takes place with respect to the U.S. dollar. For example, both the £ and the DM will be traded with prices quoted vis-à-vis the U.S. dollar. If a commercial customer asked for a DM price in terms of the £, this cross rate will be determined from the two dollar rates (see the example below). There are two major reasons for quoting all exchange rates against a common currency (a "vehicle currency"). The first has to do with information complexity. If each currency were traded directly against each other currency, it would involve an enormous number of dealing markets. For ten currencies there would be forty-five exchange rates.

□

The first currency would have an exchange rate against the other nine currencies. The second currency would have eight additional exchange rates (since the exchange rate against the first currency has already been counted). And so on, giving a total of $9 + 8 + 7 + 6 + 5 + 4 + 3 + 2 + 1 = 45$ exchange rates. For n currencies there would similarly be $n(n - 1)/2$ bilateral exchange rates. ■

A second reason for quoting all exchange rates against a common currency is to avoid the possibility of *triangular arbitrage*. If all currencies were traded against each other directly, the exchange rate of the dollar against the pound compared with the exchange rate of the pound against the DM would imply an exchange rate of the dollar against the DM. If this implied exchange rate differed from the direct dollar/DM exchange rate by an amount sufficient to cover the costs of the transactions, there would be a profit available by buying at one of the dollar/DM exchange rates and selling at the other. By contrast, when all cross rates are *derived* from the rate of the two currencies with respect to the dollar, there is only one available cross rate and no possibility of arbitrage.

There do exist, however, banks that specialize in giving cross rates. Since the bid/asked spread of a normal cross-rate quotation incorporates both bid/asked spreads from the two currencies quoted with respect to the dollar, there is room for banks to specialize and undercut the size of the total spread, provided they have enough cross-rate business to make it profitable.

If the quoted price is the dollar price of a unit of foreign exchange (or, restated, the number of dollars per unit of foreign exchange), then the quotation is said to be in *American* (or *direct*) terms. Examples of quotations in American terms include:

$1.55 = £ 1 $.40 = DM 1 $.50 = SF 1 $.0044 = ¥ 1

If the quoted price is the foreign currency price of a dollar (or, restated, the number of units of foreign currency per one U.S. dollar), then the quotation is said to be in *European* (or *indirect* or *reciprocal*) terms. Examples of quotations in European terms include:

£ .645 = $ 1   DM 2.5 = $ 1   SF 2.00 = $1   ¥ 227 = $ 1

In the interbank market, European terms are used for all currency quotations except for the £ and the Irish pound, American terms being used for the latter currencies. (Thus, one would quote DM 2.5 = $1, but $1.55 = £ 1.) Currency quotations are generally in American terms, however, in the markets for FX futures and options. (An exception is the interbank FX options market, which flip-flops between the two ways of quotation. FX futures and options are discussed in Chapters 5 and 6.)

Three general types of transactions take place in the FX market: spot, forward, and swap. Spot transactions involve an agreement on price today, with *settlement* day (actual delivery of currency for currency) usually two business days later. When, however, currencies whose home countries are in the same time zone are traded, such as the U.S dollar for the Canadian dollar, or the U.S. dollar for the Mexican peso, settlement is typically one business day later. Further detail on settlement dates is covered below. *Forward transactions* involve an agreement on price today for settlement at some date in the future (beyond the normal time lag for spot settlement). Frequently traded forward maturities are for one or two weeks, or one through twelve months. Odd maturity dates may be negotiated, however, and large banks will give forward quotations for major currencies out to five years.

Sometimes a forward transaction is called an *outright forward* to emphasize that no spot transaction is involved. Outright forward transactions usually take place between a bank and a commercial customer. For example, Exxon may have a scheduled payment of £25,000,000 in eight months and may buy that amount of British pounds forward today. No money will change hands now. The forward contract will simply lock in the price at which the transaction will take place between Exxon and Exxon's bank eight months from now. By contrast, transactions involving forward exchange in the interbank market usually take the form of swap transactions. A swap is the sale of a foreign currency with a simultaneous agreement to repurchase it at some date in the future, or the purchase of a foreign currency with an agreement to resell it at some date in the future. For example, Citibank might buy DM 2,500,000 from Deutsche Bank for $1,000,000, with a simultaneous agreement to sell the DM back in six months for $1,050,000. In a swap transaction, it is the difference between the sale price and the repurchase price (and not their absolute magnitudes) that is important. This difference is called the *swap rate* (see Chapter 4 for further details). It was estimated in 1983 that 65 percent of trading by New York banks was in the spot market, 33 percent in the swap market, and 2 percent in the market for outright forwards (Andrews, 1984).

As covered earlier, all foreign exchange trading involves two prices, a bid or buying price and an asked (offered) or selling price. However, all transactions also involve two currencies, so it is essential to keep straight which currency you have in mind. If you bid for DM with dollars, that is the same as offering dollars for DM. Thus, whether an exchange rate represents a "bid" price or an "offered" price depends on which currency you use for reference. The following example explores this in detail and establishes the convention for quoting exchange rates in this book.

EXAMPLE 3.1

A trader quotes the DM against the dollar at a bid/offer price of

DM 2.3697/2.3725 per $1

It is natural to think of the small number, DM 2.3697, as the bid price, and the large number, DM 2.3725, as the offer price. Question: Bid and offer for what? The DM? Answer: DM 2.3697 is the bid price *for the U.S. dollar,* while DM 2.3725 is the offer (or asked) price for the U.S. dollar. In order to keep this straight, keep in mind the trader's objective: to make money. The trader will make money by giving away as few DM as possible when he purchases dollars (hence his bid for the dollar is DM 2.3697), while acquiring as many DM as possible when he sells dollars (hence he offers to sell $1 for DM 2.3725).

For a rate quoted in American terms, we may again refer to the smaller number as the bid price, but in this case it would be the bid price for the foreign currency. For the bid/offer price of $1.5525/$1.5535 per £1, $1.5525 is the bid price for the pound (offer price for the dollar), while $1.5535 is the offer price for the pound (bid price for the dollar).

No fees are charged in ordinary foreign exchange transactions. Rather, *transactions costs* relate to the size of the bid/offer spread. For a standard FX contract of $1 million traded against FX, the typical cost (the spread multiplied by $1 million) of the transaction might be $200 for Canadian dollar trades; $500 for the DM and the £; $1000 for the ¥; and $1225 for the SF. For cross rates, however, the bid/asked spread enters twice, so that typical transactions costs are larger. The calculation of cross rates is shown in the following example.

EXAMPLE 3.2

A bank is currently quoting the following two exchange rates with respect to the dollar:

DM 2.3697/2.3725 per $ 1 $ 1.5525/1.5535 per £ 1

What DM per £ cross rate would the bank quote, if asked? The way to answer this question is *conceptually* to engage in two transactions with respect to the U.S. dollar. First consider the bank's bid rate for £s. In order to buy £s with DM, conceptually one would first buy $ with DM, then buy £s with $. The trader would chose the most advantageous price with each transaction. The trader will get the most dollars for DM by dealing at the DM 2.3697/$ price and will get the most £s for dollars by dealing at the $1.5525/£ price. Hence, the bid price for £s would be:

(DM 2.3697/$)($ 1.5525/£) = DM 3.6789/£.

Similarly, in order to sell £s for DM, one would first sell £s for $, then sell $ for DM. Choosing the most advantageous price at each point from the trader's perspective, we get the price at which £s are offered as:

($1.5535/£)(DM 2.3725/$) = DM 3.6857/£.

This gives a bid/offer quotation for the £ of DM 3.6789/3.6857 = £1.

THE RISK FROM AN OPEN POSITION IN FOREIGN EXCHANGE

An FX trader is a probability manager. Suppose that an FX trader intentionally or unintentionally adjusts his or her bid and asked prices in such a way that the trader is hit unequally on the bid and asked sides. Because the trader's purchases and sales of a foreign currency are not equalized, the trader begins to build up a net short or long position. (A short position is involved if the amount sold is greater than the amount purchased, while a long position is involved if the amount purchased is greater.) Having a net long or short position can be very risky, as the following example illustrates.

EXAMPLE 3.3

A trader in a bank that is concerned with dollar profits is short DM 15,000,000. The current exchange rate is DM 2.500 = $1, so that the bank's liability is $6,000,000. If the exchange rate were suddenly to jump to DM 2.600 = $1 (that is, if the DM were to depreciate in value with respect to the dollar), the bank's liability would fall to

$5,769,230.77. The trader might receive a large bonus. But if the exchange rate were to jump to DM 2.400 = $1 (that is, if the DM were to appreciate in value with respect to the dollar), the bank's liability would increase to $6,250,000. The trader might be fired. Because of exchange rate risk, most banks set *position limits* which are the maximum net FX exposure traders can have at any one time. A typical position limit for an experienced trader might be $35,000,000 in FX exposure during the trading day, or $7,000,000 in FX exposure carried overnight. Daily exchange rate movements of the size (4 percent) used in this example are rare. On the other hand, 1 percent daily movements are common.

It is important to have some empirical estimate of the risk involved in holding open positions in foreign exchange. Let today's spot rate be $S(t)$, while the spot rate one day later is $S(t + 1)$. The daily proportional change ΔS in the spot rate is:

$$\Delta S = \frac{[S(t + 1) - S(t)]}{S(t)}.$$

In many instances the expected value of ΔS can be taken as zero for all practical purposes. Even so, there may be wide variations around this expected value. That is, there is risk that the change in the exchange rate will be different from what is anticipated. One measure of foreign exchange risk is the standard deviation (SD) of ΔS. Below are standard deviations of ΔS, where S is the dollar price of the given foreign currency, for days in the calendar year 1981. In the second column is the corresponding change in the dollar value of foreign currency with an initial value of $1,000,000, given a change in the spot exchange rate over a one-day period equal in size to one standard deviation:

SD of ΔS in 1981	Equivalent change in value of an initial $1,000,000
DM .00868	$ 8,680
SF .01120	$11,200
¥ .00823	$ 8,230
£ .00850	$ 8,500

What do these numbers mean? We can give a simple interpretation in terms of probability. Assume that the values for ΔS are drawings from a normal distribution with mean zero and with the standard deviations given above. (This is not an entirely valid assumption empirically, but will be close enough for our purposes.) Recall that for a normal distribution, we can expect that the values of our drawings will fall within plus or minus one standard deviation around the mean about 68 percent of the time, within plus or minus two SDs about 95 percent of the time, and within plus or minus three SDs about 99 percent of the time. For example, since a change in the dollar/Swiss franc exchange rate in an amount equal to one SD is $11,200, we can expect that over the course of a day our foreign currency — which had an initial value of $1,000,000 — will have an ending value in the range of $988,800 to $1,011,200 with a probability of 68 percentage. Below is a summary based on the SD rate of the dollar price of Swiss francs:

Range in terms of SD	Probability for drawings from a normal distribution	Change in value of SF position
±1	.6826	±$11,200
±2	.9544	±$22,400
±3	.9974	±$33,600

A trader operating on a .2 percent ($2000) profit margin might find this degree of exchange risk large indeed. In about 32 percent of the cases, the change in the value of the position from foreign exchange rate changes over a day's time would be more than five times as large as the entire profit margin. This exchange rate change could work to the trader's advantage, increasing his profit, but it could just as easily go the other way.

☐

The normal probability distribution will be used for illustration throughout this book. The intention is that the reader learn to think in terms of probability, and it is the author's belief that the introduction of multiple distributions will get in the way of this objective. However, it is well established that daily proportional exchange rate changes are too "leptokurtic" to represent drawings from a normal distribution. That is, by reference to the normal distribution, they have (1) a greater proportion of very small deviations from the mean; (2) a greater proportion of very large deviations from the mean; but (3) a smaller proportion of intermediate deviations from the mean. Imagine two erratic drivers driving along a highway. The mean location of each is on the center line. Let the normal distribution represent the proportion of time the first spends on each part of the highway. If the second driver has a leptokurtic distribution, this second driver spends relatively more time close to the center line and relatively more time driving in the ditch than does the first, but spends proportionately less time driving on the shoulders.

Leptokurtosis as measured in empirical samples of exchange rates may be the result of a time-varying scale parameter (such as a standard deviation that changes over time), in which case case ΔS may be normal once an adjustment for scale changes has been made. Or ΔS may be drawn from the class of infinite-variance stable distributions (with or without time-varying scale), as has been suggested by Cornell and Dietrich (1978); MacFarland, Pettit, and Sung (1982); So (1982); and Westerfield (1977). An infinite-variance stable distribution might result from the fact that information arrives in "lumps." If ΔS had a normal distribution, the total price change over a period of time would be the result of a large number of very small changes. But in an infinite-variance stable market, the total price change would more likely be the result of a few very large changes (Mandelbrot, 1963), which could result from the lumpy arrival of information that affects the market exchange rate. ∎

SETTLEMENT DATES

Settlement of a spot or forward contract always takes place by giving the other party a bank deposit denominated in the relevant currency. If the relevant currency is DM, then a DM deposit in a German bank is transferred to the other party. If the relevant currency is the $, ⟨...⟩ bank is transferred to the other party. The loca ⟨...⟩ currency's home country: the settlement ⟨...⟩ rencies can themselves be physically loca ⟨...⟩ currency they trade. This is referred to a ⟨...⟩ wo banks in London can trade DM. The d ⟨...⟩ tle-ment location would be Germany.

The first principle involved in settl ⟨...⟩ ttle-ment location are not open, no settlem ⟨...⟩ y are not open on a particular day, then a tr ⟨...⟩ ce on that date.

A **spot** settlement date is usually ⟨...⟩ ate for either the European currencies or ⟨...⟩ r. (The time gap results from the practic ⟨...⟩ ing and clearing the trades through the ⟨...⟩ FT and CHIPS.) Thus if a London bank s ⟨...⟩ lars, then two business days later the Lon ⟨...⟩ it in Germany to the New York bank, wh ⟨...⟩ er a dollar deposit in the United States to the Londo ⟨...⟩ ted value" principle says that settlement of both sides of a FX contra ⟨...⟩ place on the same working day. This principle is intended to reduce credit risk, and is followed in all FX trading except that of some Middle Eastern currencies. (The latter exception is due to the fact that Islamic banks are closed on Friday but open on Saturday and Sunday. So for a U.S. dollar – Saudi riyal trade on Wednesday, for example, dollars will normally be delivered at a U.S. bank on Friday but riyals will be delivered at a Saudi bank on Saturday.)

But what is meant by "two business days after"? This is easily answered if the two banks that are trading have the same holidays. For example, both London and New York banks are closed on Saturday and Sunday, so if spot trading between a New York and a London bank takes place Friday, two business days later is Tuesday. Thus, spot settlement would be Tuesday if banks in the settlement location are also open. However, if the DM was being traded and Tuesday was a holiday in Germany, settlement would have to be postponed until Wednesday. Also if Tuesday were a holiday in either New York or London, settlement would also be put off until Wednesday. Finally, there is the question of Monday. What if, say, Monday is a holiday in New York, but not in London? Then "two business days" later, for a trade on Friday, would be Wednesday in New York but Tuesday in London. On which of the two dates would settlement take place? The answer is that normally (in the absence of special arrangements) the value date (settlement date) of the bank making the market is applied (Coninx, 1982). Thus, if the New York bank called the London bank, the London bank's value date (Tuesday) would be applied, while if the London bank called New York, the New York bank's value date (Wednesday) would be applied.

For U.S. dollar trades against the Canadian dollar and the Mexican peso, settlement is one day later. The shorter time to settlement stems from the fact that most trading takes place in the United States, so that both the dealing banks and the settlement banks are in similar time zones.

One- through twelve-month *forward* maturities follow a simple pattern. To determine the one-month (or "30-day") forward settlement date for forward trading that takes place today, first determine the spot settlement date. Then go to *the same day of the month, one month forward.* For example, if the spot settlement date for a trade taking place on June 21 is June 23, then the one-month forward settlement date would be July 23.

What if, in the previous example, July 23 is a holiday in the dealing center, or the banks are not open in the settlement location? Answer: Move the date forward to the first suitable day. However, a rule followed in the market is that you can never move the date forward into the next month (into August, in our example). If you hit the end of the month, then you go backward to the first suitable settlement date.

A final rule for forward maturity dates is the "end-end" rule. If the spot value date takes place on the last business day of the current month, then all forward value dates are also for the last business day of the appropriate month. For example, if the spot value date for trades made today is March 28 and this is the last business day in March, then a two-month forward contract traded today will mature on the last business day of May. If the last business day is May 31, then May 31 (not May 28) is the value date.

These rules will sometimes cause bunching of forward maturity dates, as the following example shows.

EXAMPLE 3.4

Exchange is traded one month forward on Monday, January 26; Tuesday, January 27; and Wednesday, January 28. The corresponding spot settlement dates are, respectively, Wednesday, January 28; Thursday, January 29; and Friday, January 30. What are the one-month forward settlement dates? The one-month forward value date would be the same in all three cases. First, going forward one month from January 28, we get February 28. But February 28 would be a Saturday, so we go backward to Friday, February 27, and this would be the settlement date if February 27 were a business day for both banks. Otherwise, the last business day in February. Similarly, going forward one month from January 29 and January 30 would take us to the last business day in February, since we cannot have a March settlement date for one-month forward trades in January.

EXCHANGE CONTROLS

Most countries of the world set a price (or a small range of prices) at which their currencies can be traded for a foreign currency. This price usually represents a *political equilibrium:* the price is chosen so as to benefit one economic group while penalizing another. The principles involved can be stated simply: *If the domestic currency price is chosen so as to undervalue foreign currency, then the price acts to subsidize buyers of foreign exchange and to tax sellers of foreign exchange. If the domestic currency price is chosen so as to overvalue foreign currency, then the price acts to subsidize sellers of foreign exchange and to tax buyers of foreign exchange.*

Suppose that in an ordinary market, where the price adjusts to equate the supply of a foreign currency with the demand for that currency, a particular exchange rate would be 85 pesos = 1 dollar. The local government, however, sets the exchange rate at 39 pesos = 1 dollar. What are the consequences? Assuming that the dollar is the foreign currency in this case, the exchange rate chosen *undervalues* foreign exchange. It treats the dollar as though it were worth only 39 pesos, whereas in normal market equilibrium the dollar would be worth 85 pesos. One consequence is that buyers of dollars are subsidized. Buyers of dollars can get them at the cheap price of 39 pesos instead of the normal price of 85 pesos. One group of dollar buyers will be *importers* of dollar-priced goods. To buy dollar goods, they will first exchange pesos for dollars. A good with a price of $1 would normally cost 85 pesos, but they are able to buy it for 39 pesos. As a consequence, imports of dollar goods are likely to soar. Another buyer of dollars will be tourists who travel to the dollar's home country. The local government will in effect pay travelers 85 − 39 = 46 pesos per dollar to take a vacation.

Dollar sellers, however, are penalized by a tax. In ordinary circumstances, they would be able to sell each dollar for 85 pesos. However, at the chosen exchange rate they are only able to get 39 pesos. One group of dollar sellers will be exporters of goods to the dollar's home country. They will receive dollars for goods sold and will then sell dollars for pesos in order to pay local wages and other costs. Since the local government extracts 85 − 39 = 46 pesos directly from each dollar's worth of goods sold, exporters may soon find themselves going broke. Exports will drop.

Initially, the local government may find the exchange control scheme entirely workable. The tax of 46 pesos on dollar sellers can be used to pay the subsidy of 46 pesos to dollar buyers. But this will not last for long. Soon the government's supply of foreign exchange will disappear. First, consider dollar sellers such as exporters. Exporters will try to get back the 46 pesos they are paying to the government. One way might be to raise the dollar price of their goods sold in the dollar's home country. But this may be self-defeating; raising the dollar price of goods sold may result in fewer sales. If the markets in which they sell their goods in the dollar's home country are characterized by perfect competition, an increase in the dollar price of the exporter's goods will result in sales falling to zero. In general, the feasibility of raising prices depends on the elasticity of demand for their product, and only in rare circumstances would they be able to significantly reduce the 46-peso tax by increasing the foreign-currency price of their goods.

As another alternative, they may decide to leave the dollar proceeds from the sales of foreign goods deposited in foreign banks. They may hope that the exchange rate will be changed later (say to 70 pesos = 1 dollar), which would reduce the size of the tax on selling dollars to the local government. In the meantime, they may attempt to pay local wage and other costs through local borrowing. The local government, seeing its inflow of cheap dollars drying up, will likely respond by passing a law that says companies must repatriate the proceeds from foreign sales immediately. To attempt to enforce this law, the government will require companies to keep and turn in elaborate records to the government concerning foreign sales and the management of foreign-currency funds.

Meanwhile, the government will have found that a reduction in the supply of foreign exchange did not bring about a reduction in the demand. Rather, long lines of people who wish to buy dollars at 39 pesos each will have formed at the central bank. The government will not have enough dollars to go around at that price, so it will begin to ration foreign exchange. Travelers will be allowed a maximum number of dollars they can buy per year. To keep track of who has purchased foreign exchange and who has not, the government will have to keep careful records, and buyers of foreign exchange will have to fill out elaborate forms. Importers of goods may be required to obtain a license before they can buy dollars at the cheap 39 peso rate. There may be a long waiting period before a license is granted, and the actual permission to purchase dollars will be subject to "legitimate need." Importers who import goods the government favors will be granted a license, while others will be turned away. Importers who support the current regime politically will almost certainly be found to have needs more legitimate than those who oppose the current regime or those who fail to show support by making the appropriate political contributions. Government officials in charge of licenses may be offered (or may demand) side payments in return for their services.

Since many people who want dollars, and who are not able to get them from the government, would be willing to pay more than 39 pesos per dollar, a black or parallel market will develop. Those willing to pay more than 39 pesos per dollar will get together with those who want to sell dollars but who want to sell them for more than 39 pesos per dollar. Travelers returning from vacation in the dollar's home country will sell dollars on the black market. Word will spread that dollars may be exchanged for pesos at a better rate at offices of travel agents, or in the back room of the Casa del Gallo, or in taxicabs, or on the sidewalk in front of the local bank. Local companies may also sell their export proceeds on the black market, but they will have a more difficult time escaping detection than will individuals. And, of course, there will be those who deal in foreign exchange but who were not able to deal with the government in the first place because their trade is declared illegal. It may be illegal to buy foreign TVs, to export wheat, to buy or sell cocaine, or to purchase bibles or foreign books. Importers or exporters of these goods and services will also buy and sell on the parallel market.

The black market in Brazil is so well organized that the cruzeiro/U.S. dollar black market exchange rate is reported daily in major newspapers. The premium paid for the dollar on the black market rises and falls with dollar inflows and outflows associated with tourist trade at the time of the Festival, with seasonal smuggling of grain, and with expectations of maxidevaluations of the cruzeiro. In one Central American country in early 1984, citizens could take out a local currency loan at their bank, buy the maximum number of U.S. dollars that the government permitted, sell part of the dollars at a higher price on the black market — enough to repay their local currency loan from the bank — and have enough dollars left over to purchase a round-trip airline ticket to the United States. The level at which the exchange rate was fixed not only subsidized travel to the United States, it also discouraged any capital inflows into the country. In Mexico in 1984 the central bank faced shortages of foreign exchange because it was maintaining an exchange rate for the Mexican peso that overvalued the peso with respect to the U.S. dollar. In one attempt to acquire artificially cheap U.S. dollars, the government told foreign auto companies that their exports from Mexico would have to match their imports into Mexico. Since the companies concerned needed to import parts before they had finished cars to sell, they had to close automotive assembly plants. Then, in order to generate a sufficient volume of exports that would then allow them to import parts, the auto companies turned to the export of local commodities like horsemeat, chickpeas, and coffee. Tourists to East Germany from West Germany are required to change a small amount of West German marks to East German marks as the price of an entrance ticket to the country. The exchange rate is 1 West German mark = 1 East German mark. The black market rate in 1985 was 1 West German mark = 17 East German marks. Thus tourists were led to subsidize the East German government by giving up their West German marks at an artificially low price. Foreign exchange control regulations in France fill four published volumes. The services of lawyers who know these regulations by heart are much in demand. After the Iranian Revolution under the Ayatollah Khomeini, the former head of the central bank was sentenced to death for maintaining an "incorrect" exchange rate for the Iranian rial with respect to the U.S. dollar. (In a humanitarian gesture, the sentence was later commuted to life imprisonment.)

There can be little doubt that exchange controls usually stem from political motives, and seldom — if ever — have any net positive benefit to *both* the buyers and sellers of foreign exchange. Instead, controls impose dead-weight costs to all users of the foreign exchange market. And it is usually fixed exchange rates, or fixed par values, that lead to exchange controls, because governments that fix exchange rates seldom pursue economic policies consistent with the chosen rate. Although economists have contributed a great deal of literature to a debate on "fixed versus flexible" exchange rates, this analysis (as important as it may be) seems to have had little impact either way on the political process that results in the selection of an official trading value for the local currency. When in the 1920s Winston Churchill set the dollar/pound rate at $4.86 = £1, so "the pound can look the dollar in the face," the decision was not based on a simple economic cost-benefit analysis. And in the 1980s, when countries claim they have imposed exchange controls for "balance of payments reasons," the explanation is circular, since it is generally the existence of fixed prices and exchange and other controls that created the payments "imbalance" in the first place (see Chapter 9).

Fixed exchange rates frequently also lead to capital controls. In many Latin American countries today, domestic interest rates are fixed and there is in addition high inflation, so the inflation-adjusted (real) return to domestic deposits or interest-bearing securities is negative. Holders of deposits or other assets would normally switch to foreign currency deposits in order to escape the inflation tax, so governments legally prohibit or restrict the ownership of foreign deposits or securities. In such cases, governments consider (correctly) that the purchase of foreign currency securities is a vote against their domestic economic policies. Having created a climate in which their own citizens will not voluntarily hold the domestic currency, governments then resort to controls as an attempt to force people to hold and use it anyway. Occasionally, however, a country will impose controls to make its currency *less* attractive. Switzerland at one time even set negative interest rates on foreign-owned Swiss franc-denominated assets in order to discourage foreign purchases.

The use of *multiple exchange rates* is similarly related to a political decision to favor certain transactions over others. Often a distinction is made between current account transactions (those involving goods and services) and capital account transactions (those involving only the exchange of financial assets). The best-known example is the system in Belgium, where one exchange rate ("the commercial franc") is freely determined in the market, and exchange purchased at this rate may be used for transactions in goods and services. A slightly different rate ("the financial franc") must be used to purchase foreign securities. Venezuela in 1984 had a three-tier system in which U.S. dollars for debt repayments could be purchased at a low bolivar price, U.S. dollars from oil sales were exchanged at a somewhat higher bolivar price, while most other transactions took place at a still higher number of bolivars per U.S. dollar.

□

Some of the economic effects of exchange controls are explored in Bank of England (1981), Culbertson (1977), and Kruger (1966). An annual listing of controls in force in IMF member countries can be found in the IMF's *Annual Report on Exchange Arrangements and Exchange Restrictions.*   ■

PROBLEMS FOR CHAPTER 3

1. If you could reorganize the foreign exchange market, which currency would you choose as the vehicle currency? What advantages would there be in using this currency? What problems?

2. How many bilateral exchange rates can be created using twenty currencies?

3. If the U.S. dollar price of the Japanese yen is $.0042, what is the Japanese yen price of the U.S. dollar?

4. Consider the following bid/asked prices: DM 4.085–4.095/£. Which is the asked price for the pound sterling? Which is the bid price for the DM?

5. A bank quotes bid/asked rates of SF 2.5110–2.5140/$ and ¥ 245–246/$. What ¥/SF bid and asked cross rates would the bank quote?

6. A bank is currently quoting spot rates of DM 3.2446–3.2456/$ and BF 65.30–65.40/$. What would be the bank's bid price for the Belgian franc in terms of DM?

7. At the end of the day, an FX trader has a net FX position totaling $45 million. If the expected proportional overnight exchange rate change is zero with a standard deviation of .6 percent, what is the probability distribution of the position's dollar value on the next day? (Assume a normal probability distribution and state the values corresponding to plus or minus 1, 2, and 3 standard deviations, along with the corresponding probabilities.)

8. Refer to today's calendar and assume that a spot trade of dollars for pounds takes place between a New York bank and a London bank. Assume there are no special banking holidays. Determine the spot settlement date, the one-month forward settlement date, and the two-month forward settlement date. Is the length in days of the two-month forward contract exactly twice the length of the one-month forward contract?

9. Comment on the following news item, which appeared in *The Wall Street Journal* on March 7, 1984:

The black market rate for U.S. dollars in Brazil rose sharply last week. Dealers said the rate jumped to 1600 Brazilian cruzeiros for $1, or about 30 percent above the official exchange rate. A week earlier, the black-market rate was only 13 percent above the official rate. The jump was surprising because it came just ahead of the long carnival weekend, which lasts from Saturday through today. In previous years, the spread between the black-market and official rates often narrowed before the carnival as foreign tourists brought in dollars. On Monday, Brazil made a small devaluation of the cruzeiro, the 13th this year. The official rate is 1225 to the dollar for buyers and 1231 for sellers.

10. Comment on the following news item, which appeared in *The Wall Street Journal* on March 7, 1985:

Pressured by high inflation and the strong U.S. dollar, Mexico said it will devalue the peso at a faster rate and implement export policies designed to right its economic recovery. Beginning yesterday, the dollar was raised against the Mexico peso by 21 centavos a day, rather than 17 centavos. There are 100 centavos in a peso. The change means that the controlled peso rate, used for most imports and exports, will fall about 27 percent annually against the dollar, contrasted with a projected decline of 23 percent at the old pace. . . .

Exporters have complained that, because inflation boosts their costs, an earlier increase in the peso devaluation rate in December wasn't enough to keep their goods competitive in foreign markets. Exporters say they have especially had problems competing with European exporters because European currencies have fallen faster against the dollar than the peso.

FORWARDS, SWAPS, AND INTEREST PARITY

FORWARD RATE QUOTATIONS

As noted in the preceding chapter, forward exchange is traded in the interbank market in connection with spot exchange. Although banks will quote "outright forwards" (that is, forward prices quoted without reference to the spot rate) to their corporate customers, market-making banks trade among themselves in the form of swaps, which involves both a spot and a forward contract. Thus forward rates are always quoted by reference to spot rates. (There is a special type of swap, a "forward-forward" swap, that involves trading one forward contract for another forward contract of different maturity. However, in this case each of the forward rates involved has been determined by reference to the spot rate, so that the existence of this type of swap does not provide an exception to the rule that forward rates are determined in reference to spot rates.)

If the value of a foreign currency (in terms of the domestic currency) is greater forward than it is spot, the foreign currency is said to be at a *premium* (which implies that the domestic currency is at a forward *discount*). If the forward value of a foreign currency is less than is the spot value, then the foreign currency is at a *discount* (which implies that the domestic currency is at a *premium*). For example, if the spot DM is DM 2.4370 = \$1 and the one-month forward DM is DM 2.4320 = \$1, then the one-month forward DM is at a premium. The one-month forward DM is at a premium here because the forward DM is more valuable. It takes fewer DM (namely, DM 2.4320) to buy \$1 forward than it takes to buy \$1 spot. By the same criterion, the forward dollar is at a discount in this example because the forward dollar buys fewer DM (namely, DM 2.4320) than does the spot dollar (DM 2.4370).

Because forward exchange is traded at a premium or discount to spot exchange in the interbank market, forward rates are quoted in terms of the premium or discount that is to be added to the spot rate. Since two numbers (the bid price and the asked price) are quoted in the spot market, discounts or premiums are quoted as two numbers: one number to be added to or subtracted from the bid price and one number to be added to or subtracted from the offered price. For example, a forward premium for the one-month forward DM might be 30/20. Then if the spot DM is quoted as DM 2.4273/90, the one-month forward DM would be DM 2.4243/70. In this case, .0030 ("30") is subtracted from 2.4273 to give 2.4243, and .0020 ("20") is subtracted from 2.4290 to give 2.4270.

How would one know to *subtract* 30/20 instead of adding in this example? To keep the calculations straight, keep in mind that the bid/asked spread will always widen as we go forward. By subtracting in this case, we got a wider spread on one-month forward exchange (DM 2.4270 − DM 2.4243 = .0027) than on spot exchange (DM 2.4290 − DM 2.4273 = .0017). If we had added 30/20, the spread on forward exchange would have narrowed to .0007. An alternative way to keep the calculations straight is to note that 30/20 has the form "large number/small number" while, say, 30/40 would have the form "small number/large number." Then follow the rule to *subtract* if the form is "large number/small number" but *add* if the form is "small number/large number."

EXAMPLE 4.1

An FX trader quotes the spot DM against the U.S. dollar as 2.5005/10 and one-month forward margins as 100/95. What are the one-month outright forward rates? Answer: Since 100/95 has the form large number/small number, the margins should be subtracted to yield an outright forward rate of DM 2.4905/15. The one-month forward DM is at a premium (the dollar is at a discount). On the other hand, if the quotation had been 95/100, then the margins would have been added to yield DM 2.5100/110.

INTEREST PARITY

What determines whether a foreign currency will be quoted at a premium or discount with respect to the domestic currency? The answer lies in interest rates, and the relationship between spot and forward exchange can be summarized in the form of an arbitrage condition called interest parity. *By "arbitrage we mean the simultaneous buying and selling (or borrowing and lending) of two commodities or assets in such a way that the action locks in a sure, known profit.* The calculation of this profit in no way depends on the outcome of random events or on people's expectations. (There is, however, usually a presumption that people will honor their contracts. That is, when we use the term *arbitrage* we will be excluding the possibility that random events determine the profit outcome, given that there is no risk of default on contracts.)

The interest parity theorem is an arbitrage condition relating the discount or premium on forward exchange to the term structure of interest rates on financial assets denominated in the two currencies involved in an exchange rate. In particular, if interest rates are *higher* in the domestic country than in the foreign country, then the foreign country's currency will be selling at a *premium* in the forward market, while if interest rates are *lower* in the domestic country, then the foreign currency will be selling at a *discount* in the forward market. For example, if interest rates are higher in the United States than Germany, then the forward DM will cost more U.S. dollars than will the spot DM. The forward DM will be at a premium and the forward dollar at a discount. If interest rates are higher in the United Kingdom than in the United States, then the forward £ will cost fewer dollars than will the spot £. The forward £ will be at a discount and the forward dollar at a premium.

Before getting to the arbitrage strategy that brings about interest parity, we should explore a few market conventions about how interest rates are quoted. In particular, for reasons mentioned later, we will be especially concerned with interest rates on eurocurrency deposits. Eurocurrency interest rates, like all interest rates, are always quoted at a yearly rate. Thus if a 30-day rate of "8 percent" is quoted, that does not literally mean 8 percent over the 30-day period but is an artificial construction. It is a "yearly" rate with the year in question a 360-day year. A 30-day rate of "8 percent" means that, for a $1 deposit, at the end of 30 days one will receive $(1 + .08(30/360)) = $1.006667 back. That is, one adjusts the "yearly" interest rate by changing it to a decimal and then multiplying by the fraction of a 360-day year involved in the time period of the deposit. (*Note:* You do it this way because that is the agreed meaning of "8 percent" in the market. You are not free to make up your own interpretation. That means, for example, that if you take $1.08 to the power $\frac{1}{12}$ and get $1.0064, your answer is wrong.)

The 360-day year applies to most eurocurrencies. Notable exceptions, however, are the British pound and the Belgian franc, which use 365-day years. Therefore "8 percent" paid on a eurosterling deposit for 30 days would, for an initial deposit of £1, yield

£(1 + .08(30/365)) = £1.006575

at maturity.

Eurocurrency deposits are traded over the phone, just like foreign exchange, with a bid/offer spread (the bid price being the rate one will pay on deposits and the offer price being the rate one charges on loans). Settlement dates follow the same conventions as in the FX market. For example, if one-month DM deposits are traded today, the deposit is actually made (at the interest rate agreed today) on the settlement date for spot DM. The DM deposit will mature on the same date as does a one-month forward DM contract traded today.

Now we are ready for the interest parity theorem. We will need some notation. At first we will simplify, and ignore the difference in bid and offer prices. That is, we will assume there is only one price quotation for spot exchange, for forward exchange, and for interest rates. After we have derived the theorem under these simplifying assumptions and seen some examples, we will then redo it taking into account bid and offer prices. Let $S(t)$ be the *domestic currency price of spot foreign exchange* at time t. For example, if the domestic currency is taken to be the dollar, and the foreign currency is the DM, then we might have $S(t) = \$.40/$ DM. Thus, $S(t)$ is in "American" terms if we take the dollar as our domestic currency. But if we take the DM for our domestic currency, then $S(t)$ would be in European terms. We can treat any currency as the domestic currency just as long as we are consistent. Let $F(t,T)$ be the *domestic currency price of forward exchange* at time t, for a contract that matures at time $t + T$. Let i and i^* be the yearly rates of interest paid on eurocurrency deposits denominated in the domestic (i) or foreign (i^*) currency. The maturity of the deposits is chosen to coincide with the maturity of the forward contract. Notice that matching maturities here is no problem, since eurocurrency deposits have settlement dates that correspond to those for forward contracts. We will assume for the following calculation that i and i^* are for a 360-day year.

Consider a trader with access to the interbank market in foreign exchange and eurocurrency deposits. At time t, this trader can borrow one unit of the domestic currency at an interest rate i, for which he will have to repay $1 + i(T/360)$ at time $t + T$:

Time t	Time $t + T$
Borrow 1 unit domestic currency	Repay $1 + i(T/360)$ units of domestic currency

With one unit of domestic currency in hand at time t, the trader can buy $1/S(t)$ units of foreign currency. If this amount is placed on deposit, he will receive $[1/S(t][1 + i^*(T/360)]$ back at time $t + T$. This amount of foreign currency will, however, have an uncertain value in domestic currency terms. So to lock in a domestic currency value now he can sell this amount forward at the forward rate $F(t,T)$. The domestic currency value of the amount sold forward is therefore $[1/S(t)][1 + i^*(T/360)] F(t,T)$. To summarize:

Time t	Time $t + T$
Purchase $[1/S(t)]$ units of foreign currency; sell forward $[1/S(t)][1 + i^*(T/360)]$ units of foreign currency at forward rate $F(t,T)$	Deposit matures and pays $[1/S(t))][1 + i^*(T/360)]$ units of foreign currency; deliver this amount of foreign currency in fulfillment of forward contract, receiving $[1/S(t)][1 + i^*(T/360)] F(t,T)$ units of domestic currency

Notice that the trader has put up no money in the process of making these transactions. Therefore, if the investment in foreign currency deposits, after covering through the forward market, yielded an amount greater than that which the trader would have to repay on his loan, the trader would make a riskless profit, having used none of the trader's own capital. And in the contrary case, if the investment in foreign currency deposits, after covering through the forward market, yielded an amount less than the trader would have to repay on his loan, the trader could reverse this procedure (by borrowing foreign currency) and also make a riskless profit using only borrowed money. Either way, the trader would realize he had hold of a money machine, and would keep repeating the process as long as the market kept giving him a free profit. Other traders would have a similar idea, so their volume of trading would cause prices to adjust in such a way that a free, riskless profit was no longer available.

To summarize, in economic equilibrium (an absence of free profit opportunities like those above) we must have equality between the rate of return on domestic assets and covered foreign assets:

$$1 + i(T/360) = [1/S(t)][1 + i^*(T/360)]F(t,T)$$

Or, rearranging this equation,

$$F(t,T) = S(t) \frac{[1 + i(T/360)]}{[1 + i^*(T/360)]} \tag{4.1}$$

The last equation is the famous interest parity "theorem." It relates the forward exchange rate to the spot exchange rate and the interest rates on eurodeposits denominated in the domestic (i) and foreign (i^*) currencies. Notice that if i is greater than i^* (the domestic interest rate is higher than the foreign interest rate), then the domestic currency price of forward exchange [$F(t,T)$] will be higher than the domestic currency price of spot exchange [$S(t)$]. Foreign currency would be at a forward premium and domestic currency at a forward discount. Finally, notice that 360 appears in the equation because a 360-day year is assumed as the basis for the interest-rate quotation. If one currency were quoted on the basis of a 365-day year, however, 365 should be substituted adjacent to the relevant interest rate.

EXAMPLE 4.2

Let the spot rate $S(t) = \$.40000/DM$ and the 1-year forward rate $F(t,T) = \$.42026/DM$. Assume that the forward contract will mature in $T = 365$ days from the spot value date. Let the rates on eurodollar deposits and euro-DM deposits be, respectively, $i = 11.3\%$ and $i^* = 6.0\%$. Then, comparing the return on domestic borrowing with the return on covered foreign lending,

$$1 + i(T/360) = 1 + .113(365/360) = \$1.114569.$$
$$[1/S(t)][1 + i^*(T/360)]F(t,T) = (1/.40)[1 + .06(365/360)](.42026) = \$1.114565$$

For each dollar borrowed domestically, a trader would have to repay $1.114569. The return from using the $1 to buy spot foreign exchange, placing the deposit at the foreign rate of interest, and selling the total return forward would be $1.114565. These two amounts are so close that it would in all probability not be worth anyone's time trying to exploit the difference. So in this case, interest parity can be said to hold. In fact, as we will see when we look at the realistic case involving both bid and ask prices, the two sides of the transaction can differ by a good bit more than they do here, and still there may be no profit opportunity.

INTEREST PARITY AND SWAPS

How do interbank swaps relate to the interest parity theorem? There are several parts to the answer. First, referring back to the interest parity formula, we see that it gives the forward rate as a function of the spot rate. Therefore the swap rate should be the difference between $F(t,T)$, as given by the formula, and the spot rate $S(t)$. That is, the swap rate $F(t,T) - S(t)$ should have the value:

$$F(t,T) - S(t) = S(t) \left(\frac{1 + i(T/360)}{1 + i^*(T/360)} - 1 \right)$$

$$= S(t) \left(\frac{(i - i^*)(T/360)}{1 + i^*(T/360)} \right) \tag{4.2}$$

To see what this implies in practice, consider the situation of a commercial bank. Suppose the bank assigns a group of traders to do arbitrage between the spot and forward markets in the way described in deriving the interest parity theorem. If the traders do the task correctly, soon there will be no arbitrage opportunities left and the traders will serve no useful purpose. That is, they will put themselves out of a job if they do their job of arbitraging well; thus the bank may not consider it a good idea to assign a lot of people to do covered interest arbitrage.

Neither, on the other hand, does the bank want to give money away by quoting prices inconsistently, whereby other banks can arbitrage against it. Even if the bank does not think it will find long-lasting arbitrage opportunities, it still may worry that other banks will and that it will be a source of arbitrage profit to the benefit of other banks. How can the first bank ensure that this never happens? Answer: Quote forward rates according to the interest parity theorem. This is, in fact, what essentially all money-center banks—those that make the market in interbank trading—do. They use the interest parity theorem to calculate the swap rate.

This, of course, does not mean there will *never* be an arbitrage opportunity. The first qualification comes from the fact that because there are many traders in the market, there is always a spectrum of spot exchange rates being quoted simultaneously throughout the foreign exchange market. These spot prices are not the same, so the forward rates derived from them will not be exactly the same across banks at any one time either. Second, the size of the discount or the premium on forward exchange relates to eurocurrency interest rates on the domestic and foreign currencies. These interest rates may not be quite the same as seen by different traders at any point in time in the market, so the size of the discount or premium quoted on forward exchange will vary from trader to trader.

Why should the trader be looking at eurocurrency interest rates as opposed to some other set of rates? There are many reasons. Recall from the history in Chapter 1 that the eurocurrency market grew out of the Merchant Banks' Market of the late 1950s. At that time, eurocurrency dealing was done in foreign exchange trading rooms by foreign exchange traders. Therefore conventions in the eurodeposits market such as settlement and maturity dates were chosen to correspond to foreign exchange conventions. A trader could thus arbitrage using eurocurrency deposits and never have to worry about the deposits maturing on a different day than the forward contract. Moreover, eurocurrencies corresponded precisely to that set of money market instruments that could be freely traded internationally, usually without controls, taxes, and other restrictions. Thus an arbitrage could be done in the simple manner described by the interest parity theorem, without incurring so many additional transactions costs as to rule out any possible profit opportunity.

Therefore a bank will quote its swap rate using eurocurrency rates as reference rates in the interest parity formula. For some currencies with forward markets, however, eurocurrency rates do not exist. As of 1985, for example, there were functioning interbank forward markets for about twenty-one currencies but eurocurrency rates for only fifteen of them. In cases where no relevant euromarket exists, or exists but is too thin to be really useful, then some money market instrument other than eurocurrency deposits may be relevant.

Here is an example of how banks use swaps to manage outright forward exposures incurred in dealing with corporate customers.

EXAMPLE 4.3

A company buys £1 million six months forward from a bank. The bank selling the £1 million has done an "outright forward" deal with the company. The bank now has a foreign exchange exposure in that it is short (it has sold) £1 million. To cover this exposure, the bank will *buy* £1 million forward. This purchase forward, if done in the interbank market, must be done in the form of a swap, so the bank will do a swap involving a *spot sale and forward purchase* of £1 million. After doing the swap, the bank has now matched its forward commitments. But it is now short (it has sold) £1 million spot. So to even out its spot position, the bank does a separate spot purchase of £1 million. To summarize:

Company	Bank
Purchases £1 million in the forward market	Sells £1 million as an "outright forward" Does a swap in which it buys £1 million forward and sells £1 million spot Purchases £1 million spot

---

DIVERGENCES FROM INTEREST PARITY

Let's now consider some examples where interest parity does not hold. We will see how to use the interest parity relation to detect arbitrage opportunities and to compare hedging costs. (We will continue to simplify in this section by ignoring bid/asked prices.)

EXAMPLE 4.4

Suppose an interbank trader noticed the following market prices:

$S(t) = \$.40/DM, \qquad F(t,T) = \$.42/DM$ for $T = 360$ days,
$i = 10\%$, and $i^* = 6.0\%$.

Is there an arbitrage opportunity available? A quick way to check for arbitrage possibilities is to calculate both sides of the interest parity theorem. Since interest rates do not have to be adjusted (since $360/360 = 1$), the trader observes:

$$F = \$.42/DM \qquad S\frac{(1+i)}{(1+i^*)} = \$.40/DM\frac{(1.10)}{(1.06)} = \$.41509/DM.$$

The actual forward rate, \$.42/DM, is larger than the synthetic forward rate (\$.41509/DM) calculated from the other side of the equation. Following the principle "buy low, sell high," the trader will want to sell forward because forward exchange is overvalued by relation to spot exchange and the two interest rates. That is, the actual forward rate is overvalued by reference to the synthetic forward rate. She will end up selling forward, if she borrows the dollar, buys DM, and sells DM forward. Hence *she will borrow the dollar and undertake an interbank swap.* A typical transaction size will be $1 million, but it is simpler to think in terms of $1. She will borrow $1, buy $1/.40 =$ DM 2.5, place the DM at 6 percent interest to yield DM 2.65 in 360 days. Meanwhile, she has sold the DM 2.65 forward for (DM 2.65)($.42/DM) = $1.113. She will pay off her $1 loan with $1.10, so that her net gain is $.013. For a $1 million transaction, the profit would be $13,000. (Profit of this magnitude would be enormous and would occur rarely, if ever, on a single transaction in the interbank market.)

Let's now consider a corporation. Because the relevant interest rates seen in the interbank market are eurocurrency rates, while the relevant interest rates as seen by a corporation may be something else, interest parity may not hold for the corporation, even if it does in the interbank market. That does not mean that the corporation is necessarily in a position to do arbitrage: probably it will not be since the corporation would have to deal at larger spreads than will the bank. But the corporation may be in a position to alter its hedging costs.

EXAMPLE 4.5

A U.S. importer of machinery must pay DM 2 million in 6 months (180 days). The company's borrowing rate for dollars is 10 percent, while its lending rate for DM is 5.5 percent. The company is quoted a bank rate of $.3752/DM for spot exchange, and $.3900/DM for six-months forward exchange (180 days). The company wishes to lock in the dollar cost of the DM 2 million now, and has decided to use a forward hedge or a money market equivalent. Given the prices faced by the company, which should it use?

To hedge through the forward market, the company will buy forward DM 2 million at a cost of (DM 2 million)($.3900/DM) = $780,000 to be paid in 180 days.

To use a money market equivalent, the company calculates the amount of DM it needs now, which, if placed on deposit, will yield DM 2 million in 180 days. The interest over 180 days would be (180/360)(.055) = .0275, so the company will need to deposit DM 2 million/1.0275 = DM 1,946,472. The dollars the company would need now to buy this amount of DM is (DM 1,946,472)($.3752/DM) = $730,316.30. So the company will need to borrow $730,316.30 in order to buy DM, and it will pay back its loan in the amount of ($730,316.30)(1.05) = $766,832.12, as interest in the amount of (180/360)(.10) = .05 will be paid on each dollar borrowed.

The money market equivalent is cheaper by $780,000 − $766,832.12 = $13,167.88. The only reason the two hedging procedures give different numbers is that interest parity in this case doesn't hold at interest rates that are relevant to the company.

The reader should not be deceived into thinking that examples like that above never occur in practice. Hilley et al. (1981) cite instances in which money market hedges were considerably more advantageous to corporations than were three- to five-year forward contracts being contemporaneously offered by banks.

INTEREST PARITY WITH BID/ASKED SPREADS

Let's now turn to the realistic case where all prices are quoted with bid/asked spreads. We will need slightly different notation. Let $Sb(t)$ and $Sa(t)$ be, respectively, the bid and asked domestic currency prices of spot exchange. Let $Fb(t,T)$ and $Fa(t,T)$ be the bid and asked domestic currency prices of forward exchange.

And let *ib*, *ib*** and *ia*, *ia*** be the bid and asked interest rates on eurodeposits denominated in the domestic and the foreign (*) currency. Again, assume a 360-day year as the basis for the interest quotations although a 365-day year should be substituted if relevant.

Consider now a trader in the interbank market. He will have to buy or borrow at the other party's asked price while he will sell or lend at the bid price. If the trader wishes to do arbitrage, there are two approaches he can take: borrow domestic currency or borrow foreign currency. Let's consider each case in turn.

BORROW DOMESTIC CURRENCY

The trader can borrow $1/[1 + ia(T/360)]$ units of domestic currency at time t, and repay 1 unit at time $t + T$. Using the borrowed domestic currency, he can engage in a swap to buy spot foreign currency and sell the currency forward, meanwhile placing the foreign currency at the foreign rate of interest. This would yield, in terms of domestic currency:

$$(1/[1 + ia(T/360)]) \, ([1/Sa(t)][1 + ib^*(T/360)]Fb(t,T)).$$

For this procedure to yield no profit, which is the requirement for economic equilibrium, it must be the case that it gives an amount less than or equal to the 1 unit of domestic currency that must be repaid on the loan:

$$(1/[1 + ia(T/360)])([1//Sa(t)][1 + i^*b(T/360)]Fb(t, T) \le 1.$$

Rewriting, we get

$$Fb(t,T) \le Sa(t)\,\frac{1 + ia(T/360)}{1 + ib^*(T/360)}. \tag{4.3}$$

So, to eliminate arbitrage, the forward bid price must be less than the spot asked price multiplied by the ratio of one plus the domestic asked interest divided by one plus the foreign bid interest.

BORROW FOREIGN CURRENCY

The trader can borrow $1/[1 + ia^*(T/360)]$ units of foreign currency at time t and repay 1 unit of foreign currency at time $t + T$. With the foreign currency, he can buy spot domestic currency, place it at the domestic interest rate, and sell it forward. This will yield a foreign currency amount of

$$(1/[1 + ia^*(T/360)])(Sb(t)[1 + ib(T/360)][1/Fa(t,T)]),$$

which must, in economic equilibrium, be less than or equal to the one unit of foreign currency that must be repaid. From this inequality, we get

$$Fa(t,T) \ge Sb(t)\,\frac{1 + ib(T/360)}{1 + ia^*(T/360)}. \tag{4.4}$$

To avoid arbitrage, the market prices must be such that the forward asked price is greater than or equal to the spot bid price multiplied by one plus the domestic bid interest divided by one plus the foreign asked interest.

Notice that *both* conditions must hold simultaneously at all times, else the market will be offering a riskless profit to the trader. These relationships are illustrated in Figure 4.1.

Conditions: $Fb(t,T) \leq Sa(t) \dfrac{1 + ia(T/360)}{1 + ib^*(T/360)} = Y$

$Fa(t,T) \geq Sb(t) \dfrac{1 + ib(T/360)}{1 + ia^*(T/360)} = X$

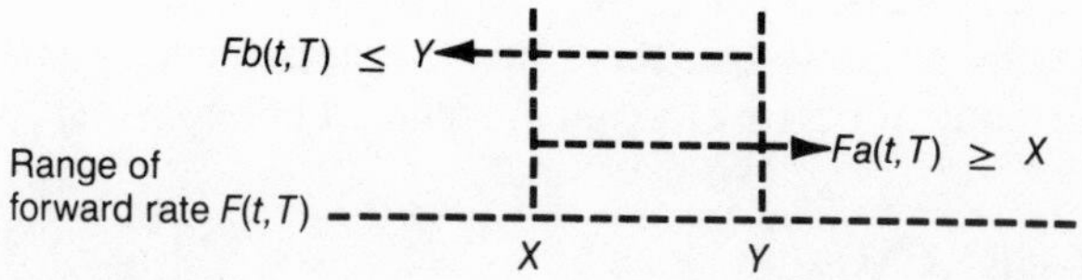

FIGURE 4.1
Constraints on forward exchange rate to avoid covered interest arbitrage. Allowable ranges for *Fb*, *Fa* (conditional on *Fb* < *Fa*) are shown.

EXAMPLE 4.6

Suppose, at market prices, we have the spot price of DM at $.4428 − .4438/DM, while the one-month forward rate (with $T = 30$ days) is $.4450 − .4460/DM. The rate on one-month euro-DM deposits is $5\frac{7}{8} − 6$ percent, while the rate on one-month eurodollar deposits is $10\frac{11}{16} − 10\frac{13}{16}$ percent. Is there an arbitrage possibility?

If a trader borrows dollars, he will borrow $1/[1 + (.10\frac{13}{16})(30/360)]$ and repay $1. If he buys spot DM, places them at the DM interest rate, and sells forward, he will obtain

($1/[1 + (.10\frac{13}{16})(30/360)])([1/$.4438/DM][1 + (.05\frac{7}{8})(30/360)][$.4450/DM])
= $.9986.

Therefore there is no arbitrage opportunity. For each $1 the trader would have to repay he would receive $.9986 in return. This is a losing proposition.

If a trader borrows DM, he will borrow DM $1/[1 + .06(30/360)]$ and repay DM 1. If he now buys spot dollars and places them at the dollar interest rate, and sells forward, he will obtain

(DM $1/[1 + .06(30/360)])([$.4428/DM][1 + (.10\frac{11}{16})(30/360)][1/$.4460/DM])
= DM .9966.

Again, there is no arbitrage profit available this way. For each DM 1 the trader would have to repay on his loan, he would receive only DM .9966 in return.

In Example 4.6, there was no arbitrage possibility in the interbank market. That does not mean, however, that a corporation will necessarily be indifferent to hedging costs at the rates given. We see this in Example 4.7.

EXAMPLE 4.7

Consider a corporation not set up for arbitrage but large enough to have access to the interbank market. The corporation is buying DM to make payment 30 days hence. The prices are those in Example 4.6. There are two obvious routes the corporation can take to have DM on hand to make payment in 30 days. The corporation can set aside an amount in dollars for 30 days, meanwhile receiving interest, and sell the dollars forward for DM. For each $1 set aside this way, it will receive

$$\$1[1 + (.10\tfrac{11}{16})(30/360)](1/\$.4460/DM) = DM\ 2.2621.$$

Alternatively, the company can take $1, buy spot DM, and place these at interest for 30 days. This will yield DM in the amount of

$$\$1(1/\$.4438/DM)[1 + (.05\tfrac{7}{8})(30/360)] = DM\ 2.2643.$$

Thus the second route will yield more DM per dollar. For each $1 million, the company will receive an additional DM 2200 by following the second procedure.

□

The range within which the forward rate can move without covered interest arbitrage possibilities is explored empirically in Frenkel and Levich (1975, 1977). The narrower range illustrated in Example 4.7 for corporations choosing the least-cost method of obtaining foreign currency is discussed in Deardorff (1979) and Bahmani-Oskooee and Das (1985). ∎

INTEREST PARITY AND THE COST OF INFORMATION

Examples 4.5 and 4.7 illustrate an important principle. Some companies may pay more than they need to by dealing through the forward market. Even given the fact that on average interest parity will hold in the interbank market — because of the method of forward rate quotation — it does not follow that currency or hedging costs will be the same whether undertaken through the forward market or spot market in connection with the money markets. A simple difference in costs of twenty-five basis points would amount to $25,000 on the purchase or sale of $10 million. Presumably corporate treasurers are not so highly compensated that it would fail to be worth a few minutes of their time to do the simple calculation necessary for comparing two equivalent hedging methods.

If the interest parity relation holds exactly, there is no advantage in choosing a money market hedge over a forward hedge, or vice versa. But interest parity may not hold when rates relevant to the corporation are used, and sometimes the money market hedge will be more advantageous. Does this mean the market is inefficient? Not necessarily, because of the costs of information. If a company were continually dealing in the interbank market, borrowing and lending and buying and selling currencies, the prices at which it made transactions would be immediately transmitted as information throughout the market, and any riskless arbitrage opportunities would be quickly eliminated. But a company such as the one in our hedging example may not do continuous dealing. It may only come to the market occasionally. Suppose we take the price at which spot exchange is available to the company as given and the rate at which the company can borrow the domestic currency as given. Now assume the company goes to the market and asks for a quotation on forward exchange and also asks for a quotation on the rate for lending a foreign currency. If the market quotes one rate on forward exchange, then there is one and only one lending rate that is consistent with this forward rate without interest parity being violated. But, likely as not, the two rates quoted will not be entirely consistent. The market is not inefficient, however, unless this difference is big enough to pay someone in the market a normal level of profit to collect and exploit the information concerning differences in quotations to companies. But from a specific company's own point of view, however, it is virtually costless to compare hedging costs using the rates quoted to it. For an individual company's decision to be efficient, the company must choose the least-cost hedging method.

FORWARD MARKETS AND INTEREST RATES: HISTORICAL BACKGROUND

While forward contracts have existed for thousands of years, forward markets are a more recent innovation. FX forward markets in their modern form have, however, existed at least since the 1880s. On the Vienna stock exchange at that time, one could make forward contracts for the German mark for one-, three-, four-, and six-months' delivery. In Berlin there were forward markets for the Austrian gulden and the Russian ruble, while a smaller forward market for the German mark existed in St. Petersberg. The Russian ruble in particular was subject to considerable fluctuations in value. British importers and exporters of that era insisted that trade contracts with Russia be denominated in the pound sterling. German traders were able to gain a competitive advantage by their willingness to denominate trade in terms of the Russian ruble. The Berlin forward market in the ruble had an essential part in their risk-exposure management (Schulze-Gaevernitz, 1899).

Later in the 1890s the emergence of forward markets in the pound sterling and French franc in Berlin and Vienna led to some aggressive interest arbitrage between those two cities and London and Paris. The existence of such an operation as interest arbitrage was considered a trade secret, however, and was jealously guarded (Einsig, 1937, p. 42).

It was another thirty years before an extended public exposition of the interest parity relation was given. This account appeared in the *Manchester Guardian Reconstruction Supplement* on April 20, 1922, and was written by an economist named John Maynard Keynes. Keynes' article was expanded into a book, *A Tract on Monetary Reform* (1923), which described the postwar forward markets in detail. Keynes cited some dramatic examples of profitable interest arbitrage despite the fact that large bid/asked spreads were common in the forward market.

Keynes' lucid exposition of forward contracts and interest parity did not prevent economists from treating forward markets as an institutional development devoid of any major theoretical interest. When Paul Einsig published his *Theory of Forward Exchange* fifteen years later, in 1937, he complained: "Whatever may be the reason, Forward Exchange is one of the neglected branches of financial literature. The majority of economists avoid the subject if they can; the majority of bankers leave it to their Foreign Exchange dealers; as for the general public, they regard Forward Exchange as something deeply mysterious and infinitely complicated, like Relativity, and consider it futile even to try to understand the workings of the system." Einsig himself produced long charts comparing the forward premium to "parities" involving various interest rates. He calculated "discount rate" parity, "bank rate" parity, and "call money rate" parity.

If we jump ahead another thirty-five years, to 1972, the confusion over the relevant interest rates had disappeared. In the late 1950s the dealing of eurocurrency deposits had grown up in foreign exchange trading rooms, and settlement dates and procedures followed those for foreign exchange. The costs (as embodied in bid/asked spreads) of doing interest arbitrage using eurocurrency deposits were very small. Not only was the interest parity relation well understood, but it had also acquired increasing relevance as transactions costs fell, because the range of possible forward quotations was correspondingly narrowed. Soon banks dropped the pretense of maintaining a separate forward market and simply quoted the swap rate using the interest parity relation. Even if they were not engaged in interest arbitrage, it was not worth taking the risk that some *other* bank might be.

□

Since the re-emergence of foreign exchange markets at the end of the 1950s, economists have conducted numerous "tests" of the interest parity "theorem." The usefulness or importance of many of these tests is unclear. Typically the discount or premium on forward exchange—usually measured without taking into account bid/asked spreads—was compared to an interest differential—again measured without bid/asked spreads. The assets whose interest rates were used in the tests might mature on different dates from the spot or forward exchange contracts or might have different credit risk or tax characteristics. Moreover, the tests were usually done with observational data on interest rates that were collected at times of the day different from the exchange rate data.

Since the interest parity relation is an arbitrage relation, the real empirical question was whether there were unexploited, essentially riskless profit opportunities. This question is difficult to answer on the basis of statistical tests. Profit is measured after the payment of transactions costs, which include the bid/asked spread omitted in the tests. The tests did not consider taxes, which become important (Levy, 1977) if, say, gains on forward contracts are taxed at a capital gains rate while interest rate gains are taxed as ordinary income. Political risk—the threat of capital or exchange controls—becomes important if arbitrage takes place across national borders (Aliber, 1973). Apparently riskless opportunities as shown in the data may simply indicate periods of high political risk. Of a more subtle nature, the tests involved regressions that measure "average" deviations from interest parity. Such an average measure is misleading because deviations may be large enough for profit opportunities yet zero on average, or too small for profit opportunities but nonzero on average (Frenkel and Levich, 1975).

Because eurocurrency deposits mature when forward contracts do, have similar credit risks, and face a similar absence of taxes and capital controls, tests using eurocurrency rates have generally found that any deviations from interest parity were sufficiently small as to be ascribable to transactions costs [see Aliber (1973), Frenkel and Levich (1975, 1977), and Herring and Marston (1976)]. Given that traders now use interest parity and eurocurrency rates to set the forward rate, it is not surprising that interest parity holds well when tested with eurocurrency data.

■

FORWARD CONTRACTS AND DUAL-CURRENCY BONDS

FX forward contracts show up in many different contexts. One important example is that of *dual-currency* bonds. A dual-currency bond is one that is purchased in terms of one currency—with coupon interest paid in that same currency—but is redeemed in terms of another currency. An example of a dual-currency bond was the issue led by the Swiss Bank Soditic for First City Financial in July 1985. Each bond could be purchased for its full face value of SF 5,000. Interest on the bonds is paid in Swiss francs. But when the bonds mature, at the end of ten years, the bond principal will be repaid in the amount of $2800.

At the time of issue, this bond could be viewed as the combination of (1) an ordinary ten-year Swiss-franc bond that would repay principal in the amount of SF 5,000, plus (2) a ten-year forward contract to buy $2800 at SF 1.7857/$. The reason is simple. As a dual-currency bond, the bond repays $2800. Alternatively, if one had a regular bond that repaid SF 5000, plus the forward contract, one would have to give up the SF 5000 in payment for the $2800 that would be received on the forward contract, since ($2800)(SF 1.7857/$) = SF 5000 (except for minor round-off error). In either case, one would end up with $2800.

Viewing a dual-currency bond as the sum of an ordinary bond and a forward contract helps elucidate the nature of the exchange risk involved. With a forward contract, one has locked in an exchange rate. For the dual-currency bond above, the locked-in exchange rate is SF 1.7857/$. When a forward contract to purchase foreign currency matures, one will have an opportunity gain if the market price of foreign currency is higher than the price embodied in the contract. One will have an opportunity loss if the market price is lower. In the above example of a dual-currency bond, the holders of the bond will enjoy an exchange gain if the Swiss franc price of the dollar is higher than SF 1.7857 at bond maturity in 1995, but suffer an exchange loss if the Swiss franc price of the dollar is lower than SF 1.7857.

The motives for issuing such bonds are as various as the motives for using FX forward contracts in general. The chief reason a company might issue a dual-currency bond rather than issuing an ordinary bond and then taking out a forward contract is that the FX forward market provided by banks does not generally extend out to ten years. (For more on this, see Chapter 19.) In some cases there is a risk/return tradeoff, as dual-currency issues often pay higher coupons than the equivalent single-currency issue (*Financial Times*, July 12, 1985). The pattern of a company's cash flows may be such that repayment in a different currency is less risky from the company's point of view. In order to obtain this risk reduction, the company is willing to give up some earnings now in the form of higher coupon payments.

PROBLEMS FOR CHAPTER 4

1. Calculate the settlement day, as well as the maturity date, for a three-month eurodollar deposit traded on the first Wednesday in September of the current year.

2. A bank's spot quotation is ¥244.95 – ¥245.15/$. If the three-month forward yen is quoted as 3.12 – 3.07, what is the actual three-month forward exchange rate?

3. A bank sells a company DM 2,500,000 three months forward. What would be the customary way for the bank to cover its forward DM exposure?

4. A bank is currently quoting one-month forward rates of $1.2410 – 1.2425/£ and $1.0185 – 1.0200/Irish pound. What is the bank's one-month forward asked price for the Irish pound in terms of the British pound?

5. Consider two 92-day eurodeposits, one denominated in the U.S. dollar and the other denominated in the pound sterling. Each pays interest at a yearly rate of 9⅞ percent. Calculate the actual amount of interest paid on each deposit over the 92 days.

6. The interest rate on three-month (89-day) eurodollar deposits is $11\frac{7}{16} - 11\frac{9}{16}\%$ (bid/asked), while that on three-month euro-DM deposits is $5\frac{5}{16} - 5\frac{7}{16}\%$. Spot exchange is available at DM 3.0215–3.0280/\$ while three-month forward is available at DM 2.9852–2.9910/\$. Is there an arbitrage opportunity from borrowing either DM or dollars? If so, explain the steps that would be taken to exploit the arbitrage opportunity. What profit would be obtained from 1,000,000 units of currency? At what point in time would this profit be realized?

7. A company has a known cash payment of SF 50,000,000 to be made to a Swiss supplier in 100 days. The company wishes to fix or lock in the nominal dollar price of this payment using currently available rates. The spot rate available to the company is SF 2.50/\$, the forward rate for maturity in 100 days is SF 2.465/\$, and the company faces a dollar interest rate of 12 percent and a SF interest rate of 6 percent. Given this information, what is the smallest dollar price on its SF 50,000,000 that the company can lock in with certainty? Explain the procedure the company will follow to obtain this price.

FOREIGN CURRENCY FUTURES

INTRODUCTION

FX futures contracts are different from the FX forward contracts covered in Chapter 4. It is important not to get futures and forwards confused. Many years ago, FX forward contracts were sometimes referred to as "futures" by interbank traders, a practice which was probably harmless at the time. Today, however, given the existence of organized exchange trading in FX futures contracts, it is important to use the terms correctly, since futures involve a *different type of contract* from forwards.

The first important thing to realize about foreign currency futures is that when you have a futures contract, you do *not* own foreign exchange. A **futures contract** instead represents a pure *bet on the direction of price (exchange rate) movement of the underlying currency.* What this means is that the futures price is not a monetary amount you pay to anyone. Rather, the futures price is the variable about which you are betting. You can bet either that the price will go up or that it will go down. If you *buy* a futures contract, (go *long*) and the futures price goes up, you make money. If the futures price goes down, you lose money. Thus if your total FX portfolio consisted of a *long* position in FX futures, you would be betting that the price would go *up.* If you *sell* a futures contract (go *short*) and the futures price goes down, you make money. If the futures price goes up, you lose money. Thus if your total FX portfolio consisted of a *short* position in FX futures, you would be betting that the price would go *down.*

Futures trading in countries such as the United States takes place only on government-regulated exchanges. Buyers or sellers of futures contracts place orders through brokers or exchange members. These orders are communicated to the exchange floor and then transferred to a trading pit, where the price (or prices) for a given number of contracts will be negotiated by open outcry between floor brokers or traders. A futures trade will result in a futures contract with two sides—someone going long at the negotiated price and someone going short at that same price. Thus, if there were no transactions costs, futures trading would represent a zero-sum game: what one side will win will exactly match what the other side will lose. The futures price itself will change minute by minute. The futures price is a market price that adjusts to bring about equilibrium between the number of long positions and the number of short positions. If more people want to go long than want to go short at the current futures price, the futures price will be driven up until an equilibrium between desired short and long positions is reached. If desired short positions are greater than desired long positions at the current futures price, the price will be driven down. The number of two-sided futures bets in existence at any time is called the **open interest**.

Many publications, written by people who really know better, state that a "futures contract is a binding agreement to buy or sell an underlying asset at a specified date in the future." Such a definition is not only technically false, it is also misleading. A futures contract is really a binding agreement to pay up your bet on a daily basis, for every day the market is open and your bet is still in effect. There may be, however, certain specified dates on which, *if your bet is still in force at that time,* you will be legally obligated to acquire (if long) or deliver (if short) the underlying asset on whose price you are betting. For foreign currency futures, these dates correspond to the **last trade dates** covered below. If you stop an FX futures bet prior to the end of trading on the last trade date, you are never obligated to buy or to deliver anything. The way to stop a bet is to reverse whatever you did to get into it. If you are long a contract, then going short the same contract (at the same exchange) will kill the bet. If you are short, then going long will kill the bet. (Killing a bet results in a reduction in open interest.)

The size of the bet you take by opening a futures contract is governed by the face amount of the contract. If you have gone *long* a futures contract at a price $P(0)$, then at the end of the day there will be a positive or negative cash flow to your futures account in the amount of

$$[P(1) - P(0)] \times \text{Face value of contract,}$$

where $P(1)$ is the settlement price at the end of the trading day. The next business day the cash flow to your account will be

$$[P(2) - P(1)] \times \text{Face value of contract,}$$

where $P(2)$ is the next day's settlement price. If you go *short,* the cash flows are the reverse of those above. For example, suppose a £25,000 futures contract is opened during Day 1 at a negotiated price of $1.4500/£ and the settlement prices at the end of Day 1 and Day 2 are

Opening price	$1.4500/£
Settlement price, Day 1	$1.4460/£
Settlement price, Day 2	$1.4510/£,

then the respective cash flows for long and short positions in a single contract opened at $1.4500/£ are

Long	Short
($1.4460/£ − $1.4500/£) × £25,000 = −$100	+$100
($1.4510/£ − $1.4460/£) × £25,000 = +$125	−$125

On Day 1, the long side will lose $100 while the short side will gain $100 on each contract. On Day 2, the long position gains $125 and the short position loses $125 on each contract.

It is important to realize that these cash flows take place every business day. If you win money, you can withdraw your winnings immediately. If you lose, you pay up immediately. But how can you be sure that the loser will pay up immediately, or even at all? The way this is taken care of is that the brokerage firm will require a certain amount of cash to be deposited with it as a security bond. The brokerage firm will in turn post margin with a **clearing house**, which will then guarantee both sides of the futures contract against default by the other party. The amount per contract you have to deposit with the broker is called **margin**. If the money won on a particular day leaves the account balance above the required margin, the surplus cash can be withdrawn immediately. If the money lost leaves the account balance below the required margin, more cash must be added. Margin requirements and the clearing house are discussed more fully below.

THE IMM AND LIFFE

The two most important places where FX futures contracts can be traded are at the International Money Market (**IMM**) of the Chicago Mercantile Exchange and at The London International Financial Futures Exchange (**LIFFE**). At each exchange FX futures contracts are for standardized foreign currency amounts, terminate at standardized times (last trade dates), and have minimum allowable price moves (called "ticks") between trades. The available contracts in 1985 were

Contract	Face amount	Minimum price move	
British pound (IMM)	25,000	$.0005	($12.50)
British pound (LIFFE)	25,000	$.0001	($2.50)
Deutschemark (IMM)	125,000	$.0001	($12.50)
Deutschemark (LIFFE)	125,000	$.0001	($12.50)
Swiss franc (IMM)	125,000	$.0001	($12.50)
Swiss franc (LIFFE)	125,000	$.0001	($12.50)
Japanese yen (IMM)	12,500,000	.0001¢	($12.50)
Japanese yen (LIFFE)	12,500,000	.0001¢	($12.50)
Canadian $ (IMM)	100,000	$.0001	($10.00)
Mexican peso (IMM)	1,000,000	.001¢	($10.00)
French franc (IMM)	250,000	.005¢	($12.50)

For most types of futures contracts there are also maximum allowable daily price movements ("limit moves") up or down from the previous day's settlement price. The IMM, however, removed all daily price limits on currency futures in February 1985.

FX futures prices at both the IMM and LIFFE are quoted in American terms—the U.S. dollar price of a unit of foreign exchange. Contracts are traded on a standard three-month cycle of March, June, September, and December. The IMM has, in addition, some maturities for other months, but these contracts are not much traded. The month during which a contract expires is referred to as the **spot month**. Daily limits, if they exist, do not apply during the spot month.

The process of actually turning over a foreign currency bank deposit in return for a dollar deposit is referred to as **delivery**. Delivery takes place on the third Wednesday of the spot month at the IMM or, if that is not a business day, the next business day. Trading in a contract ends two business days prior to the delivery day. If a futures bet is still in effect at the end of trading on the last trade date, then the long side of the FX futures contract has acquired the obligation to pay U.S. dollars for the face amount of foreign currency involved in the contract, at an exchange rate given by the last trading day's settlement price. The short side has the obligation to deliver the amount of foreign currency specified in the contract. The transfer of U.S. dollars for foreign currency (delivery) between the long and short positions then takes place two days later on the delivery date, according to procedures set by the exchange.

REGULATION AND GUARANTEES

Futures trading at the IMM and elsewhere in the United States is regulated by the **Commodities Futures Trading Commission (CFTC)**, a regulatory body created by Congress in 1974. LIFFE is run by the International Commodities Clearing House (ICCH), which is a clearing system owned by the British clearing banks of Barclays, Lloyds, Midland, and National Westminster and by Standard Chartered Bank.

Because of regulation, different participants in the futures markets face different legal constraints on the type of business they conduct. In the United States, **futures commission merchants** (who accept margin payments) and other *associated persons* (who do not) are authorized to solicit and accept orders from the public. Futures commission merchants may or may not be members of a clearing house. (A similar distinction is made at LIFFE.) **Clearing members** are those members who hold accounts at the clearing house. The clearing houses guarantees both the long and short sides of a futures contract against the risk of default by the opposite party. The clearing house, in effect, takes the short side of every long futures position and the long side of every short futures position. This guarantee, however, applies only to futures contracts made by the customers of clearing member firms, and then only after transactions have been registered and confirmed by the clearing house and margin on the transactions has been received from clearing members. Futures commission merchants who are not clearing members must have their trades cleared by a clearing member. Such a nonmember firm will then have its own contracts guaranteed by the clearing house (since the firm is a customer of a clearing member). But customers of the non-clearing member firm will still face default risk.

A customer's order is transmitted to the exchange floor by the futures commission merchant, who acts as the customer's agent. There a floor broker — an exchange member who acts as agent for the clearing house — will attempt to complete the trade by open outcry in the trading pit. The trade may be completed either with another floor broker or with a **floor trader**. A floor trader is an exchange member or nominee who trades for his or her own account. Floor traders may take speculative futures positions, or they may act as marketmakers, similar to marketmakers in the interbank FX market; this is discussed more fully below. Floor traders must have their trades cleared by a futures commission merchant who is a clearing member. Finally, there is a category of *broker-traders* or **dual traders** who trade both for their own and customer accounts.

MARGIN REQUIREMENTS

The amount of margin required on an FX futures contract is related to the volatility of price movement of the underlying currency, and hence to the probability distribution of daily losses or gains. Margin requirements on the Swiss franc, whose price is highly variable with respect to the U.S. dollar, are greater than margin requirements on the Canadian dollar, whose U.S. dollar price shows lower variability. Margins are negotiable, and therefore will vary from broker to broker. However, there is a *minimum margin* for each contract that will hold throughout the market, a minimum given by the margin the clearing house charges clearing members. Clearing members sign an agreement with the clearing house that says they will set margins for their customers that are not less than the margins the clearing members have to hold with the clearing house. There is nothing, however, to prevent clearing members as well as brokerage firms (futures commission merchants) who are not clearing members from requiring higher margins, and most of them do so.

In the United States a distinction is made between **initial margin,** which is the amount of money that must be deposited when a contract is opened, and **maintenance margin,** which is the minimum level to which the margin is allowed to fall (if there are losses after opening the contract) before additional money must be added to the account. If the balance in the account falls below the maintenance level, additional money called *variation margin* must be added to the account to restore the account balance to the initial margin level. At LIFFE in the United Kingdom there is no separate maintenance level, so the initial margin level must be maintained at all times. Initial and maintenance margin required in July 1985 for IMM contracts by one brokerage firm were:

Contract	Initial	Maintenance
British pound	$2000	$1400
Deutschemark	$2000	$1500
Japanese yen	$1500	$1000
Swiss franc	$2000	$1500
Canadian $	$1200	$900
French franc	$2000	$1500
Mexican peso	$10000	$8000

Because price movements on currency futures contracts are sometimes more volatile during spot months, margin requirements go up. (For example, for the British pound, the required level during July 1985 for the brokerage firm above was $2500 initial and $2000 maintenance during spot months.) Margin requirements will similarly be altered if general market conditions change.

To the extent margin is posted in cash, there is an opportunity cost involved, because the cash could otherwise be held in the form of an interest-bearing asset. Generally in the United States, but not at LIFFE in the United Kingdom, initial margin can be posted in the form of treasury bills. Hence, there will be no interest lost on initial margin deposited with a broker. However, variation margin must usually be paid in cash. Remember that people with positive cash flows (the winning side of the daily price bets) will generally be withdrawing their cash to put it into interest-bearing accounts (or spend it on something suitable). Hence if the brokerage firm did not require the losers to pay up in cash, the firm would have to pay winners from its own cash holdings.

Actually, it is slightly more complicated than the preceding paragraph suggests. Generally only a part of initial margin can be posted in the form of T-bills. One firm, for example, will allow 90 percent margin in the form of T-bills and 10 percent in cash, if the T-bills have face values totaling $25,000 or more, but for smaller face amounts 40 percent of the initial margin must be posted in cash. Then if the cash position falls below the initial level, a "T-bill call" results, and the customer has three days to restore the cash to the initial level. If the cash level falls below zero, then a "cash call" ensues and the initial cash margin level must be restored the same day.

As an additional transaction cost to the public user of the futures markets, there is a brokerage fee associated with each futures contract. Such fees are usually quoted *round turn,* covering both the opening and closing of a futures position. The round turn commission is charged at the time the contract is closed. As of July 1985, a round turn commission for public customers was typically less than $30 per futures contract at discount brokerage firms.

FUTURES CONTRACTS COMPARED TO FORWARD CONTRACTS

There are a number of differences between a *forward* contract as used in the interbank market for foreign exchange and a *futures* contract as traded on exchanges like the IMM and LIFFE. The most important difference is the daily cash flows ("marking to market") that take place on a futures contract. In a forward contract, by contrast, no money will change hands until the contract expires. Then, on expiration day, currencies will be traded at the prearranged price, the forward price. The absence of daily cash flows in a forward contract is an important economic distinction. The reader should not be misled, however, into thinking that real-world forward contracts never involve any cash flow prior to maturity. There is potential credit risk in the corporate and the interbank market just like there is in the futures market. If a bank enters into a forward contract (via a swap) with another marketmaking bank, this credit risk is considered small enough for nothing more to be involved in the forward contract than the verbal agreement on the price. But if a corporation is involved, the corporation's line of credit at the bank will usually be reduced by the amount of the forward contract, provided the corporation has such a line of credit. If the company does not have a line of credit, usually a deposit of about 5 percent of the amount of the forward contract must be made with the bank. This insures the bank against the loss that might be incurred if the company defaulted on the forward contract and the spot exchange rate had in the meantime moved to the bank's disadvantage.

Leaving aside these minor qualifications, however, it is easy to see intuitively why a simple purchase of a futures contract is different from a simple purchase of a forward contract. Suppose you buy September British pound futures for $1.50 per pound. You have decided to take delivery on the contract, so on the third Wednesday in September you will receive £25,000 for which you will have to pay a dollar price determined by the settlement price on the expiration day (which will occur two business days prior to the third Wednesday). During the meantime, the dollar price of the pound may have gone up or it may have gone down.

In either case, your positive or negative cash flow will be such that it just offsets any change in the pound price from $1.50. For example, if the price has gone to $1.60, you have to pay $0.10 more for each pound than the $1.50 at which you opened the contract. However, you will have made $0.10 net on your futures bet because you were long the contract; the $0.10 offsets the difference between $1.50 and $1.60. Similarly, if the price had gone to $1.40, you would get the pounds at a cheaper price of $1.40, but in the meantime you will have lost $0.10 per pound on futures because you were long the contract and the price went down. So the net cost is still $1.50 per pound. However, *because the time pattern of cash flows was different in the two cases, your opportunity cost was different.* In the first case, you had generally positive cash flows. These cash flows could have been reinvested and earned interest. In the second case, you had negative cash flows. You had to forego interest by putting up more variation margin during the life of the contract. In the first case, you earned interest on the $0.10/£ positive cash flow, while in the second case you lost interest on the $0.10/£ negative cash flow. The cash flow in the first case is an *average* positive cash flow of $0.05 per pound, so that the dollar amount of interest earned would be about $0.05 per pound multiplied by the rate of interest and by the face amount of the contract. For example, for a £25,000 contract and 12 percent interest for one year, the interest earned would be roughly

$$(\pounds 25{,}000)(\$.05/\pounds)(.12) = \$150.$$

A forward contract would not have earned this amount of interest. In the second case, the negative cash flow on the futures contract would entail a loss of interest. Again, this loss would not be present in a forward contract.

The above example shows an intrinsic difference between forwards and futures to the purchaser of a contract. It does not automatically follow from that discussion, however, that forwards and futures will have different *prices.* Nevertheless, it can be shown as a theoretical proposition that futures prices ought in general to be different from forward prices. This difference in prices should result from the random unpredictable behavior of interest rates. The behavior of interest rates is crucial, for it can also be shown as a theoretical proposition that *if interest rates were nonstochastic, then the forward price and the futures price should be equal.* That is, if interest rates were either constant or else predictable with certainty, there exists an arbitrage strategy that would yield the arbitrager a sure profit if the market were quoting a particular futures price differently from the equivalent forward price. Hence the cash flow distinction between forwards and futures would not be sufficient by itself to make their prices differ. [This arbitrage strategy is not important for our purposes, so will not be covered here, but a description can be found in Cox, Ingersoll, and Ross (1982).] But it can be shown, conversely, that when interest rates are stochastic (as they are in the real world), forward and futures prices should differ by an amount whose magnitude depends on the covariance between futures price movements and interest rate movements. Is this covariance important in practice for FX futures and FX forwards? Apparently not. For the few currencies in which futures markets exist, FX futures prices rarely differ from FX forward prices by an amount even as large as twice the bid-ask spread in the interbank forward market. [See Cornell and Reinganum (1981).]

There are a number of other more obvious, though less important differences between FX forward contracts and FX futures contracts. *Forward* contracts are usually traded in standardized amounts equivalent to $1 or $2 or $3 million. However, any amount is negotiable. *Futures* contracts traded on an exchange are completely standardized, so it is only possible to take a position in the futures market that is a multiple of the size of one standardized contract. *Forward* contracts are mostly traded for maturities of one week, two weeks, and one through twelve months. But again, any maturity can be negotiated, and major banks will give quotations out to five years for the major currencies. *Futures* contracts expire at standardized intervals. In practice, for currency futures that means in March, June, September, and December at both the IMM and LIFFE. What this implies is that you will seldom, if ever, use the futures market as a way of actually acquiring or selling foreign exchange, since you could only do so on four dates during the year. The real purpose of futures is for hedging and speculation.

Forward contracts are traded over the counter: banks and brokers can be located anywhere and deal with each other over the phone. FX *futures* are traded on the market floor of the IMM, LIFFE, the Sydney Futures Exchange, the New Zealand Futures Exchange, the MidAmerica Commodities Exchange, the New York Cotton Exchange (which trades an ECU/U.S. dollar contract), the Toronto Futures Exchange, and the Singapore International Monetary Exchange (SIMEX). *Forward* contracts are contracts made directly between two parties, and there is no secondary market. To reverse a forward position, you would have to make a separate additional forward contract. Unless this happens to be with the same bank, the first contract will not kill the second: you will still have two contracts to deal with, and there may be credit risk on both contracts. *Futures* contracts are netted out through a clearing house, so that the clearing house stands on the other side of every contract cleared through it. Moreover, as long as you are dealing through a single exchange, you are only responsible for *net* positions. If you go long a futures contract and then go short the same contract, the second cancels the first. (The IMM and SIMEX have, in addition, an arrangement that allows one to net a futures position between the two exchanges.)

Forward contracts have no daily price limit. That is, that forward contracts were traded at $1.50 yesterday does not imply anything about today's price, which could differ from $1.50 by an arbitrarily large amount. *Futures* contracts, as explained previously, may have daily price limits set by the exchange (though the IMM has no daily limits on FX futures). *Forward* contracts in the interbank market have a delivery rate of about 90 percent. In the futures market, delivery is made or taken on less than 5 percent of FX contracts. The forward market is self-regulated. Forward contracts are subject, however, to the ordinary laws of contracts and taxation. In the United States, futures trading is regulated by the Commodity Futures Trading Commission. In the United Kingdom, LIFFE is self-regulated.

EXCHANGE TRADING AND MARKETMAKING

Orders to buy or sell futures contracts take the form of either **limit orders** — orders to buy or sell at prestated prices — or **market orders** — orders to buy at the prevailing level of offers in the trading pit or to sell at the prevailing level of bids. An example of a limit bid order might be "Buy 2 DM futures at $.3323/DM or lower." An example of a market order might be "Buy 2 DM futures at the market." The market order would then be filled with the purchase of 2 DM futures contracts at the lowest available offered price prevailing in the trading pit. Limit orders provide liquidity to the market because they enable others to take the opposite sides of the futures contract at the price embodied in the limit order. Market orders, by contrast, consume liquidity. Market orders to sell will fill some of the limit bid orders existing in the pit, while market orders to buy will fill some of the existing limit offer orders.

Futures trading is governed by a number of rules intended to ensure that orders will be executed in such a fashion as to produce a single market price determined on the basis of competition among floor brokers and traders. All bids and offers must be announced publicly. The highest bid price takes precedence over all other bid prices, and the lowest offer price takes precedence over all other offered prices. These rules are intended to ensure that the sale of a futures contract will take place at the highest price currently bid, while the purchase of a futures contract will take place at the lowest price currently offered.

As a result, the spectrum of prices at which trades simultaneously take place in the interbank FX market is mostly eliminated in the FX futures market. In addition, since most major banks also deal in the FX futures market and are able continually to observe FX futures prices, the existence of a single price quotation in the futures market acts as a common information variable that helps standardize price quotations in the interbank markets for spot and forward exchange. It was estimated that in 1983 roughly one-tenth of total FX dealing by New York banks involved the IMM (Andrews, 1984).

Like the interbank market, the futures market has marketmakers and bid/asked spreads. Floor traders may, at their option, provide marketmaking services by quoting two-way prices. Traders who perform these services are called "scalpers." By contrast to the interbank market, where an FX marketmaker is in continuous contact only with a limited number of other market participants, all marketmaking in the futures markets is concentrated in the trading pit. Since only one price may prevail in the market at any one time, a marketmaker will be constantly tempted to raise his or her bid price above that of other marketmakers, or to lower his or her offered price, in order to capture more business. As a result it is difficult to determine the actual size of the effective bid/offered spread (the spread at which trades actually take place). But the effective spread will generally be smaller than the average bid/offered spread quoted by marketmakers.

☐

Roll (1984) has suggested the following measure of the effective bid/asked spread in an efficient market. Let $\text{cov}[\Delta Z, \Delta Z(-1)]$ represent the average covariance of successive price changes on a futures contract (the "first order serial covariance" in statistical terminology). These successive price changes have a negative correlation because of trading across the bid/asked spread. This fact was used by Roll to derive a measure of the effective spread ("spr"), which in percentage terms is

$$\text{spr} = 200\sqrt{-\text{cov}[\Delta Z, \Delta Z(-1)]}. \qquad \blacksquare$$

As in the interbank market, marketmakers quote a bid/asked spread around an equilibrium market value. As supply and demand conditions change, the market equilibrium futures price changes. Marketmakers who are not interested in taking positions on the direction of futures price movements must be adroit in adjusting their bid and offered prices so as to buy and sell equal numbers of futures contracts and to keep their net futures positions as close to zero as possible. In a study of scalper behavior on the New York Futures Exchange, Silber (1984) found that a representative scalper held a net long or short futures position for an average time of less than two minutes. In addition, he found that the net profit per traded contract was significantly less than the value of the bid/asked spread. That is, the effective bid/asked spread was much smaller than the quoted spread.

HEDGING WITH FUTURES

The idea of **hedging** with futures is simple. You have a fixed position in an underlying asset or liability. For example, you have accounts receivable denominated in British pounds. There is exchange risk: the dollar value of the accounts receivable will drop if the British pound loses value with respect to the dollar. To hedge this risk, you take out a side bet in the futures market. *The futures bet must be chosen in such a way that whenever the underlying asset loses value, the futures bet generates a positive cash flow.* Because you have an underlying *long* position in pounds, to offset you should go *short* pound futures. (If you had an underlying short position in pounds, then to offset you would go long pound futures.) If the pound loses value in dollar terms, you will make money on your short futures position, which will offset the loss in value of your accounts receivable.

By the same criterion, if the value of the pound increases in dollar terms, the short futures position will generate a cash flow loss, which will offset the gain in value of your accounts receivable. So by hedging you avoid exchange rate loss, but also give up the possibility of exchange rate gain. This is the nature of hedging. It assumes you would prefer $10 million for sure rather than a fifty-fifty bet that would give you $20 million with probability .5 and $0 with probability .5. Restated, it assumes you are (or your company is) **risk-averse**. (By definition, risk aversion is the preference for a sure amount of wealth over a bet involving the same mathematical expectation. Hence risk aversion is one justification for hedging. A different justification for hedging in terms of ruin probabilities is given at the end of this chapter. This alternative interpretation relies on the practical assumption of limited capital and does not require risk aversion in order for hedging to be a desirable activity.)

In order to be hedged perfectly in dollar (or local currency) terms, the value of the futures position must change one-for-one (but with the opposite sign) with the value of the underlying position being hedged. Assuming that the amount of foreign currency involved in your futures bet exactly matches the amount of foreign currency involved in the underlying position, a perfect hedge requires that the futures price move one-for-one with the spot or cash price of the underlying currency.

☐

To see why, let x represent the change in the spot dollar (or local currency) price (S) of foreign exchange, while y represents the change in the futures price (Z).

That is, $x = \Delta S$ and $y = \Delta Z$. Let the total portfolio consist of one unit of cash or spot foreign currency held long that is hedged with one unit of foreign currency futures held short. The change u in the value of the total portfolio can then be represented as

$u = x - y.$

As long as $x = y$ (the change in the spot price equals the change in the futures price), we have $u = 0$ (no change in total portfolio value). The same would obviously also be true for a portfolio of arbitrary size, or for a short spot position hedged with a long position in futures. ∎

The difference between the spot or cash price and the futures price is called the basis. That is,

Basis = Spot price − Futures price.

If the movement in the spot price and the futures price is one-for-one, the basis is constant. When you hedge with futures, there is always a risk that the movement in the spot and futures prices will not be one-for-one. This is referred to as *basis risk*. Hedging with futures will never eliminate exchange risk entirely. There will always be basis risk. Basis risk, however, is normally much smaller than would be the open position without the futures bet.

EXAMPLE 5.1

You are long a £25,000 asset and you go short one futures contract to offset this. The spot rate is $1.1545/£, and you go short at a futures price of $1.1620/£. One month later the spot price is $1.1350 and the futures price is $1.1460. The basis has changed, so the hedge has not been perfect:

	Spot price	Basis	Futures price
Beginning price	$1.1545	−.0075	$1.1620
One month later	$1.1350	−.0110	$1.1460

Loss in value   Cash flow from
of spot asset $487.50   futures contract $400.00

The net loss is

$487.50 − $400.00 = $87.50.

An alternative way to do the calculation is to observe that the change in the basis is

$-.0110 - (-.0075) = -.0035.$

This yields a net cash flow of

$-\$.0035/£\ (£25,000) = -\$87.50.$

The hedge was not perfect, but the loss of $87.50 was much smaller than the unhedged loss of $487.50.

☐

In terms of the notation used above, here we have

$x = \$1.1350 - \$1.1545 = -\$.0195$

while

$y = \$1.1460 - \$1.1620 = -\$.0160.$

Thus

$u = x - y = (-\$.0195) - (-\$.0160) = -\$.0035.$

The change in portfolio value per foreign currency unit is $-\$.0035$. The total change is

$25,000(-\$.0035) = -\$87.50.$ ■

It should be clear from this example that *the ability to set up a good hedge depends on finding a futures contract whose price movement has a high degree of correlation with the underlying asset being hedged.* If the current time is February and you are hedging spot pounds with March pound futures, the movement in the two prices should be very close. But if the current time is February and you are hedging spot Danish krone with March deutschemark futures (an example of cross-hedging), there will be more risk involved because the correlation between price movements in spot krone and March DM futures will not be as high as the correlation between price movements in spot £s and March £ futures.

In practice, no futures hedge is perfect. There is always some risk that the actual value of a position hedged with futures will change with movements in the spot exchange rate. However, the amount of risk — in the sense of the variation in dollar (or local currency) value of the underlying position — can usually be reduced with an appropriately chosen futures hedge.

☐

There is a simple way to estimate the risk on a position that is hedged with an equal amount of currency futures. Recall from statistics that for two random variables x and y, the variance ("var") of $u = x - y$ is

$$\text{var}(u) = \text{var}(x) + \text{var}(y) - 2\,\text{cov}(x,y)$$

where $\text{cov}(x,y)$ denotes the covariance of x and y. As before, let x represent the change in the dollar (or local currency) spot or cash price of one unit of foreign currency, while y represents the change in price of one unit of foreign currency futures. The risk of the hedged position compared to the unhedged underlying position can be gotten by comparing the square root of $\text{var}(u)$ to the square root of $\text{var}(x)$:

$$\text{Hedged risk as \% open risk} = \sqrt{\frac{\text{var}(u)}{\text{var}(x)}}\; 100.$$

EXAMPLE 5.2

Suppose that x and y have the *same* variance and a correlation ("corr") of .95. Then, since $\text{cov}(x,y) = \text{corr}(x,y) \cdot \sqrt{\text{var}(x)}\,\sqrt{\text{var}(y)} = .95\sqrt{\text{var}(x)}\,\sqrt{\text{var}(x)}$, we get that

$$\text{var}(u) = \text{var}(x) + \text{var}(x) - 2(.95) \sqrt{\text{var}(x)} \sqrt{\text{var}(x)} = .1 \text{ var}(x).$$

Therefore

$$\text{Hedged risk as \% open risk} = \sqrt{\frac{.1 \text{ var}(x)}{\text{var}(x)}} \, 100 = 31.6\%.$$

That is, given a correlation of .95 between changes in the futures price and changes in the spot price, and assuming that the two price changes have equal variance, hedging a currency position with an equal amount of currency futures will result in a position with risk reduced to 31.6 percent of its original value.

■

The hedging procedure considered thus far has involved the matching of a currency asset or liability with an offsetting futures position of equal currency amount. The hedge assumed an expected (though not a certain) one-for-one price movement between spot prices and futures prices. For some practical purposes this approximation will suffice. In general, however, movements in spot and futures prices cannot be expected to be one-for-one even if the spot position and futures hedge involve the same currency. The amount of the futures hedge should be adjusted to compensate for this fact. This point is explored in the following two sections.

THE RELATION OF FUTURES PRICES TO SPOT (CASH) PRICES

Previously we noted that if interest rates were nonstochastic there should be no difference between futures and forward prices. And even though interest rates are in fact stochastic, the empirical evidence cited indicated little difference between FX forward prices and FX futures prices. In Chapter 4, we saw that forward exchange rates were related to spot exchange rates by the interest parity theorem, where the relevant interest rates were eurocurrency rates. This implies, then, that FX futures prices are related to spot (or cash) prices by interest parity.

Let the price of a futures contract at time t for delivery at time $t + T$ be denoted $Z(t, T)$. If, as an empirical matter, FX futures prices do not differ materially from FX forward prices, we then have by the interest parity condition (ignoring bid/asked spreads):

$$Z(t, T) = b \, S(t)$$

where

$$b = \frac{1 + i(T/360)}{1 + i^*(T/360)}.$$

Note that as $T \to 0$ (the contract matures), we have $b \to 1$, and thus $Z(t, T) \to S(t)$. That is, the futures price converges to the spot price at maturity. This is as it should be. On the final trading day for an FX futures contract, for example, one has two alternative ways to get foreign exchange: buy spot foreign exchange in the interbank market or buy an FX futures contract and take delivery. In either case, the foreign exchange will actually be delivered two days later. Thus, on the final trading day, simple arbitrage between the spot and futures markets will ensure that the prices are the same on that day.

This fact should be kept in mind in making hedging decisions. Price movements between the spot rate and the futures rate cannot be the same over the *entire* life of the contract if the prices themselves are not the same when a position is opened. For example, if spot DM is $.3552/DM and the December DM futures price is $.3576/DM when a position is opened, and if the spot (and futures) price on the last day of trading in December is $.3665/DM, the spot price will have moved by

$$\$.3665 - \$.3552 = \$.0113,$$

while the futures price will have moved by

$$\$.3665 - \$.3576 = \$.0089.$$

The relation between movements in the futures price and movements in the spot price prior to maturity is given in the equation above by b, which is referred to as the **futures delta**. The delta b can be greater than, or less than, 1. If b is greater than 1, the futures price will move more than the spot price. Hence, the hedge should involve a smaller amount of currency futures than the actual amount of underlying currency being hedged. If b is less than 1, the futures price moves less than the spot price, so a greater amount of currency futures is needed to form the hedge. It is easy to see that for each unit of an underlying currency you are long, you should go short $1/b$ units in futures of the same currency. For each currency unit you are short, you should go long $1/b$ units in futures of the same currency.

To see why this is true, first note that by interest parity

$$\Delta Z(t,T) = b \, \Delta S(t).$$

If you are long one unit spot and short $1/b$ futures, your position can be represented as

$$S(t) - (1/b) \, Z(t,T).$$

So for a change in the spot rate, the change in the value of your position will be

$$\Delta S(t) - (1/b) \, \Delta Z(t,T) = \Delta S(t) - (1/b) \, b \, \Delta S(t) = 0,$$

provided that the interest parity relation holds perfectly.

Note, however, that even if we assume that interest parity holds perfectly, the amount of the hedge must be adjusted over time, because b, the futures delta, is a function of time. As the contract matures, $b \rightarrow 1$, a process referred to in the futures markets as *convergence*. As contracts mature, the futures price converges to the spot price. Simultaneously, the futures hedge must be continually adjusted because the futures delta is changing.

EXAMPLE 5.3

Suppose the spot rate is $.3645/DM, while the futures price is $.3733. The futures delta in this case is $b = 1.024$, indicating that you should go short $1/b = .9764$ in DM futures for each DM 1 in the underlying position being hedged. Of course, you cannot go long or short a piece of a futures contract. However, if you are hedging a long position of DM 5,000,000, which is equivalent to 40 IMM futures contracts (40 $\times$ DM 125,000 = DM

5,000,000), this calculation indicates you should go short 39 IMM DM futures contracts, as $(40)(.9764) \cong 39$.

☐
CALCULATING THE RISK IN A DELTA HEDGE

When the futures contract is denominated in the same currency as the asset being hedged, we can use interest parity to get the futures delta b. For cross-hedging, such as a U.S. dollar/Danish krone position being hedged with U.S. dollar/DM futures, the concept of the futures delta is still meaningful. For cross-hedging, we similarly define the futures delta as a number b that gives the best linear relationship between changes in the spot price and changes in the futures price:

$$\Delta Z = b \, \Delta S.$$

For a cross-hedge, however, the futures delta b is not determined by interest parity. Consequently, b must be estimated using historical data.

In either case—whether b is derived from interest parity or from historical data—the futures hedge will not be perfect. How can you estimate the risk or variance of a delta hedge?

First, suppose that you use historical data to estimate the futures delta by means of a simple regression equation. Such an equation might involve regressing y and on x, where y is measured by weekly changes in the futures price, and x is measured as weekly changes in the spot price of the underlying asset being hedged. Assuming x and y have zero means, we can write the regression equation as

$$y = b \, x + e,$$

where b is the futures delta being estimated, and e is an error term. From statistics, we know that the least-squares estimate of b, $\hat{b}$, will have the value $\hat{b} = \text{cov}(x,y)/\text{var}(x)$. For example, we might have $\hat{b} = .8$. Given $\hat{b}$, the hedging rule is the same as above: for each unit of currency asset held long, sell short $1/\hat{b}$ units of currency futures. For each change x in the spot or cash price, you would then expect to see a change $\hat{b} x + \hat{e}$ in the futures price, where $\hat{e}$ results from the fact that your equation will not hold exactly. The expected value of $\hat{e}$ should be zero. Then, as prices change, the change u in the value of your portfolio, for each unit of foreign currency hedged with futures, would be

$$
\begin{aligned}
u &= x - (1/\hat{b}) \, y \\
&= x - (1/\hat{b})(\hat{b} \, x + \hat{e}) \\
&= -(1/\hat{b})\hat{e}.
\end{aligned}
$$

Thus if the error term $\hat{e}$ is zero, the change in the value of your portfolio is zero, and you are perfectly hedged. However, the error term will in general not be zero. The variance of the portfolio position can be easily calculated. It is

$$\frac{\text{var}(\hat{e})}{\hat{b}^2}$$

so that the hedged risk as a proportion of open risk is

$$\text{Hedged risk as \% open risk} = \sqrt{\frac{\text{var}(\hat{e})}{\hat{b}^2 \, \text{var}(x)}} \, 100.$$

EXAMPLE 5.4

Dutch guilders are being hedged using DM futures. Let x be weekly changes in the spot dollar price of the Dutch guilder, and let y be weekly changes in the dollar price of DM futures (for a particular delivery date). Suppose the regression equation gave the result

$$y = 1.26\ x.$$

This equation implies that for each unit of Dutch guilders held long, one should be short $1/1.26 = .79$ units of DM in futures. The risk of the hedged position depends on var(x) and on var(e). The future values of $é$ cannot now be known, but their variance can be estimated from the variance of the residuals in the regression. For example, suppose that in the data sample used to estimate the above equation, var(x) = 6.28, while var($é$) = 1.03. Then the hedged risk as a percentage of the unhedged risk can be estimated as

$$100 \times \sqrt{1.03/[(1.26)^2(6.28)]} = 32.14\%.$$

This estimate of the reduction in risk relies, of course, on the estimate of b, which is derived on the basis of past history. It will not be a reliable guide if historical relationships change in a material way.

A final qualification that should be made is that the above risk calculations assume you can buy futures in arbitrary amounts. But, as noted previously, you have to use futures in minimum amounts of £25,000, DM 125,000, and the like. Thus the *hedged* risk in the above calculation only applies to the portion of your portfolio that can be matched with multiples of standardized futures contract amounts. Anything left over is unhedged and faces ordinary foreign exchange risk.   ■

FX RISK MANAGEMENT AND THE GAMBLER'S RUIN PROBLEM

Many people assume that the futures price represents a fair bet. That is, they assume that the probability of an upward movement in the futures price is equal to the probability of a downward movement, and hence the mathematical expectation of a gain or loss is zero. They use the analogy of flipping a fair coin. If you bet $1 on the outcome of the flip, the probability of your winning $1 is one-half, while the probability of losing $1 is also one-half. Your expected gain or loss is zero. For the same reason, they conclude, futures gains and futures losses will tend to offset each other in the long run.

There is a hidden fallacy in such reasoning. Taking open positions in foreign exchange (whether in the futures market or just in accounts payable) is not analogous to a single flip of a coin. Rather, the correct analogy is that of a *repeated series of coin flips with a stochastic termination point.* Why? Because of limited capital. Suppose you are flipping a coin with a friend and betting $1 on the outcome of each flip. At some point either you or your friend will have a run of bad luck and will lose several dollars in succession. If one player has run out of money, the game will come to an end. The same is true in the futures market. If you have a string of losses on a futures position, you will have to post more margin. If at some point you cannot post the required margin, you will have to close out the contract. You are forced out of the game, and thus you cannot win back what you lost. In a similar way in 1974, Franklin National and Bankhaus I. D. Herstatt had a string of losses on their interbank foreign exchange positions. They did not break even in the long run because there was no long run. They went broke in the intermediate run. This phenomenon is referred to in probability theory as the **gambler's ruin problem** [see Feller (1968), chap. 14].

The gambler's ruin problem will be explored further in Chapter 7, where we will see that even if an FX futures price represented a "fair" bet when viewed as a single flip of the coin, when viewed as a series of flips with a stochastic ending point the odds are different. The probabilities of the game then depend on the relative amounts of capital held by the different players. This fact is important for FX risk management in general. Any company with foreign currency exposure is in a position to make or lose money when the exchange rate moves. Even if the probability of an upward move in the exchange rate were equal to the probability of a downward move, it would not generally be true that a company will in the long run make neither exchange-rate gains or losses. Instead, because the company has limited capital, the odds are stacked against it if it plays against the market. Thus, if any company has a large foreign currency exposure, the existence of significant ruin probability would constitute a strong argument for hedging away at least some portion of the risk.

ECONOMIC FUNCTIONS OF FX FUTURES MARKETS

The services provided by FX futures are not unlike those provided by FX forward contracts. Such contracts allow for long and short positions. If two hedgers are on either side of the contract, each views his or her risk as reduced: the gain is the perceived advantage of an increase in price certainty. But the market could not function if there were only hedgers. The reason is that the risks that are being hedged are endemic to the economy: the outcome of economic decisions made today depends on the uncertain course of events, prices, and currency exchange values in the future. This risk cannot be eliminated from the economy; it can only be transferred. In futures and forward markets, the transfer of risk is from hedgers to speculators. Speculators assume the risks that hedgers prefer to avoid. We will see in Chapter 11, however, that there is no reason to expect this risk transfer ever to be complete. That is, **speculators** will be increasing their risk exposure through futures contracts while hedgers will be reducing risk. But both will have some optimal risk/return tradeoff, and as a result—provided there is uncertainty in the economy—everyone will remain a net speculator.

In many cases the opposite sides of a futures contract will be held by two speculators: the contract increases the risk exposure of each. But this too has a useful economic purpose—price discovery. If two speculators are on opposite sides of a contract, this is probably due to different expectations, so the futures price will in part represent an expectational equilibrium. Some speculators may spend considerable time and money in acquiring and processing information about the economy and about future exchange rates. By position-taking in the futures market, they cause futures prices to reflect this information about potential supply and demand. In the case of exchange rates, however, the price discovery role is already played by the much larger interbank market. Nevertheless, the FX futures market would appear to have a secondary value to interbank market-makers since the joint participation by many banks in the futures market causes the FX futures price to represent the temporary equilibrium price in this segment of the larger market.

PROBLEMS FOR CHAPTER 5

1. Determine the last day of trading as well as the settlement day for IMM DM futures for March of the current year. Compare the corresponding dates for the LIFFE DM contract.

2. At the beginning of the week, you buy seven British pound IMM futures contracts, and two days later sell four Canadian dollar IMM futures contracts. As a result of your transactions, open interest has increased by eleven contracts. The brokerage fee is $26 per round turn. What is the total brokerage fee actually paid so far?

3. Check the futures page in today's *Wall Street Journal,* and calculate the gain or loss on a short position of one contract in each of the listed currencies.

4. On February 8, you go long one IMM DM contract at an opening price of $.3423. There is an initial margin of $1500 and a maintenance margin of $1200. The settlement prices for February 8, 9, 10 are $.3393, $.3441, and $.3496, respectively. On February 11, you close out the contract at a price of $.3483. Round-turn commission was $28.56. Calculate the daily cash flows on your account, assuming that the beginning balance was $1500 and there were no cash additions or withdrawals other than the cash flows from gains or losses on the futures position or from additional required variation margin.

5. Explain why U.S. futures contracts can be said to involve a *fixed* amount of foreign currency, but a *variable* amount of U.S. dollars. Consider now the case of a Japanese company using U.S. futures contracts to hedge against a change in value of the U.S. dollar. In what way will the number of futures contracts chosen to hedge $1,000,000 change as the dollar/yen exchange rate changes?

6. On June 15, a U.K. firm is planning to import computers worth $5 million from the United States on September 3. The firm decides to hedge its position using LIFFE futures contracts. The spot rate is $1.3139/£; the September LIFFE futures price is $1.3080/£. The firm chooses an amount of futures contracts that matches as closely as possible, at the current exchange rate, its $5-million position. Later, on September 3, the spot rate is $1.2590/£, while the September futures price is $1.2550/£. Calculate the net gain or loss, in terms of £s, of the hedged position as of September 3. (Ignore any interest rate opportunity gain or loss from the time pattern of cash flows.)

7. In the preceding problem, what was the change in the basis? How did this affect the net gain or loss on the hedged position?

8. A Philadelphia importer goes short one DM in futures for each DM in accounts receivable. The change in the dollar price of DM futures over a selected time interval has a variance of .40, while the change in the dollar price of each DM in receivables has a variance of .45. These two variables have a correlation coefficient of .93. Estimate the importer's hedged risk as a percentage of the risk inherent in the underlying long position in DM accounts receivable.

9. In what way does the level of interest rates affect the amount of FX futures used in a delta hedge?

10. A regression reveals the following recent relationship between changes in the $A/\$$ futures price and the $B/\$$ spot rate:

$$\Delta A/\$ = .79 \, \Delta B/\$.$$

In the sample data used,

$$\text{var}(\Delta A/\$) = .012, \text{var}(\Delta B/\$) = .009,$$

while the variance of the residual in the regression was .001. A dollar-based company with a short position in currency B takes an off-setting $A/\$$ futures contract, using the above equation to establish a delta hedge. Estimate the risk inherent in the company's hedged position as compared to the risk of the original position.

CHAPTER

6

FOREIGN CURRENCY OPTIONS

Options are a unique type of financial contract that have a throwaway feature. They give you the right, but not the obligation, to do something. You only use the contract if you want to. This contrasts with forward contracts, which obligate you to make a transaction at the preagreed price even if the market has changed and you would rather not. Options normally also differ from futures in that there are no daily cash flows ("marking to market") on the long side of an option. (Futures-style options, explained below, are exceptions.) In any case, potential loss on a long position in an option is limited if the price moves in the wrong direction. It is this limited-loss feature that distinguishes options from forward and futures contracts.

Options are usually classified according to whether they are options to buy (calls) or options to sell (puts), and according to whether they can be used only on a specific date (European) or at any time prior to a specific date (American). The terms "European" and "American" refer to *types* of options and have nothing to do with the geographical location of trading or the manner in which exchange rates are quoted. We will divide foreign currency options into three further categories: as options on spot exchange, options on foreign currency futures, and futures-style options. The latter category comprises both futures-style options on spot and futures-style options on futures.

OPTIONS ON SPOT EXCHANGE

An *American call* option in this category is a security issued by an individual that gives its owner the right to purchase a given amount of one currency, at a price stated in terms of a second currency (the **exercise** or **strike** price), on or before a stated date (the **expiration** or *maturity* date). For example, a call option on the British pound might give one the right to purchase £12, 500 at $1.50/£ on or at any time before the Saturday prior to the third Wednesday in December 1988. An *American put* option is similar, except that it gives the right to sell a given amount of currency. For example, a put option on the yen might give one the right to sell ¥100,000,000 at $.0040/¥ on or before June 13. American-style options on spot exchange are traded over the counter, at the **Philadelphia Stock Exchange (PHLX)** and the London Stock Exchange (LSE), and at the member exchanges of the International Options Clearing Corporation (the European Options Exchange, the Montreal Exchange, the Vancouver Stock Exchange, and the Sydney Stock Exchange).

A *European option* differs from an American option in that it may be exercised (used) only on the expiration date. If the call option in the preceding paragraph were European, then it could be exercised only on, but not prior to, the Saturday prior to the third Wednesday in December 1988. If the put option in the preceding paragraph were European, it could be exercised only on June 13. European-style options on spot exchange are traded over the counter, and at the **Chicago Board Options Exchange (CBOE)**.

There are two sides to every option contract. There is the *buyer* of the option, who *purchases the right* either to buy (call) or sell (put) the asset contained in the option contract, and there is the **writer** of the option, who *sells the right* either to buy or sell the asset contained in the option contract. The buyer of an option on spot pays the price (or **premium**) of the option up front, and subsequently has the right to exercise or not to exercise the option contract. For example, the buyer might pay $86,000 to purchase a put which allows him to sell SF 25,000,000 at a strike price of $.50/SF. The other side of the put contract is the writer who sells this right. The writer receives the $86,000 premium the buyer pays. Then if the buyer decides to exercise his right to sell SF 25,000,000, the writer has to purchase the SF 25,000,000 at $.50/Swiss franc from the buyer of the put option. The buyer might be, for example, a U.S. company and the writer a U.S. bank. If the bank writes the put to the company, then if the company exercises its right to sell Swiss francs at the strike price of $.50/SF, the bank has to accept the SF 25,000,000 and pay the company $12,500,000 in return.

OPTIONS ON FOREIGN CURRENCY FUTURES

Options on FX futures contracts are somewhat different from options on spot foreign exchange. A **call option** gives the buyer of the option the right to establish a *long* position in an FX futures contract at a price given by the exercise price of the option. A **put option** gives the buyer of the option the right to establish a *short* position in an FX futures contract at a price given by the exercise price of the option. For reasons given later, all currently traded options on FX futures contracts are American in type, and can be exercised on any business day prior to expiration. For example, if you have an American call on September DM futures with a strike price of $.32/DM and the current futures price is $.3323/DM, exercising the option will give you a long position of one September DM futures contract at an opening futures price of $.32/DM. Since the current futures prices is $.3323/DM, the value of this futures position is

$$\$.3323/DM - \$.32/DM = \$.0123/DM.$$

This profit can be realized immediately by closing out the futures position (going short to offset), or by withdrawing the cash from the account (if futures margin requirements are otherwise already met). Options on IMM foreign currency futures are traded at the Chicago Mercantile Exchange (CME).

Note that for options on FX futures, if a call buyer exercises his or her right to go long, then the call writer has to take the other side of the futures contract. The call writer ends up with a short futures position if the call is exercised. Similarly, if a put buyer exercises his or her right to go short a futures contract, then the put writer assumes the long side of the futures position. (A clearing house will, in the usual manner, guarantee both sides of the futures contract once appropriate conditions have been met.)

FUTURES-STYLE OPTIONS

A futures-style option is like a futures contact in one respect: a futures-style option represents a bet on the direction of price change of the option contract. A buyer of a futures-style call goes long the call price, while the writer of the call goes short the call price. On any day that the price of the call goes up, the buyer makes money, while the writer loses money. On any day that the price of the call goes down, the buyer loses money, while the writer makes money. In a similar fashion, a buyer of a put option goes long the put price, while the writer goes short the put price. But a futures-style option is unlike a futures contract in that the long side of the option position can exercise the option either on any business day (if American) or at option expiration (if European). American futures-style options on spot exchange are traded at LIFFE.

Both the buyer and writer of a futures-style option (call or put) post margin, just as is done with an ordinary futures contract. The margin is a security bond which ensures that the loser pays up each day. The option price itself is not paid to anyone; it is just the variable about which the long and short sides are betting. The price of the option is **marked to market** daily. If money has been lost, more margin must be posted. If money has been gained, any excess over required margin may be withdrawn. For example, suppose a firm "buys" (goes long) a LIFFE put option on £25,000 at a strike price of $1.35/£. Suppose the option price at that time is $.0265/£, for a total value of

£25,000 ($.0265/£) = $662.50

If the option price subsequently moves to $.0375/£, for a total value of

£25,000 ($.0375/£) = $937.50,

then the put buyer has a positive cash flow of

$937.50 − $662.50 = $275,

while the put writer has a negative cash flow of the same amount. The difference in this case between the futures-style option and an option on spot or futures is that the buyer of an option on spot or futures would have paid the initial option premium ($662.50) up front, whereas the "buyer" of a futures-style option does not pay the option premium but simply posts margin. (The amounts of margin the buyer and writer have to post is, however, related to the option premium.) The buyer of an option on spot or futures does not have a further cash flow until the option is either sold or exercised. But cash flows take place daily on both the long and the short sides of a futures-style option.

Figure 6.1 summarizes the different types of FX options and their current location of trading.

	European	American
Option on spot	CBOE, OTC	PHLX, LSE, OTC
Option on futures	Not traded	CME
Futures–style option on spot	Not traded	LIFFE
Futures–style option on futures	Not traded	Not traded

CBOE: Chicago Board Options Exchange
CME: Chicago Mercantile Exchange
LIFFE: London International Financial Futures Exchange
LSE: London Stock Exchange
OTC: Over-the-Counter
PHLX: Philadelphia Stock Exchange

FIGURE 6.1
Types of FX options.

THE FOREIGN CURRENCY OPTIONS MARKET

As of November 1985, the market for foreign currency options consisted of an interbank market centered in London and New York, and exchange-based markets in Philadelphia (the PHLX), Chicago (the CME and CBOE), and London (LIFFE and LSE). Open interest (option contracts in existence) was 376,248 at the PHLX on November 14; 127,214 at the CME; 27,514 at the CBOE; and 27,252 at LIFFE. There was additional open interest at the LSE and the International Options Clearing Corporation. No data were available on the interbank market, but it appeared to be of a comparable magnitude to the exchange-based market.

Exchange options in the United States are traded in standardized sizes that match the foreign currency amounts in the IMM's FX futures contracts (described in Chapter 5). Each CME FX option represents the right to go long or short a single IMM FX futures contract. CBOE and LIFFE options involve spot FX in an amount equal to one IMM futures contract, while PHLX options are one-half the size of CBOE and LIFFE options. (That is, PHLX options on the British pound, DM, Swiss franc, Japanese yen, Canadian dollar, and French franc are, respectively, options on £12,500; DM 62,500; SF 62,500; ¥ 6,250,000; Can$ 50,000; and FF 125,000.)

The expiration dates of most exchange FX options contracts are likewise set to correspond to the March, June, September, December delivery dates on IMM FX futures. PHLX and CBOE FX options, for example, are opened with terms to maturity of one, two, three, six, and twelve months. As a consequence, option contracts that expire in March, June, September, December, and, in addition, the two nearby months not part of this cycle are always trading.

As we saw in Chapter 5, IMM futures contracts for a particular month expire on the second business day prior to the third Wednesday. PHLX and CBOE FX options expire on the Saturday prior to the third Wednesday. CME FX options expire on the second Friday prior to the third Wednesday. This usually means that the last day of FX options trading at the PHLX and CBOE will be on a Friday, since no trading takes place on Saturday. This same Friday will also be the last day of options trading at LIFFE. The last day of IMM FX futures trading will then be the following Monday. Settlement for any options exercised on the last trade day at the CBOE, PHLX, and LIFFE takes place on the third Wednesday, corresponding to the IMM futures settlement date. The last day for trading CME FX options is also on a Friday, but the Friday a week prior to the last trading day at the PHLX, CBOE, and LIFFE.

Each of the exchanges trades options with standardized strike price intervals, in addition to standardized expiration dates and currency amounts. The exercise price of an option at the PHLX, CBOE, LIFFE, or CME is stated as the U.S. dollar price of a unit of foreign currency. ("Foreign" here means foreign by reference to the dollar.) Exercise price intervals at the PHLX are $.05 for the British pound; $.01 for the German mark, Swiss franc, and Canadian dollar; $.005 for the French franc; and $.0001 for the Japanese yen. If the spot price of the British pound is $1.42/£ when June options open for trading, options will begin trading with exercise prices set at $1.40/£ and $1.45/£. If the British pound then drops to $1.40/£, a new option series with an exercise price of $1.35/£ will be opened. Options at the CME and CBOE are similar, except that exercise intervals are $.025 for the British pound.

Over-the-counter options, by contrast, can be tailor-made as to amount, maturity, and exercise price. The currency amount involved in over-the-counter options is usually much larger than exchange-traded options (typically involving a minimum of $1,000,000 or so of foreign currency) and over-the-counter options have been written on a larger variety of currencies — including some currencies in which there is little spot or foward trading, such as the Venezuelan bolivar. As of mid-1985, the interbank FX options market was still closely related to the exchange market. Commercial banks, investment banks, and brokerage houses wrote over-the-counter options to companies, but did little direct interbank trading with each other. Instead, to manage their risk by keeping short and long options positions in rough balance, the banks relied on foreign currency options brokers, such as Exco International, Bierbaum-Martin, and Butler Treasury Services. These brokers operated to match buy and sell orders between banks. In addition, both the banks and the brokers regularly bought and sold FX options on the available exchanges. In effect, they created tailor-made interbank options by buying and selling standardized exchange options contracts and repackaging them to the user's specification.

As with exchange-traded futures contracts, exchange-traded options are registered with a clearing house that guarantees both the long and short sides of puts and calls. FX options contracts at the CME are guaranteed by the Chicago Mercantile Exchange Clearing House, while PHLX and CBOE contracts are guaranteed by the **Options Clearing Corporation (OCC)**, the clearing house for all options traded on U.S. securities exchanges. LIFFE FX options, like LIFFE FX futures, are cleared through the International Commodities Clearing House (ICCH). Once an FX option has been exercised, there is a time gap before the currency exchange takes place (for options on spot) or the futures position is established (for options on futures). Exercise of an option at the CME is effective the next business day, while exercise is effective four business days later at the PHLX. CBOE options can only be exercised on the last trading day, and are effective the following Wednesday.

The process of trading FX options on an exchange will vary, depending on the exchange and the regulatory environment. FX options trading at the PHLX and the CBOE is regulated by the SEC, while that at the CME is regulated by the CFTC, and that at LIFFE by the ICCH. Trading of options on FX futures at the CME is similar to the trading of futures contracts themselves (discussed in Chapter 5). At the CBOE, in addition to floor brokers and floor traders, there is an *order book official,* who keeps track of limit orders from the public. Bids and offers are placed in order from the lowest to the highest, and the current highest bid and lowest offered are continuously displayed. Market-order trades by floor brokers and marketmakers must take place within the range set by the order book official's highest bid and lowest offer. At the PHLX a *specialist* system is used. A specialist can be viewed as an exchange-appointed marketmaker who is required to quote two-way prices and maintain a continuous market in the FX option. (Other marketmakers, by contrast, make markets at their discretion.) Specialists act both as brokers, executing orders for other brokers for a commission, and as marketmakers, buying and selling for their own account.

FX OPTIONS AS FOREIGN CURRENCY INSURANCE

We now turn to the use of FX options in hedging from the point of view of an option buyer. For the moment, we will simply treat options as contracts that are available to the buyer or the writer at a market-determined price, without concerning ourselves with the separate question of what the fair value (fair to both the buyer and writer) of an FX option is. Questions concerning FX option pricing will be dealt with in later sections.

For the purpose of hedging, foreign currency options can be viewed as exchange-rate insurance. Consider how insurance works in general. Suppose you buy fire insurance on a $100,000 house. You insure the house for its full value of $100,000, and the insurance is good for one year. If, by the end of the year, your house has not been damaged by fire, the insurance will have proved worthless. You throw away the unused insurance policy. Your total cost has been the cost of the insurance premium. On the other hand, suppose that fire does $40,000 worth of damage to your house. In this case, you have a $40,000 loss. But the insurance policy pays off the difference between the amount of the insurance ($100,000) and the current value of the insured asset ($60,000), making up exactly the amount of your loss ($40,000). Thus your total loss is zero, except again for the insurance premium, which you pay in any case.

An option works in the same way. Suppose you buy a put option on the value of a house. In particular, suppose the strike price of the put is $100,000. That is, it gives you the right to sell the house for $100,000. You buy an American put (so that it can be used at any time), and it expires in one year. If the market value of the house stays at $100,000 or greater for the year, there would be no advantage in exercising the put. Thus the put would expire worthless. You would throw it away rather than use it to your disadvantage. But if, because of fire or for some other reason, the value of the house dropped to $60,000, you could exercise the put and sell the house for $100,000. The put has then served as insurance. It paid off the difference between the strike price ($100,000) and the current value of the house ($60,000), thus making up the entire loss in value ($40,000). In any case, whether or not the house lost value, you pay for the cost of the put. The price paid for an option is (conveniently) referred to in the options market as the premium and is analogous to an insurance premium. Overall, then, the put serves as an insurance policy. (Or, as some prefer to say, insurance itself is just a put option.)

Let's extend the analogy to deductible insurance. Suppose that, instead of insuring your house for $100,000, you insured it for $80,000. In this case if your house is damaged by fire, you will have to bear the loss of the first $20,000. On the other hand, the insurance premium on $80,000 will be less than the premium on $100,000, so that you may be willing to trade off the greater risk of loss in the case of fire with the lower fixed cost of the insurance premium. In the same way, if you purchased a put option on the house with a strike price of $80,000 instead of a strike price of $100,000, the premium (purchase price) of the put would be lower. But the insurance level of the put will be lower, because it will only pay to exercise the put if the value of the house falls below $80,000. Thus, buying a put option with a strike price that is lower than the current market value of the asset involved is like buying deductible insurance. Whether you like deductible insurance depends on your attitude to trading off lower insurance premiums with the risk of greater loss in the event disaster strikes.

Both foreign currency options on spot and foreign currency options on futures can be considered types of insurance against adverse exchange-rate movements. Options on spot represent insurance bought or written on the spot rate, while options on futures represent insurance bought or written on the futures price. Futures-style options are slightly different. No insurance premium is paid or received for futures-style options. Rather, the buyer goes long the value of the insurance policy while the writer goes short. If the value of the policy goes up, this added value automatically accrues to the option buyer as a daily cash flow, without the need to make a claim (to exercise or sell the option). On the other hand, if the value of the policy goes down, this loss of policy value is automatically reflected in a loss on the margin account.

An individual with foreign currency to sell can use put options on spot to establish a floor price on the domestic currency value of the foreign currency. For example, a put option on 1 DM with an exercise price of $.40/DM will ensure that, in the event the value of the DM falls below $.40/DM, the 1 DM can be sold for $.40/DM anyway. If the put option costs $.01/DM, this floor price can be roughly approximated as

$.40/DM − $.01/DM = $.39/DM,

or the strike price minus the premium. That is, if the option is used, you will be able to sell the 1 DM for the $.40/DM strike price, but in the meantime you have paid a premium of $.01/DM. Deducting the cost of the premium leaves $.39/DM as the floor price established by the purchase of the put. (This ignores fees and interest rate adjustments. A more exact calculation is shown in the example below).

Similarly, an individual who has to buy foreign currency at some point in the future can use call options on spot to establish a ceiling price on the domestic currency amount that will have to be paid to purchase the foreign exchange. For example, a call option on 1 DM with an exercise price of $.40/DM will ensure that, in the event the value of the DM rises above $.40/DM, the 1 DM can be bought for $.40/DM anyway. If the call option costs $.01/DM, this ceiling price can be approximated as

$.40/DM + $.01/DM = $.41/DM,

or the strike price plus the premium. To summarize these two important points involving FX puts and calls:

1. Foreign currency *put* options on spot can be used as insurance to establish a *floor price on the domestic currency value* of foreign exchange. This floor price is approximately

   Floor price = Exercise price of put − Put premium.

2. Foreign currency *call* options on spot can be used as insurance to establish a *ceiling price on the domestic currency cost* of foreign exchange. This ceiling price is approximately

   Ceiling price = Exercise price of call + Call premium.

The calculations above are only approximate for essentially two reasons. First, the exercise price and the premium of the option on spot cannot be added directly without an interest rate adjustment. The premium will be paid now, up front, but the exercise price (if the option is eventually exercised) will be paid later. The time difference involved in the two payment amounts implies that one of the two should be adjusted by an interest rate factor. Second, there may be brokerage or other expenses associated with the purchase of an option, and there may be an additional fee if the option is exercised. The two examples below illustrate the insurance feature of FX options on spot and show how to calculate floor and ceiling values when some additional transactions costs are included.

EXAMPLE 6.1

A U.S. importer will have a net cash outflow of £50,000 in payment for goods bought. The payment date is not known with certainty, but should occur in late November. On September 16 the importer locks in a ceiling purchase for pounds by buying four PHLX calls on the pound, with a striking price of $1.50/£ and an expiration date in December. The option premium on that date is $.0220/£. There is a brokerage commission of $8 per option contract. Thus the total cost of the four contracts is:

4(£12,500)($.0220/£) + 4($8) = $1132.

Measured from today's viewpoint, the importer has essentially assured that his purchase price for pounds will not be greater than

$1132/£50,000 + $1.50/£ = $.02264/£ + $1.50/£ = $1.52264/£.

Notice here that the add factor $.02264/£ is larger than the option premium of $.0220/£ by $.00064/£, which represents the dollar brokerage cost per pound.

The number $1.52264/£ is the importer's ceiling price. He is assured he will not pay more than this, but he could pay less. The price the importer will actually pay will depend on the spot price on the November payment date. To illustrate this, we can consider two scenarios for the spot rate.

Case A

The spot rate on the November payment date is $1.46/£. The importer would not use the call options but would buy pounds spot for the cheaper rate of $1.46. He would then sell the four calls for whatever market value they had remaining. Assuming a brokerage fee of $8 per contract for the sale, the options would be sold as long as their remaining market value was greater than $8 per option. The total cost per pound will have turned out to be

$1.46 + $.02264 − (Sale value of options − $32)/50,000.

If the resale value is not greater than $32, then the total cost per pound is

$1.46 + $.02264 = $1.48264.

The $.02264/£ that was the original cost of the premium and brokerage fee turned out in this case to be an unnecessary expense.

Now, to be strictly correct, a further adjustment to the calculation should be made. Namely, the $1.46 and $.02264 represent cash flows at two different times. Thus, if x is the amount of interest paid per dollar over the September 16 to November time period, the proper calculation is

$1.46 + $.02264(1 + x) − (Sale value of options − $32)/50,000.

Case B

The spot rate on the November payment date is $1.55/£. The importer can either exercise his options or sell them for their market value. Assume he sells them at a current market value of $.055 and pays $32 total in brokerage commissions on the sale of four option contracts. The importer then buys the pounds in the spot market for $1.55/£. The total cost is, before subtracting out the premium and commission costs paid in September:

($1.55/£)(£50,000) − ($.055)(£50,000) + 4($8) = $74,782

or

$74,782/£50,000 = $1.49564/£.

Adding in the premium and commission costs paid back in September, the total cost is

$1.49564/£ + $.02264(1 + x)/£.

If the importer chooses instead to exercise the option, the calculations will be similar except that the brokerage fee will be replaced by an exercise fee.

EXAMPLE 6.2

A Japanese company wants to lock in a minimum yen value of $50 million, this amount to be sold between July 1 and December 31. Since the company wishes to sell dollars and get yen, the company will buy a put option on dollars, with an exercise price stated in terms of yen. (Or, what is the same thing, the company will buy a call option on yen, with an exercise price stated in terms of dollars.) Suppose the company buys from its bank a put on $50,000,000 with a strike price of ¥230/$. The put is American, in that it can be used at any time prior to expiration. However, there is no resale value to the option. The company pays a premium of ¥4/$. In this case, assume there are no additional fees in dealing with the bank. Approximately, then, the Japanese company has established a floor value for its dollars at ¥230/$ − ¥4/$ = ¥226/$. Again, we can consider two scenarios, one in which the yen falls in value to ¥245/$ and the other in which the yen rises in value to ¥215/$.

Case A

The yen falls to ¥245/$. In this case the company will not exercise the option to sell dollars for yen at ¥230/$, since the company can do better than this in the exchange market. The company will have obtained a net value of

$$¥245/\$ - ¥4(1 + x)/\$,$$

where x is the opportunity cost of yen borrowing and reflects the fact that the ¥4 premium is paid up front. If the opportunity cost is 5 percent per year for one-half year, then $x = .025$, so the company will have obtained a net value of ¥245 − ¥4(1.025) = ¥240.9 for each U.S. dollar.

Case B

The yen rises to ¥215/$. The company will exercise the put and sell each U.S. dollar for ¥230/$. The company will obtain, net,

$$¥230/\$ - ¥4(1 + x)/\$,$$

or about ¥226/$. This is ¥11 better than would have been available in the FX market and reflects a case where the "insurance" paid off.

WRITING FOREIGN CURRENCY OPTIONS

The writer of a foreign currency option on spot or futures is in a different position from the buyer of one of these options. The buyer pays the premium up front and afterward can choose to exercise the option or not. The buyer is not a source of credit risk once the premium has been paid. The writer *is* a source of credit risk, however, because the writer has promised either to sell or to buy foreign currency if the buyer exercises his option. The writer could default on the promise to sell foreign currency if the writer did not have sufficient foreign currency available, or could default on the promise to buy foreign currency if the writer did not have sufficient domestic currency available. If the option is written by a bank, this risk of default is small. But if the option is written by a company, the bank may require the company to post margin or other security as a hedge against default risk. For exchange-traded options, as noted previously, the relevant clearing house guarantees fulfillment of both sides of the option contract. The clearing house covers its own risk, however, by requiring the writer of an option to post margin. At the PHLX and CBOE, for example, the Options Clearing Corporation will allow a writer to meet margin requirements by having the actual foreign currency or U.S. dollars on deposit, by obtaining an irrevocable letter of credit from a suitable bank, or by posting cash margin. If cash margin is posted, the required deposit is the current market value of the option plus 4 percent of the value of the underlying foreign currency. This requirement is reduced by any amount the option is out of the money, to a minimum requirement of the premium plus .75 percent of the value of the underlying foreign currency. These percentages can be changed by the exchanges based upon currency volatility. Thus, as the market value of the option changes, the margin requirement will change. So an option writer faces daily cash flows associated with changing margin requirements.

Other exchanges have similar requirements for option writers. The CME allows margins to be calculated on a net basis for accounts holding both CME FX futures options and IMM FX futures. That is, the amount of margin is based on one's total futures and futures options portfolio. LIFFE makes a similar allowance for accounts holding both LIFFE futures-style FX options and LIFFE FX futures. The risk of an option writer at the CME is the risk of being exercised and consequently the risk of acquiring a short position (for call writers) or a long position (for put writers) in IMM futures. Hence the amount of margin the writer is required to post is related to the amount of margin required on an IMM FX futures contract. The risk of option writers at LIFFE is similarly related to the risk of a futures contract, because (as pointed out above) LIFFE options partially represent a futures contract on the value of an FX option. The exact calculation of margins at LIFFE or the CME relies on the concept of an option delta, which will be explained later in this chapter.

From the point of view of a company or individual, writing options is a form of risk-exposure management of importance equal to that of buying options. It may make perfectly good sense for a company to *sell* foreign currency insurance in the form of writing FX calls or puts. The choice of strike price on a written option reflects a straightforward tradeoff. For reasons explained below, FX call options with a lower strike price will be more valuable than those with a higher strike price. Hence the premiums the option writer will receive are correspondingly larger. However, the probability that the written calls will be exercised by the buyer is also higher for calls with a lower strike price than for those with a higher strike. Hence the larger premiums received reflect greater risk-taking on the part of the insurance seller (the option writer).

The following example will illustrate this risk/return tradeoff for the case of an oil company that chooses to become an option writer.

EXAMPLE 6.3

Isis, a U.S.-based oil company, has a large foreign currency exposure in the form of a Canadian-dollar cash flow from Canadian operations. The risk to Isis is that the Canadian dollar will depreciate against the U.S. dollar in such a way that Isis' total U.S. dollar revenues will fall.

Isis chooses to reduce its long position in Canadian dollars by writing Canadian-dollar call options with a U.S.-dollar strike. The particular option strategy chosen is one of "fully covered call writing," which involves writing call options with a face amount equal to the anticipated Canadian-dollar cash flow over the period of maturity of the options. By writing options, Isis will receive an immediate U.S.-dollar cash flow representing the market value of the options written. This cash flow will increase Isis' total U.S.-dollar return in the event the Canadian dollar depreciates against the U.S. dollar, remains unchanged against the U.S. dollar, or appreciates only slightly against the U.S. dollar.

To implement its strategy, Isis will write Canadian-dollar call options involving an amount of currency that matches its anticipated cash flow prior to the maturity of the options. This strategy will involve only a minimal amount of management of the option position. At the extreme, Isis could simply allow the options to expire or to be exercised. In either case, Isis walks away with the full amount of the option premium. If the U.S.-dollar value of the Canadian dollar remains unchanged, the option premium received is simply additional profit. If the value of the Canadian dollar falls, the premium received on the written option will offset part or all of the opportunity loss on the underlying Canadian-dollar position. If the value of the Canadian dollar rises sharply, Isis will only participate in this increased value up to a ceiling level, where the ceiling level is a function of the exercise price of the option written.

In short, the payoff to Isis' strategy will depend both on exchange rate movements and the selection of the strike price of the written options. To illustrate Isis' strategy, consider an anticipated cash flow of Can\$ 300,000,000 over the next 180 days. Assume that Isis writes CBOE options with a six-month expiration. Assume also that the current spot rate is \$.75/Can\$, while the six-month forward rate is \$.7447/Can\$. For this level of spot rate, logical strike price choices for the calls might be \$.74, \$.75, or \$.76. For the illustration, we will assume that Isis pays a brokerage fee of \$8 per written option and will let the hypothetical market values of the options be those listed below.

Strike price	Option value	No. of options (CBOE)	U.S. \$ credit from written options	Brokerage fees
74	\$1197.00	3,000	\$3,591,000	\$24,000
75	\$ 650.00	3,000	\$1,950,000	\$24,000
76	\$ 313.00	3,000	\$ 939,000	\$24,000

The payoff to the total position will depend on the "terminal" value of the spot rate S (\$/Can\$) as well as the choice of strike price. The terminal spot rate is the market spot rate at the expiration date of the options. If the options are exercised, assume an additional clearing corporation fee of \$70 per option, or a total fee of \$210,000 for 3000 contracts. The value of the total long Canadian dollar plus short option position will be:

Strike price	Spot rate			
	$S < 74$	$74 < S < 75$	$75 < S < 76$	$76 < S$
74	S(Can\$300 m.) +\$3,567,000	\$225,357,000	\$225,357,000	\$225,357,000
75	S(Can\$300 m.) +\$1,926,000	S(Can\$300 m.) +\$1,926,000	\$226,716,000	\$226,716,000
76	S(Can\$300 m.) + \$915,000	S(Can\$300 m.) + \$915,000	S(Can\$300 m.) + \$915,000	\$228,705,000

As illustrated above, *the lower the strike price chosen, the better the protection against a depreciating Canadian dollar. On the other hand, a lower strike price corresponding limits profitability if the Canadian dollar appreciates.* The optimal decision will turn out to be, after the fact, a function of the terminal spot exchange rate. Table 6.1 summarizes the optimal decision for all possible values of the spot exchange rate, given our assumptions. The assumptions are that the company either maintains an open long position of Can\$ 300,000,000, or (in addition) writes 3000 CBOE calls with 180-day

TABLE 6.1
Optimal Decision under Isis' Strategy, as a Function of the (Now Unknown) Terminal
Spot Rate*

Terminal spot rate (U.S. cents/Can$)	Optimal decision
$S > 76.235$	Hold long currency only
$75.267 < S < 76.235$	Write options with 76 strike
$74.477 < S < 75.267$	Write options with 75 strike
$S < 74.477$	Write options with 74 strike

* Current spot rate is $.75/Can$.

maturity. Possible strike prices are $.76/Can$, $.75/Can$, $.74/Can$. Here the terminal spot rate is the market exchange rate when the options expire. It is assumed the company pays a brokerage fee of $8 per option contract and an additional fee of $70 per option to the clearing corporation if the options are exercised.

There are some additional points worth noting for Isis' strategy. Because of the large fee ($70) assumed to be charged by the clearing corporation if the options are exercised, it might be less expensive for Isis to buy back the options (and pay a brokerage fee of $8) in the event the options were in danger of being exercised. In addition, it is assumed that Isis will have the Canadian dollars on hand if the options are exercised. This would not be the case if actual Canadian-dollar revenues were less than anticipated. In that event, the options would need to be repurchased prior to expiration.

Each of the three choices of strike price will have a different payoff, depending on the movement in the exchange rate. But Isis' expectation regarding the exchange rate is not the only relevant criterion for choosing a risk-management strategy. The possible variation in the underlying position should also be considered. Below are the maximal and minimal payoffs for each of the call-writing choices, compared to the unhedged position and a forward market hedge:

Strategy	Maximal value	Minimal value
Unhedged long position	None	Zero
Sell forward	$223,410,000	$223,410,000
Strategy A, 76 strike	$228,705,000	Unhedged minimum plus $915,000
Strategy A, 75 strike	$226,716,000	Unhedged minimum plus $1,926,000
Strategy A, 74 strike	$225,357,000	Unhedged minimum plus $3,567,000

SOME ELEMENTARY PRINCIPLES OF FX OPTION PRICING

In this section we will look at some basic principles of pricing FX options. These principles will enable us to narrow down the possible range of FX option values in terms of the values of other assets. Some more advanced principles, as well as exact pricing formulas, are given in the following sections.

First, here is some notation that will be used below. Let $C(t)$ and $P(t)$ denote the domestic currency prices of, respectively, American call and American put options on one unit of *spot* foreign exchange. The reason for looking at option prices on *one* unit of foreign exchange is simple. If $C(t)$ is the dollar price of an American call on 1 DM, then the dollar price of an American call on 1000 DM is 1000 $C(t)$, the dollar price of an American put on 79681 DM is 79681 $P(t)$, and so on. So it is convenient to think in terms of an option on one unit of foreign exchange. Similarly, let $c(t)$ and $p(t)$ denote the domestic currency prices, respectively, of a European call and a European put on one unit of spot foreign exchange.

In a similar way, let $C^*(t)$, $P^*(t)$, $c^*(t)$, $p^*(t)$ denote the prices of American and European calls and puts on one unit of FX *futures*. And let $C^{**}(t)$, $P^{**}(t)$, $c^{**}(t)$, $p^{**}(t)$ denote the prices of *futures-style* American and European FX calls and puts.

The exercise price of an option will be indicated by X. The current time will be t, and the option will be assumed to expire in T days from the present — at time $t + T$. The current spot exchange rate (the domestic currency price of a unit of foreign currency) will be designated as $S(t)$, and $Z(t)$ will be the current futures price. The maturity of the futures contract will be left unspecified, as the futures contract may or may not expire at the same time the option on the future expires. Finally, let $B(t,T)$ be the current price of a discount (or "zero-coupon") bond that matures at time $t + T$ and pays one unit of *domestic* currency at maturity. That is, $B(t,T)$ is expressed as a fraction of its maturity value. $B(t,T)$ is inversely related to the interest yield on the security. For example, if $B(t,T) = \$.95$ then, since at maturity the bond will have a value of $\$1$, the interest yield over the time period T will be

$$1/.95 - 1 = .05263.$$

If T is 360 days, then .05263 corresponds to a yearly interest rate of 5.263 percent. But if T is 180 days, the corresponding money market interest rate would be

$$i = .05263(360/180) = .10526$$

or 10.526 percent.

An alternative way to think of $B(t,T)$ is that it is just the discount factor corresponding to the interest rate i, where i is quoted at a yearly rate:

$$B(t,T) = 1/[1 + i(T/360)].$$

Thus for $i = .10526$ and $T = 180$ days,

$$B(t,T) = \$1/[1 + i(180/360)] = \$.95.$$

A similar variable will be $B^*(t,T)$, where $B^*(t,T)$ is the price at time t of a discount bond that pays one unit of *foreign currency* at time $t + T$. For example, we might have

$$B^*(t,T) = DM .975.$$

Principle 1

An option is a limited liability contract to the option buyer. If you own an option, you can exercise it but you do not have to. You can always throw it away. That means that the value of an option you own can only go to zero, where zero corresponds to the case you throw the option away rather than exercise it or sell it.

Hence, expressing this fact mathematically,

$$C(t), C^*(t), \text{ and } C^{**}(t) \geq 0. \qquad P(t), P^*(t), \text{ and } P^{**}(t) \geq 0.$$
$$c(t), c^*(t), \text{ and } c^{**}(t) \geq 0. \qquad p(t), p^*(t), \text{ and } p^{**}(t) \geq 0.$$

(6.1)

The owner of an option would never sell the option for a negative amount. The price can go down, but cannot become less than zero. (Notice, however, that for a futures-style [**] option, the change in the option price can generate both positive and negative cash flows for the buyer, even though the option price itself must remain positive.)

Principle 2

At the *expiration date,* an American or a European call option on spot will be worth either its immediate exercise value or zero, whichever is higher. Since call options allow you to buy one unit of foreign exchange for a domestic currency amount X, and the value of the unit of spot exchange on the maturity date, day $t + T$, will be that day's spot market price, $S(t + T)$, the immediate exercise value is $S(t + T) - X$. Thus

$$C(t + T) = \text{maximum } [0, S(t + T) - X]$$
$$c(t + T) = \text{maximum } [0, S(t + T) - X].$$

(6.2)

For example, the dollar value of a European call option on 1 DM, with an exercise price of \$.40/DM and expiration on a day when the spot exchange rate is \$.42/DM, is maximum $(0, \$.42 - \$.40) = \$.02$. A corresponding European call on DM 10,000,000 would have a value of DM 10,000,000 (\$.02/DM) =\$200,000.

Notice that similar relations hold for calls on futures, $C^*(t)$ and $c^*(t)$, if we substitute the futures price $Z(t)$ for the spot price $S(t)$. Moreover, if the futures contract expires on the same date as the option, on that day $Z = S$ and hence $Z - X = S - X$, so the equations are identical to (6.2). In general, however, as is the case at the IMM, the options and the futures may expire on different dates. Hence the general relation is

$$C^*(t + T) = \text{maximum } [0, Z(t + T) - X]$$
$$c^*(t + T) = \text{maximum } [0, Z(t + T) - X].$$

(6.3)

For futures-style calls $C^{**}(t)$ and $c^{**}(t)$, the relation is similar to (6.2) if they are futures-style calls on spot or (6.3) if they are futures-style calls on futures.

Principle 3

At the expiration date, an American or European put option on spot will be worth either its immediate exercise value or zero, whichever is higher. Since a put gives one the right to sell one unit of foreign exchange for a domestic currency amount of X, while the market price of the unit of spot exchange at expiration is $S(t + T)$, the immediate exercise value of the put is $X - S(t + T)$. Thus

$$P(t + T) = \text{maximum } [0, X - S(t + T)]$$
$$p(t + T) = \text{maximum } [0, X - S(t + T)].$$

(6.4)

For example, the value of an American put option on 1 £, with an exercise price of $1.50/£ and expiration when the spot exchange rate is $1.41/£, would be maximum $(0, \$1.50 - \$1.41) = \$.09$. If it expires when the spot exchange rate is $1.51/£, the put's value would be maximum $(0, \$1.50 - \$1.51) = \$0$.

Similarly, for put options on futures

$$P^*(t + T) = \text{maximum } [0, X - Z(t + T)]$$
$$p^*(t + T) = \text{maximum } [0, X - Z(t + T)].$$

(6.5)

Futures-style puts $P^{**}(t)$ and $p^{**}(t)$ obey equations similar to (6.4) if they are puts on spot exchange but (6.5) if they are puts on FX futures.

Principle 4

At all times prior to expiration, an American option has a value that is at least as large as its immediate exercise value. This holds true for both American puts and American calls because an American option can be exercised at any time, so that by exercising it one can force an option to have a value at least as large as its immediate exercise value. But, at all times prior to expiration, an American option has a value that is also at least as large as the corresponding European option. This is due to the fact that one chose to wait until maturity to exercise an American option. One can simply treat it like a European option. Combining these relationships, we have, for time $t < T$,

$$C(t) \geq \text{maximum } [c(t), S(t) - X]$$

$$P(t) \geq \text{maximum } [p(t), X - S(t)].$$

$$C^*(t) \geq \text{maximum } [c^*(t), Z(t) - X]$$

(6.6)

$$P^*(t) \geq \text{maximum } [p^*(t), X - Z(t)].$$

For example, if a European FX call option on 1 French franc had a value of $.02, and $S(t) = \$.125$ and $X = \$.101$, then

$$C(t) \geq \text{maximum } (\$.02, \$.125 - \$.101) = \$.024.$$

This example illustrates the advantage of an American FX option. Sometimes European FX calls will have a value less than $S(t) - X$, but not American FX calls.

American futures-style options $C^{**}(t)$ and $P^{**}(t)$ obey relations similar to the first two equations of (6.6) if they are on spot but similar to the second two equations if they are on futures.

Principle 5

Given two American options on the same amounts of the same currency and with the same domestic currency exercise price, the one with the longer term to maturity has a value at least as large as the one with the shorter term to maturity. For example, consider a nine-month option and a six-month option. If you had a nine-month option, you could always choose to exercise it during the first six months. Therefore it could be used as a six-month option. But if not, the option is still good for an additional three months. The additional three months could never hurt the holder of the option. Thus the nine-month American option would have a value at least as great as the six-month American option. The same does not hold true for European FX options, however. A nine-month European option could not be exercised at the end of six months even if one wanted to. Under certain circumstances a nine-month European FX option (either call or put) can have a value that is less than a six-month European FX option (an example is given later). This distinction between American and European options holds true for FX options on spot, FX options on futures, and futures-style FX options on spot. (See Problem 14 for futures-style FX options on futures.)

Principle 6

Given two call options identical in every way except that one has a larger exercise price, the call option with the larger exercise price will have a value less than or equal to the one with the smaller exercise price. The opposite holds for put options. Given two put options identical in every way except that one has a larger exercise price, the put option with the larger exercise price has a value greater than or equal to the one with the smaller exercise price. It is easy to see why. With a higher exercise price, a call is less valuable because it obligates you to pay more domestic currency for a unit of foreign exchange. But with a higher exercise price, a put is more valuable because it gives you the right to sell foreign exchange at the higher exercise rate. These relations hold for FX options on spot, FX options on futures, and futures-style options. For example, given two six-month call options on the spot Swiss franc, one with an exercise price of $X = \$.50/SF$ has a value larger than one with $X = \$.55/SF$. But for the corresponding puts on the Swiss franc, the put with $X = \$.55/SF$ has a value larger than the put with $X = \$.50/SF$.

Principle 7

An FX call option on a foreign currency can be considered an FX put option on the domestic currency. Similarly, an FX put option on a foreign currency can be considered an FX call option on the domestic currency. These relations follow from the fact that an exchange rate has two sides. For example, a call option on DM 100,000,000 with an exercise price of SF.80/DM gives one the right to buy DM100,000,000 for SF80,000,000. Restated, this option gives one the right to sell SF80,000,000, for which one receives in return DM100,000,000. Thus it is a put option on SF80,000,000 with an exercise price of DM 1.25/SF. As another example, the PHLX American put option on ¥6,250,000, with an exercise price of $.0042/¥, is simultaneously an American call option on $26.250, with an exercise price of ¥238.095/$.

Principle 8

Consider a European option on futures where the futures contract under consideration expires at the same time as the option. Since the futures contract expires when the option does, at option maturity the futures price will be equal to the spot price: $Z(t + T) = S(t + T)$. And since the option is European, it can only be exercised at maturity, in which case the option gives the right to buy (if a call) or sell (if a put) $Z(t + T)$ in exchange for the exercise price X. Compare this to a

European option on spot. It also gives the right to buy (if a call) or sell (if a put) $S(t + T)$—which is the same as $Z(t + T)$—in return for the exercise price X. The European option on spot and European option on futures give the purchaser exactly the same privileges. Hence, *for an FX futures contract expiring at the same time as the option, a European option on FX futures has the same value as the equivalent European FX option on spot exchange*. That is,

$$c(t) = c^*(t)$$
$$p(t) = p^*(t). \tag{6.7}$$

This value equivalent between European options on spot and European options on futures does not apply to American options, however. The reason is simple: if an American option on FX futures is exercised prior to expiration, it has the value $Z(t) - X$, while an American FX option has the value $S(t) - X$ if exercised. Since $Z(t)$ will generally differ from $S(t)$ by an amount determined by interest parity (as we saw in Chapter 5), the two options will not have the same value. The "boundary constraints" differ, and thus the probability of early exercise differs between the two American options.

Principle 9

Consider futures-style options as compared to ordinary options on spot or futures. The special characteristic of the futures-style option is that the buyer of the option does not have to pay the option premium up front. Therefore the buyer does not forgo, and the writer does not receive, any interest on the money that would otherwise be needed to pay the option premium. (The buyer must post margin, but there will be no loss of interest as long as the buyer can post margin in the form of interest-bearing securities.) Except for this special feature of no forgone interest, the futures-style option on spot gives the buyer the same privileges as an option on spot, and the futures-style option on futures gives the buyer the same privileges as an option on futures. Therefore the value of the futures-style option is the same as the value of an ordinary option, once an adjustment for interest has been made. Restated, *the payoff to a futures-style option is not discounted*. Since the discount factor for any payoff at option expiration is the price of a domestic discount bond $B(t,T)$, we obtain the following equations for European calls and puts:

$$c(t) = B(t,T)\, c^{**}(t)$$
$$p(t) = B(t,T)\, p^{**}(t) \tag{6.8}$$

For two American options (one ordinary, the other futures-style) the relationship is more complex, because there is no single discount factor that relates the payoff boundaries between the two options.

All of the preceding principles (1 though 9) have been stated assuming no transactions costs. In practice, the relations will hold within a margin of error given by the relevant costs of making the transaction. These include bid/asked spreads and brokerage or exchange fees.

There are several important terms frequently used in connection with options. A call option on spot (futures) is said to be **in the money** if the current spot rate (futures price) is higher than the option exercise price. It is said to be **out of the** money if the current spot rate (futures price) is less than the exercise price, while it is at the money if the current spot rate (futures price) is equal to the exercise price. A put option on spot (futures) is said to be in the money if the current spot rate (futures price) is less than the exercise price; it is out of the money if the current spot rate (futures price) is greater than the exercise price; and it is at the money otherwise. Similar terminology is applied to futures-style options. The terminology comes from the fact that in-the-money options would have a positive value if they were exercised immediately (if American) or if they could be exercised immediately (if European.)

Sometimes the terms "intrinsic value" and "time value" are used. The intrinsic value is the amount the option is in the money, while the time value is the option premium minus the intrinsic value. For example, if the spot rate is $.41/SF, a call with a strike price of $.40/SF and a premium of $.03/SF would have an intrinsic value of $.01/SF (since it is $.41/SF − $.40/SF = $.01/SF in the money) and a time value of $.02/SF. A put with a strike price of $.40/SF and a premium of $.01/SF would have an intrinsic value of zero and a time value of $.01/SF. These two terms, while widely used, are somewhat misleading, so we will not use them further here. The reason they are misleading is that the value of the option in excess of its immediate exercise value is not just a function of the time to maturity. This excess is also a function of the exchange rate volatility and the domestic and foreign interest rates.

☐

MORE ADVANCED PRINCIPLES OF FX OPTION PRICING

This section gives some further conditions that must be satisfied by the market prices of FX call and put options in order to avoid arbitrage. Since these relations will involve our keeping track of several variables simultaneously, call and put prices will be written as general functions of several option characteristics. For example, in the previous section a European call on spot exchange at time t was denoted as "$c(t)$." In this section, the more general form "$c(S(t),X,t,T)$" will sometimes be used. This notation simply reminds us that the European option price is a function of the spot rate $S(t)$, the exercise price X, and the term to maturity T. One new variable that will be used in this section is $F(t,T)$, which — as we saw in Chapter 4 — denotes the price of forward exchange at time t, where the forward contract matures at time $t + T$. The notation will be simplified in cases where the meaning is clear.

Principle 10

Consider the following two portfolio strategies undertaken at time t when the spot exchange rate is $S(t)$:

Strategy A: 1. Purchase for $c(S(t),X,t,T)$ a European call option, with an exercise price of X and that expires in T units of time, on one unit of spot exchange.

2. Purchase X domestic currency discount bonds, which mature in T units of time, at the current price $B(t,T)$.

Total Domestic Currency Investment: $c + XB$.

Strategy B: 1.   Purchase one foreign discount bond, which matures in T units of time, at a domestic currency price of $S(t)B^*(t,T)$.

Total Domestic Currency Investment: SB^*.

At time $t + T$, the spot exchange rate $S(t + T)$ will either be less than X or greater than or equal to X. The bonds will have values, in their respective currencies, of

$B(t + T,0) = 1$, $B^*(t + T,0) = 1$.

The call option will have a value

$c(S(t + T),X,T,0) = \max [0, S(t + T) - X]$.

Therefore:

	Value of Strategy A	Value of Strategy B
$S(t + T) < X$	X	$S(t + T)$
$S(t + T) \geq X$	$S(t + T)$	$S(t + T)$

In either case, the payoff to strategy A will always be as good as or better than strategy B. Hence the cost of A must, in economic equilibrium, be at least as great as that of B. Thus

$c + XB \geq SB^*$ or $c \geq SB^* - XB$.

Since an American call must be at least as valuable as its European counterpart (because it has all the same features plus the additional one that it can be exercised at any time), we get

$$C(S(t),X,t,T) \geq c(S(t),X,t,T) \geq S(t)B^*(t,T) - XB(t,T) \tag{6.9}$$

For example, if 360-day eurodollar deposits have an interest rate of 11.11 percent $[B(t,T) = 1/1.1111 = 0.9]$, 360-day euro-SF deposits have an interest rate of 5.26 percent $[B^*(t,T) = 1/1.0526 = 0.95]$, and the spot rate $S(t) = \$.55/SF$, then a 360-day American option on one Swiss franc with an exercise price of $X = \$.50/SF$ will have a value

$C(.55, .50, t, 360) \geq c(.55, .50, t, 360) \geq (.55)(.95) - (.50)(.9) = \$.0725$.

Since an American option can be exercised at any time and must have a value at least as large as its immediate exercise value, we get the stronger inequality

$$C(S(t),X,t,T) \geq \max [S(t) - X, S(t)B^*(t,T) - XB(t,T)]. \tag{6.10}$$

Notice that, depending on the bond prices B and B^*, sometimes $S - X$ will be greater than $SB^* - XB$, and sometimes $S - X$ will be smaller. This shows that the American call on spot has a constraint,

$C(t) \geq S - X$,

that is not subsumed in any constraint that applies also to the European call on spot. As a consequence, American calls will have values greater than European calls as long as there is a positive probability this additional constraint will be binding.

Similar reasoning shows that for European and American puts on spot:

$$p(S(t),X,t,T) \geq XB(t,T) - S(t)B^*(t,T) \tag{6.11}$$

$$P(S(t),X,t,T) \geq \max [X - S(t), XB(t,T) - S(t)B^*(t,T)]. \tag{6.12}$$

Principle 11

The interest parity relation of Chapter 4 may be rewritten using the notation of this chapter as

$$F(t,T) = S(t)\frac{B^*(t,T)}{B(t,T)}. \tag{6.13}$$

Substituting for $S(t)B^*(t,T)$ in equation (6.10), we obtain the relation

$$C(S(t),X,t,T) \geq c(S(t),X,t,T) \geq B(t,T)[F(t,T) - X]. \tag{6.14}$$

A call option on one unit of spot exchange must have a value at least as great as the discounted difference between the forward exchange rate and the exercise price. The intuition is clear if we consider the case $F > X$. An owner of a European call can sell foreign currency forward for $F(t,T)$ even though the purchase price will be X. Thus such an option has a value at least as large as this difference, $F - X$, once it is discounted to the present.

Similarly, we have for puts

$$P(S(t),X,t,T) \geq p(S(t),X,t,T) \geq B(t,T)[X - F(t,T)]. \tag{6.15}$$

Now consider futures-style options on either spot or futures. Combining the relations (6.7) and (6.8) in the previous section with (6.14) and (6.15) above, we get

$$C^{**}(S(t),X,t,T) \geq c^{**}(S(t),X,t,T) \geq [F(t,T) - X] \tag{6.16}$$

$$P^{**}(S(t),X,t,T) \geq p^{**}(S(t),X,t,T) \geq [X - F(t,T)]. \tag{6.17}$$

Principle 12

Here we derive a direct relation between the prices of European calls on spot and European puts on spot. Consider the following two portfolio strategies:

Strategy A: 1. Buy, at a domestic currency price of $p(S(t),X,t,T)$, a put option on one unit of foreign currency with exercise price X.

Strategy B: 1. Issue a foreign-currency-denominated discount bond at $B^*(t,T)$ and sell the foreign currency for $S(t)B^*(t,T)$.

2. Buy X domestic discount bonds at a price of $B(t,T)$ each for a total domestic currency amount $XB(t,T)$.

3. Buy, at a domestic currency price of $c(S(t),X,t,T)$, a European call option on one unit of foreign currency with an exercise price of X.

Total Domestic Currency Investment: $c - SB^* + XB$.

At time $t + T$ the spot exchange rate $S(t + T)$ will be such that either

$$S(t + T) < X \text{ or } S(t + T) \geq X.$$

In each case, since

$$p(S(t + T), X, T, 0) = \max[0, X - S(t + T)],$$

the strategies will have the payoffs:

	Value of Strategy A	Value of Strategy B
$S(t+T) < X$	$X - S(t+T)$	$X - S(t+T)$
$S(t+T) \geq X$	0	0

Since each strategy gives the same payoff, each must cost the same in economic equilibrium. Hence

$$p(S(t),X,t,T) = c(S(t),X,t,T) - S(t)B^*(t,T) + XB(t,T). \qquad (6.18)$$

Thus *the price of a European put on spot is totally determined by the price of the corresponding European call, the spot exchange rate, and the prices of discount bonds denominated in the two currencies.* Equation (6.18) is a put-to-call conversion equation for European FX options on spot.

Principle 13

Using the interest parity relation (6.13), and substituting into equation (6.18), we obtain

$$p(S(t),X,t,T) = c(S(t),X,t,\text{T}) + B(t,T)[X - F(t,T)]. \qquad (6.19)$$

The price of a European FX put differs from the price of the corresponding call by a factor which represents the discounted difference between the exercise price and the forward exchange rate.

Combining the relations of (6.8) with (6.19), we obtain a similar put-to-call conversion equation for futures-style European FX calls and puts as:

$$p^{**}(S(t),X,t,T) = c^{**}(S(t),X,t,T) + [X - F(t,T)]. \qquad (6.20)$$

The prices of European futures-style puts and calls on spot or futures differ by the difference between the exercise price and the forward exchange rate.   ∎

PRICING MODELS FOR FX OPTIONS

Option-pricing models price options through arbitrage relationships. Think, for the sake of analogy, of the interest parity equation. The interest parity equation gives the forward rate as a function of the spot rate and two eurocurrency interest rates. It shows that there cannot be four independent markets for spot exchange, forward exchange, and domestic- and foreign-currency eurodeposits. Once you specify three of these variables, the other can be solved for by interest parity. Given the spot rate and the two interest rates, you can solve the equation for a synthetic forward rate. If this synthetic forward rate is different from the market forward rate (by more than a margin of error allowed by transactions costs), a profit opportunity is available. Arbitrage will eliminate riskless profit opportunities and will thus tend to equalize the forward rate derived from the equation with the market forward rate.

Option-pricing models are derived using the same principle. A synthetic option is created using other market assets. The value of these assets is then the value of the option. In particular, *a European FX option on spot can be created synthetically by a portfolio consisting of eurocurrency deposits (or bonds) denominated in both the domestic and foreign currencies.* The cash flows involved in this portfolio will exactly duplicate the cash flows involved in a European FX option on spot. Keeping our previous notation, let $B(t,T)$ and $B^*(t,T)$ be the prices of discount bonds denominated in the domestic and foreign currency, respectively. To convert the value of the foreign bond into domestic currency terms, it must be multiplied by the spot exchange rate, so the domestic-currency value of the foreign bond would be $S(t)B^*(t,T)$. The assertion that a European FX call option on spot can be created synthetically using domestic and foreign bonds can be written as:

$$c(t) = a[S(t)B^*(t,T)] + b[B(t,T)], \tag{6.21}$$

where a and b are the amounts of the foreign and domestic bonds, respectively, in the portfolio.

It remains only to specify the exact values of a and b. It turns out that a and b are themselves functions of five variables: $S(t)$, $B^*(t,T)$, $B(t,T)$, T, and v, where v is related to the variation of the forward rate. Since most of these variables are changing with time, the values of a and b change with the passage of time. That is, *the portfolio of domestic and foreign currency assets must be adjusted continuously.* As a practical matter, this latter requirement is very strict, since real-world transactions costs would make it costly to continuously adjust such a portfolio. That means, as a practical matter, that it would be difficult to duplicate closely a European FX option synthetically. This fact has two implications: (1) Transactions costs will allow a proportionately larger range of prices at which a European FX option can trade without arbitrage possibilities than would be the case for an FX forward rate; (2) the creation of an FX options market serves a real economic need, since transactions costs make it difficult to create synthetic FX options using other market instruments (Ross, 1976).

To derive a European FX option-pricing formula, we must make some assumptions about the distribution of asset prices. The main assumption made for the formulas presented here is that the logarithmic change in the forward rate, $1n[F(t + u, \ T - u)] - 1n[F(t,T)]$, is a normally distributed random variable with mean $m\,u$ and variance $v^2\,u$. That is, both the mean and the variance are proportional to the passage of time u. Hence, there is a mean drift m per unit time, and a variance rate v^2 per unit time. (The variable v, which is the standard deviation rate per square root of unit time, is commonly referred to as **volatility** by options market participants.) Similar assumptions are made for logarithmic changes in bond prices:

$$1n[B(t + u, \ T - u)] - 1n[B(t,T)]$$

and

$$1n[B^*(t + u, \ T - u)] - 1n[B^*(t,T)].$$

With these probability assumptions, it is shown in Grabbe (1983) that the portfolio proportions a and b in (6.21) have the values $a = N(d1)$, and $b = -X\ N(d2)$, where X is the option strike, and $N(d1)$ and $N(d2)$ are the cumulative normal distribution evaluated at $d1$ and $d2$, respectively:

$$c(t) = S(t)B^*(t,T)\ N(d1) - XB(t,T)\ N(d2), \tag{6.22}$$

where

$$d1 = \frac{1n(SB^*/XB) + .5\ v^2 T}{v\sqrt{T}}$$

$$d2 = \frac{1n(SB^*/XB) - .5\,v^2 T}{v\sqrt{T}}$$

and

$$N(d) = \frac{1}{\sqrt{2\pi}} \int_{-\infty}^{d} \exp(-x^2/2)\,dx.$$

The expressions "v^2/T" and "$v\sqrt{T}$" are unit-free. That is, if T is measured in days, then v^2 must be the daily variance rate. If T is measured in years, then v^2 must be the yearly variance rate. Commonly calculated values for v usually assume that T is measured in years.

EXAMPLE 6.4

The mechanics of the formula can be illustrated making the following data assumptions:

$$S(t) = \$1.5449/\pounds \qquad B(t,T) = .99465$$

$$X = \$1.50/\pounds \qquad B^*(t,T) = .99315$$

$$T = .05833 \qquad v = .15705.$$

The intermediate formula variables may be calculated as:

$$1n(SB^*/XB) = 1n((1.5449)(.99315)/[(1.50)(.99465)]) = .027985$$

$$v\sqrt{T} = (.15705)\,(\sqrt{.05833}) = .03793$$

$$.5\,v^2 T = .5\,(.15705)^2(.05833) = .0007193$$

$$d1 = \frac{(.027985) + (.0007193)}{.03793} = .7567$$

$$d2 = \frac{(.027985) - (.0007193)}{.03793} = .7188$$

$$N(d1) = .7754$$

$$N(d2) = .76387$$

$$c(t) = SB^*\,N(d1) - XB\,N(d2)$$

$$= (\$1.5449/\pounds)(.99315)(.7754) - (\$1.50/\pounds)(.99465)(.76387)$$

$$= \$.05/\pounds.$$

Some sample European call option values are given in Table 6.2, for a spot rate of $S(t) = \$1.60/\pounds$. The value of v is assumed to be $v = .10$ per year; maturities are for three, six, and nine months with various sets of domestic and foreign bond prices; and strike prices are $\$1.55/\pounds$, $\$1.60/\pounds$, and $\$1.65/\pounds$. Diagonal cells in the table illustrate that a lower level of interest rates (higher level of bond prices) yields higher call values when the term structure is the same in both the domestic and foreign countries. Cells below the diagonal show that call values are an increasing function of the positive difference of domestic over foreign interest rates. Cells above the diagonal demonstrate that call prices are a decreasing func-

TABLE 6.2
Values of European FX Calls on Spot*

	$\sigma = .10$								
	3 mo.	6 mo.	9 mo.	3 mo.	6 mo.	9 mo.	3 mo.	6 mo.	9 mo.
B	.97	.94	.91	.98	.96	.94	.99	.98	.97
B^*	.97	.94	.91	.97	.94	.91	.97	.94	.91
1.55	6.07	6.94	7.55	4.99	5.07	4.98	4.03	3.55	3.08
1.60	3.10	4.24	5.03	2.38	2.88	3.07	1.78	1.86	1.74
1.65	1.30	2.36	3.15	0.92	1.47	1.77	0.63	0.88	0.92
B	.97	.94	.91	.98	.96	.94	.99	.98	.97
B^*	.98	.96	.94	.98	.96	.94	.98	.96	.94
1.55	7.31	9.29	11.03	6.13	7.09	7.80	5.05	5.21	5.22
1.60	3.98	6.08	7.87	3.13	4.33	5.19	2.41	2.96	3.22
1.65	1.80	3.64	5.32	1.31	2.41	3.26	0.93	1.52	1.86
B	.97	.94	.91	.98	.96	.94	.99	.98	.97
B^*	.99	.98	.97	.99	.98	.97	.99	.98	.97
1.55	8.64	11.93	15.02	7.37	9.44	11.27	6.19	7.23	8.05
1.60	4.98	8.26	11.34	4.01	6.16	8.02	3.16	4.42	5.36
1.65	2.42	5.30	8.18	1.81	3.69	5.41	1.32	2.46	3.36

* Entries in the table are prices, in U.S. cents, of a European call option on one British pound, with the designated standard deviation rate (σ), strike price ($1.55, $1.60, $1.65), time to maturity (3 months, 6 months, 9 months), and domestic (B) and foreign (B^*) bond prices, when the spot rate is $1.60 per pound.

tion of the positive difference of foreign over domestic interest rates. They also show that the European FX call on spot can have an ambiguous time derivative. For $X = \$1.55$,

$$B \in \{.99, .98, .97\}, \; B^* \in \{.97, .94, .91\},$$

for example, the value of the option decreases from 4.03 cents for a three-month term to maturity to 3.08 cents for a nine-month term to maturity.

The formula for the European put can be derived from (6.22) and the put-call conversion equation (6.18) as

$$p(t) = XB(t,T)[1 - N(d2)] - S(t)B^*(t,T)[1 - N(d1)]. \tag{6.23}$$

Equations (6.22) and (6.23) can also be written in a form that contains the forward exchange rate. To do this, simply substitute $F(t,T)B(t,T)$ for the expression $S(t)B^*(t,T)$ in equations (6.22) and (6.23), since from the interest parity relation (6.13), we have

$$F(t,T)B(t,T) = S(t)B^*(t,T).$$

Note that as a result of (6.7), equations (6.22) and (6.23) also serve to price European options on futures, provided the futures price and forward rate for option expiration can be treated as equivalent.

For futures-style European options on spot, we have from (6.8) combined with (6.22), (6.23), and (6.13):

$$c^{**}(t) = F(t,T)\, N(d1) - XN(d2) \tag{6.24}$$

$$p^{**}(t) = X[1 - N(d2)] - F(t,T)\, [1 - N(d1)]. \tag{6.25}$$

□

A more exact statement of the probability assumptions used to derive the pricing equations above is that log S, log B, and log B^* are assumed to follow Wiener-Levy processes. These assumptions imply that log changes in exchange rates and bond prices have normal distributions. (A similar assumption for stock prices was made by Black and Scholes (1973) in deriving their famous equation for pricing European options on non-dividend-paying stock.) If the FX option price is assumed to be twice-continuously differentiable in these variables, then stochastic calculus may be used to construct a riskless hedge portfolio using the option, the domestic-currency bond, and the foreign-currency bond. As shown in Grabbe (1983), the construction of the hedge results in a partial differential equation whose solution is the option price. A slightly different equation is derived in Garman and Kohlhagen (1983), since they assume that bond prices (interest rates) are constant. The Garman-Kohlhagen pricing equations are similar to (6.22) and (6.23), except that with constant interest rates, the volatility parameter v becomes the volatility of the spot rate instead of the forward rate.

As noted in Chapter 3, it is well known that log changes in exchange rates are leptokurtic, which implies that the normal distribution is at best an approximation to the true empirical distribution. An alternative probability assumption that allows for leptokurtosis is made by McCullough (1984), who derives an FX option-pricing formula assuming that log S has an infinite-variance stable distribution. McCullough's formulation, however, requires an additional purchasing-power parity assumption.   ■

AMERICAN FX OPTION PRICING

The European FX pricing model gives a *minimum* price for American FX options as a consequence of equation (6.6), but American options will generally have higher prices. Unfortunately there is no known simple, closed-form pricing equation for American FX options generally. However, there are algorithms for getting the right answer, so American options are easily priced on the computer. The lack of a simple equation, however, makes it difficult to summarize the characteristics of the pricing formula easily.

The difference between American and European FX options is that American options can be exercised on any business day. Thus any variable that would influence the holder of an American option to exercise it prior to expiration increases the value of the American option relative to a European option. The chief influence in this regard is interest rates. In particular, higher foreign interest rates relative to domestic rates increase the probability that American FX calls will be exercised prior to expiration and decrease the probability that American FX puts will be exercised early. As a consequence, the higher foreign interest rates above domestic interest rates, the greater will be the differential between American FX call prices and European FX call prices and the smaller the differential between American FX put prices and European FX put prices. On the other hand, the higher domestic interest rates above foreign interest rates, the greater will be the differential between American FX put prices and European FX put prices and the smaller the differential between American FX call prices and European FX call prices. (A numerical example is given in the following section.) In the early days of foreign currency options trading at the PHLX (in 1983), many participants used European FX pricing models, even though the options were American. Since U.S. dollar interest rates were greatly above rates in Switzerland, Germany, and Japan, the use of European pricing models for the PHLX American options mispriced the puts on those currencies more than they mispriced the calls.

□

In some exceptional cases, the American formula is known. First, as shown in Merton (1973), sometimes American and European option prices are the same — for example, they are the same for calls on non-dividend-paying stock but not for puts. In addition, Merton (1973) obtained the pricing equation for a perpetual (infinite-maturity) American put on stock. Grabbe (1985) has obtained pricing equations for perpetual American FX calls and puts.

Most algorithms for pricing American options without a known formula follow a common procedure. Imagine a two-dimensional graph in which the option term-to-maturity is placed on the horizontal axis, while the spot exchange rate is placed on the vertical axis. Divide the time axis into a discrete number of time points and divide the price axis into a discrete number of price points. The option price will be evaluated at each time-point, price-point pair. First consider the expiration time point. For each price point at that time we know the value of the option, because the option value is the maximum of either its immediate exercise value or zero. Next consider the time point immediately preceding expiration. The option value for any price point will then be the maximum of either the immediate exercise value of the option or the option's discounted expected value at the following time point. We thus work backward from option expiration in a dynamic programming fashion. For each time point we evaluate the option values at all price points. Then, when we reach the current time point and current price point, we have obtained the current value of the American option.

The trick in the above procedure is the proper calculation of the discounted expected value of the option at each time-point, price-point pair. This requires knowledge of the transition probabilities for movement of the price from the current time point, price point to any price point at the following time point. Parkinson (1977) obtains transition probabilities by using a trinomial approximation to the assumed normally distributed log price changes. Cox, Ross, and Rubinstein (1979) use transition probabilities from a multiplicative binomial distribution. Brennan and Schwartz (1977) take a different approach which involves replacing the option partial differential equation by a set of difference equations. More recently, Geske and Johnson (1984) have derived an exact analytical equation for pricing American options. This equation has an infinite number of terms, but the authors suggest a numerical simplification that requires dividing the time axis into only three time points.

Numerical pricing of American FX options has been used in two empirical examinations of the FX options market at the PHLX. Bodurtha and Courtadon (1984) show the superiority of the American FX model over the European in terms of the model's correspondence with observed market prices. Even so, they found that the American model tended to overprice (relative to market prices) options at or in the money. Shastri and Tandon (1985) found a similar result, but they also found that the American model tended to underprice (relative to market prices) out-of-the-money options. It was not clear whether these differences were the fault of the model or the market. Neither study found significant exploitable profit opportunities from the point of view of nonmembers of the exchange, but the Shastri-Tandon results leave open the possibility that there may have been profitable model-based strategies from the point of view of exchange members.   ∎

SOME OPTION CONCEPTS FOR HEDGING AND RISK MANAGEMENT

This section introduces some basic option concepts—the option delta, gamma, theta, elasticity, and lambda. Each of these variables will be illustrated by reference to Table 6.3, which gives comparative American and European call and put values for FX options on spot, options on FX futures, and futures-style FX options on spot. The underlying price assumptions for the spot rate, interest rates, exercise price, term-to-maturity, and volatility are listed at the top of Table 6.3. The futures contract embodied in the option on futures is assumed to expire at the same time the option expires, and the futures price is assumed to be related to the spot rate by interest parity. (The rates listed in the table imply a futures price of 35.20573.) The European values given in the table were generated by the European pricing formulas presented above. The American values were calculated by a numerical technique that uses a binomial approximation to the normal distribution.

TABLE 6.3
Comparison of Options on Spot, Options on Futures, and Futures-Style Options*

	Value	Delta	Gamma	Theta	Elasticity	Lambda
Option on spot						
Call						
European	1.069	.540	.159	−.007	17.58	.069
American	1.072	.540	.160	−.007	17.52	.069
Put						
European	.869	−.447	.159	−.003	−17.92	.069
American	.915	−.479	.180	−.004	−18.23	.068
Option on futures						
Call						
European	1.069	.540	.159	−.007	17.58	.069
American	1.079	.539	.159	−.005	17.58	.069
Put						
European	.869	−.447	.159	−.003	−17.92	.069
American	.876	−.445	.159	−.005	−17.91	.069
Futures-style option on spot						
Call						
European	1.096	.553	.163	−.008	17.58	.070
American	1.098	.552	.164	−.008	17.51	.070
Put						
European	.890	−.458	.163	−.003	−17.92	.070
American	.928	−.483	.179	−.004	−18.12	.070

* *Assumptions:* Current spot rate = 34.82; Exercise price of option = 35; Days to option expiration = 93; Eurocurrency rate on domestic currency = 9.47%; Eurocurrency rate on foreign currency = 5.125%; Yearly standard deviation rate = .14; Current futures price determined by interest parity.
Source: Author's calculations.

Value

For the sake of concreteness, we may think of the spot rate as being the price of the DM in terms of U.S. cents. Thus the spot rate is 34.82 cents per DM, while the strike price is 35 cents per DM. An option value generated by a pricing formula will appear in the same units used to measure the spot rate and exercise price. So the option values listed in Table 6.3 under the column heading "Value" are in terms of U.S. cents. For example, the value of the European call on one unit of spot DM is 1.069 cents.

Several characteristics of the relative option values should be noted. First, all the American options have values larger than their European counterparts. This will always be true for American FX options, just as long as neither interest rate is zero. (If the rate on domestic currency were zero, then American and European FX puts would have the same value. If the rate on foreign currency were zero, then the American and European calls would have the same value.) Second, each of the futures-style options on spot has a value larger than the corresponding option on spot. (For example, the value of the futures-style American put on spot is .928, versus .915 for the American put on spot.) This is a consequence of Principle 9. An option on spot is the discounted value of the corresponding futures-style option on spot. Hence, for a positive discount rate, the value of the ordinary option is always smaller than the value of the futures-style option. Third, the value of a European option on futures is equal to the value of the corresponding European option on spot. (For example, both puts have values of .869.) This is an illustration of equations (6.7). Finally, the value of the American call on futures is greater than the value of the American call on spot (1.079 versus 1.072), but the value of the American put on futures is less than the value of the American put on spot (.876 versus .915). This reflects the fact that the FX futures price is at a premium. If the FX futures price were at a discount, then the relative prices between the option on spot and the option on futures would be reversed on both the call and the put.

Delta

The **option delta** measures the amount the option price changes relative to a small increase in the spot rate (for options on spot) or futures price (for options on futures). The option price change is always less in absolute magnitude than the price change in the spot or futures. Hence an option delta always has an absolute value between 0 and 1. For example, for the American put option on spot, the delta value is given as $-.479$. This delta value implies that if the spot rate increases by .1 cent (from 34.82 to 34.92), the option value will increase by $(.1)(-.479) = -.0479$ cents (from .915 to .8671).

In Chapter 5 we looked at delta-hedging with futures contracts. Option deltas may be similarly used for delta-hedging between options and spot exchange, options and futures, or just between options. For example, the delta on the American call on futures is .539. This indicates that if one is long 1 IMM DM futures contract and short 1 IMM DM option on futures, the net delta of the position (per DM) is

$$1 - .539 = .461.$$

That is, the total position is equivalent to a long position in .461 IMM DM futures contracts. Since there are DM 125,000 in a futures contract, the net position is equivalent to a long position in future DM of (.461)(DM 125,000) = DM 57,625. As a second example, if one is long 2 IMM DM futures contracts, and short 4 IMM DM call options on futures, the net delta is

$$2 - 4(.539) = -.156.$$

This total position is equivalent to a short position in .156 IMM DM futures contracts. As a final example, suppose one is long ten CBOE European calls on spot DM and also long twelve CBOE European puts on spot DM. The net delta is

$$10(.540) + 12(-.447) = .036 \text{ (per DM)}.$$

Since a CBOE DM option represents DM 125,000, the net position is equivalent to a long position in spot DM of (.036)(DM 125,000) = DM 4500.

Because the net delta of a position represents the equivalent long or short position in foreign currency, it is a measure of one's total portfolio risk. For that reason, both the IMM and LIFFE use delta factors as a basis for margin requirements. Hedgers use delta factors to determine their actual FX exposure. It should be emphasized, however, that the delta value is only valid for small changes in the spot rate (or futures price), because the delta value itself changes with a change in the underlying price. This implies an additional source of risk once one has established a desired delta position. Suppose, for example, that one has a net delta position of zero. One is then said to be delta-neutral. For small changes in the spot rate, the change in the value of the position will be zero. One is fully hedged for small exchange-rate fluctuations. Marketmakers who do large amounts of trading relative to their capital often attempt to remain delta-neutral. But there is still risk involved, because the net delta will itself change for any significant change in the spot rate.

Gamma

The option **gamma** measures the amount the option delta changes relative to a small increase in the spot rate (for options on spot) or futures prices (for options on futures). It is thus a measure of the risk inherent in a delta-neutral hedge. If the gamma is positive, then the delta will increase with an increase in the underlying price and decrease with a decrease in the underlying price. If the original delta were zero while the gamma was positive, then a rising price would result in a positive delta position. A falling price would result in a negative delta position. This is a very desirable state of affairs, because one would like to have a positive delta (net long position) if prices are rising but a negative delta (net short position) if prices are falling. Hence marketmakers who attempt to maintain a delta-neutral position can control their risk by maintaining a positive gamma position also.

Consider the American option on spot. The delta is .540 and the gamma is .160. If the spot rate increased by 1 cent (from 34.82 to 35.82), the gamma of .160 indicates that the delta will increase from approximately

$$.540 \text{ to } .540 + .160 = .700.$$

Suppose that one were initially long a PHLX DM call option on DM 62,500. The initial delta of .540 indicates that being long 1 PHLX DM call is equivalent to a long position in $(.540)(DM\ 62,500) = DM\ 33,750$. But this equivalent long position would be increasing with the spot rate, and at a spot rate of 35.82 would represent a long position of approximately

$$(.700)(DM\ 62,500) = DM\ 43,750.$$

All of the options have a positive gamma. This is viewed from the long side of the option. The gamma is negative to the option writer. Suppose one is long one PHLX American call on spot DM and short one PHLX American put on spot DM. The net delta (per DM in the option contract) would be

$$.540 - (-.479) = 1.019,$$

while the net gamma would be

$$.160 - (.180) = -.020.$$

The net delta for DM 62,500 is

$$(1.019)(DM\ 62,500) = DM\ 63,687.5.$$

The net gamma for DM 62,500 is

$$(-.020)(DM\ 62,500) = -DM\ 1250.$$

The small negative value for gamma here indicates that there will be only a small negative change in net delta as the spot rate moves. If the spot rate goes up, the net delta will fall, but only slightly. If the spot rate goes down the net delta will rise, but only slightly.

Using gammas can be tricky because a gamma is not unit-free. For example, if the spot rate and exercise price in Table 6.3 were measured in U.S. dollar terms ($.3482 instead of 34.82 cents, and $.35 instead of 35 cents), all of the gammas would be multiplied by 100. That is, dividing the spot rate and exercise price by 100 multiplies the gamma value by 100. But the meaning of gamma has not changed in any way.

Theta

The option theta is a measure of the change in an option value with the passage of time. For example, the futures-style American call on spot has a theta of $-.008$. This indicates that if the option maturity goes from ninety-three days to ninety-two days while none of the other variables listed at the top of Table 6.3 changes, the value of the option will fall by .008 cents per unit of foreign currency. That is, the option value will go from 1.098 to $1.098 + (-.008) = 1.090$ cents. Notice that to the buyer (long side) the option theta is always negative: the value of the option premium decays with time. The theta value is of great interest to people who write options The reduction in the option value with the passage of time accrues as income to the option writer. A higher theta value implies a higher income stream.

For example, suppose one has written ten LIFFE futures-style American calls on DM. Then the daily cash flow to the option writer—assuming no other variable changes—would be $(10)(.008)(125,000) = 10,000$ cents, or $100 per day.

Elasticity

The **elasticity** of an option represents the percentage change in the option premium for a 1-percent increase in the underlying price. For example, the elasticity of the American put on spot of -18.23 indicates that if the spot rate increases by 1 percent (from 34.82 to $(1.01)(34.82) = 35.1682$), the option value will decrease by approximately 18.23 percent (from .915 to .748). As a second example, if the futures price increases by 1 percent, the value of the American call on futures will increase by 17.58 percent.

Lambda

The option **lambda** represents the change in the option value for a unit increase in volatility. The unit used here is an increment of .01 to the volatility. For example, the lambda value for the European put on spot is .069. This indicates that if the volatility (yearly standard deviation rate) goes from .14 to $.14 + .01 = .15$, the option premium will increase by .069 cents (from .869 to .938). Call and put lambdas on otherwise similar European options are always equal, but call and put lambdas on similar American options can differ.

The sensitivity of the option price to the volatility is of great importance in the market for FX options. The pricing equations used above were derived under the assumption that the volatility v is a known variable. However, in the real world this is not true. One can calculate the yearly standard deviation rate over some recent time period from historical data, but one can't be sure that the actual value of v over the life of the option will be exactly the same. So any option position involves a risk that the assumed value for volatility will not be correct. So, unless one is extremely adroit in forecasting volatility, the only way to reduce volatility risk is to reduce the net lambda of the option position. For example, suppose one bought the European call on spot and wrote the American call on spot. The lambda for each option is .069, so the net lambda is $.069 - .069 = 0$. The net lambda of zero indicates that the value of the position should not change even if the volatility v changes. Thus there is little volatility risk in this position.

☐

The concepts in this section are based on the partial derivatives of the option price with respect to the underlying variables that determine it. The delta is the partial derivative of the option price with respect to the spot rate (or futures price, for options on futures). The gamma is the second partial derivative of the option price with respect to the spot rate (or futures price, for options on futures). That is, the gamma is the partial derivative of the delta with respect to the spot rate (or futures price, for options on futures). The theta is the partial derivative of the option price with respect to the term-to-maturity. The lambda is the partial derivative of the option price with respect to the volatility. The elasticity is calculated as the delta multiplied by the (spot rate/option value) [or (futures price/option value) for options on futures]. ■

IMPLIED VOLATILITY

The implied volatility is that unique value of the volatility v that generates a model price of an option that is identical with an observed market price of the option — given market observations on the spot rate and the domestic and foreign interest rates, and given the strike price and term-to-maturity of the option.

The way implied volatility is calculated in practice is that an arbitrary starting value for v (say $v = .12$ or 12 percent) is used to generate a model price (MOD) of the option. MOD is then compared with the observed market price (MAR). If MOD > MAR, then the value for v needs to be decreased (since the MOD price always decreases with decreasing v). If MOD < MAR, then the value for v needs to be increased. When MOD = MAR (or the difference in the two is less than some predefined small number, the "convergence criterion"), the final value of v is the implied volatility.

The chief reason for looking at implied volatility is that it is the only real way to get a handle on whether an option is underpriced or overpriced. For example, one may feel that option prices are "lower" or "higher" than they were last week, but how can one be sure? The spot rate may have changed, and the maturity of the options has also changed. So there is no reason that the same option should be priced the same as it was last week. The question is: Has the price of the option changed *after adjustment for changes in other market factors* such as the spot rate and term-to-maturity. The answer is no if implied volatility has not changed, yes if implied volatility has changed. The same concept would apply to comparing two options with different strike prices: How can I know if one is overpriced relative to another? The answer hinges on whether they have the same implied volatility. Since they are both options on the same underlying currency, they should presumably have the same implied volatility if correctly priced relative to each other.

The calculated implied volatility (which generates a MOD value equal to the MAR value) is totally dependent on the option-pricing model used. If the model is irrelevant, then the implied volatility will also be irrelevant. For an extreme example, suppose the model for the call price (C) were

$C = 100v - 3.$

If a value of $C = 7$ is inserted into this equation, then solution will yield an implied volatility of $v = .10$, because

$100(.10) - 3 = 7.$

This implied volatility value is meaningless, however, because the option model is meaningless. For example, one can input a foreign currency option price into a stock option model and solve the stock option model backward to generate an implied volatility. This implied volatility would not be useful because the option model is incorrect. Similarly, a market price of an American FX option can be inserted into a European FX model. The resulting implied volatility will be too high, not necessarily because the American FX option is overpriced in the market but rather because the European FX model will normally generate smaller values for the options and thus compensate for the higher American price by returning a higher volatility.

Taken at face value, a correctly measured implied volatility represents an estimate of the actual volatility of the underlying currency over the life of the option. Thus, whether a given volatility is too "high" or "low" in absolute terms is partly a matter of forecasting judgment. One would expect implied volatilities to resemble recent historical actual volatilities (annual standard deviation rates) of the underlying currency. There is a very subtle issue involved here. Option-pricing models are universally derived on the assumption that the value for v over the life of the option is known in advance. Most people accept that this is not really true—they know v is probably a random variable—but letting v be stochastic in the model derivation makes the mathematics so messy as to be usually beyond solution. So they use models derived on the basis of a known v and then fudge by inserting continually updated v estimates. This uncertainty in the true value for v results in practice in implied volatilities being on average larger than the actual volatilities of the underlying currency.

OPTIONS AND FUTURES: A BRIEF HISTORICAL PERSPECTIVE

The history of options is interconnected with that of futures. Neither contract is a recent development. The Osaka rice market in eighteenth-century Japan provides an early example of an organized exchange that included standardized spot and futures contracts and the settlement of trades through a clearing house. In the United States, the first spot commodity exchange was established in New York City in 1691. Exchanges provided a common meeting place to collect information as well as to trade commodities. Trade was facilitated because exchange members could agree on commercial standards and on rules for handling disputes.

Futures contracts grew out of delayed delivery contracts in the commodities markets. These delayed delivery contracts were actually forward contracts. A cotton grower in the southern United States might ship cotton to New York in return for a price that was fixed in advance. The cotton buyer faced the risk that the market price might change before the cotton arrived in New York. This risk could be transferred if the cotton buyer made a separate forward contract to sell the cotton to another party. But the chain of transfer could only terminate when someone voluntarily bore the price risk. To reduce the costs of arranging such risk transfer as well the costs of obtaining credit information on counterparties to a contract, trading in futures contracts was organized on exchanges in a manner similar to spot commodities. Trading in grain futures began at the Chicago Board of Trade (CBT) around the time of the Civil War, while cotton futures began a few years later with the New York Cotton Exchange.

Clearing houses were originally bookkeeping organizations. They confirmed trades but did not guarantee each side of a contract. But when clearing houses became guarantors, toward the end of the century, they began to require the marking to market of open positions. Margin requirements were first imposed on clearing members and later extended to retail customers. Marking to market created a clear distinction between futures and forward contracts.

Option contracts arose in connection with futures. Members of the CBT would sometimes protect a futures position by taking out an option to make or take delivery of grain. But options were not universally accepted. Some said that options disrupted the futures market. When grain markets collapsed in the Great Depression of the 1930s, commodity options trading was prohibited by the Commodity Exchange Act (1936). By the late 1900s option trading had appeared in connection with the stock market. The Securities Exchange Act of 1934 placed exchange-based stock option trading under the jurisdiction of the SEC. Stock options, however, continued to trade only in an over-the-counter market until February 1973, when the Chicago Board Options Exchange (CBOE) opened.

The advent of financial futures trading began about the same time, in 1972, when contracts on several foreign currencies were listed at the IMM. In 1974 the Commodities Futures Trading Commission Act created the CFTC. This act gave the CFTC jurisdiction over futures contracts generally, including foreign currency futures. The act continued to ban agricultural options (the ban was lifted in 1982), but the CFTC was given discretion to allow options trading on other commodities and financial instruments. Trading in stock index futures and options on certain debt securities resulted in a jurisdictional dispute between the SEC and CFTC. This was resolved by an accord between the two agencies in 1981. One provision of the accord was that options on foreign currency traded on a national securities exchange would be regulated by the SEC, while the CFTC would have jurisdiction over options on foreign currency not traded on a securities exchange as well as over options on foreign currency futures. The accord was enacted into law by Congress a year later, and the SEC approved FX options trading at the PHLX in December 1982. [An overview of the accord, as well as of U.S. regulation generally, can be found in Board of Governors et al. (1984).]

PROBLEMS FOR CHAPTER 6

1. Suppose you had purchased 2 March DM PHLX calls with a 38 strike ($.38/DM) at the price shown in the following *Wall Street Journal* excerpt.

FOREIGN CURRENCY OPTIONS

Friday, November 29, 1985

Philadelphia Exchange

Option & Underlying	Strike Price	Calls Last			Puts – Last		
		Dec	Jan	Mar	Dec	Jan	Mar
12,500 British Pounds-cents per unit.							
BPound	115	33.60	s	r	r	s	r
148.98	.130	18.70	r	18.90	r	r	0.25
148.98	.140	8.70	r	8.80	r	0.25	1.35
148.98	.145	3.80	r	5.50	0.30	1.10	2.80
148.98	.150	0.55	1.50	3.10	1.70	3.10	r
148.98	.155	r	r	1.70	r	r	r
50,000 Canadian Dollars-cents per unit.							
CDollr	...72	0.33	r	r	0.18	0.43	0.73
72.24	...73	r	r	0.32	0.55	0.72	r
72.24	...74	r	r	r	r	r	2.05
62,500 West German Marks-cents per unit.							
DMark	..35	4.85	r	5.00	r	r	r
39.80	...36	3.80	r	4.12	r	r	0.10
39.80	...37	2.84	2.92	3.27	r	r	0.18
39.80	...38	1.84	1.90	2.44	0.01	r	0.35
39.80	...39	0.86	1.21	1.77	0.07•	r	r
39.80	...40	0.24	0.62	1.23	0.40	0.69	r
125,000 French Francs-10ths of a cent per unit.							
FFranc	.120	r	r	r	r	r	0.80
130.45	.125	r	r	6.60	r	r	1.65
130.45	.130	r	r	3.85	r	r	r
6,250,000 Japanese Yen-100ths of a cent per unit.							
JYen	... 39	10.40	s	r	r	s	r
49.44	...42	7.38	r	r	r	r	r
49.44	...46	r	r	3.42	r	r	0.08
49.44	...47	r	r	2.66	r	r	r
49.44	...48	1.46	1.62	r	r	r	0.32
49.44	...49	0.74	0.90	1.26	0.12	0.39	0.75
49.44	...50	0.15	0.39	0.69	0.60	r	r
49.44	...51	0.06	s	s	r	s	s
62,500 Swiss Francs-cents per unit.							
SFranc	..40	8.00	s	r	r	s	0.02
48.03	...41	6.98	s	r	r	s	r
48.03	...42	6.10	s	r	r	s	r
48.03	...44	4.03	r	4.65	r	r	0.14
48.03	...45	3.03	r	r	r	r	r
48.03	...46	r	r	3.04	r	r	r
48.03	...47	1.24	1.55	2.27	r	r	0.75
48.03	...48	0.43	0.88	1.75	0.30	r	r

		Feb	May	Aug	Feb	May	Aug
62,500 West German Marks-cents per unit.							
DMark	41	0.52	s	s	r	s	s
62,500 Swiss Francs-cents per unit.							
SFranc	49	0.94	s	s	s	s	s
Total call vol.	19,587			Call open int.	211,409		
Total put vol.	7,523			Put open int.	168,078		

r – Not traded. s – No option offered.
Last is premium (purchase price).

[Chicago Mercantile Exchange]

BRITISH POUND (CME) 25,000 pounds; cents per pound

Strike	Calls – Settle			Puts – Settle		
Price	Dec-C	Mar-C	Jun-C	Dec-P	Mar-P	Jun-P
1425	6.40	7.05	7.75	0.05	2.00	3.65
1450	3.95	5.55	6.35	0.10	2.85	4.60
1475	1.65	4.20	5.15	0.35	4.00	5.80
1500	0.50	3.20	4.20	1.65	....	....
1525	....	....	....	....	....	....
1550	....	....	....	....	....	....

Est. vol. 747, Wed.; vol. 1,019 calls, 598 puts
Open interest Wed.; 12,094 calls, 14,841 puts

W. GERMAN MARK (CME) 125,000 marks, cents per mark

Strike	Calls – Settle			Puts – Settle		
Price	Dec-C	Mar-C	Jun-C	Dec-P	Mar-P	Jun-P
38	1.86	2.51	3.06	.0008	0.33	0.62
39	0.88	1.79	2.40	.02	0.60	0.94
40	0.19	1.22	1.84	0.33	1.02	1.32
41	0.02	0.82	1.37	1.16	1.58	1.81
42	....	0.52	1.00	....	....	....
43	....	....	....	....	....	....

Est. vol. 6,885, Wed.; vol. 4,985 calls, 1,851 puts
Open interest Wed.; 42,333 calls, 37,633 puts

SWISS FRANC (CME) 125,000 francs; cents per franc

Strike	Calls – Settle			Puts – Settle		
Price	Dec-P	Mar-P	Jun-P	Dec-P	Mar-P	Jun-P
46	2.19	3.05	3.79	.0008	0.40	0.70
47	1.20	2.32	3.10	0.01	0.67	0.99
48	0.36	1.71	2.49	0.17	1.02	1.35
49	0.06	1.23	1.98	0.87	1.52	1.80
50	....	0.86	1.56	....	2.14	2.34
51	....	....	....	....	....	....

Est. vol. 1,439, Wed.; vol. 770 calls, 995 puts
Open interest Wed.; 12,972 calls, 15,357 puts

Source: The Wall Street Journal,
Friday, November 29, 1985.

    (a)   What dollar amount (ignoring broker fees) would you have paid?

    (b)   What approximate ceiling cost of DM 125,000 would you have locked in?

    (c)   Suppose you had held the two options for 30 days, and then sold them for "2.60" (U.S. cents per DM). What was the net dollar profit, assuming entry costs of $4/option, exit costs of $4/option, and a dollar interest opportunity cost of 9% per annum (360 days) on the premium?

2. Suppose you had purchased 1 June DM 41 IMM futures put at the price shown in the *Wall Street Journal* excerpt for Problem 1.

    (a)   What dollar amount would you have paid?

    (b)   Explain exactly what would take place if you exercised the put at a time when the futures price was $.4021/DM.

    (c)   Compare the prices of PHLX options on spot exchange for Friday, November 29, with the prices of equivalent (same strike and maturity) options on IMM futures. What do you think accounts for the difference in prices between the two types of options?

3. A Japanese company buys a European call on ¥200,000,000 with a strike price of ¥240/$, and pays a premium of ¥4/$. The company's interest opportunity cost is 10% per year. There are no additional fees.

    (a)   What is the minimal end-of-year dollar cost of the yen that would result in a net positive pay-off on this insurance?

    (b)   What range of end-of-year exchange rates would result in exercise of the option (assuming no exercise fees)?

    (c)   Suppose the one-year forward rate were ¥238/$. For what range of end-of-year spot exchange values would the option contract prove more advantageous than the forward contract? For what range would it prove less advantageous?

4. Verify the numbers in Table 6.1. That is, given the option prices and assumptions, derive the sets of terminal spot-rate ranges that would make (after the fact) each decision the optimal one.

5. Explain why American FX calls and puts generally have values larger than European FX calls and puts. Under what circumstances would an American FX call *not* have a value larger than a European FX call? Answer the same question for FX puts.

6. Explain why futures-style FX calls and puts on spot generally have values larger than ordinary calls or puts on spot. Under what circumstances would a futures-style option have the same value as the corresponding ordinary option?

7. A trader buys a "bear spread" on the British pound that consists of a long CBOE 130 March put and a short CBOE 125 March put.

    (a)   If the price of the 130 put is $.055/£ while the price of the 125 put is $.022/£, what is the net dollar amount paid for the bear spread?

    (b)   What is the maximum amount the trader can make if the British pound depreciates with respect to the U.S. dollar?

    (c)   Answer similar questions for a "bull spread" that consists of a long CBOE 125 March call priced at $.043/£ and a short CBOE 130 call priced at $.015/£. What is the trader's maximum profit? Maximum loss?

8. The spot price of pounds is $1.25/£, the eurodollar interest rate is 10 percent, and the eurosterling interest rate is 8 percent. Given only this information, determine the minimum value an American FX call option could rationally trade for in the market, if the exercise price of the option is $1.25/£ and there are ninety days until expiration.

9. Using the European FX call formula and a table of the normal distribution, calculate the value of a FX call on the DM, given a strike of $.30, a spot rate of $.2950, a eurodollar rate of $8\frac{3}{4}$ percent, a euro-DM rate of $5\frac{1}{2}$ percent, a term-to-expiration of ninety days, and a volatility parameter (yearly standard deviation rate) of .15.

10. Explain in what sense being long an FX futures call and short an FX futures put is similar to being long an FX futures contract.

11. Show that an American futures-style option on spot always has a larger value than an American futures-style option on futures. [*Hint:* Examine equations (6.16) and (6.17) carefully. In what way is the boundary constraint for an American futures-style option on futures already included in the boundary constraint for an American futures-style option on spot? What additional boundary constraint does an American futures-style option on spot have?]

12. Show that American and European futures-style options on futures have equal values. [*Hint:* Show that an American futures-style option on futures would never be exercised early. Use the relation

$$FN(d1) - XN(d2) \geq F - X.]$$

13. Using the relationships covered in this chapter and, in addition, Problems 11 and 12, show that the value relationships among FX options are those summarized in the figure below.

Value relationships among FX option. [*Note:* Values for similar options only (both options are calls or both puts; same strike price; same *date of expiration*). The futures contract is assumed to expire at the same time as the option. When applying these relationships to traded options, keep in mind that CME options expire a week earlier than PHLX, LSE, CBOE, and LIFFE options.]

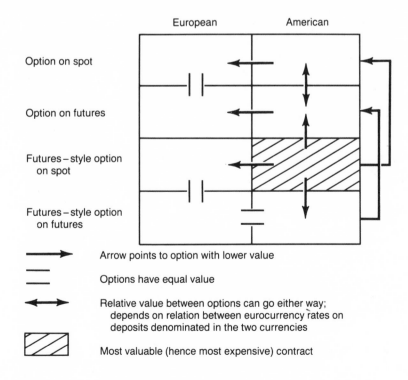

14. Explain how to set up a delta-neutral position, being long calls and short spot exchange, whose dollar value will remain essentially unchanged for small movements in the exchange rate. What would be the preferred gamma of such a position? The preferred theta?

15. A U.S. multinational has annual cash flows of £100,000,000. The company believes the pound may either depreciate slightly or remain at the current exchange rate with respect to the U.S. dollar. The company wishes to increase the immediate dollar value of its pound sterling cash flow, and in order to obtain this the company is willing to forego the possibility of exchange rate gains if the pound were to appreciate strongly against the dollar.

    (a) Explain why the company can meet its objectives by writing call options on the British pound (with a U.S. dollar strike price).

    (b) How is the tradeoff between up-front cash inflow and foregone exchange-rate gains affected by the choice of strike price in the calls that the company writes?

THE DETERMINATION OF EXCHANGE RATES

EXPECTATIONS, INFORMATION, AND EXCHANGE RATE SPECULATION

In Chapter 3 we saw that only a small percentage of foreign exchange trading represents commercial business. The majority of transactions arise from an endless round of purchases and sales among marketmakers. We saw that FX marketmakers are a special category of inventory specialists who make the market by their willingness to deal at two-way prices and to become the counterparty to either a purchase or sale of foreign exchange. In the absence of marketmakers, the random flow of buy and sell orders would result in large fluctuations in the exchange rate. The marketmaker provides a price-smoothing service by his willingness to buy or sell at a stated price. In the process the marketmaker acquires (if only temporarily) net long or short exchange positions.

But is all the trading that actually occurs really necessary to make the market? For each commercial transaction he handles, the marketmaker may do ten additional trades with other marketmakers. What is going on? The answer is that foreign currency traders have become *information dealers.* The bulk of their trading is related to the ebb and flow of economic and political events. In the words of Walter Wriston, "The information standard has replaced . . . the system invented at Bretton Woods." Each new piece of information may bring with it a shift in trader expectations. For example, "The words of a prime minister or a president appear on the screens of the trading rooms all over the world in minutes, and are reflected in the currency cross-rate immediately" (Wriston, 1984).

Much of the discussion of the FX spot, forward, futures, and option markets in Part II was concerned with arbitrage — the simultaneous buying and selling of the same or equivalent assets at two different prices. But an important additional force at work in the market is deliberate risk-taking: the acquiring of an open long or short position in foreign currency with the expectation of a profit. Some risk-taking is unavoidable. We saw in Chapter 5 that speculators are required in order to bear the risks that hedgers are trying to avoid. But of equal importance is the close connection between speculation and marketmaking itself. They differ only by degree, since the same decision process is at work in either activity. The marketmaker's ability to make a profit relies on his closing out a long position (short position) at a net price that is higher (lower) than that at which the position was acquired. How long a short or long position is retained, or how often a marketmaker adjusts his bid and asked prices, depends on the marketmaker's view as to whether the current state of FX supply and demand is temporary or permanent. So whether the trader is "just marketmaking" or engaged in active speculation, his expectations are a key determinant in how he manages his position. And what expectations he has will in turn depend on the available information.

An interbank trader is not allowed the luxury of ignoring the news. Since most FX supply and demand comes from the interbank market itself, the trader knows that any news event may bring about a reaction on the part of other traders. And, perceiving an impending shift in the market, he must immediately adjust his own position according to how he thinks other traders will react. Traders are like the judges in the Keynesian beauty contest (Keynes, 1936) who, rather than voting for the girl they thought was most beautiful, instead voted for the girl they thought the other judges would think was the most beautiful. Market equilibrium will depend in part on what traders think other traders think about equilibrium.

The interplay of expectations and information in the process of bringing about market equilibrium is the subject of this chapter. In the course of the discussion, we will introduce a number of concepts that will be used throughout Part III.

EXPECTATIONS AS A FUNCTION OF INFORMATION

The fact that news moves exchange rates can hardly be taken as cause for alarm. Suppose the contrary were true. If no one bothered to become informed, for example, news events might have little immediate impact on the market. Such would hardly be a rosy state of affairs. Few companies would contemplate seeking financial advice from a bank that employed sleepy traders. When people complain about the fact that news moves exchange rates, what they really mean is that they wish the bad news (to them) would go away. Even the European Monetary System, formed "to provide a zone of monetary stability in Europe" requires the existence of well-informed exchange traders. The system is implicitly built around the notion that the exchange rate mirrors the economy. (The "community average," as we saw in Chapter 2, is based on the market value of the ECU, which represents an average of community exchange rates.)

A trader's buy and sell decisions are based on the trader's expectations or forecasts—his or her view of the future movement of the exchange rate. The direction of spot rate movement that a trader foresees is a function of what the trader knows—his or her *information set*. Information includes not only "facts" but also the technology or human capital required to evaluate facts. A shorthand way of denoting a trader's information set at time t is by the symbol $I(t)$. Then, a simple way of writing "the expected exchange rate for the next period, given information at time t" is:

$$E\,[S(t+1)|I(t)].$$

Traders trade because they have different information and hence different expectations. No one who does not earn an economic reward for the effort is going to bother to collect information in the first place. If uninformed people could get along as well in the market as informed people, there would be no incentive for anyone to incur the expense of reading the news media, watching the Telerate monitor, doing research, employing a stable of econometricians and technical analysts, talking to policymakers, or hiring Wharton or Stanford MBAs. Information equilibrium requires market participants to collect information only up to the point where the benefit of additional information no longer justifies the cost. Therefore the market will always be composed of different groups who have different information sets. The information sets of group i at time t will be denoted by $I(i,t)$.

EXAMPLE 7.1

You are an interbank FX trader, and your bank has the best available forecasting model, purchased from Nostradamus, Inc. It predicts FX rates better than anything else on the market. Should you use this model to make speculative bets? In order for you to make a profit, it would have to be the case that some other FX traders were not in possession of the same model (the same information). Other traders would have to have expectations different from your own before they would take speculative positions against you, thus allowing you to win a profit when they are proved wrong. This means that they would have to be less informed than you. On the other hand, if the use of the model allowed one to earn excess profits, other people would attempt to acquire the same model. If more people began to form their expectations on the basis of the model, the advantage of using the model would diminish. Eventually market participants would become indifferent between having or not having the model, since the advantage of having the model would be no greater than the additional expense. We will call this the *Model Theorem:* Good models generate their own obsolescence. A different way of stating the same thing: Good models become bad. They lose their usefulness.

□

An interesting question arises as to whether people who have less information can learn what informed people know just by watching their trading decisions. If one FX trader knows that another FX trader is better informed, the first trader would never be willing to take a long or short position against the second trader. If others reacted the same way, the second, informed trader would never find anyone to trade with. Hence the value of his information would be useless. As a result, neither he nor anyone else would have an incentive to acquire information. This apparent paradox is solved by Grossman and Stiglitz (1980), who show that under conditions of market uncertainty, informed traders will still retain an advantage over uninformed traders, but the value of the informed trader's information will vary inversely with the number of other traders who acquire the same information. As a result, additional traders will continue to acquire information only up to the point at which the marginal benefit is equal to the marginal cost.   ■

EXPECTATIONAL EQUILIBRIUM

In the introduction to this chapter we mentioned the Keynesian beauty contest: the notion that market equilibrium depends on what traders think other traders think about equilibrium. How is the market equilibrium exchange rate determined by the simultaneous actions of many traders with diverse expectations?

Here we will focus on the aggregate point of view — on the "market" information set $I(M,t)$. We can think of the market information set as embodying the sum total of the different information sets $I(i,t)$ of individual traders.

One notion of expectational equilibrium is the concept of *rational* expectations. Rational expectations are expectations that are *self-fulfilling* on average. That is, expectations are rational if by holding and acting on the basis of these expectations, traders would bring about an economic equilibrium that confirms their original expectations. Clearly, expectations that were not self-fulfilling could not represent an expectational equilibrium. If traders did not on average find their expectations concerning the exchange rate fulfilled, they would have an incentive to change them. If they changed their expectations, they would change their trading decisions. A change in their trading decisions would result in a change in the market rate. Hence the market could not have been originally in equilibrium. Only if expectations are self-fulfilling on average will market participants have no incentive to alter their behavior.

This process is most easily illustrated by a simple numerical example. Suppose the foreign exchange market operated according to the following natural law:

$$S(t + 1) = .6 \; E[S(t + 1)|I(M,t)] + .4 \; S(t) + e(t + 1), \tag{7.1}$$

where $e(t + 1)$ is a random error term with

$$E[e(t + 1)|I(M,t)] = 0.$$

This equation says that next period's spot rate will be equal to a weighted average (with weights .6 and .4) of the market's expected spot rate for next period,

$$E[S(t + 1)|I(M,t)],$$

and today's actual spot rate, $S(t)$, plus an error term. The equation implies that today's expectation for next period is an important variable determining next period's actual spot rate.

Suppose now that the market has the following expectation:

$$E[S(t + 1)|I(M,t)] = 1.1 \; S(t). \tag{7.2}$$

Substituting this expectation into equation (7.1), we get that

$$S(t + 1) = .6 \; [1.1 \; S(t)] + .4 \; S(t) + e(t + 1) = 1.06 \; S(t) + e(t + 1).$$

The market expectation in this case would be wrong on average, since on average $S(t + 1)$ would be equal to $1.06 \; S(t)$, and not $1.1 \; S(t)$. Hence the expectation in equation (7.2) would not be rational since it is not self-fulfilling.

On the other hand, if people *lowered* their expectation to some number between $1.1 \; S(t)$ and $1.06 \; S(t)$, then equation (7.1) will yield a value for $S(t + 1)$ that is on average *less* than $1.06 \; S(t)$, but which is still not self-fulfilling. (Try it and see. For example, substitute

$$E[S(t + 1)|I(M,t)] = 1.07 \; S(t)$$

into equation (7.1).) Some experimentation will show that the only value for $E[S(t + 1)|I(M,t)]$ that *is* self-fulfilling on average is

$$E[S(t + 1)|I(M,t)] = S(t).$$

This value is the rational expectations solution to equation (7.1).

□

The rational expectations approach to expectational equilibrium is credited to John Muth (1961), who assumed that "expectations, since they are informed predictions of future events, are essentially the same as the predictions of the relevant economic theory." This approach implies that if a particular model is used to explain market behavior, it should also be assumed that the market formed its expectations on the basis of the same model. For example, if a trader really thought that equation (7.1) was the correct equation governing the spot exchange rate, this approach says he ought to credit other informed people with the same knowledge. That is, equation (7.1) is itself part of the market information set $I(M,t)$ and would be used in the process of forming the expectation

$$E[S(t + 1)|I(M,t)].$$

This approach yields a straightforward way of generating solutions to equations like (7.1).

EXAMPLE 7.2

Suppose a trader believed that equation (7.1) was the best available equation for forecasting next period's spot rate. In order to use the equation, some number must be inserted for

$$E[S(t + 1)|I(M,t)].$$

If she adopts the rational expectations approach, this trader would assume that other people in the FX market formed their expectations using equation (7.1). To solve for

$$E[S(t + 1)|I(M,t)],$$

then, the trader first takes the conditional mathematical expectation of both sides of equation (7.1) with respect to $I(M,t)$:

$$E[S(t + 1)|I(M,t)] = E[.6\ E[S(t + 1)|I(M,t)]|I(M,t)] + E[.4\ S(t)|I(M,t)] \\ + E[e(t + 1)|I(M,t)]. \tag{7.3}$$

As noted previously, we have

$$E[e(t + 1)|I(M,t)] = 0.$$

Since $S(t)$ is part of one's information set at time t, we have

$$E[.4\ S(t)|I(M,t)] = .4\ E[S(t)|I(M,t)] = .4\ S(t).$$

Finally, the term

$$E[.6\ E[S(t + 1)|I(M,t)]|I(M,t)] = .6\ E[S(t + 1)|I(t)]$$

because the expectation of an expectation, conditional on the same information, is just the original expectation. Substituting these results back into equation (7.3), we obtain

$$E[S(t + 1)|I(M,t)] = .6\ E[S(t + 1)|I(M,t)] + .4\ S(t). \tag{7.4}$$

Finally, solving for $E[S(t + 1)|I(M,t)]$ in equation (7.4), we obtain

$$E[S(t + 1)|I(M,t)] = S(t). \tag{7.5}$$

That is, applying the rational expectations approach to the original equation (7.1), we get that the expected spot rate for next period, conditional on $I(M,t)$, is just the current spot rate. Having reached this conclusion on the basis of rational expectations, we can now substitute the conclusion (7.5) back into the original equation (7.1) to obtain:

$$S(t + 1) = .6\ S(t) + .4\ S(t) + e(t + 1)$$
$$= S(t) + e(t + 1). \tag{7.6}$$

In this case, the two assumptions (a) that equation (7.1) describes the movement of exchange rates and (b) that expectations are rational leads to the conclusion that next period's spot rate will not differ in any systematic way from the current spot rate. Next period's spot rate will be this period's spot rate plus a random error term.

■

THE SPECULATIVE EFFICIENCY HYPOTHESIS

One appealing view of the world is the notion that there may be market variables that embody the sum total of the market's information about the future. Suppose that there are N different groups in the market, each with a corresponding information set $I(i,t)$, for $i = 1, 2, \ldots, N$. Meanwhile, the sum total of their information is contained in a "market" information set $I(M,t)$. If there existed market variables that reflected all of $I(M,t)$, then by observing these variables each group would be able to ensure that its information set was identical to the market's total information set: $I(i,t) = I(M,t)$ for all i. For example, suppose it were the case that the forward price $F(t,T)$ was conditional on the current market information set $I(M,t)$, an unbiased predictor of the spot price that would occur at time $t + T$:

$$F(t,T) = E[S(t + T)|I(M,t)]. \tag{7.7}$$

Then by observing $F(t,T)$ everyone could ensure that his private expectation

$$E[S(t + T)|I(i,t)]$$

was identical to that conditional on having the largest information set $I(M,t)$. As a result, everyone would have the same information concerning the future spot rate; everyone would be fully informed.

In particular, because forward contracts involve transactions that will take place at some time in the future, forward prices are often taken to be implicit forecasts. Is it rational to form expectations of future spot rates on the basis of forward rates? The notion that forward (or, alternatively, futures) prices represent expected spot rates relies on the belief that if the current forward rate is less than the expected spot rate,

$$F(t,T) < E[S(t + T)|I(M,t)],$$

speculators will buy forward exchange in unlimited amounts now, in the expectation of making a profit at time $t + T$ by taking delivery of exchange at the forward rate and turning around and selling at the higher spot rate at that time. This process of buying forward exchange will bid up its price until

$$F(t,T) = E[S(t + T)|I(M,t)].$$

A similar story can be told if

$$F(t,T) > E[S(t + T)|I(M,t)].$$

Speculators will sell unlimited amounts of forward exchange until

$$F(t,T) = E[S(t + T)|I(M,t)].$$

Equation (7.7) has been termed the **speculative efficiency hypothesis (SEH)**. The SEH is the proposition that the T-period forward rate is the best unbiased predictor of the spot rate T periods in the future. For example, it assets that the six-month forward exchange rate is the best unbiased predictor of what the spot exchange rate will be on the day the six-month forward rate matures. (If this six-month period is $T = 182$ days, it says that this forward rate is the best unbiased predictor of the spot rate in 182 days.) Alternative propositions to the SEH are that

$$F(t,T) > E[S(t + T)|I(M,t)]$$

(a condition referred to as **contango**), or that

$$F(t,T) < E[S(t + T)|I(M,t)]$$

(**normal backwardation**).

□

Equation (7.7) has also been termed the "efficient market" hypothesis, a term avoided here because it is ambiguous and misleading (LeRoy, 1982).   ■

We will dwell on the SEH at some length because it is an important empirical proposition. First, if it is true, it implies that all market participants have the same information set. Second, there are many corporations that hedge FX risk using the forward market, and thus any systematic divergences between the forward rate and the eventual spot rate would give an estimate of the cost of this hedging procedure. Third, many people subscribe to forecasting services. Since it does not cost anything to observe the forward rate, one would certainly expect that a forecasting service that had a non-zero cost would predict as well as (or not worse than) the forward rate did.

If we subtract the spot rate $S(t)$ from both sides of equation (7.7) and then divide both sides by $S(t)$, we obtain

$$\frac{F(t,T) - S(t)}{S(t)} = \frac{E[S(t + T)|I(M,t)] - S(t)}{S(t)}. \tag{7.8}$$

Written in this form, the SEH says that the forward premium is an unbiased forecast of spot exchange depreciation. To test for unbiasedness we can run the regression equation

$$a + b\frac{F(t,T) - S(t)}{S(t)} + e(t + T) = \frac{S(t + T) - S(t)}{S(t)}, \tag{7.9}$$

where a and b are the coefficients to be estimated and e is an error term. If the SEH is correct, then a should be statistically indistinguishable from 0, while b should be statistically indistinguishable from 1. (A brief review of hypothesis testing with the simple linear regression model is given in the appendix to this chapter.) If the error terms e are drawings from a normal distribution, then the coefficient estimates of a and b, $\hat{a}$ and $\hat{b}$, can—for sufficiently large sample sizes — be treated as drawings from a normal distribution. Thus we can assign a probability of obtaining $\hat{a}$ and $\hat{b}$, given that the SEH is true. If this probability is sufficiently low, we may elect to reject the SEH.

□

There are a number of alternative formulations of the SEH. Some formulations assume a constant liquidity premium, and so do not require that $a = 0$, but do require $b = 1$.   ∎

In a sophisticated multicurrency test of equation (7.9), Bilson (1981) obtained the values $\hat{a} = 3.123$ (± 1.18) and $\hat{b} = .178$ ($\pm .18$), where the numbers in parentheses are the standard errors. This result, which involved weekly observations on nine currencies, enabled him to reject the hypothesis $b = 1$ with a high degree of confidence. That is, it is highly improbable that this estimated value would have occurred if the SEH were empirically true.

On the other hand, he could not — with the same regression results — reject the hypothesis that $b = 0$. That is, he could not rule out the proposition that the percentage discount or premium on forward exchange is entirely unrelated to future changes in the spot exchange rate. This implies that the forward rate $F(t,T)$ does not give any additional information about the future spot rate $S(t + T)$ that is not already contained in the current spot rate $S(t)$, at least for the forward rates that Bilson investigated.

On the basis of these results, Bilson reasoned that one might want to distinguish between discounts or premiums that are "large" (he defined "large" as a discount or premium greater than 10 percent when converted to a yearly rate) and ones that are "small" ("small" was defined as a discount or premium less than 10 percent when converted at a yearly rate). He found evidence that, once the large/small distinction was made, the forward premium or discount did give useful information. In this case, large discounts or premiums went in the wrong direction, suggesting that — if the discount or premium is greater than 10 percent per annum — one should on average bet against the forward rate getting even the direction of exchange rate change correct. For small discounts/premiums, the indicated change was in the right direction, but on average the subsequent depreciation in the spot rate was only about 25 percent of the magnitude of the forward premium.

Similar rejections of the SEH have been found by Hansen and Hodrick (1980), Hodrick and Srivastava (1984), Huang (1984), Korajczyk (1985), and Longworth (1981). The forward exchange market is characterized by contango or normal backwardation and not by speculative efficiency. Thus the forward rate appears to be a generally biased estimate of the future spot rate. What does this rejection tell us about exchange market speculators?

SPECULATOR CHARACTERISTICS

The failure of the forward exchange rate to equal the expected spot rate would appear to be rooted in three speculator characteristics: speculators are not risk-neutral; the information set of speculators is not identical with the full market information set; speculators do not have unlimited wealth. Let us examine each of these characteristics in turn.

Risk Neutrality

Are people willing to take fair bets involving large amounts of money? During the eighteenth century, mathematician Daniel Bernoulli observed that people wouldn't and suggested the reason for this was that an amount of money won was worth less to an individual than the same amount of money lost. For example, suppose that you can — for a fee — participate in the following bet. A fair coin will be flipped. If it comes up heads, you win $20,000. If it comes up tails, you win $0. How much would you pay to enter into the bet? Since the probability of heads is equal to that of tails, the expected winning is .5($20,000) + .5($0) = $10,000. Thus a mathematically fair entry fee to take part in the bet is $10,000, because the expected profit becomes $0 after paying an entry fee of $10,000. Most people, however, will not pay $10,000 to enter into this bet. They may be willing to pay, for example, only $3000. Such behavior is termed *risk-averse*.

If participants in the market are risk-averse there is no reason to expect the forward rate to be equal to the expected spot rate. The forward rate will adjust to clear the market between sellers and buyers of forward exchange, but could differ from the expected spot rate by an amount dependent on market risk aversion. Since there are two sides to an exchange contract, the risk aversions of both the buyers and sellers of forward contracts would be important. Thus the "risk premium" (the difference between $F(t,T)$ and $E[S(t + T)|I(M,t)]$) could be either positive or negative. In addition, it might change over time. Thus a market participant's information set $I(i,t)$ could include knowledge of the forward rate $F(t,T)$, but it would not be true that $F(t,T) = E[(S(t + T)|I(M,t)]$.

Full Information

Even if speculators were not risk-averse, their actions will not drive the forward rate to equality with $E[S(t + T)|I(M,t)]$ if the information set of speculators is not the total market information set $I(M,t)$. As we saw in the preceding section, becoming informed usually involves incurring a cost of acquiring information. Certainly speculators can't just observe the forward rate $F(t,T)$, because — in the story — it is up to them to determine whether $F(t,T)$ is greater than or less than the expected spot rate. So speculators will have to acquire information at a cost. They will do this only up to the point at which the expected cost of further information is equal to the expected benefit.

Wealth Constraints and Ultimate Ruin

In the real world speculators do not have infinite wealth. Wealth limitations impose an important constraint. Even if a speculator is not risk-averse, and even if he has sufficient information to know a fair bet when he sees one, a knowledge of probability will tell him that playing a fair betting game can lead to ultimate ruin if his wealth is limited. As explained in Chapter 5, a game may be fair when viewed as a single coin flip, yet not fair when viewed as a series of coin flips with a stochastic termination point. The probabilities of the game depend on the speculator's capital, among other variables.

Suppose we consider a betting process in which you will win $1 with probability p and lose $1 with probability q (where $q = 1 - p$). You start off with an amount W. If your money drops to zero, the game stops. Your betting partner — the person on the other side of your bet who wins when you lose and loses when you win — has an amount of money R. What is the probability you will eventually lose all of your wealth W, given p and R? From probability theory the answer is (Feller, 1968):

$$\text{Ruin probability} = \frac{(q/p)^{W+R} - (q/p)^W}{(q/p)^{W+R} - 1}, \text{ for } p \neq q$$

(7.10)

$$\text{Ruin probability} = 1 - (W/(W + R)), \text{ for } p = q = .5.$$

EXAMPLE 7.3

You have $10 and your friend has $100. You flip a fair coin. If heads comes up, he pays you $1. If tails comes up, you pay him $1. The game ends when either player runs out of money. What is the probability your friend will end up with all your money? From the second equation in (7.10), we have $p = q = .5$, $W = \$10$, and $R = \$100$. Thus the probability of your losing everything is:

$1 - (10/(10 + 100)) = .909.$

You will lose all of your money with 91 percent probability in this supposedly "fair" game.

For the same reason, if speculators have limited wealth, they may only be willing to take speculative positions in the forward market when they view the odds sufficiently in their favor. This may require large divergences of $F(t,T)$ from $E[S(t + T)|I(M,t)]$.

THE MARTINGALE CHARACTER OF SPOT RATES

If next period's exchange rate is expected to be a constant multiple $(1 + k)$ of this period's exchange rate, given $I(M,t)$,

$$E[S(t + 1)|I(M,t)] = (1 + k) S(t)$$

(7.11)

then the exchange rate $S(t)$ is said to be a **martingale** with drift k.

The notion of a martingale is an important one. There is considerable empirical evidence suggesting that for the major currencies and over short time horizons, spot exchange rates follow a martingale. (See Bilson (1981), Huang (1984), Meese and Rogoff (1983), and Mussa (1979).) Thus, one of the contributions of foreign exchange traders is that, having established a trend k, they proceed to eliminate any predictable variations of the spot exchange rate around this trend.

□

The same is not true for the forward rate. Samuelson (1972) has shown that if the forward rate were equal to the conditional expected spot rate at maturity (that is, if the SEH were true), then the forward rate would be a martingale. The failure of the SEH allows for predictable divergences between forward rates and realized spot rates. ■

☐

APPENDIX TO CHAPTER 7

SIMPLE LINEAR REGRESSION AND STATISTICAL INFERENCE

The simple linear regression equation can be written as

$$y(t) = a + b\,x(t) + u(t).$$

It is assumed that the error terms $u(t)$ are independently normally distributed with mean 0 and variance v. The sample size is n.

Let $SXY = \Sigma(x(t) - \bar{x})(y(t) - \bar{y})$, $SXX = \Sigma(x(t) - \bar{x})^2$, $SYY = \Sigma(y(t) - \bar{y})^2$, where $\bar{x}$ and $\bar{y}$ are the sample means of x and y. Then the coefficient estimators for a and b are:

$$\hat{b} = SXY/SXX \qquad \hat{a} = \bar{y} - \hat{b}\bar{x}.$$

Let $RSS = \Sigma(y(t) - \hat{a} - \hat{b}x(t))^2 = SYY - (SXY)^2/(SXX)$.

1. Then $\hat{a}$ has a normal distribution with mean a and variance

    $$\text{var}(\hat{a}) = v(\,(1/n) + (\bar{x}^2/SXX)\,).$$

2. Then $\hat{b}$ has a normal distribution with mean b and variance

    $$\text{var}(\hat{b}) = v/SXX.$$

3. Then RSS/v has a chi-squared distribution with $n - 2$ degrees of freedom, and $\hat{v} = RSS/(n - 2)$ is an unbiased estimator for v.

4. The standard errors (SE) for $\hat{a}$ and $\hat{b}$ are the same as the standard deviations of $\hat{a}$ and $\hat{b}$, except that $\hat{v}$ is substituted for v (which is unknown):

    $$SE(\hat{a}) = \sqrt{\hat{v}(\,(1/n) + (\bar{x}^2/SXX)\,)}, \ SE(\hat{b}) = \sqrt{\hat{v}/SXX}.$$

5. Then $(\hat{a} - a)/SE(\hat{a})$ and $(\hat{b} - b)/SE(\hat{b})$ have a t-distribution with $n - 2$ degrees of freedom. For large values of n (such as $n > 32$), the t-distribution is approximately the normal distribution. Therefore the probability of the estimators $\hat{a}$ and $\hat{b}$ being within 1, 2, or 3 standard errors of the mean values of a and b are:

	Probability	
$\hat{a} \in (a \pm 1\ SE(\hat{a}))$	.6826	$\hat{b} \in (b \pm 1\ SE(\hat{b}))$
$\hat{a} \in (a \pm 2\ SE(\hat{a}))$	.9544	$\hat{b} \in (b \pm 2\ SE(\hat{b}))$
$\hat{a} \in (a \pm 3\ SE(\hat{a}))$	.9974	$\hat{b} \in (b \pm 3\ SE(\hat{b}))$

6. In hypothesis testing (for example, to test the hypothesis $a = 0$, $b = 1$) we substitute our hypothesized values for a, b in the intervals above and evaluate the probability of having obtained the current sample for these values. ■

PROBLEMS FOR CHAPTER 7

1. Assume an exchange rate evolves according to the equation

    $$S(t + 1) = .5\ E[S(t + 1)|I(M,t)] + .4\ S(t) + e(t + 1).$$

    (a)   Assuming expectations are rational, determine $E[S(t + 1)|I(M,t)]$.

    (b)   Determine the equation by which the exchange rate evolves (that is, the equation written without expectational terms).

    (c)   If the market expectation were

$$E[S(t + 1)|I(M,t)] = S(t),$$

    why would this expectation not be sustained?

    (d)   If over three successive time periods we have

$$e(t + 1) = .05 \ S(t), \ e(t + 2) = -.1 \ S(t), \ e(t + 3) = .02 \ S(t + 2),$$

    determine the market exchange rate for each of these periods using your answer in (b).

2.   A regression equation testing speculative efficiency for a particular currency yields the result

$$S(t + 1) = .08 + .90 \ F(t,1) + e(t + 1)$$
$$(.04) \ (.02),$$

where standard errors are in parentheses. Assume that requirements are met so that we may interpret the coefficient estimates $\hat{a} = .08$, $\hat{b} = .90$ as drawings from a normal distribution and interpret the standard errors as standard deviations.

    (a)   Could we reject the hypothesis $b = 1$? Under what probability criterion?

    (b)   If we assume domestic and foreign interest rates are the same, what does the above regression imply about the drift term k in equation (7.11)?

3.   The value of a tick (.0001) on a DM IMM futures contract is $12.50. Suppose initial margin is $1500 and maintenance margin is $1200. You take a long position in one futures contract and plan to hold the contract until your account balance falls from $1500 to $1200 or until the account balance rises to $3000, whichever comes first.

    (a)   If the probability of an upward tick is .6 and a downward tick is .4, what is the probability that you will end up with $3000? [*Hint:* Pretend you are playing against "the market" and assume the market's initial wealth is $3000 − $1500 = $1500, while your initial wealth is $1500 − $1200 = $300. Translate the dollar amounts into the number of betting units (ticks), and use equation (7.10).]

    (b)   Answer the same question if the probability of upward and downward ticks are equal.

    (c)   Assume the same values as in (a) but assume that tick values are $300. Calculate the probability of ending up with $3000.

    (d)   Comparing your answers in (a) and (c), what conclusions would you draw in general for risk-taking (exposure) in FX risk management? (Consider the limited capital of the firm compared to the size of FX risk exposure.)

PURCHASING POWER PARITY

INTRODUCTION

What determines the level of the spot exchange rate? We saw in Chapter 3 that marketmakers in the interbank market will keep adjusting the level of their bid and ask prices in such a way that they are being hit in equal proportions on their bid and asked sides, except to the extent they may choose deliberately to take speculative positions (Chapter 7) by becoming long or short in their holdings of a particular currency. If a marketmaker's customers are hitting him equally at his current bid and ask prices, the marketmaker's own market is in equilibrium. The supply of foreign currency is equal to the demand for foreign currency at the trader's current prices. Thus the quick answer to our question is: The spot exchange rate is the rate that brings about equality between the supply of and the demand for spot exchange as seen by marketmakers.

But what are the fundamental economic factors that ultimately give rise to this supply and demand, and why do supply and demand factors change over time? To answer this question, we now turn to the different facets of foreign commerce. Foreign commerce includes transactions in goods, services, bank deposits, bonds, and equity between domestic residents and foreigners. Most countries maintain a record of all such transactions they know about. This record is referred to as the *balance on international transactions* or the **balance of payments (BOP)**. The total accounting record that makes up the balance of payments can be viewed as a list of factors giving rise to demand and supply in the FX market.

It is traditional to separate out two general categories of FX supply and demand: factors relating to goods and services (the **current account**), and those relating to financial assets and ownership (the **capital account**). The present chapter will focus on the first of these two categories. In particular, we will explore the relation between international trade in goods and services and the level of the spot exchange rate. As we shall see, it is a two-sided relationship. The exchange rate influences the level of trade, and the level of trade influences the exchange rate.

PURCHASING POWER PARITY

Consider the following chimpanzee economy. In circulation in the chimpanzee economy are blue plastic chips the chimpanzees know can be exchanged for bananas from gullible psychologists. Because of this, the otherwise uninteresting plastic chips are prized in the chimpanzee economy. Prudent chimps hoard chips by carefully concealing them under hemp mats which serve as bedding. Other chimps give chips as gifts to desirable companions in return for various favors. Such an economy is similar to one created by brain researcher Karl Pribram in experiments with chimpanzees during the 1950s. One can draw the obvious conclusion: any chimpanzee knows that the value of money is found in what you can trade it for.

Suppose we extend this economy a bit and do an experiment Karl Pribram didn't do. We introduce two types of plastic chips: small blue ones that trade for one banana, and big red ones that trade for two bananas. Clever chimps, if they think like the economist Gustav Cassel, will reason as follows: two blue chips give me the same number of bananas as one red chip, namely two bananas. Therefore two blue chips have the same value as one red chip. Therefore the exchange rate between blue chips and red chips should be 2 blue chips = 1 red chip. Certainly a clever chimp would never accept less than two blues for each red, since she knows that a gullible psychologist will give her two bananas for each red chip, but only one for each blue chip. Only dumber, unevolved chimps will fail to make the proper calculations.

Chimpanzees acting in this manner will have created **purchasing power parity (PPP)**. The basic idea of the purchasing power parity, in its different formulations, is that different currencies represent purchasing power over goods and services. The exchange rate adjusts to keep purchasing power constant. This adjustment will occur through commodity arbitrage. If, for example, the market will only give a chimp 1.9 blue chips for one red chip, the chimp will trade her red chip directly for two bananas and then buy two blue chips, paying one banana each. With her blue chips, she will now buy cheap red chips at the market exchange rate of 1.9 blue chips = 1 red chip, and repeat the process, all with the help of the gullible psychologist. With each transaction she gains .1 blue chip, and if the market exchange rate does not change, she will eventually own all chips in the economy. Presumably other primates will catch on before that happens and change the exchange rate.

There is, of course, an alternative to exchange rate adjustment that would prevent the chimp from becoming a millionaire before the age of four. The gullible psychologist could have wised up and started giving out only 1.9 bananas for each red chip. If so, this would be an example in which prices adjusted to the exchange rate rather than vice versa. PPP does not necessarily imply any direction of causality between price adjustments and exchange rate adjustments. It could happen either way.

☐

The causality issue here is important. It is sometimes stated on the basis of purchasing power concepts that an exchange rate is "over-" or "undervalued." A priori, such statements have no more validity than the assertion that domestic or foreign prices are "too high" or "too low."   ■

THE LAW OF ONE PRICE

The simplest concept of PPP is the so-called *law of one price,* which says that bananas will cost the same whether purchased directly with red chips or whether the red chips are first converted to blue chips at the going rate of exchange and the blue chips then used to purchase bananas. Let $S(t)$ be the current exchange rate (the domestic currency price of foreign exchange), and $P(i,t)$ and $P^*(i,t)$ the current domestic and foreign (*) currency prices of commodity i. Then the law of one price says

$$P(i,t) = S(t)\, P^*(i,t), \text{ for any commodity } i. \tag{8.1}$$

EXAMPLE 8.1

Gold in New York is trading for $400 per ounce, while in London the price is £250 per ounce. Then the law of one price implies

$400 = S(t)\, £250$

or that

$S(t) = \$1.60/£.$

This proposition has strong intuitive appeal. It also involves a lot of hidden assumptions that make it somewhat less than a law of nature or even sufficiently well defined to be easily testable empirically.

1. The first assumption is that there are no transactions costs involved in buying a commodity in one market and selling it in another. This, of course, is not true in the real world. So for the "law of one price" (LOP) to have any empirical content, it must be adjusted to say that (8.1) holds within a margin given by transactions costs. For some commodities, say for similar futures contracts available simultaneously at the IMM in Chicago and LIFFE in London, the transactions costs are so small that the proposition still holds considerable theoretical interest once we modify it to include transactions costs. That is, the transactions costs are not so large that arbitrage would be ruled out over all reasonable ranges of price deviation. On the other hand, in cases where transactions costs are large, the LOP may be meaningless as an empirical proposition. For illustration, recall that the interest parity theorem holds up well empirically because interbank traders use it to set the forward rate. They do so because if they did not set prices according to the interest parity theorem, other banks could arbitrage against them if their prices deviated from parity more than the small amount allowable by bid/ask spreads. On the other hand, if the zloty price of coal in Poland multiplied by the cruzeiro price of zlotys differs from the cruzeiro price of coal in Brazil, there is an arbitrage possibility only after the costs of shipping coal from Poland to Brazil (or vice versa) have been taken into account. Coal, unlike money, does not exist as an accounting entry in a computerized data bank, and so cannot be transferred electronically at the speed of light and at very low cost. If transactions costs are very large in comparison to the value of the

underlying commodity, then it makes little sense to appeal to a "law" of one price. One might just as well appeal to a law of large transactions costs.

2. A second condition for the LOP to hold in a rational market is that there be no barriers to trade. This would include prohibitions on trade (for example, certain countries may be blacklisted by the local government, or trade in certain items—ranging from machine guns to laser technology—may be proscribed); tariffs, taxes, and quotas that may apply differentially to a good in different countries; and exchange controls of all sorts that might prevent the exchange rate from adjusting to the market price that would prevail under free exchange. To the extent that such barriers could be quantified, (8.1) would have to be adjusted to include their effects wherever they exist.

3. A third, perhaps obvious, point is that we must be comparing homogeneous goods. There is no reason to expect (8.1) to hold if $P^*(i,t)$ is the price of a barrel of Saudia Arabian light crude while $P(i,t)$ is the price of a barrel of West Texas intermediate crude. They both represent barrels of oil, but not homogeneous goods.

THE ABSOLUTE VERSION OF PURCHASING POWER PARITY

The *absolute* version of PPP postulates a relationship similar to (8.1), except that it uses price levels instead of particular commodity prices. Let $w(i)$ be the weight of good i in the domestic economy, and let $w^*(i)$ be the weight of good i in the foreign economy. The *price levels* of the domestic and foreign countries are, respectively, defined as

$$P(t) = \sum_i w(i) P(i,t)$$
$$P^*(t) = \sum_i w^*(i) P^*(i,t).$$

Note that $P(t)$ and $P^*(t)$ are price levels, and *not* price indexes. Each domestic price $P(i,t)$ is measured in, say, dollar terms, so $P(t)$ is measured in dollars. Each price $P^*(i,t)$ of a foreign good is measured in, say, French franc terms, so $P^*(t)$ is measured in French francs. Then the absolute version of purchasing power parity states:

$$P(t) = S(t) P^*(t). \tag{8.2}$$

EXAMPLE 8.2

Suppose the average price of a good in the U.S. economy is $3000. That is, $P(t) =$ $3000. Meanwhile, the average price of a good in the French economy is FF24,000. $P^*(t) =$ FF24,000. Then, according to absolute PPP,

$3000 = S(t)$ FF24,000

or

$S(t) = \$.125/FF.$

What are the conditions necessary for absolute PPP to hold? We can see by comparing (8.2) with (8.1) that *if the law of one price holds for each good i, then* *absolute PPP holds if the weights of each good in the domestic and foreign economies are the same:* i.e., if $w(i) = w^*(i)$, for all goods i. This means that if weights are not the same for all goods, then absolute PPP may not hold, even if the LOP holds for each good individually.

EXAMPLE 8.3

Consider the following two hypothetical economies:

Economy A		Economy B	
Goods (units)	Price ($/unit)	Goods (units)	Price (¥/unit)
4 gold	1	20 gold	200
20 wheat	2	11 wheat	400
6 oil	2	1 oil	400

The current exchange rate is ¥200 = $1. Does the absolute version of PPP hold between these economies?

First notice that the LOP holds for each of the three goods, since the ratio of prices in each case is equal to the exchange rate. The exchange rate is ¥200/$ and also

¥200/$1 = ¥400/$2 = ¥400/$2 = ¥200/$.

In order to check absolute PPP, we must first calculate the price levels for each economy. In order to calculate the price level, we weight the price of each good by its share in the economy. The dollar value of the goods in Economy A is

4($1) + 20($2) + 6($2) = $56.

The share of gold in Economy A is 4($1)/$56. The share of wheat is 20($2)/$56. The share of oil is 6($2)/$56. Thus the price level in Economy A is

$P(A) = (4(\$1)/\$56)(\$1) + (20(\$2)/\$56)(\$2) + (12(\$2)/\$56)(\$2) = \$1.928.$

In a similar fashion, we calculate the price level of Economy B as

$P(B) = (20(¥200)/¥8800)(¥200) + (11(¥400)/¥8800)(¥400)$
$+ (1(¥400)/¥8800)(¥400) = ¥309.09.$

Given the price levels $P(A) = \$1.928$ and $P(B) = ¥309.09$, we then use equation (8.2) to obtain

$P(B)/P(A) = ¥309.09/\$1.928 = ¥160.32/\$1,$

which is *not* equal to the exchange rate ¥200/$1. Hence absolute PPP does not hold, due to the fact that the two economies have a different composition of goods, even though the LOP holds for each of these goods individually.

RELATIVE VERSION OF PURCHASING POWER PARITY

As a practical consideration, price levels are seldom if ever calculated. Calculation of a price level would require observation of all prices and all quantities in the economy—a very costly endeavor. Countries therefore typically calculate a variety of price *indexes.* Instead of taking the prices of all goods and services in the economy and calculating a weighted average, a country will take a sampling of the prices of a small subset of the economy's goods. Then an index—such as the GNP deflator or the consumer price index (CPI)—is calculated based on the sample. This index number has no meaning in itself. It is not, for example, denominated in terms of the domestic currency. Rather, the index number is measured as a pure number relative to a base year, and the base-year number is usually set at 100 for the year in which the current list of goods to be sampled was first chosen. If the representative bundle of goods costs $10.43 in the base year while it costs $11.06 in the second year, then the first year's index is 100 while the second year's index is

$$(\$11.06/\$10.43)\,100 = 106.04.$$

For the same reasons that price indexes, not price levels, are tabulated in practice, in practice people do not make absolute PPP calculations, but instead appeal to *relative purchasing power parity.* Relative PPP involves looking at price index ratios.

Let us extend our use of $P(t)$ and $P^*(t)$ at this point to denote price indexes as well as price levels. The difference will be that $P(t)$ as a price level will be in units of the domestic currency and include all goods and services while $P(t)$ as an index will be a pure number and include only a subset of all goods and services. Then *relative* PPP postulates:

$$\frac{P(t+T)}{P(t)} = \frac{S(t+T)}{S(t)}\frac{P^*(t+T)}{P^*(t)}, \tag{8.3}$$

where t is one date and $t + T$ is a later date.

EXAMPLE 8.4

Between the end of December 1978 and the end of December 1979 the dollar price of DM went from $.53217/DM to $.57671/DM. Meanwhile the U.S. CPI went from 195.4 to 217.4 and the German CPI went from 160.2 to 166.6. Suppose we postulate that relative PPP holds when consumer price indexes are used in equation (8.3). Then using five of these variables, we can substitute into equation (8.3) and solve for the sixth. If we solve for $S(t + T)$, then, since

$$S(t + T) = S(t)\,\frac{P(t+T)/P(t)}{P^*(t+T)/P^*(t)}$$

we have

$$S(t + T) = \$.53217/DM\,\frac{217.4/195.4}{166.6/160.2} = \$.56934/DM.$$

The calculated rate of $.56934/DM is somewhat less than the actual market rate of $.57671/DM. In this case, however, the calculated value for $S(t + T)$ is in the right direction, and it is of the same order of magnitude as the calculated value from relative PPP.

Relative PPP may hold in circumstances where absolute PPP does not. For example, the formulation of equation (8.3) compensates for the fact that two economies may not have the same composition of goods.

EXAMPLE 8.5

In Example 8.3 we saw a case where absolute PPP did not hold between Economy A and Economy B. Suppose that all prices double in the two economies of Example 8.3 but the spot exchange rate remains unchanged. Does relative PPP hold?

Recalculating the prices levels of Economies A and B with doubled prices for all goods yields $P(A) = \$3.856$ and $P(B) = ¥618.18$. In terms of an index, if the price index in Economy A was at 100 in the original time period, it is now at 200. Or, what is equivalent, if the original index was at 1.928, it is now at 3.856. Similarly, in Economy B the index goes from 309.09 to 618.18. Thus equation (8.3) implies

$$S(t + T)/S(t) = (3.856/1.928)/(618.18/309.09) = 1,$$

or that $S(t + T) = S(t)$. Since the actual exchange rate is also still at its original level, relative PPP holds.

On the other hand, relative PPP cannot be expected to hold, even if the LOP holds, if *relative* prices change. This is illustrated in the following example.

EXAMPLE 8.6

Let the prices in Economy A and Economy B at time t be those originally given in Example 8.3, while at time $t + T$ the price for oil has increased to \$3 in Economy A and to ¥600 in Economy B. (That is, oil has become more expensive in terms of gold and wheat.) Does relative PPP hold, assuming the exchange rate remains unchanged at ¥200/\$?

The original price levels at time t were previously calculated to be $P(A) = \$1.928$ and $P(B) = ¥309.09$. The new price levels with the changed oil price are:

$$P(A) = (4(\$1)/\$62)(\$1) + (20(\$2)/\$62)(\$2) + (6(\$3)/\$62)(\$3) = \$2.226;$$

$$P(B) = (20(¥200)/¥9000)(¥200) + (11(¥400)/¥9000)(¥400)$$
$$+ (1(¥600)/¥9000)(¥600) = ¥324.44.$$

Dropping the currencies of denomination, the price levels here correspond to price indexes, so we have for relative PPP:

$$S(t + T)/S(t) = (2.226/1.928)/(324.44/309.09) = 1.10.$$

Hence relative PPP implies

$$S(t + T) = (1.10)S(t) = (1.10)(\$1/¥200) = \$.0055/¥ \text{ or } ¥181.82/\$.$$

Since the actual exchange rate is ¥200/\$, relative PPP does not hold, even though LOP holds for each good. This is a consequence of the relative increase in the price of oil in terms of wheat and gold.

RELATIVE RATES OF INFLATION

Relative PPP can be converted into a version using inflation rates. Let μ be the rate of inflation in the domestic country and μ^* the rate of inflation in the foreign country. These rates of inflation are for the time period extending between t and $t + T$. Then, observing that

$$P(t + T)/P(t) = 1 + \mu, \; P^*(t + T)/P^*(t) = 1 + \mu^*,$$

we have from equation (8.3):

$$\frac{S(t + T)}{S(t)} = \frac{1 + \mu}{1 + \mu^*}$$

or, rewritten

$$\frac{S(t + T) - S(t)}{S(t)} = \frac{\mu - \mu^*}{1 + \mu^*}. \tag{8.4}$$

The last equation says that the proportional appreciation or depreciation of the foreign currency depends on whether inflation is higher in, respectively, the domestic or the foreign country.

EXAMPLE 8.7

Suppose that there is inflation in Germany over the course of a year in the amount of 6 percent while there is inflation in France in the amount of 13 percent. Then, interpreting $S(t)$ as the DM price of the FF, we would expect to find on the basis of relative PPP:

$$\frac{S(t + T) - S(t)}{S(t)} = \frac{.06 - .13}{1 + .13} = -.0619.$$

The DM price of the French franc would fall. Over the course of the year the French franc would become 6.19 percent cheaper in terms of the DM.

The above equation should be modified slightly if inflation is not constant or not exactly predictable. In that case, μ and μ^* should be interpreted to be *expected* inflation rates derived from *expected* changes in price levels. This different interpretation is primarily important when an inflation rate is random with a large variation. In that case, expected and actual inflation may differ by significant amounts.

□

Equation (8.4) is sometimes combined with interest parity in the following manner. The difference in interest rates is said to equal the difference in inflation (or expected inflation) rates, because "real" interest rates are the same everywhere. That is, (nominal) interest rates are divided up by the *Fisher equation* into the sum of the rate of inflation (μ, μ^*) and a "real" component (β, β^*) that represents the return to capital in the absence of inflation:

$$i = \beta + \mu$$
$$i^* = \beta^* + \mu^*.$$

The difference between the (nominal) interest rate and *expected* inflation is referred to as the *ex ante* real rate, while the difference between the (nominal) interest rate and *actual* inflation is called the *ex post* real interest rate.

If the real interest rate is the same in both the domestic and foreign country, $\beta = \beta^*$, it follows that $\mu - \mu^*$ in equation (8.4) is the same as $i - i^*$. That is, the rate of depreciation of the spot rate is roughly equal to the difference in interest rates. (If all variables are measured in continuous time, this approximate equality can be converted to an exact equality.) Furthermore, since the premium on forward exchange is approximately equal (exactly equal in continuous time) to the difference in interest rates by interest parity, it follows that the premium on forward exchange represents the expected rate of depreciation of the spot rate.

This combination of concepts is objectionable on several grounds. First, it combines a well-defined market arbitrage relationship (interest parity) with a crude macroeconomic simplification (purchasing power parity). Second, it requires the assumption that the real return to capital (the real interest rate) is everywhere the same. Most current evidence contradicts that assumption. Theoretical models indicate that real interest rates should vary across countries and across time. [See Dornbusch (1983), Fama and Farber (1979), Hansen and Hodrick (1983), Solnik (1973), and Stulz (1981).] Empirical tests constructed so that their power is high have also rejected the hypothesized equality of real eurocurrency rates across countries. [See Cumby and Obstfeld (1981) and Mishkin (1984).] ∎

THE REAL EXCHANGE RATE

Does empirical violation of PPP matter? It may matter a great deal to those engaged in international commerce. Consider, for example, the case of an industrial plant whose energy supply comes from imported oil. Oil will usually be priced in U.S. dollar terms. Suppose the dollar appreciates in value 10 percent with respect to the local currency. The industrial plant's fuel bill has now increased 10 percent in local currency terms. What are the plant's options? The plant may wish to pass its cost increase on to its final customers, by increasing the price of its product. There may be obstacles, however. If the final price of the plant's product is changed, it may alter demand for the product and reduce the total revenue the plant receives. Alternatively, the plant may attempt to compensate by cutting other costs. Wage costs may be fixed, however, as the plant's workers may have long-term contracts. The plant may wish to substitute other sources of energy, but to do so may take time and may involve fixed investment in equipment of a new technological vintage.

The law of one price, equation (8.1), implies that either the price of the plant's product will be adjusted or else that the exchange rate will adjust back in the other direction, all in such a way that the LOP will be preserved. However, as indicated in the previous paragraph, a complex set of circumstances may dictate that such does not happen. The exchange rate may have moved 10 percent without the local currency price moving at all. If the price of the product in the foreign country has not changed, then the LOP has been violated. And there may be nothing the plant—or anyone else—can do about it in the short run. The change in the exchange rate has had a *real* impact on the industrial plant's profits. Its net income has fallen as a result of the exchange rate-induced rise in energy costs.

Similarly, consider the situation of a U.S. equipment manufacturer who exports to Germany. The supply of and demand for the dollar with respect to the DM in the foreign exchange market is related to a great many more factors than U.S. equipment exports to Germany, so the exchange rate may change in ways totally unrelated to equipment prices in the U.S. and Germany. If so, the competitiveness of the exporter in foreign markets will be affected. The *nominal* changes in the exchange rate may be accompanied by *real* changes, because prices do not adjust in such a way as to totally offset these exchange rate changes.

A Bolivian tin mine in the hyperinflationary summer of 1985 will serve as a final example. U.S. dollars obtained by the sale of tin were supposed to be turned over to the Bolivian government at an official exchange rate of $1 = Bolivian pesos 75,000. But the mine's wage costs were tied to the black market exchange rate. In the black market (the free trade environment of city streets), the exchange ratio was 850,000 pesos per dollar and rising. A comparison of the price of tin in Bolivia and in world markets did not yield the official exchange rate. The tin mine manager was understandably concerned at this violation of PPP.

The *real exchange rate* is a variable defined to represent cases where purchasing power parity does not hold. We will designate the real exchange rate by $R(t)$. There are, in practice, two different ways of quoting real exchange rates, so you must interpret them in line with the source you are using. We will define $R(t)$ in such a way that the following interpretations are appropriate:

$R(t) < 1$: The relative purchasing power of domestic currency over foreign goods has fallen; there has been an improvement in export competitiveness.

$R(t) > 1$: The relative purchasing power of domestic currency over foreign goods has risen; there has been a loss of export competitiveness.

By analogy with equation (8.2), we may define, for price *levels:*

$$R(t) = P(t)/[S(t)P^*(t)], \tag{8.5}$$

while for price *indexes:*

$$R(t + T) = \frac{P(t + T)/P(t)}{[S(t + T)/S(t)][P^*(t + T)/P^*(t)]}. \tag{8.6}$$

If, respectively, absolute and relative PPP hold for the price variables under consideration, then the real exchange rate $R(t) = 1$. Roughly speaking, if the domestic currency depreciates less rapidly than the differential between domestic and foreign inflation, then the real exchange rate will rise, $R(t) > 1$. While if the domestic currency depreciates more rapidly than the differential between domestic and foreign inflation, the real exchange rate will fall, $R(t) < 1$.

EXAMPLE 8.8

Using the data from Example 8.4, we can calculate the change in the real exchange rate of the dollar with respect to the DM over the period December 1978 to December 1979. Using equation (8.6),

$$R(t) = \frac{217.4/195.4}{(.57671/.53217)(166.6/160.2)} = .9872.$$

The value $R(t) = .9872$ implies that the dollar, once converted through the FX market, would not buy as much of a basket of German goods in December 1979 as in December 1978. On the other hand, U.S. consumer goods were cheaper to DM holders in December 1979 than in December 1978, and exporters of such goods to Germany may have seen an increase in their export competitiveness. This interpretation, on the basis of the calculations, assumes of course that it was not changes in *relative* prices of goods (as illustrated in Example 8.6) that caused relative PPP not to hold.

Two final terms involve an extension from the concept of bilateral (two-country) index measures to multilateral (many-country) index measures. The *nominal effective exchange rate* refers to a weighted average of bilateral nominal exchange rates. An index is constructed by weighting each foreign currency by the country's share in the domestic country's foreign trade. For example, if trade with Japan represents 25 percent of U.S. foreign trade, then the exchange rate for the yen is weighted by .25. Thus the nominal effective exchange rate represents how much of a basket of foreign currencies you can get for one unit of the domestic currency. A bigger number, measured relative to a base year, implies that you will get a bigger basket of foreign currency than in the base year. The data given in Table 8.1 are taken from Morgan Guaranty's *World Financial Markets*.

TABLE 8.1
Real and Nominal Effective Exchange Rates

	United States	Canada	Japan	France	Germany	United Kingdom	Switzerland
Nominal Effective Exchange Rates[a]							
1980	90.7	100.4	95.5	106.5	100.0	99.8	95.4
1981	99.5	100.2	105.8	100.4	97.2	102.1	98.3
1982	109.8	99.4	98.6	93.1	102.8	98.1	106.3
1983	114.2	100.8	107.8	87.3	107.6	91.6	111.5
1984	122.4	97.3	113.0	84.4	107.4	88.1	110.5
1985							
March	136.8	93.2	111.3	83.7	106.0	84.0	105.9
August	124.0	92.8	113.6	86.3	108.7	91.4	112.2
Real Effective Exchange Rates[b]							
1980	89.4	99.6	103.0	102.1	103.5	99.8	98.7
1981	100.6	100.0	104.6	100.2	97.3	102.3	98.8
1982	109.9	100.4	92.3	97.7	99.2	97.9	102.6
1983	112.6	103.1	96.6	95.9	99.3	92.0	105.3
1984	118.1	101.2	97.6	96.4	96.5	89.2	102.0
1985							
March	130.2	97.8	94.5	96.8	95.0	86.9	97.7
August	117.8	97.5	93.7	103.0	95.5	94.7	99.5

[a] Index numbers, 1980–1982 average = 100. Each index shows a currency's trade-weighted appreciation or depreciation measured against 15 other currencies, using averages of daily noon spot exchange rates in New York and bilateral trade weights based on 1980 trade in manufactures. Annual figures are calendar-year averages.

[b] Index numbers, 1980–1982 average = 100. Each index is the corresponding nominal effective exchange rate adjusted for differential inflation in wholesale prices of nonfood manufacturers. Underlying price data are partly estimated.

Source: Morgan Guaranty, *World Financial Markets*.

Morgan Guaranty's index is set at 100 for the 1980–1982 base period. For example, the nominal effective exchange rate for the U.S. is at 136.8 in March 1985. Compared to the base-period index of 100, this number indicates that the U.S. dollar would buy 36.8 percent more foreign currency in March 1985 than in the base period of 1980–1982.

The *real effective exchange rate* is just a multilateral version of the real exchange rate. Changes in bilateral real exchange rates are weighted by a foreign country's share of trade with the domestic country. So the real effective exchange rate measures how much of a basket of foreign goods you can get for one unit of domestic currency. A bigger number relative to a base year implies you will get a bigger basket of foreign goods with the domestic currency than in the base year. For example, as measured in Table 8.1, the real effective exchange rate for the U.S. dollar in March 1985 was 130.2. This indicates that the U.S. dollar would buy 30.2 percent more foreign goods than in the base period. That is, you would get 36.8 percent more foreign currency in March 1985 but that foreign currency would only buy 30.2 percent more foreign goods.

An alternative measure of nominal and real effective exchange rate changes is given in Figure 8.1, which is taken from the 1985 *Economic Report of the President.* The chart indicates that from 1980 to the end of 1984, the U.S. dollar's real effective exchange rate rose by approximately 60 percent. This was only slightly less than the increase in the nominal effective exchange rate. That is, a

FIGURE 8.1
Nominal and real effective exchange rates as calculated by the U.S. Council of Economic Advisors. [*Source:* U.S., *Economic Report of the President* (1985).]

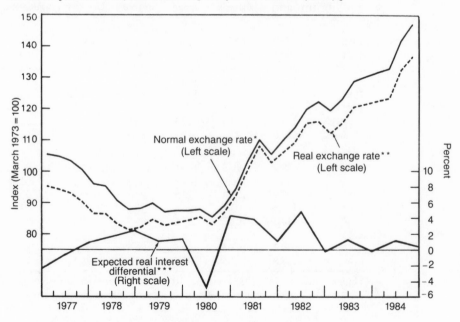

*Multilateral trade-weighted dollar
**Nominal exchange rate adjusted by relative consumer prices
***U.S. interest rate (3-month) minus trade-weighted average interest rate (also 3-month)
for six industrial countries adjusted by corresponding OECD inflation forecasts

change in the dollar's nominal exchange rate translated almost one-for-one into a change in the real exchange rate. Hence, for some ecnomic units, a change in the dollar's nominal exchange rate translated directly into a change in competitiveness.

EMPIRICAL EVIDENCE AND THEORETICAL REFORMULATION

PPP calculations are widely used in policy formation. Central banks have relied on PPP calculations in establishing par values for their currencies. Others may appeal to PPP to pronounce even market-determined rates as "overvalued" or "undervalued." For example, throughout the year 1983, many observers declared that the U.S. dollar was overvalued and that it would soon fall in the FX market. Apparently these observers were not in the market selling dollars, for the dollar continued to rise in value. But what they *said* was based largely on calculations such as those embodied in equation (8.6). They assumed that there should be a tendency for $R(t)$ to return to $R(t) = 1$. One of the arguments is that barriers to trade tend to erode over time, as individuals and companies find ways to get around them. But the argument is flawed to the extent that it assumes that all LOP deviations are the result of trade barriers.

Few people would argue with the fact that international trade does take place in the real world. In order for trade to flow from one destination to another, there has to be a price differential sufficient to pay shipping, capital, insurance, and other costs. That means that the "law of one price" can never hold in unidirectional trade from one location to another. Price differentials must exist in order to motivate trade, and they must *persist* in order for unidirectional trade to persist. These price differentials are consistent both with commodity market equilibrium and with the absence of commodity arbitrage opportunities. The shipment of oil from the Middle East to Japan implies that delivered oil in Japan commands a higher price than does the same oil at Kharg Island in the Persian Gulf. This higher price compensates the shipper and allows the shipper to earn a normal economic profit. There is no necessary reason the price of oil in Japan should *ever* equal the price at Kharg Island. Nor should we expect a "long-run" tendency for prices to adjust between the two locations. Thus it is not surprising that studies such as Isard (1977), Kravis and Lipsey (1978), Protopapadakis and Stoll (1982), and Richardson (1978) find large and persistent deviations from the "law" of one price, which is the least problematical version of PPP. As customarily formulated, PPP is not a necessary consequence of economic rationality.

Roll (1979) has indicated, however, that normal economic maximizing behavior implies that the real exchange rate $R(t)$ [see equation (8.6)] is a martingale without drift:

$$E[R(t + T)|I(M,t)] = R(t). \tag{8.7}$$

Given the current market information set $I(M,t)$, real exchange rate changes should not be predictable if the available information is used efficiently. For example, referring back to Table 8.1, if we assume that the real effective exchange rate changes for the U.S. dollar are not simply the product of measurement error or statistical jerry-rigging, then what is implied by equation (8.7) is that the change in the index from 1982 to 1983 ($114.2 - 109.8 = 3.4$) was not predictable based on the information that was available in 1982. The intuition behind equation (8.7) is that the current level of the real exchange rate $\overset{\prime}{R}(t)$ embodies the costs of trade and does not imply commodity arbitrage possibilities. But if real exchange rate *changes* were predictable, one could engage in successful commodity speculation.

□

As noted in Chapter 7, however, there may be costs to acquiring information, which would induce a modification in equation (8.7). Since the collection of information is a costly enterprise, those who invest in information should also find occasional speculative opportunities sufficient to justify the cost of their research. Be that as it may, there is a good bit of evidence that says that real exchange rates, as commonly measured, are martingales. See Adler and Lehmann (1982), Darby (1982), Rogalski and Vinso (1977), and Roll (1979). Further discussion can be found in Shapiro (1983) and Adler and Dumas (1983).

■

Empirical tests of equation (8.7) have been generally supportive (see references above). On the other hand, tests of (8.1)–(8.4) have generally rejected PPP as formulated in those equations except over long-run time horizons. Most people will not find the empirical rejection of equations (8.1)–(8.4) surprising, since they may have experienced "bargain countries" as tourists as well as "expensive countries." The purchasing power of their currency was found to vary from place to place and over time. In this context, equation (8.7) may be formulated as the *Tourist Theorem:* the best forecast of next season's bargain country is this season's bargain country. The usefulness of this theorem depends on the variance of the forecast errors $e(t + T)$, where

$$e(t + T) = R(t + T) - R(t) \tag{8.8}$$

and

$$E[e(t + T)|I(M,t)] = 0.$$

That is, if the error variance were large, then even if we correctly expected no change in the real exchange rate, there would be considerable risk that we could be wrong.

The implication of this evidence is that, under freely floating exchange rates, the current real exchange rate should be taken to represent long-run market equilibrium, given current information. From (8.7), a change in the real exchange rate at time t would *not* imply a change in the opposite direction at time $t + 1$. Meanwhile, if empirical data show that any of equations (8.1)–(8.4) are violated, then the size of the violation could be used as a guide indicating the magnitude of transactions or transport costs, the degree of uncertainty, the presence of barriers to trade, or the existence of measurement or statistical error.

Current deviations from the LOP (equation (8.1)) can be used by producers as a forecast of future deviations, since by equation (8.7) these deviations would not be expected to change. Hence, deviations from the LOP could be used as a guide to plant location, based on differences in local costs of inputs to the production process. There will be risk, however, depending on the variance of the errors in (8.8).

EXAMPLE 8.9

The following excerpt from *Business Week* reports on a company decision that reflects an application of equation (8.7):

Beckman Instruments Inc., a medical and laboratory-equipment subsidiary of Smith-Kline Beckman Corp., recently moved the production of two product lines sold overseas from the U.S. to plants in Europe. "With a strong dollar today, it makes absolute sense to have overseas manufacturing," says Mr. Michael T. O'Neill, director of international operations for Beckman's bioanalytical-systems group. "We're looking to expand operations in Ireland and Scotland." He has good reason: Some of the parts Beckman buys from suppliers in Europe cost 33 percent less than what U.S. suppliers charge for the same parts. Says O'Neill: "It is a permanent shift."

—October 8, 1984

PROBLEMS FOR CHAPTER 8

1. Suppose the inflation version of relative PPP holds true in terms of the U.S. dollar price of EMS currencies.
   (a) Explain the proportional change in the U.S.$/ECU rate in terms of the proportional change in the U.S. dollar prices of the individual EMS currencies.
   (b) Answer the same question for the French franc/ECU exchange rate. Why do the two answers differ?

2. For this problem and the next, assume that the stated price indexes are truly representative of purchasing power (i.e., transactions costs do not bias the calculations, and there are no changes in the relative prices of the individual goods that compose the index). Between the end of the first quarter and the end of the fourth quarter in 1979, the U.S. price index went from 207.0 to 227.6, while the Japanese price index went from 254.0 to 267.6. Meanwhile, the U.S. dollar price of the yen went from .0048470 to .0041613. Explain what the impact was on
   (a) U.S. exporters to Japan and
   (b) Japanese consumers of U.S. goods.

3. Below are data from the U.S. and Chile for the years 1975–1980.

	1975	1976	1977	1978	1979	1980
Peso/dollar	8.5	17.4	28.0	34.0	39.0	39.0
Chile CPI	100	312	599	838	1118	1511
U.S. CPI	161.2	170.5	181.5	195.4	271.4	257.0

   (a) Based on these data, would you argue that the peso is over- or undervalued at the end of 1980?
   (b) What would you guess concerning Chile's current account?

4. The expected yearly inflation rate is 4 percent in the United States and 2 percent in Switzerland. The current exchange rate is SF 2.3/$. Assuming that the inflation version of relative purchasing power parity holds, what is the expected exchange rate in one year?

5. Two countries, A and B, have economies with the following compositions of goods and prices:

Economy A		Economy B	
Units	Price/unit	Units	Price/unit
1.5 oil	$20	3 oil	DM80
1 wheat	$10	4 wheat	DM60

The market exchange rate is DM 4/$1.
(a) Does the law of one price hold?
(b) Does absolute purchasing power parity hold?
(c) If all prices double in Economy A, and the exchange rate moves to DM 2/$1, does relative purchasing parity hold?

6. Evidence that real exchange rates are a martingale without drift suggests all of the following *except* [choose one]:
   a. The best forecast of next year's bargain country is this year's bargain country.
   b. The elimination or lessening of barriers to trade is a process that is not generally forecastable.
   c. Real exchange rate changes do not typically imply opportunities for commodity arbitrage.
   d. If real exchange rates are measured with statistical error, such measurement errors are not generally forecastable.
   e. There is a natural tendency for the real exchange rate to return to its initial value.

FOREIGN EXCHANGE RATES AND THE BALANCE OF PAYMENTS

THE BALANCE ON INTERNATIONAL TRANSACTIONS

In Chapter 8 we looked at possible relationships between the prices of goods and the foreign exchange rate. The notion of commodity arbitrage, even though it provides some intuitive insight, does not succeed in clarifying the relation of foreign exchange supply and demand to more fundamental economic forces. In particular, government policy, national consumption and savings, and the accumulation and allocation of financial assets are all variables having a direct impact on the exchange rate. It would seem desirable to deal with these variables explicitly and not just through their implicit impact on commodity prices. This consideration leads us to the balance of payments.

The accounting record of all of a country's commercial transactions with respect to the rest of the world is called *the balance on international transactions* or, more commonly, *the balance of payments.* The balance of payments (BOP) is divided into two principal divisions: the *current account,* which is the record of all purchases and sales of goods and services with respect to the rest of the world, and the *capital account,* which represents the flows of financial assets — either bought and sold outright, or in payment for goods and services. Many, but not all, of these transactions involve the foreign exchange market. Imported or exported goods will usually be priced in terms of a foreign currency on at least one side of the transaction, and sometimes the currency of denomination of trade will be foreign to both countries. (*Countertrade,* the direct barter of goods between countries, is a notable exception that circumvents the financial markets altogether.) Similarly, foreign currency transactions are involved when financial assets are bought and sold, or borrowed and lent, across national boundaries.

The term "balance of payments" is commonly abused in conversation, financial publications, and newspapers. Sometimes the term will be used to refer to the entire accounting balance sheet, and sometimes it will be used in reference to a particular item on the balance sheet, such as the current account balance or capital account balance or reserves balance. In addition, it will appear often in phrases like "balance of payments problems" — which could be construed to mean a variety of things, including the possibility the speaker or writer does not know what he's talking about and is just throwing out political or economic buzzwords. One should take care to determine what, if anything, is actually meant in a particular context.

Items recorded on the BOP balance sheet are classified into *accounts* according to the *type* of transaction. A typical balance sheet will have accounts for the yearly flow of goods and services, the yearly flow of capital, and the yearly changes in official reserves. In addition, transactions within each account will be given plus signs if they represent ways of getting money ("sources of funds") or minus signs if they represent ways of spending money ("uses of funds"). Sources of funds include exports of goods and services, sales of financial assets to foreigners, and foreign borrowing. Uses of funds include importing goods and services, purchases of financial assets, and foreign lending. By the principles of double-entry bookkeeping, sources and uses always match. The dollar amount of plus items equals the dollar amount of minus items. The sum of all items is thus zero. In order to get a non-zero amount (a "surplus" or a "deficit"), you have to leave something out.

THE CURRENT ACCOUNT

Let us begin our discussion with the *balance on current account* (*CA*). This is an accounting measure of the total domestic currency value of exports of goods and services (*X*) over a period of time, minus the total domestic currency value of imports of goods and services (*M*) over the same time period:

$$CA = X - M. \tag{9.1}$$

The current account is typically divided into three subcategories: the merchandise trade balance, the services balance, and the balance on unilateral transfers. *Merchandise trade* refers to physical goods like automobiles, oil, machinery, coffee, and beef. *Services* include interest payments, shipping and insurance, tourism, dividends, and military expenditures. **Unilateral transfers** are gifts, such as foreign or military aid, or money sent by immigrant workers in the host country to the folks back home. In each of these three categories, items will be given a plus sign if they are sources of funds (export of goods, provision of tourist services, receipt of transfer payments from abroad), or a minus sign if they are uses of funds (imports of goods, taking foreign trips, sending money home). The sum of all plus and minus items in a category is the "balance," which will be positive if the amount of plus items is greater than of minus items, and negative otherwise. The sum of the merchandise trade balance, the services balance, and the unilateral transfers balance is the current account balance.

Table 9.1 gives current account balances for the United States and West Germany for several recent years. We see that, for example, the United States has large deficits on the merchandise trade balance (− $36.469 billion in 1982), while West Germany has large surpluses (+ DM 52.445 billion in 1982). On the other hand, the United States has large surpluses on the services balance (+ $35.328 billion in 1982), while West Germany has large deficits (− DM 16.289 billion in 1982). Both countries have deficit balances on unilateral transfers. It is important to keep in mind that the merchandise trade balance has no unique implication

TABLE 9.1
Current Account Balances for the United States and West Germany.

	United States ($ millions)				West Germany (DM millions)			
	Merchandise trade	Services	Unilateral transfers	Current account	Merchandise trade	Services	Unilateral transfers	Current account
1980	−25,512	34,487	−7,077	1,898	8,901	−12,898	−24,544	−28,541
1981	−28,001	41,128	−6,833	6,294	28,551	−16,380	−26,864	−14,693
1982	−36,469	35,328	−8,058	−9,199	52,445	−16,289	−28,089	8,067
1983	−61,055	28,143	−8,651	−41,563	47,713	−10,195	−27,011	10,507
1984	−108,281	18,163	−11,414	−101,532	53,460	−4,039	−31,614	17,807

Sources: U.S., *Economic Report of the President;* Deutsche Bundesbank, *Monthly Report.*

for the foreign exchange rate. The merchandise trade balance is widely reported in the media in the United States and is frequently referred to as the "trade balance." But actually merchandise trade is only part of total trade. A dollar's worth of foreign exchange earned in exporting goods is no different from a dollar's worth of foreign exchange earned in the provision of services. In terms of supply and demand for foreign exchange, merchandise trade is no more important than any other kind of trade.

As we saw in the last chapter, export competitiveness, as well as the purchasing power of the domestic currency over imported goods, is affected by the real exchange rate $R(t)$. Therefore we can write the CA flow at any particular time as a function of the real exchange rate at that time:

$$CA = CA[R(t)]. \tag{9.2}$$

Generally speaking — looking at the feedback of exchange rate influences on the current account — with a higher real exchange rate we would expect fewer exports and more imports, while a lower real exchange rate would imply more exports and fewer imports. Conversely — looking at the feedback of the current account on the exchange rate — if the CA is negative (a deficit), adjustment of the balance to zero would usually require the real exchange rate to fall, while if the CA is positive (a surplus), adjustment of the balance to zero would usually require the real exchange rate to rise. Whether there is any tendency for the CA to adjust to zero depends on other factors (such as the desire to accumulate or sell foreign assets, discussed below).

The explanation in the previous paragraph focused on the relation between the real exchange rate and competitiveness in international trade in goods and services. By broadening our focus somewhat, we can see that the real exchange rate will in turn depend on the underlying savings and investment behavior of the national population. Consider the standard GNP identity

$$Y = C + I + G + CA[R(t)] \tag{9.3}$$

where Y is national income, C is consumption spending, I is private-investment spending, and G is government spending. Rewriting and subtracting total national taxes T from each side of the equation, we obtain

$$Y - C - T = I + G - T + CA[R(t)].$$

The expression $Y - C - T$ represents total *after-tax private savings*. Denote this by S. The expression $G - T$ is the *government deficit*. Thus, as a GNP accounting identity,

$$CA[R(t)] = S - [I + (G - T)]. \tag{9.4}$$

This is an identity, so it will always hold in equilibrium. That is, in ex post economic equilibrium, *the current account balance will identically equal the excess of private after-tax saving over the sum of private investment spending and the government deficit*. This shows that the level of the real exchange rate $R(t)$ is related to the consumption/savings decision, and the desire to invest. If, in economic equilibrium, after-tax savings is not sufficient to finance both private investment and the government deficit, then the current account will be in deficit. Conversely, to *reduce a current account deficit* (or to cause a fall in $R(t)$), one of the following must occur in equilibrium:

1. For a given level of I and $G - T$, private after-tax savings S must be increased.
2. For a given level of S and $G - T$, private investment must fall.
3. For a given level of S and I, the government deficit $G - T$ must be reduced.

Since all of these variables will influence the equilibrium value of the current account $CA[R(t)]$, it follows that they will influence, and be influenced by, the real exchange rate $R(t)$. The real exchange rate in turn will change as the nominal exchange rate $S(t)$ changes, to the extent that economic equilibrium does not imply completely offsetting price changes.

THE CAPITAL ACCOUNT

The *capital account* is an accounting measure of the total domestic currency value of financial transactions between domestic residents and the rest of the world over a period of time. It includes financial transactions associated with international trade as well as flows associated with portfolio shifts involving the purchase of foreign stocks, bonds, and bank deposits. Leaving aside counter-trade, every international transaction that gives rise to a current account entry also gives rise to a capital account entry. For example, a payment for $10,000,000 of Brazilian steel will involve a minus item of $10,000,000 being recorded in the merchandise trade part of the current account, while a plus item of $10,000,000 ("capital inflow") will be recorded in the capital account to represent the transfer of a $10,000,000 bank deposit to Brazil. However, there may be additional transactions that take place independently of the current account. For example, a purchase of $50,000,000 of Swiss franc bonds will involve two capital account entries of $50,000,000 — a negative one to represent the domestic purchase of foreign bonds ("capital outflow") and a positive one to represent the foreign acquisition of the domestic bank deposits that were used to pay for the bonds ("capital inflow").

Since the sum of all plus items and all minus items is zero, it follows that the sum of current account and capital account transactions (leaving nothing out) is zero. A current account surplus equals a capital account deficit. A current account deficit equals a capital account surplus. This means that the *current account surplus or deficit represents a net change in the ownership of foreign assets*.

For example, in 1974 Saudi Arabia was running a current account surplus. Saudi Arabia was earning much more on its oil exports than it was spending on imports. Since it was earning more than it was spending, it was accumulating foreign IOUs, or financial assets, in the form of bank deposits in New York and other places. These bank deposits might, in turn, be transformed into U.S. Treasury bills or eurocurrency deposits in London or real estate in Beverly Hills.

Let FA denote a country's ownership of foreign assets. Since the current account flow over the year gives rise to a positive or negative change in the value of these foreign assets, we may write

$$CA[R(t)] = \Delta FA. \tag{9.5}$$

If the current account is in deficit, $CA < 0$, then the country is either accumulating debt or else running down its current stock of foreign assets. If the current account is in surplus, then the country is either repaying debt or building up its stock of foreign assets. A country that already has a large stock of foreign-asset-denominated wealth can run a current account deficit and draw down its stock of foreign assets without the need for any protracted macroeconomic adjustment. On the other hand, a country that is financing its current account deficit by foreign borrowing can only continue to do so as long as creditors are willing to extend loans to the country.

EXAMPLE 9.1

In the year 1984, the United States ran a large current account deficit, and yet the United States dollar remained very strong in the FX markets. How was this possible? It was easily possible as long as foreigners wished to continue to accumulate dollar assets given the current exchange rate. In fact, foreigners wished to accumulate dollar assets at a rate even faster than represented by the U.S. current account deficit. As a result the dollar improved in value in the FX market as foreigners switched directly out of domestic assets and into U.S. dollar assets.

EXAMPLE 9.2

As a country Japan has a high savings rate relative to the rest of the world. Referring back to equation (9.4), this fact implies a large value for after-tax savings S relative to Japan's national income Y. National after-tax savings will be absorbed either in private domestic investment I, or by a government deficit $G - T$, or by a current account surplus $CA > 0$. Thus, depending on I and $G - T$, Japan may run a current account surplus without any change in the real yen exchange rate. That is, one should not necessarily expect to see the value of the yen rise in the FX market and the CA surplus eliminated at an early date. As long as Japan maintains a high savings rate relative to the rest of the world, the current account surplus need not ever be eliminated through exchange rate adjustment. The Japanese desire to save corresponds to a desire to accumulate financial assets. If all saving were done in the form of domestic assets, then risk-adjusted rates of return would be driven down in Japan. Thus, to keep risk-adjusted rates of return equalized, some of the Japanese savings will take the form of the accumulation of foreign assets. A current account surplus would thus correspond to the desire to add to the stock of financial wealth. (On the other hand, Chapter 2 indicated that the rate of return on Japanese domestic assets was in the past kept at an artificially low rate through interest-rate ceilings, a feature apparently stemming from the government's desire to borrow at cheap interest rates. This in turn gives rise to an excess demand for foreign assets.)

THE CAPITAL ACCOUNT AND CENTRAL BANK INTERVENTION

As we saw in Chapter 2, most nations of the world fix or peg their exchange rates to one or more of the major currencies such as the U.S. dollar, the French franc, or the currencies that make up the SDR. In addition, major European currencies are pegged within the bands of the parity grid system of the EMS. And even for currencies like the U.S. dollar, the Japanese yen, the Swiss franc, and the British pound — which are not pegged to any other currency or set of indicators — there is occasional or frequent central bank intervention to influence the market exchange rate.

Central bank intervention creates a link between the BOP balance sheet and the balance sheet of the central bank. Since this link has important implications for the domestic money supply, a common way of dividing up the capital account in the BOP is to separate out those items that involve the central bank. Let $\Delta FACB$ denote the change in the foreign asset position of the central bank and ΔFAO denote all other items not involving the central bank:

$$CA[R(t)] = \Delta FA = \Delta FACB + \Delta FAO. \tag{9.6}$$

It follows from this identity that

$$CA - \Delta FAO - \Delta FACB = 0.$$

Previously, we treated both $-\Delta FAO$ and $-\Delta FACB$ as parts of the capital account. Let us now change terminology and call $-\Delta FAO$ the capital account and $-\Delta FACB$ the reserves account. They would appear on the BOP balance sheet as:

Balance of Payments	
CA	Current account
$-\Delta FAO$	Capital account
$-\Delta FACB$	Reserves account

Of course, the total sum of items on the BOP balance sheet will sum to zero, just as before. Since, however, the amount of intervention the central bank has to undertake to peg or to influence the FX value of the domestic currency is a variable of considerable interest, one may wish to separate out this item by placing it "below the line" — which means that we draw an arbitrary line on the balance sheet and calculate a "balance" that leaves out what is below the line:

Balance of Payments	
CA	Current account
$-\Delta FAO$	Capital account
$-\Delta FACB$	Reserves account

The line could have been drawn anywhere. Drawn at another point, it would imply a different "balance" on the BOP, but we will not concern ourselves here with alternative concepts.

Notice that the absolute value of the numbers above the line and below the line are equal (since they sum to zero). Thus an economic explanation of the balance below the line cannot be different from the economic explanation of the balance above the line. There is, however, a difference in the focus of attention. Looking at the current account and the capital account above the line, we are led to think about competitiveness in international trade (current account) and the portfolio determinates of capital flows (capital account). Looking at the reserves account below the line, we are led to think about central bank policy. The following discussion will focus on central bank behavior in order to explore the relationship among the central bank's intervention policy, domestic monetary policy, and the exchange rate.

Table 9.2 gives a rough measure of CA, ΔFAO, and $\Delta FACB$ for the United States and Germany over the years 1980–1984. Note, for example, that in 1980 the loss in foreign assets represented by West Germany's current account deficit of DM 28.541 billion was mostly a loss in foreign exchange reserves by the Bundesbank. This reserve asset loss was DM 27.894 billion. These numbers indicate that the German central bank was undertaking massive sales of foreign exchange.

Let us now connect the balance sheet of the BOP to the balance sheet of the central bank. We saw in Chapter 1 that the major items on a central bank balance sheet were:

Central Bank

Assets	Liabilities
DA	H
FACB	

where DA are domestic assets such as government bonds; $FACB$ are foreign assets such as foreign exchange, gold, and SDRs; and H is the domestic high-powered money base, which includes items like commercial banks' reserve deposits with the central bank and printed currency. (There may be, in addition, other types of central bank liabilities. This will not, however, materially affect the following discussion.)

TABLE 9.2
Balance on International Transactions for the United States and West Germany

	United States ($ millions)			West Germany (DM millions)		
	CA^a	ΔFAO^b	$\Delta FACB^c$	CA^a	ΔFAO^b	$\Delta FACB^c$
1980	1,898	−6,257	8,155	−28,541	−647	−27,894
1981	6,294	1,119	5,175	−14,693	−12,410	−2,283
1982	−9,199	−14,164	4,965	8,067	4,990	3,078
1983	−41,563	−42,759	1,196	10,507	14,581	−4,074
1984	−101,532	−104,662	3,130	17,807	20,907	−3,099

[a] CA: Current account.
[b] ΔFAO: Changes in nonreserve assets (for U.S.: residual item setting $CA = \Delta FAO + \Delta FACB$; for West Germany: sum of "balance of capital transactions" and "balance of unclassifiable transactions," with sign reversed).
[c] $\Delta FACB$: Change in reserve assets (for U.S.: change in "U.S. Official Reserve Assets" — gold, convertible currencies, SDRs, and reserve position in IMF — with sign reversed; for West Germany: "balance of all transactions" — change in Bundesbank's net external assets at transactions values excluding SDRs.
Sources: U.S., *Economic Report of the President;* Deutsche Bundesbank, *Monthly Report.*

Central bank monetary and FX policies can be characterized according to the changes they give rise to on the balance sheet of the central bank. Common central bank policies for some (not all) countries are *open-market operations* and *foreign exchange intervention.* Open market operations involve changing the monetary base by buying and selling some domestic asset such as government bonds, bills of exchange, or even corporate stock:

$$\Delta DA = \Delta H.$$

The change in the monetary base, ΔH, will in turn lead to a change in the domestic money supply $(M1)$, which is a multiple of ΔH. Similarly, when the central bank does foreign exchange intervention, it changes the monetary base by buying or selling foreign exchange:

$$\Delta FACB = \Delta H.$$

In general, then, the change in the monetary base over any period of time can be viewed as stemming from either domestic or foreign operations:

$$\Delta H = \Delta DA + \Delta FACB \tag{9.7}$$

Since the change in the monetary base gives rise to a change in the domestic money supply, it is natural to organize the above facts in terms of the supply of, and demand for, money, denoted respectively by MS and MD. Let's begin with the money market in equilibrium at the current real exchange rate $R(t)$:

$$MS = MD[R(t)]. \tag{9.8A}$$

Of course money demand is a function of more than just the real exchange rate, but we write it this way because $R(t)$ is the variable in which we are primarily interested. The supply of money can be written in terms of the monetary base H and the money multiplier m as:

$$MS = m\,H. \tag{9.8B}$$

Thus

$$MD[R(t)] = m\,H \tag{9.8C}$$

Then, from a position of equilibrium at time $t + T$, we can calculate:

$$MD[R(t+T)] - MD[R(t)] = m\,\Delta H$$
$$\Delta MD = m\,\Delta H$$
$$\Delta MD = m\,(\Delta DA + \Delta FACB)$$

or, rewriting,

$$[(1/m)\,\Delta MD] - \Delta DA = \Delta FACB. \tag{9.9}$$

Let's analyze the last equation. The expression $[(1/m)\,\Delta MD]$ is the change in the demand for the monetary base, which is a function of the real exchange rate at t and $t + T$. The expression ΔDA is the amount of monetary base supplied by the central bank in the form of domestic assets. The expression $\Delta FACB$ is the amount of monetary base supplied by the central bank in the form of foreign assets. The real exchange rate $R(t)$ adjusts until supply and demand are equal at $R(t + T)$.

We can now summarize the implications of (9.9) under three different central bank policy regimes:

Case 1

First, consider the case where there is no central bank intervention in the FX market. Exchange rates float freely. Since there is no intervention, $\Delta FACB = 0$. (This assumes, of course, that foreign exchange is valued at historical rates and the central bank takes no action to offset valuation changes in its reserves position that might result from the divergence of market rates from the historical rates at which the central bank intervened.) With no foreign exchange intervention,

$$[(1/m) \Delta MD] = \Delta DA.$$

The real exchange rate adjusts so that supply and demand for the monetary base ("high-powered money") are equal. If, for example, the central bank supplies too much of the monetary base, at the margin the public will use the increased supply of money to buy foreign currency, or domestic goods, or foreign goods. This will cause a depreciation of the domestic currency in the foreign exchange market (the nominal domestic currency price of foreign exchange, $S(t)$, will rise), and this depreciation will continue until foreign currency and foreign goods become sufficiently expensive that the demand for the monetary base is equal to the supply. While the nominal exchange rate $S(t)$ will rise, the real exchange rate $R(t)$ may or may not change. What happens to $R(t)$ depends on what relative prices do.

Case 2

Second, consider a regime of completely fixed exchange rates. The nominal exchange rate is fixed at some level by central bank intervention: $S(t) = S^*$. Since the nominal exchange rate is not free to change to bring about an adjustment in monetary demand (and hence the demand for foreign exchange) all adjustment must occur through relative price changes. That is, $R(t)$ can only adjust through domestic and foreign price level adjustments, and not through the adjustment of $S(t)$. Thus we see that fixed exchange rate systems, by constraining the adjustment of $S(t)$, require greater price-level adjustments than do floating exchange rates.

In addition, equation (9.9), along with fixed exchange rates, implies that the central bank will not be able to conduct a domestic monetary policy (in the form of open market operations ΔDA) independent of its foreign exchange policy (foreign exchange intervention $\Delta FACB$). That is, $\Delta FACB$ will be determined by the need to intervene in the foreign exchange market. Thus from (9.9) we see that the central bank will have to adjust its position in DA in order to make up any resulting difference between supply and demand for the monetary base.

Countries that fix the exchange rate $[S(t) = S^*]$ and also engage in inflationary policies (via large values of ΔDA from year to year) will have chronic deficits on their reserve accounts. The central bank will have a "shortage" of foreign currency. If ΔDA is large relative to $[(1/m) \Delta MD]$, it follows that

$$\Delta FACB = [(1/m) \Delta MD] - \Delta DA$$

will be negative, and will remain negative unless either a devaluation of the domestic currency takes place (S^* is increased) or else the rate of growth of the money supply is curtailed (ΔDA takes place at a less rapid rate). Countries that do not have large reserve positions will not be able to maintain fixed nominal exchange rates and also indulge in inflationary domestic policies. As we saw in Chapter 3, if the current nominal exchange rate S^* overvalues the domestic currency (undervalues foreign currency), then everyone will want to buy foreign currency from the central bank and no one will want to sell foreign currency to the central bank. Thus, to avoid running out of foreign exchange reserves, the central bank will have to change S^* or else impose a system of quotas and exchange controls. The latter "solution" will only lead to a black or free market that will take place outside official channels. In the summer of 1985, for example, Bolivia supposedly had a "fixed" rate of 75,000 pesos = \$1. But virtually no foreign exchange transactions took place at this rate; the Bolivian peso was actually floating, since almost all transactions took place at privately negotiated rates.

The task of an exchange-rate forecaster is simplified under fixed exchange rates. The exchange rate will remain unchanged unless there is a devaluation or revaluation of the current fixed rate. The forecaster's task becomes one of evaluating the consistency of policy goals to evaluate the timing and magnitude of devaluations or revaluations, using as his or her data the level of central bank reserves, the availability of credit lines, the political probability the central bank will change monetary policy, the size of the black market premium on foreign currencies such as the U.S. dollar (if there are exchange controls), and so on. There should be no problem in getting the *direction of change* correct. That is why commercial banks and corporations made a lot of money betting against central banks in the last years of the Bretton Woods system.

Case 3

A third case involves countries that engage in "dirty floating." That is, they do some intervention ($\Delta FACB \neq 0$) to influence the exchange rate $S(t)$ but do not attempt to peg the rate at a fixed level or keep it within a fixed band. In this case, equation (9.9) implies that greater foreign exchange intervention implies less freedom to conduct an independent domestic policy (make changes in DA), while greater independence in domestic policy implies less freedom to intervene in the FX market. The less $S(t)$ is allowed to adjust to bring about market equilibrium, the greater must be the adjustment in relative prices. And so on. This third case is intermediate between cases 1 and 2.

If central bank policy is predictable, then central bank actions are part of the market information set $I(M, t)$. For example, it has been claimed that 55 to 70 percent of German central bank intervention can be explained on the basis of a statistically estimated "policy reaction function" (Neumann, 1984). It was indicated in Chapter 8 that rational economic decision-making should yield the result that

$$E[R(t + T)|I(M, t)] = R(t).$$

If central bank behavior is part of the market information set, then central bank intervention should not result in predictable real exchange rate changes.

SELECTIVE CENTRAL BANK INTERVENTION IN THE FX MARKET

The third case we examined, that of "dirty floating," raises some interesting issues. Central banks have continued to intervene on a massive scale despite floating exchange rates. The Bundesbank, for example, which averaged DM 4.5 billion in yearly foreign exchange purchases over the 1949–1973 Bretton Woods period, purchased a net total of DM 20.1 billion in FX in 1978, while it sold DM 27.6 billion in foreign assets in 1980 (Neumann, 1984). Why should central banks choose to intervene selectively in the foreign exchange market? And what does this imply for equilibrium in the FX market?

If central bankers allow rates to float, one assumes that they believe that rates determined in the market are better than fixed exchange rates. A freely floating exchange rate has the property that it is the price at which the exchange market clears when all buy and sell decisions are being made in a context of utility maximization. But if the central bank intervenes in the market for other reasons, the resulting equilibrium price that emerges as a result may represent a signal whose interpretation is uncertain. The uncertainty comes from the fact that the central bank's actions may not be predictable or consistent. If central bank policy is not a part of the market information set $I(M,t)$, the central bank is a source of random noise. Tomorrow's equilibrium exchange rate will depend in part on a future random intervention by the central bank. The uncertainty over central bank action could increase exchange rate uncertainty, volatility, and risk. The prediction error

$$e(t + T) = R(t + T) - E[R(t + T)|I(M,t)]$$

in the real exchange rate (review Chapter 8) could have a greater variance than it would without central bank intervention.

So why do central banks intervene? Surprisingly, many central banks intervene because, they say, exchange markets are too volatile. Hence, they intervene to "smooth out" such volatility. The Bundesbank, for example, has said in the past that it intervened "not only to prevent erratic variations in the rate from day-to-day but also to smooth unduly large fluctuations in the rate of the deutschemark against the dollar over longer periods" (*Annual Report,* 1974). If the domestic currency has depreciated "too much" with respect to a foreign currency, the central bank will buy up domestic currency (using the relevant foreign currency to make the purchase) in order to increase the value of the domestic currency in the FX market by decreasing its supply. If the domestic currency is appreciating too rapidly, the central bank will sell domestic currency (purchasing the relevant foreign currency in the process) in the FX market to depress the value of the domestic currency by increasing its supply.

☐

A more esoteric policy is "sterilized intervention," which involves offsetting transactions in foreign and domestic assets so that the monetary base is left unchanged. For example, a purchase of $1 billion of DM by the Federal Reserve (which would increase the monetary base by $1 billion) would be accompanied by a sale of $1 billion of U.S. government securities (which would decrease the monetary base by $1 billion). Since the monetary base is not altered, any impact of this operation would rely on the fact that dollar bonds in the hands of the public are now larger by $1 billion, while DM assets are fewer by $1 billion. If dollar assets and DM assets are not perfect substitutes, there could be some impact on the exchange rate. Recent Federal Reserve staff studies conclude there is little long-run impact from sterilized intervention (Federal Reserve, 1983).

∎

Is there a rational argument that would justify such actions to correct "disequilibrium" exchange rates? It is difficult to construct one. Here is what the notion of "overvalued" or "undervalued" market exchange rates implies. First, *it implies that the central bank will realize a profit from foreign exchange intervention* (Friedman, 1953). Because the central bank is selling foreign currency when it is "overvalued" and buying foreign currency when it is "undervalued," the central bank will realize a profit as the exchange rate returns to its "proper" value. The central bank sells at a high price and buys back at a low price. The profit is the difference in the two prices multiplied by the volume of intervention.

But if the central bank can earn a speculative profit this way, why can't private market speculators perform the same role? The argument for central bank intervention needs more than a simple statement that exchange rates are over- or undervalued. For example, here are two alternative additional arguments one could make.

(1) One could argue that there is insufficient private market speculation. As noted in Chapter 7, individual speculators with limited wealth face ultimate ruin unless the odds are very much in their favor. Thus, if there is market failure due to insufficient speculation, the central bank might fill the gap to ensure the optimal degree of speculation. McKinnon (1979) has suggested that private FX speculation may be insufficient. Most central banks are, however, unwilling to argue that there is insufficient speculation in the FX market. They would prefer to believe there is too much.

(2) A different argument for central bank intervention — the one used most frequently — is that the central bank has an informational advantage. The information set of the central bank, the argument goes, is greater than that of other market participants. Thus the central bank is better able to know what the "right" exchange rate ought to be. If $I(CB,t)$ is the central bank's information set, then the forecast error

$$c(t + T) = R(t + T) - E[R(t + T)|I(CB,t)]$$

has smaller variance than the forecast errors of other exchange market participants. In addition, the notion of "over-" or "under-" valuation would seem to imply that the forecasts of other market participants are biased.

The intervention issue, then, hinges on empirical questions. The evidence cited in Chapter 8 that the real exchange rate is a martingale would seem to imply there is no meaningful sense in which free market exchange rates are over- or undervalued. Is this empirical state of affairs a result of past central bank intervention on the basis of superior information? (Have central banks made money?) The evidence suggests otherwise. Not only have central banks not "smoothed out" exchange-rate movements, but over the floating rate years of the 1970s they have increased exchange-rate volatility by buying foreign exchange when it is already overpriced and selling foreign exchange when it is underpriced. If you buy when the price is too high and sell when the price is too low, you lose money. Table 9.3 indicates the billions of dollars that central banks have lost in

TABLE 9.3
Profits and Losses from Official Intervention in the Foreign Exchange Market

Country	Period beginning	Period ending	Profit or loss (−) ($ millions)
Canada	June 1970	December 1979	−82
France*	April 1973	December 1979	1,035
			(−2,003)
Germany	April 1973	December 1979	−3,423
Italy	March 1973	December 1979	−3,724
Japan	March 1973	December 1979	−331
Spain	February 1974	December 1979	−1,367
Switzerland	February 1973	December 1979	−1,209
United Kingdom	July 1972	December 1979	−2,147
United States	April 1973	January 1980	−2,351

* For France, the profit or loss is calculated assuming intervention is done in dollars and in deutsche-marks. A profit is shown for the dollar figure and a dollar equivalent loss is shown in parentheses for the deutschemark figure.

Source: Dean Taylor, "Official Intervention in the Foreign Exchange Market, or, Bet Against the Central Bank," *Journal of Political Economy,* April 1982.

the process of central bank intervention. Of the central banks examined by Taylor (1982), only the Bank of France failed to lose money in U.S. dollar terms. (And in DM terms, which Taylor argues is more relevant for the French case, the Bank of France also lost money.) The empirical evidence does not justify the argument that central banks have superior information.

It is doubtful that much has changed since the period investigated by Taylor (although the Bundesbank, for one, undoubtedly made a large profit on its dollar sales in 1980). Since participating banks in the European Monetary System continue to intervene on a daily basis to maintain the parity grid (see Chapter 2), this intervention should prove a source of FX trader profit with respect to European-currency cross rates, especially if neither national economic policy nor parity grid par values are altered rapidly whenever the market exchange rate moves close to parity bands. Neumann (1984) notes: "As a rule realignments in the EMS are delayed. The main reason seems to be that any realignment of the currencies requires first a politically feasible realignment of the subsidization of the agricultural sectors of the European economies." Hence the agricultural subsidy may translate into an FX trader subsidy.

PROBLEMS FOR CHAPTER 9

1. Which of the following items would receive plus signs on the U.S. balance on international transactions, and which would receive minus signs if carried out by a domestic citizen or entity?
   (a) Export of 15,000 Bruce Springsteen records.
   (b) Payment for consulting services received from a Japanese securities firm in Tokyo.
   (c) Receipt of $1,000,000 from relatives in Beirut as recorded under unilateral transfers.
   (d) A sale by Exxon of $100,000,000 of eurobonds in London.
   (e) A new issue of common stock in the London market.

2. (a) In what way is the current account balance relevant to the repayment of foreign debt?

(b) If a debtor country has a current account deficit, how is the long-run growth of the country affected by the manner in which the country may choose to reduce that deficit? (Refer to the savings, investment, government-deficit equation.)

3. Country X had a government deficit of $40 billion in 1982. In addition, private investment exceeded private after-tax saving by $10 billion.
   (a) What can you conclude concerning Country X's current account?
   (b) If, relative to GNP, a country has a high proportion of after-tax savings, an average proportion of investment expenditures, and an average government deficit, will the country tend to have current account deficits or surpluses?

4. The following data are for Mexico for the year 1981:

   Government deficit   782.7 billion pesos
   Current account   − 108.0 billion pesos

   Using the analysis of the preceding question, explain Mexico's foreign debt problem in terms of consumption and savings.

5. Comment on this statement:

   When demand for money grows faster than the supply of money would have grown due to domestic sources alone, international reserves tend to accumulate and to bring actual growth in the money stock closer to desired growth.

   Under what type of exchange regime would this statement be true?

6. Comment on this statement:

   The attempts of central banks to maintain an exchange rate when there is a change in their equilibrium level explains the consistent losses from foreign exchange intervention. They are able to influence the exchange rate for a period of time. However, market forces eventually force an adjustment and the central bank realizes a loss.

7. Assume the statement in Problem 6 is accurate. Is the following conclusion then justified?

   Counterspeculation by exchange traders dampens the destabilizing effect of central bank intervention. To the extent that speculators bet against central banks, resource misallocation is reduced and central bank losses become a subsidy to foreign exchange traders.

   The following information should be used in answering the questions in Problems 8 and 9.

   Money demand in Erewhon is fixed at 400 billion wawas. The high-powered money base in Erewhon is currently 100 billion wawas and the money multiplier has a constant value of 5. The central bank of Erewhon pegs the value of the wawa to the bancor, which is a foreign currency used throughout the rest of the world. The central bank of Erewhon has two policy instruments: foreign exchange intervention and domestic open-market operations.

8. If the central bank of Erewhon does not engage in any domestic open-market operations, then — in economic equilibrium — it will be forced to intervene in the foreign exchange market and, in the process [choose the correct answer]:
   a. Sell bancors in an amount equal to 20 billion wawas.
   b. Buy bancors in an amount equal to 20 billion wawas.
   c. Sell wawas in an amount equal to 100 billion bancors.
   d. Buy bancors in an amount equal to 100 billion wawas.
   e. Sell bancors in an amount equal to 100 billion wawas.

9. If the central bank of Erewhon wishes to maintain the pegged rate but wants to avoid any loss of foreign exchange reserves, then in economic equilibrium the central bank of Erewhon will engage in the following domestic open-market operation [choose the correct answer]:
    a. Sell government securities in the amount of 20 billion wawas.
    b. Buy government securities in the amount of 20 billion wawas.
    c. Sell government securities in the amount of 100 billion wawas.
    d. Buy government securities in the amount of 100 billion wawas.
    e. Sell government securities in the amount of 100 billion bancors.

10. Holding other things constant, all of the following would intend to increase the value of the Japanese yen against the U.S. dollar *except* [choose one]:
    a. A tax on foreign-held U.S. dollar assets.
    b. An increase in the U.S. GNP real growth rate.
    c. An increase in the U.S. money supply growth rate.
    d. An income tax reduction in Japan.
    e. A reduction in the Japanese money supply growth rate.

FOREIGN EXCHANGE FORECASTING

In previous chapters we have looked at some of the macroeconomic variables that influence and are influenced by the exchange rate. These have included relative prices, consumption and savings, money supply and demand, central bank intervention, and capital flows (which will receive further attention in Chapter 11 in the context of portfolio theory). We can envision a "true" model of the economy that includes all of these variables and more, and that, in the context of economic maximization and random events (such as the weather), generates the time path of foreign nominal and real exchange rates. Chapter 7 indicated that some of the important variables in this model would be people's expectations. The expectations of foreign-exchange marketmakers would be a crucial factor influencing the nominal exchange rate, and expectations in general would be an important influence in price determination.

Forecasting can be thought of as the formal process of generating expectations. One's expectations of future economic variables, however derived, are implicit forecasts. Such expectations can be generated in various ways: through casual reading of the newspaper or the book of Revelation, from dreams and visions, or by subscribing to an economic forecasting service. The rational-expectations criterion discussed in Chapter 7 says that people form expectations of future values of the exchange rate and other variables in the same fashion that the "true" model of the economy actually generates those variables. It implies that expectations cannot be taken as arbitrary, but rather must — in expectational equilibrium — be formed in such a manner that they are self-fulfilling. One way to picture this process is to conceive of people making a model of the economy. The model will include known and expected values of different variables. To get the required expected values in the model, the model itself will be used as a forecasting device. The forecasted values will then be inserted back into the original model in place of "expected" values. Rational expectations equilibrium occurs if the final model outcome generates values for economic variables, such as the exchange rate, that are on average the same as the expected values (review Chapter 7 for an example). If expectations are self-fulfilling in this way, no one has any incentive for revising expectations or revising the way in which expectations are formed. By contrast, if expectations were *not* self-fulfilling (not rational), they cannot be expected to endure.

As a practical matter, this process seems to be pretty much the way the real world works. While most people do not engage in the formal construction of economic models, they may subscribe to the output of such models or read newspaper reports giving the projections of economic forecasters. People take these forecasts into account when they make economic decisions. These decisions then influence the direction in which the economy actually moves. (Even dreams and visions may be rational if they are a way of accessing the "true" model of the economy.)

One strong qualification is in order, however. People may not really know the "true" model of the economy. As a consequence, they are not quite sure how to react when their expectations are wrong. Suppose the current real exchange rate is $R(t + T)$ and that it is related to the expected real exchange rate by the equation

$$R(t + T) = E[R(t + T)|I(i,t)] + e(t + T).$$

In general, there will be forecasting or expectational errors $e(t + T)$. Errors result even if the "true" model of the economy is known, because actual outcomes will depend on future random events. But if errors occur, they could also be due to the fact that people may not know the true model of the economy. For example, many people did not anticipate the high real U.S. interest rates of the early 1980s. As high real interest rates emerged, economists and others asked themselves: Are these high rates simply the result of unforeseeable events that could not have been incorporated into our previous forecasts? Or were our previous forecasts wrong because our view of how the economy works was wrong? Thus, in the absence of certainty that one knows the "true" model of the economy, rational expectations cannot be expected to prevail while people are in the process of learning. Eventually, however, people can be expected to learn what the true economic model is, assuming it stays fixed. But if the true model is itself undergoing random changes in structure the learning process will be permanent, and thus expectations would never be completely rational.

And, in reality, people are always in a process of revising their perception of how the economy works. For example, the metatheory of rational expectations itself entered the economics profession as one such revision.

APPROACHES TO FX FORECASTING

The idea of forecasting is to construct a methodology that will optimally extract indications of the future FX rate from today's available set of data. Two main approaches are used.

The **fundamental** approach attempts to process a wide range of data regarding fundamental economic variables in order to determine the future course of the exchange rate. Included may be such variables as consumption, investment, savings, trade, money supplies, inflation rates, productivity indices, opinion surveys, stock prices, and the like. The methodology used to process the data may be *econometric* (information processing through mathematical equations derived from economic theory, utilizing coefficients that are usually related to historical relationships) or it may be *judgmental* (direct processing through the human biocomputer). In the latter case, a person may be employed to spend the working day looking at economic data and then come to some opinion about what will happen to exchange rates. This procedure frequently seems to work about as well as the more formal econometric methodology, at least for short-run forecasting.

The technical approach focuses on a smaller subset of the available data. For example, a technical model may look only at the past history of several exchange-rate series, including both spot and forward exchange rates. This may involve "eyeballing" charts of price series or it may involve statistical procedures. Examples of technical models using statistical methodology are "momentum" models based on the relation of short-run moving averages to long-run moving averages and vector autogressive models, which involve a simultaneous regression of several exchange rate (and possibly other) variables on a time series of observations of past values of these same variables.

In past years there has been, and perhaps there still is, strong academic bias against the use of technical models. However, the distinction between fundamental and technical analysis is not as great as many people assume. One thing is clear: the use of a smaller information set could never improve forecasting accuracy. Thus one might think that the fundamental approach is a priori the better way to do forecasting. But there are other considerations. The use of greater information implies a greater cost of collecting and processing it, and the benefits must justify this additional cost. In addition, it is not entirely clear that the fundamental approach always uses a greater information set. For example, many fundamental models use GNP data, which is only available with a considerable time lag. By the time the data become available, they may no longer be useful. In addition, such "information" is subject to considerable measurement error. By contrast, the variables generally used in technical models — interest rates, exchange rates, futures prices, and so on — are available with almost no delay and with little measurement error. Finally, it should be noted that major banks, exchange dealers, and forecasters have not only continued to use technical models, but many organizations that previously used fundamental models have also switched to technical models or added the output of a technical model to their forecasting portfolio. Why? If we grant that market participants are rational people who act in their own self-interest, then we should grant that such decisions were made on the basis of a cost-benefit analysis. Many people have come to the conclusion that, for *short-term* forecasting, good technical models outperform good fundamental models.

The Model Theorem from Chapter 7 applies equally to fundamental and technical forecasting models. Models, if they are good, should become bad. They will set in operation the events that will ensure that their use will not generate excess returns.

INFORMATION, EFFICIENCY, AND MODEL EVALUATION

A consistent record of better forecasting requires *superior information*. Superior information implies either knowing greater amounts of data or else having the ability to process data more efficiently. One type of superior information resulting from greater amounts of data would be "insider" information. The employee of a central bank, for example, may have better data concerning projected central bank intervention in the FX market than a private banker would. As an example of superior information from superior processing, consider the case of two individuals reading *The Wall Street Journal*. They have available the same facts, but one might be able to extract more information from those facts. In this case, the superior information would lie within an individual: A person who doesn't know how to read the futures page cannot gain much information from the numbers presented.

Whichever type of superior information one may possess, it will be difficult to maintain this informational superiority and at the same time earn an excess return as a result of that information. If an "insider" engages in market transactions on the basis of superior information, others may be able to deduce what the insider knows by observing his or her market transactions. Thus the "inside" information will become public if it is used. Similarly, if a forecasting firm with superior technological expertise publishes its forecasts, so as to earn a profit from its services, the forecasts can become known to everyone — whether or not they have a good forecasting model.

EVALUATION OF FUNDAMENTAL FORECASTERS

We now turn to some of the evidence on the expertise of fundamental forecasters. The results come from Richard Levich of New York University, who has made comparisons of forecasting performance for the magazine *Euromoney*.

One test Levich does is to compare the forecasting performance of various services to the forward rate. This measure of performance is in terms of *mean absolute error*. The mean absolute error is the average absolute deviation of a series of forecasts from a series of actual outcomes. Let $p(i)$ denote a forecasting service's prediction for a particular exchange rate at a particular time and let $a(i)$ be the actual value for the spot exchange rate at that time. Let $f(i)$ denote the forward rate for the same time period. Then, to calculate the mean absolute percentage error for the service as well as the forward rate over n observations we need to compute two totals:

Forecasting service	Forward rate
$|p(1) - a(1)|/a(1)$	$|f(1) - a(1)|/a(1)$
$|p(2) - a(2)|/a(2)$	$|f(2) - a(2)|/a(2)$
. . . .	. . . .
$|p(n) - a(n)|/a(n)$	$|f(n) - a(n)|/a(n)$
Service-total	Forward-total

Then the mean absolute error MA in each case is calculated as

$$MA(s) = \frac{\text{Service-total}}{n}, \quad MA(f) = \frac{\text{Forward-total}}{n}.$$

Finally, if the forecasting service shows a better record than the forward rate for the sample considered, then $MA(s) < MA(f)$.

For the sample period 1977–1980 and for twelve major forecasting services, Levich compared the percentage of times the services did better than the forward rate, based on the mean absolute error criterion. He looked at performance over time horizons of one month, three months, six months, and a year. The results were:

Time horizon	Percentage of observations with $MA(s) < MA(f)$
1 month	28.8%
3 months	24.0%
6 months	28.8%
12 months	32.7%

In terms of mean absolute error, on average the forecasting services performed worse than the forward rate more than two-thirds of the time. Since observation of the forward rate is virtually costless, and since—as noted in Chapter 7—the forward rate is not necessarily even an unbiased forecast of the future spot rate, these results suggest that paying large amounts of money to a forecasting service may be an unjustifiable expense. Forecasting services also provide other types of sage advice and commentary, however. One cannot get that from the forward rate. The forward rate just speaks for itself.

A different method of computing forecasting expertise used by Levich is in terms of the percentage of times a forecast is on the "correct side" of the forward rate. A forecast is on the correct side if the forecast diverges from the forward rate in the same direction as does the actual realized spot rate. For example, suppose the three-month forward rate is $.4205/DM and the forecast is $.4275/DM. If the actual spot rate turns out to be $.4225/DM, the forecast was "correct" in diverging from the forward rate in the same direction as the actual spot rate. On the other hand, if the forecast had been $.4200/DM, the forecast was "incorrect" because it diverged from the forward rate in the opposite direction from the actual realized spot rate.

A possible justification for this way of judging "correct" and "incorrect" forecasts has to do with the rewards from hedging or speculation. Suppose you bought foreign exchange forward because your forecast told you that the forward price was less than what the actual spot price would turn out to be. Then, as long as the spot rate turned out to be higher than the forward rate, you would have made the correct decision—regardless of how much higher the actual spot rate was. You may not have made (or saved) the exact amount indicated by your forecast, but you will not have lost money either.

EXAMPLE 10.1

Suppose the current three-month forward rate is $.4205/DM, while the forecast is $.4275/DM. A speculator who made decisions on the basis of the forecast would buy forward DM, with the intention of making a speculative profit by selling the DM received on the forward contract at the higher spot price he expects to prevail when the contract matures. If the spot rate in three months turned out to be $.4225/DM, the speculator will have made

$.4225/DM − $.4205/DM = $.0020/DM.

To be sure, this will be smaller than the amount the speculator expected to receive. His forecast indicated an earning of

$.4275/DM − $.4205/DM = $.0070/DM.

However, he will not have lost money on the transaction. Similarly, a hedger who made decisions on the basis of the forecast will have purchased DM at the forward rate of $.4205/DM and will have avoided the higher cost of $.4225/DM he would have had to pay if he had waited and purchased at the spot rate.

According to the "correct" or "incorrect" criterion, if a forecaster had *no* expertise, he should be right about half the time. Anyone could flip a coin to determine whether to make a forecast above the forward rate or below, and then choose an arbitrary number in the right direction. Or different levels of the forward rate could be painted on the wall and a monkey could throw darts. So, at the extreme case of no expertise, we can assume that the probability of a right forecast is $p = .5$. Let r be the number of right forecasts and n the total number of forecasts. Then, for a sufficiently large n, the variable

$$z = (r/n - .5)(\sqrt{n}/.5) \tag{10.1}$$

has approximately a normal distribution. Let $N(z)$ be the cumulative normal distribution evaluated at z. Then $1 - N(z)$ gives the probability that the proportion of "correct" forecasts r/n occurred purely by chance. Only if this probability is small can we be reasonably certain that we are true witnesses to forecasting expertise.

EXAMPLE 10.2

Suppose that out of 100 total forecasts, 65 are "correct." Then

$$z = (65/100 - .5)(\sqrt{100}/.5) = 3.0.$$

Looking up z in a table of the standard normal probability distribution, we see that for

$$z = 3.0, N(z) = .9987.$$

Hence the probability of a purely random occurrence of this value for z is

$$1 - N(z) = 1 - .9987 = .0013,$$

or .13%. That is, if we assume that $p = .5$ (which implies no forecasting expertise), we can still expect to see 65 correct guesses out of 100 about .13 percent of the time. Since this probability is very small, we can say that the probability the forecasters record occurred purely by chance is small. We may then choose to believe the forecaster has demonstrated expertise in forecasting.

In terms of the percentage of times on the correct side of the forward rate, Levich concluded that over the period 1977–1980 the forecasters he studied showed expertise. For some currencies, the better forecasters got the "correct" side of the forward rate between 60 and 70 percent of the time. However, when he updated his data to include the years 1981 and 1982, he concluded that there is no statistically significant record of forecasting expertise for the dozen major services he investigated. This "Case of the Disappearing Expertise" is pretty much what one would expect on the basis of the Model Theorem.

EVALUATION OF TECHNICAL FORECASTERS

An evaluation of technical forecasting services has been made by Stephen Goodman of the Singer Company. Technical models give very short-term forecasts, and Goodman has claimed that over short-term time horizons all of the major technical forecasting services have a better forecasting record than any econometric service. Unfortunately, it is difficult to compare Goodman's results with Levich's, since Goodman uses a different evaluation procedure. Goodman uses two different criteria for evaluating forecasts: *return on capital at risk* and *return on selective hedging.*

Goodman claims that "return on capital at risk is the most relevant performance measure for a speculator, portfolio investor, or a multicurrency borrower, and it is the best single measure of overall forecasting performance." Technical services generate "signals" that tell the user when to buy a currency and when to sell the currency. Return on capital at risk is calculated by assuming that the user of the service buys a currency three months forward (and closes any outstanding forward contract to sell the currency) whenever the service gives a buy signal. The user sells a currency three months forward whenever the service gives a sell signal. If there is no change in the signal during the three-month life of the contract, the contract is rolled over at maturity. The "capital at risk" is considered to be the initial dollar value of the amount of currency bought or sold forward. The "return on capital at risk" is the capital gain or loss on the foreign currency position minus the U.S. dollar interest rate. The dollar interest rate is subtracted to give the return over and above what could be earned without taking risk. The *total return* on the portfolio is then equal to the sum of the return on capital at risk and the dollar interest rate.

Notice that "capital at risk" defined this way is not the same as the amount of money invested in the foreign currency portfolio. There may be no money actually invested in a forward contract. A sufficiently large bank or company may have no forward contract margin requirement. Others may have a 5 percent margin requirement. If there is, the return to the actual amount of money invested in the foreign currency would be twenty times the total return.

Below are Goodman's results comparing the average return on capital at risk for three major technical services over the period January 1977 to December 1980 for six major currencies. The average return from using the technical services is compared to the average return over the same time period and for the same currencies that would have resulted from a simple buy-and-hold strategy. Finally, both results are compared with those that would have resulted from using one of the fundamental econometric services that had one of the best forecasting records.

	Technical services	Buy-and-hold strategy	Econometric service
Average return on capital at risk	12.1%	3.4%	2.1%
Eurodollar interest rate	8.5%	8.5%	8.5%
Total return	20.6%	11.9%	10.6%

The second form of evaluation is the return on selective hedging. The return on selective hedging, according to Goodman, "is probably the most relevant performance measure for a corporate treasurer who has some flexibility in managing his company's foreign currency exposure." In order to calculate this return, two cases are distinguished. It is assumed that a company may have a "natural short" or a "natural long" position. A natural short position would arise if the ordinary business operations of the company generated foreign currency payables or debt. A natural long position would arise if ordinary business operations generated foreign currency receipts or assets. A company that is hedging will only use the service as a guide whether to cover (decrease) its foreign currency exposure, but will not take action to increase its natural exposure as a result of the service's forecasts.

Below are the average returns on selective hedging that would have resulted from using the three technical services. Results are given for both naturally long and naturally short positions. The time period and currencies involved are the same as those mentioned previously. The results are also compared to the return on selective hedging that would have resulted from using the econometric service, as well as to a hedging policy of always covering foreign currency exposures in the forward market.

	Technical services	Econometric service	Always cover forward
Natural Short position	2.5%	−1.7%	−1.7%
Natural Long position	9.7%	3.8%	1.7%

At face value these results are impressive. There may, however, be considerable sample selection bias in that the results for technical services as a whole were not given. The average performance for all services could be less impressive than for the three presented. If we assume that sample selection bias was not the reason for the results, then it would be of further interest to see if the *same* forecasting services can maintain the same performance record over a period of years. The Model Theorem suggests that this would not happen. This year's good performers should, if a lot of people are attracted to the service, become bad performers.

PROBLEMS FOR CHAPTER 10

1. Suppose that out of 100 forecasts I got 55 "correct" in the sense that my predictions were on the same side of the forward rate as the realized spot rate. If we agree that I would guess right half the time if I had no forecasting skill at all, then what is the probability that my track record of 55 "correct" forecasts was purely due to chance?

2. The central bank of Surlandia pegs its currency at an exchange rate of 125 pesos/dollar. In addition, it has a scheduled weekly devaluation of the peso in the amount of 1 peso/dollar. A currency prognosticator is forecasting the Surlandian peso/dollar rate for one year ahead. He estimates that there is a probability of .7 that the schedule of devaluations will be adhered to exactly, and a probability of .3 that there will be an additional maxidevaluation in the amount of 10 percent of the exchange rate six

months from now. In the event of a maxidevaluation, he assumes that the weekly devaluation schedule of 1 peso/dollar will be resumed after the maxi.
(a) What is his point forecast for the exchange rate?
(b) What is the standard deviation of this forecast, given the forecaster's assumptions?

3. Using daily data for the past one year, a researcher calculates values for s and f, where

$$s = [S(t) - S(t - 1)]/S(t - 1)$$

and

$$f = [F(t) - F(t - 1)]/F(t - 1).$$

Here S is the spot dollar price of DM, F is the thirty-day forward price of DM, and t corresponds to a time period of one day. The researcher assumes that s and f are drawings from a normal distribution, and finds that in her sample s and f each have a mean $m = 0$, and each have a daily standard deviation $v = .003$. The correlation coefficient between s and f is .8. Finally, the two most recent values (not in the researcher's sample) for $S(t)$ and $F(t)$ are $S(t) = \$.3950/DM$ and $F(t) = \$.4030/DM$.
(a) Given this information, and assuming that future values of s and f will be drawings from the same probability distribution as in the sample, calculate a 68 percent probability interval for $S(t + 1)$, the next day's value of S.
(b) What, according to the Speculative Efficiency Hypothesis, is the best forecast for the spot rate in thirty days, $S(t + 30)$?
(c) Suppose that, between day 1 and 2, the spot rate S increased by 3.2 percent. On day 1, a speculator sold DM forward (the speculator sold a thirty-day forward contract) in an amount with an initial value of $1,000,000. Then, given the researcher's sample information and assumptions, what is the researcher's best guess about the change in the value of the speculator's forward contract between day 1 and 2?

4. According to the Model Theorem [choose one of the following]:
a. Technical models should perform better than fundamental models.
b. Fundamental models should perform better than technical models.
c. No fundamental or technical model should be able to maintain a good forecasting record long-term.
d. The proof of the pudding is in the eating.
e. The best forecast of next year's cheap vacation is this year's cheap vacation.

PORTFOLIO CHOICE AND FOREIGN EXCHANGE

FORECASTING ERRORS AND RISK

Expectations are not always borne out. In September 1983, a number of leading forecasters made exchange rate predictions for July 31, 1984, for the magazine *Euromoney* ("Why the Dollar Will Fall," October 1983). These bank economists and corporate treasurers had widely different views of what would happen to the spot exchange rate. Despite that fact, they all managed to be badly mistaken on the actual course of events. The range of their forecasts compared with realized spot rates are given in the table on the next page.

In previous chapters we have considered some of the macroeconomic influences on exchange rates, and in Chapter 10 forecasting was presented in this regard as the process of generating expectations, given available information. For many people, the future level of the real exchange rate will be of interest. For an individual with the information set $I(i,t)$, there is uncertainty associated with the magnitude of his or her forecast error

$$e(t + T) = R(t + T) - E[R(t + T)|I(i, t)].$$

But even though future real exchange rates are uncertain, financial decisions have to be made today. The outcome of these decisions will depend on the forecasting or expectational mistakes $e(t + 1), e(t + 2), e(t + 3), \ldots , e(t + T)$. There may be unexpected gains or losses from borrowing and lending in foreign currencies, purchasing or selling foreign currency-denominated assets, or investing in projects that generate foreign currency cash flows. Few people would be willing to make a decision without allowing for the possibility of being wrong. The uncertainty inherent in one's expectation or forecast thus implies risk. And the risk of making what may turn out to be an undesirable FX decision is related to the size of the expectational mistake $e(t + T)$.

The foregoing argument implies that financial decision-making involves at least a two-dimensional variable. One may have in mind an expected value — or forecast — of the exchange rate, but allowance will be made for the uncertainty

	Spot rate on September 1, 1983	Range of forecasts for July 31, 1984	Actual spot rate on July 31, 1984
Pound	$1.50/£	$1.50/£ – $1.89/£	$1.31/£
Deutschemark	DM 2.69/$	DM 2.57/$ – DM 2.10/$	DM 2.91/$
Swiss franc	SF 2.18/$	SF 2.05/$ – SF 1.70/$	SF 2.47/$
Yen	¥ 245/$	¥ 240/$ – ¥ 205/$	¥ 245/$

inherent in the forecast. For example, one may believe that the exchange rate in six months will be ¥205/$, as a point forecast, but this number is so uncertain that one may at the same time believe that there is only a 50 percent probability that the exchange rate will lie between ¥200/$ and ¥210/$. If one is borrowing in terms of yen and calculating profits in terms of dollars, a rate of ¥200/$ will result in a dollar loss relative to the point forecast of ¥205/$. Thus it is common in financial decision-making to measure risk in terms of probability. We may view future, as-yet-unknown exchange rates as drawings from a probability distribution and may measure uncertainty or risk by the dispersion of probability around a central (expected) value.

EXAMPLE 11.1

A decision-maker views the logarithm of the spot exchange rate that will occur in six months as a random drawing from a normal probability distribution. In particular, it is assumed that the mean and standard deviation are:

Mean = log(¥205/$)
S.D. = .0145

Since

log(205) = 5.323

there is a probability of 68 percent that the logarithm of the exchange rate in six months will lie between

5.323 − .0145 = 5.3085   and   5.323 + .0145 = 5.3375.

This means there is a probability of 68 percent that the actual level of the exchange rate will lie between

¥202.05/$ and   ¥207.99/$.

Where do people get their subjective probabilities concerning the distribution of variables like the exchange rate? If expectations are rational, then the amount of uncertainty that people will assume to be present when they make decisions will correspond to the actual uncertainty inherent in the "true" model by which the economy functions. If expectations are rational, then the amount of error or uncertainty as reflected in $var(e(t + T))$ will be on average the amount that was expected given available information:

$$var(e(t + T)) = E[var(e(t + T))|I(i,t)] + m(t + T),$$

where $E[m(t + T)|I(i,t)] = 0$. Expectations regarding risk will be self-fulfilling. In the long run, people will not act as though there is either more risk or less risk than actually exists in the economy. Their subjective probabilities will correspond to objective probabilities. We may formulate this as the *Poker Player's Theorem:* The poker player takes, as his subjective probability that another player has drawn a particular set of cards, the objective mathematical probability that that set of cards occurred. If the probabilities do not jibe in repeated play, he knows that the deck is stacked and revises his probabilities and decisions accordingly.

PORTFOLIO CHOICE IN AN INTERNATIONAL CONTEXT

How one chooses to deal with uncertainty, and hence risk, may vary according to the context. But there are many circumstances in which it would seem reasonable to assume *risk-averse behavior,* which can be defined as willingness to make a tradeoff between expected return and risk (uncertainty). Three situations can be distinguished.

1. Given a choice of two different investment opportunities that yield the same expected return, but with different levels of associated risk, a risk-averter would prefer the one with smaller risk.
2. Given a choice of two different investment opportunities that have equivalent levels of associated risk, but different levels of expected return, a risk-averter would prefer the one with higher expected return.
3. A risk-averter will trade off risk with expected return in the sense that if there were only two investment assets, one with both a higher expected return and a higher risk than the other, he or she would end up placing some portion of wealth in both assets. That is, an investor could conceivably choose as a total portfolio only the low expected return, low-risk asset. The purchase of some portion of the high expected return, high-risk asset increases both the expected return and the risk of the total portfolio. Thus the willingness to buy some of the high expected return, high-risk asset would indicate a willingness to trade off risk with expected return.

Portfolio choice arises in international financial decision-making in a number of contexts. Here are some examples.

1. Trust funds managed by commercial and investment banks involve international assets whose value is measured in hundreds of billions of dollars. These assets are spread around the world, and shifts in the location and type of assets are made according to changing perceptions in terms of risk and expected return. If the value of the U.S. dollar is expected to fall relative to the value of the DM, wealth may be shifted from dollar-denominated bank accounts, Treasury bills, and shares of common stock in U.S. companies to DM-denominated bank accounts, eurobonds, and shares of common stock in German companies. Similar shifts may occur as results of a change in economic risk (such as increased variability in the inflation rate) or a change in political risk (such as the impending Chinese takeover of Hong Kong, a war in the Persian Gulf, or the threat of capital controls in the United Kingdom).

2. So-called "cocktail currencies" like the ECU and the SDR, are themselves portfolios of currencies. Depending on the expected return and risk associated with each of the component currencies in the portfolio, an expected return and risk are associated with the total portfolio. The final portfolio — the ECU or the SDR — may give a better risk-return tradeoff than does any individual component currency. On the other hand, the ECU or the SDR could be an inefficient portfolio: the dollar or the French franc component may be too large or the yen component too small.

3. A corporation that does not have cash inflows or outflows matched 100 percent in foreign currency terms is subject to foreign exchange risk in terms of the domestic currency. The corporation may set up a foreign finance subsidiary whose job it is to keep track of these foreign currency cash flows for the company as a whole and to make hedging decisions based on forecasted exchange rates as well as on some measure of the risk of unexpected currency valuation changes.

PORTFOLIO CHOICE AND THE BALANCE OF PAYMENTS

International portfolio choice implies acquiring or selling foreign assets or debt. In Chapter 9 we saw that such activities were recorded in the balance on international transactions (balance of payments) accounting record either as pure capital flows (switching between domestic and foreign assets) or as capital flows associated with a current account surplus or deficit.

If portfolio decisions lead to switching between domestic and foreign financial or other assets, only capital account transactions are involved. These transactions can have a strong impact on the exchange rate. For example, if DM-denominated eurobonds are sold in order to purchase dollar-denominated U.S. Treasury bonds, the ensuing sales of DM for dollars may drive down the dollar price of DM. This purely capital account transaction may also have an indirect impact on the current account. This indirect impact would occur if there were changes in the real exchange rate brought about in the process of switching between DM assets and $ assets.

A current account deficit or surplus is also related to the desired portfolio composition. As noted in Chapter 9, the current account balance is identical to the net change in foreign assets, $CA = \Delta FA$. Whether this accumulation of assets is desired or not depends on the expected return and risk associated with holding those assets, as compared to the expected return and risk associated with holding alternative assets.

Suppose that newly acquired information leads portfolio managers to make a general shift out of DM-assets and into dollar assets. This shift will drive down the value of the DM relative to the dollar, until at the margin the *risk-adjusted* real return on DM and dollar assets is equalized. That is, the real return on DM and dollar assets need not be the same in equilibrium. For example, the real return on dollar assets may be higher. But, if so, the risk (which can in some cases be measured by forecasting uncertainty) of holding dollar assets must be correspondingly larger, so that at the margin portfolio managers are indifferent between holding DM assets and holding dollar assets.

In addition, in portfolio equilibrium, the rate of accumulation (or loss) of foreign assets through the current account balance must be such that it maintains the desired share of foreign assets in the total asset portfolio, given comparative real returns and risks. If a country such as Japan desires as a whole to accumulate foreign assets through a yearly flow, there will be a current account surplus. If portfolio equilibrium requires a flow reduction in foreign assets (or a flow increase in foreign borrowing) by the country as a whole, there will be a current account deficit.

For example, during the year 1984 foreigners were accumulating U.S. dollar assets at the rate of $100 billion a year, corresponding to the U.S. current account deficit. As long as this rate of addition of dollar assets to foreign portfolios was desired, there would be little pressure for any adjustment in the current account. On the other hand, if the dollar accumulation was not desired, portfolio managers would sell off their dollar assets. This would drive down the nominal and real exchange rate, which would in turn make U.S. exports more competitive and imports more expensive. A reduction in the current account deficit would in turn diminish the dollar flow into foreign portfolios.

This discussion distinguishes between *stocks of assets* (the total outstanding amounts) and *flows of assets* (the changes in those stocks over a period of time). Asset market equilibrium based on expected real return and risk says that shifts between the stocks of assets will be made up to the point risk-adjusted real rates of return are equalized between the assets denominated in different currencies. Even in stock equilibrium, however, flows will continue to take place, since total financial wealth will in general be changing. In equilibrium, the asset flow associated with the current account balance should be at a level such that the flow leaves the desired proportion of foreign assets in the total asset portfolio unchanged. [A survey of portfolio approaches to the exchange rate in macroeconomics may be found in Dornbush (1980:I).]

CALCULATING RETURNS WITH A FOREIGN EXCHANGE COMPONENT

The return on an asset held in a foreign currency contains an exchange-rate component. Consider three general types of assets: money market assets (or bonds held to maturity); bonds (not held to maturity); and equity.

The *nominal* return on foreign money market assets will be the nominal interest rate plus the gain or loss from any change in exchange rates. Suppose a foreign-currency pure discount bond is purchased at a domestic currency price of $S(t)B(t,T)$ and matures at time $t + T$, when the spot exchange rate is $S(t + T)$. At that time $B(t + T, 0) = 1$, so the total return on the bond is

$$\frac{S(t + T)B(t + T, 0)}{S(t)B(t,T)} = \frac{S(t + T)}{S(t)B(t,T)}. \tag{11.1}$$

If the exchange rate remains unchanged, the nominal return on this discount bond (or money market asset) is just one plus the interest rate. The real return is the nominal return adjusted for changes in purchasing power.

For discount bonds not held to maturity, the nominal return may contain a capital gain or loss component, since the terminal value of the bond is uncertain. If the bond is sold at time $t + x$, with a remaining time to maturity of $T - x$, the nominal return on the bond may be written as

$$\frac{S(t + x)B(t + x, T - x)}{S(t)B(t,T)}. \tag{11.2}$$

For bonds that pay periodic coupons, such as a payment of C units of currency at intervals of y units of time, equation (11.2) must be adjusted to include the coupon yield. Assuming that the bond is bought at the beginning of a coupon period and sold at the end of a coupon period, at time $t + y$, the return to the bond would be

$$\frac{S(t + y) [B(t + y, T - y) + C(t + y)]}{S(t)B(t,T)}. \tag{11.3}$$

Again, the real return to the bond would be the nominal return adjusted for inflation.

Finally, the nominal return to equity would take the form of (11.2) if there were no dividend payments, or (11.3) if there were dividends. Just substitute the stock price in place of the bond price and the amount of the dividend in place of the coupon amount.

EXAMPLE 11.2

A DM bond with a face value of DM 5000 and a 7 percent annual coupon is bought at a price of DM 4960 when the spot exchange rate is $.36/DM and sold a year later at a price of DM 5010, when the spot exchange rate is $.34/DM. What is the nominal return on the bond, assuming that the year holding period corresponds to the coupon period?

The annual coupon payment on the bond is (.07)(DM 5000) = DM 350. From equation (11.3), the return is

$$\frac{(\$.34/DM) [DM\ 5010 + DM\ 350]}{(\$.36/DM)(DM\ 4960)} = 1.02.$$

The total nominal return on $1 is $1.02, corresponding to a nominal interest rate of 2 percent. Notice that three components went into this nominal return: a coupon payment, a capital gain on the price of the bond, and an exchange rate loss.

To adjust nominal returns to real returns, the change in the price level must be taken into account. If the beginning domestic price level is $P(t)$ and the ending price level is $P(t + y)$, then equation (11.3) becomes, for the real return to bond holdings sold at time $t + y$,

$$\frac{P(t)S(t + y) [B(t + y, T - y) + C(t + y)]}{P(t + y)S(t)B(t,T)}. \tag{11.4}$$

This represents the return measured in terms of purchasing power in the domestic country. Portfolio decisions depend on the expected value of this real return as well as the dispersion of the real return around its expected value.

EXPECTED REAL RETURNS AND THE RISE OF THE U.S. DOLLAR

The increase in the value of the U.S. dollar from 1980 to February 1985 "rivals the oil shocks of the 1970s as the most dramatic relative price change in the

TABLE 11.1
Real Interest Rate Differential Between Long-Term Government Bonds in the United States and a Weighted Average of U.S. Trading Partners

Item	United States	U.S. trade partners	Differential
Long-term government bond rate			
1980	11.39	11.34	.05
1985 (February)	11.70	9.33	2.37
Real Interest Rate I[a]			
1980	−2.16	−0.05	−2.11
1985 (February)	8.16	5.25	2.90
Real Interest Rate II[b]			
1980	−0.28	1.99	−2.27
1985 (February)	7.87	4.41	3.46
Real Interest Rate III[c]			
1980	1.55	2.71	−1.16
1985 (February)	7.54	4.84	2.70

[a] Measured as difference between the government bond rate and one-year lagged inflation.
[b] Same with three-year distributed lagged inflation.
[c] Same with DRI forecasted inflation.
Source: Jeffrey A. Frankel, "The Dazzling Dollar," *Brookings Papers on Economic Activity,* I (1985).

post-World War II world economy" (Frankel, 1985). Most of this increased value can probably be attributed to portfolio shifts into U.S. dollar assets as a result of increased expected real returns relative to assets denominated in other currencies. Table 11.1 shows that in 1980 real interest rates paid on long-term U.S. government bonds were about two percentage points *below* those paid on a weighted average of similar securities among U.S. trading partners. (The measure of "real" interest rates depends on the method used to calculate expected inflation. Three different methods used here include taking as expected inflation either one-year lagged inflation, three-year distributed lagged inflation, or the three-year inflation forecast of a private forecasting firm (DRI).) By February 1985, the real interest rate on U.S. bonds was about three percentage points *above* that on bonds of U.S. trading partners. This ongoing shift of five percentage points in favor of dollar securities led investors to switch into dollar-denominated assets until such time as *expected* risk-adjusted real returns were equal.

☐

The more problematical macroeconomic question of why U.S. real interest rates rose so dramatically over this period is outside the scope of this book. The 1985 U.S. *Economic Report of the President* cites two reasons:

1. "The 1979 change to a tighter U.S. monetary stance" led to a drop in actual and expected inflation, and
2. "The Economic Recovery and Tax Act of 1981, together with reduced inflation, significantly raised the after-tax rate of return on new business investment."

Additional factors that have been cited include the large U.S. government deficit, which reduced the supply of savings relative to the demand for investment. The policy mix of easy "fiscal policy" and restrictive monetary policy is discussed in Sachs (1985).   ■

BENEFITS OF FOREIGN CURRENCY DIVERSIFICATION

For simplicity, let us consider nominal returns. (Assume that governments of the world have not discovered the miracle of inflation.) Suppose a bank, a company, or an individual will have the following pattern of monthly cash flows over the immediate future

U.S. dollar	Swiss franc	DM
1,000,000	−600,000	800,000

where the current exchange rates are $.42/DM and $.50/SF. What is the magnitude of the exchange risk in nominal dollar terms? Converting the above amounts to dollars, we have

Unexposed	Exposed in SF	Exposed in DM
$1,000,000	−$300,000	$336,000

The net exposure, in nominal dollar terms, depends on how the dollar price of SF moves compared to the dollar price of DM. For example, suppose that percentage changes in the dollar prices of SF and DM were always equal. Then long and short positions would automatically offset each other, so the net dollar exposure would be

$$-\$300,000 + \$336,000 = \$36,000,$$

a small net exposure. But suppose, at the other extreme, percentage changes in the dollar prices of SF and DM always had the opposite sign but were equal in magnitude. Then the net FX exposure would be

$$\$300,000 + \$336,000 = \$636,000$$

in nominal dollar terms. We can see that the magnitude of exchange risk depends on how currencies fluctuate with respect to each other. Thus portfolio risk depends on the *covariance* of exchange returns. If we only had one foreign asset, we might need only consider the variance of the dollar return on one foreign currency. But with several foreign assets, covariances are important in addition to variances.

CALCULATION OF PORTFOLIO EXPECTED RETURN AND VARIANCE

Consider the three foreign assets listed below.

	Expected monthly dollar return
DM asset	$-.500\%\ (=\ -.00500)$
Yen asset	$.670\%\ (=\ \ \ .00670)$
£ asset	$.872\%\ (=\ \ \ .00872)$

A portfolio is, by definition, an allocation of weights to each of these assets. The weights $w(i)$ are the fractions of each unit of wealth (here, each U.S. dollar) to be invested in each asset. For example, if $10 million is allocated as $5 million in DM, $3 million in yen, and $2 million in pounds sterling, the respective weights are

$w(1) = \frac{5}{10} = .5$ in DM,
$w(2) = \frac{3}{10} = .3$ in yen, and
$w(3) = \frac{2}{10} = .2$ in the £.

Three possible portfolios are:

	$w(1)$	$w(2)$	$w(3)$	Sum of weights
Portfolio A	$\frac{1}{3}$	$\frac{1}{3}$	$\frac{1}{3}$	1
Portfolio B	$\frac{1}{4}$	$\frac{1}{4}$	$\frac{1}{2}$	1
Portfolio C	$-\frac{1}{3}$	$\frac{2}{3}$	$\frac{2}{3}$	1

The expected return on each of these portfolios is

$$E(R) - A = \quad (\tfrac{1}{3})(-.500) + (\tfrac{1}{3})(.670) + (\tfrac{1}{3})(.872) = \ \ .347\%$$
$$E(R) - B = \quad (\tfrac{1}{4})(-.500) + (\tfrac{1}{4})(.670) + (\tfrac{1}{2})(.872) = \ \ .480\%$$
$$E(R) - C = -(\tfrac{1}{3})(-.500) + (\tfrac{2}{3})(.670) + (\tfrac{2}{3})(.872) = 1.195\%$$

Portfolio C has the highest return, but we do not know whether to prefer it over either A or B until we have taken the relative risks of each portfolio into account. Notice that a negative weight, such as $w(1) = -\frac{1}{3}$, implies borrowing in, having an account payable in, or otherwise being short, a foreign currency.

Suppose the expected returns among the three assets have the following covariance matrix:

$$
\begin{array}{c}
\quad \quad \ \text{DM} \quad \text{Yen} \quad \ £ \\
\begin{matrix} \text{DM} \\ \text{Yen} \\ £ \end{matrix}
\begin{bmatrix} 7.70 & 5.75 & 4.82 \\ 5.75 & 15.82 & 5.03 \\ 4.82 & 5.03 & 4.01 \end{bmatrix} \times \dfrac{1}{10{,}000}
\end{array}
$$

The variance of the monthly expected return on the DM is .00077. The covariance of the expected return on the DM with the expected return on the yen is .000575. And so on.

In order to calculate the variance of a portfolio, using the covariance matrix, write the weights of the portfolio across the top and down the side of the covariance matrix:

$$
\begin{array}{c}
\begin{array}{ccc} w(1) & w(2) & w(3) \end{array} \\
\begin{array}{c} w(1) \\ w(2) \\ w(3) \end{array}
\begin{bmatrix}
7.70 & 5.75 & 4.82 \\
5.75 & 15.82 & 5.03 \\
4.82 & 5.03 & 4.01
\end{bmatrix} \times \dfrac{1}{10,000}
\end{array}
$$

Then add together every number of the matrix multiplied by the weights in the corresponding row and column:

$$
\begin{aligned}
& 7.70\ w(1)\ w(1) + 5.75\ w(1)\ w(2) + 4.82\ w(1)\ w(3) \\
& + 5.75\ w(2)\ w(1) + 15.82\ w(2)\ w(2) + 5.03\ w(2)\ w(3) \\
& + 4.82\ w(3)\ w(1) + 5.03\ w(3)\ w(2) + 4.01\ w(3)\ w(3)
\end{aligned}
$$

Substituting the values for $w(1)$, $w(2)$, and $w(3)$, for each of portfolios A, B, C, we obtain the portfolio variances:

Variance of return on portfolio A ($\times 10,000$) = 6.53.
Variance of return on portfolio B ($\times 10,000$) = 5.65.
Variance of return on portfolio C ($\times 10,000$) = 9.44.

Thus we discover that portfolio B dominates (is preferred to) portfolio A, since B has both a higher expected return and a lower risk as measured by the variance. On the other hand, portfolio C has a higher expected return than B, but it also has a higher variance.

Note the probability interpretation of portfolio C, assuming that returns have a normal distribution. The expected return, $E(R) - C = .01195$, while the standard deviation is

$$
\sqrt{(9.44)/(10,000)} = .03072.
$$

This means that there is a 68 percent probability that R will lie between

.01195 + .03072 and .01195 − .03072,

a 95 percent probability that R will lie between

.01195 + 2 (.03072) and .01195 − 2 (.03072),

and a 99 percent probability that R will lie between

.01195 + 3 (.03072) and .01195 − 3 (.03072):

Range for R	Probability
(.04267, −.01877)	.68
(.07339, −.04949)	.95
(.10411, −.08021)	.99

If we let R be the incremental return to \$1,000,000 invested in portfolio C, the expected value of the investment at the end of one month is \$1,011,950. The corresponding intervals and their probabilities are:

Range of value	Probability
(\$1,042,760, \$981,230)	.68
(\$1,073,390, \$950,510)	.95
(\$1,104,110, \$919,790)	.99

Even though the expected value is \$1,011,950, there is only a 68 percent probability that the actual value will lie somewhere between \$1,042,760 and \$981,230.

OPTIMAL ALLOCATION OF PORTFOLIO SHARES

The example in the previous section shows that different choices of portfolio weights give differing amounts of expected return and variance. The basic idea of portfolio theory is to choose weights so that you get an optimal tradeoff. How do you do this? First, determine your attitude toward risk. At what rate are you willing to trade off expected return for variance? Second, gather together your forecast returns for the available assets, along with expected variances and covariances. Finally, using as inputs your risk attitude and the expected variances and covariances, calculate weights that will give an optimal tradeoff. This optimal tradeoff is a function of your attitude toward risk, and is also a function of your information.

In order to do these calculations, a number of additional assumptions, such as one concerning the probability distribution of returns, will need to be employed. Given standard assumptions, however, a variety of computer programs that will calculate portfolio weights are available.

□

A number of studies have indicated that international portfolio diversification is one of the most effective avenues for risk reduction. See, for example, Solnik (1974) and Lessard (1983). The amount of risk reduction available by diversifying internationally rather than restricting oneself to domestic assets is, however, difficult to measure. As noted by Adler and Dumas (1983), "The availability of risk reduction will depend upon which one [model of portfolio selection] is true. This point should put an end to all further attempts to base measures of such quantities as 'risk reduction' or 'diversifiable risk' on sample estimates of the means and variances of and correlations among market or industry indices."

Models of international portfolio selection can be found in Solnik (1973) and Sercu (1980). Adler and Dumas (1983) give a comprehensive survey of these and other models. ■

PORTFOLIO SHARES OF OFFICIAL RESERVE ASSETS

Little useful empirical work exists testing whether capital movements in fact correspond to the implications of portfolio theory. The main problem is that data on currencies in private holdings of foreign assets are not generally available.

However, it is clear that asset managers employed by investment banks, commercial banks, insurance companies, and pension and trust funds do regularly use portfolio theory in deciding where and how to invest their funds. Therefore a good guess is that actual capital movements between the major currencies are similar to the implications of the theory.

Good data exist on the currency composition of official reserve assets. The amount of these assets is small compared to private holdings of assets; and, in the past, it probably would not have been a good assumption to suppose that official reserve assets were deployed in the direction of the greatest risk-adjusted return. However, in more recent years central banks and monetary authorities have begun to manage assets more aggressively along the lines of comparative risk and return. Official reserve assets are held mostly in the form of either foreign currencies or gold.

Table 11.2 shows the changing composition of official reserve assets since the breakdown of Bretton Woods. We see that the U.S. dollar share changed little until the formation of the European Monetary System after 1978. The DM has risen from 5.5 percent (1973) to 11.9 percent (1983) of the FX component of official reserves, while the £ has fallen from 6.5 percent to 2.6 percent. The role of the yen has increased slightly, but — as noted in Chapter 2 — has been hindered by Japanese capital controls. Looking at the top section of Table 11.2, we see that the major portion of official reserve assets at the end of 1983 was held in the form of gold. The rise in the market value of gold was responsible, as the stock of physical gold had been decreased slightly to 946 million ounces from 1022 million ounces.

TABLE 11.2
Currency Distribution in Official Reserve Portfolios

Total Foreign Exchange and Gold Reserves (SDR billions)				
Year end	1973	1978	1981	1983
Foreign exchange	102.7	224.2	299.0	310.1
Gold (valued at London market price)	95.0	179.9	325.0	344.6
Gold (millions of ounces)	1022	1037	952	946

Currency shares of official reserve portfolio (Percent of total foreign currency holdings)				
	Beginning 1973	End 1978	End 1981	End 1983
U.S. dollar	78.4	75.6	69.4	69.1
Deutschemark	5.5	11.0	13.2	11.9
Japanese yen	—	3.2	4.1	4.2
Swiss franc	1.1	2.3	2.8	2.4
Pound sterling	6.5	1.7	2.2	2.6
French franc	0.9	1.2	1.4	1.2
Dutch guilder	0.3	0.9	1.2	0.8
Unspecified currencies	7.3	4.2	5.7	7.8

Source: International Monetary Fund, *Annual Report.*

PROBLEMS FOR CHAPTER 11

1. Suppose we have two assets, one denominated in DM and one in £, whose dollar returns have a joint normal distribution with the following expected values and covariances:

Expected return		Covariance matrix	
		DM	£
DM asset	.08	DM	.0064	.0020
£ asset	.06	£	.0020	.0052

Portfolio A contains the DM asset with a weight of .5 and the £ asset with a weight of .5. Portfolio B has the DM asset with a weight of .3 and the £ asset with a weight of .7.

(a) Calculate the expected return and standard deviation of portfolios A and B.

(b) Interpret your results in terms of probability.

(c) Would a risk-averse individual prefer A over B, B over A, or can you tell from the given information?

2. Under what circumstances would one buy an asset with a zero expected real return?

3. Comment on the following observation:

There is no reason to believe that variance of forecast errors or correlations will remain constant over time. The high correlation between the DM and the French franc would, for example, be drastically reduced if the EMS broke up.

EUROCURRENCY MARKETS

EUROBANKING AND EUROCURRENCY CENTERS

THE BUSINESS OF EUROBANKING

The balance sheet of a typical **eurobank** provides a convenient framework for organizing our discussion of the eurocurrency market. As illustrated on the next page, eurobanks have as *liabilities* time deposits, floating rate notes, and negotiable CDs (certificates of deposit), while their *assets* include loans to banks and loans to companies and governments. As we saw in Chapter 1, the liabilities side of the balance sheet is, by definition, made up of *eurocurrencies.* If denominated in dollars, these liabilities are called eurodollars, while if denominated in DM they are called euro-DM. The criterion that designates the liability as "euro" is that the bank be located outside the country where the currency is issued as legal tender. Sometimes other regional terms are used (Asian dollars, for example), but here we will simply use "eurocurrency" to refer to all external currency funds.

A *time deposit* has a fixed maturity date, on which the bank's obligation is repayable with interest. **Certificates of deposit (CDs)** differ from ordinary time deposits in that there exists a secondary market. If a CD owner wants the money back prior to maturity, the CD can be sold on the secondary market for its current value in that market. A **floating rate note** differs from ordinary time deposits and CDs in that it pays interest at periodic intervals, not just at maturity. The interest payments will be at a mark-up or spread above some reference rate (see below). Floating rate notes typically have longer maturities than other liabilities, and a secondary market exists for these notes.

On the asset side of the balance sheet are the eurobank's loans. "Loans to banks" will usually be to other eurobanks or to money-center banks in major financial centers. These loans arise from the *interbank market* in eurocurrency deposits. Eurocurrency borrowing and lending between major banks is done over the phone in a fashion similar to trading in foreign currencies. A eurocurrency trader will quote bid and asked interest rates. The bid interest rate is the rate at which the eurobank will accept deposits from other banks (which will increase the eurobank's time-deposit liabilities), and the asked interest rate is the rate at which the eurobank will lend to other banks (which will increase the eurobank's loan assets). The bank's objective is to make a profit on the spread between the bid and asked prices.

	Eurobanks	
Assets	Liabilities
Loans to banks	Time deposits
Loan to	CDs
companies	Floating rate notes
and	
governments	

Deposits denominated in about fifteen eurocurrencies are regularly traded in the London interbank market. These currencies include the Austrian shilling, Belgian franc, Canadian dollar, Danish krone, French franc, German mark, Italian lira, Japanese yen, Netherlands guilder, Norwegian krone, Spanish peseta, Swedish krona, Swiss franc, U.K. pound sterling, and U.S. dollar. Some other eurocurrencies exist in special regional markets. Banks in Bahrain trade deposits denominated in Saudi riyals, for example. A typical bid-ask spread for traded eurocurrency deposits is one-eighth of 1 percent for the U.S. dollar, German mark, Swiss franc, and Netherlands guilder. The other currencies usually have equivalent bid/asked spreads, but a spread may widen in thin market trading. As an illustration, Table 12.1 gives interest rates on eurodeposits traded in the London market on October 19, 1984.

The other asset category, "loans to companies and governments," arises from the eurocredits market. Loans in this market are generally longer term and entail

TABLE 12.1
Bid and Asked Eurocurrency Interest Rates Between Prime London Banks on October 19, 1984

	Interest rates on external currency funds*					
	48 hours	7 days	1 month	3 months	6 months	12 months
Austrian shilling	6.50– 6.63	6.63– 6.75	6.75– 6.88	6.88– 7.00	7.00– 7.13	NA
Belgian franc	10.38–10.50	10.38–10.50	10.63–10.75	10.63–10.75	10.63–10.75	10.88–11.00
Canadian dollar	–	12.00–12.50	11.94–12.19	12.06–12.31	12.19–12.44	12.19–12.44
Danish krone	11.00–11.13	11.00–11.13	10.75–10.88	11.38–11.50	11.63–11.75	11.63–11.75
French franc	10.50–10.63	10.63–10.75	10.88–11.00	11.13–11.25	11.69–11.81	12.13–12.25
German mark	5.44– .5.56	5.44– 5.56	5.50– 5.63	5.81– 5.94	5.81– 5.94	5.94– 6.06
Italian lira	15.38–15.50	15.38–15.50	15.75–15.88	15.88–16.00	16.00–16.13	15.88–16.00
Japanese yen	5.88– 6.00	5.88– 6.00	5.88– 6.00	6.13– 6.25	6.13– 6.25	6.25– 6.38
Netherlands guilder	5.75– 5.88	5.75– 5.88	5.88– 5.94	6.08– 6.19	6.13– 6.25	6.31– 6.44
Norwegian krone	12.13–12.25	12.38–12.50	12.56–12.69	12.56–12.69	12.56–12.69	12.56–12.69
Spanish peseta	4.88– 5.00	7.88– 8.00	11.75–11.88	12.50–12.63	12.94–13.06	13.25–13.38
Swedish krona	12.88–13.00	12.88–13.00	13.13–13.25	13.13–13.25	12.88–13.00	12.88–13.00
Swiss franc	2.00– 2.13	1.88– 2.00	5.13– 5.25	5.31– 5.44	5.25– 5.38	5.06– 5.19
U.K. sterling	9.83– 9.75	10.13–10.25	10.44–10.56	10.63–10.75	10.69–10.81	10.56–10.69
U.S. dollar	9.94–10.08	10.00–10.13	10.19–10.31	10.56–10.69	10.81–10.94	11.31–11.44

* Percentage based on current transaction rates between prime banks and other institutions in London.
Source: International Reports, *Statistical Market Letter.*

a greater possibility of default by the borrower. Therefore the spread the bank charges over its cost of funds is higher than in the interbank market. In addition, the concept of *rollover pricing* was created so eurobanks could avoid the possibility of paying higher interest rates on the bank's liabilities than the bank was receiving on its eurocredits. A credit extended through rollover pricing involves a succession of short-term loans that are periodically rolled over at a different interest rate. The interest rate on the loan is *fixed for the duration* of an interest period but *updated at the beginning* of the next interest rate period. If a new interest period begins at time t, then the interest rate $i(t)$ will be set according to a market reference rate $r(t)$ by the formula:

$$i(t) = r(t) + \text{Lending margin.}$$

The reference rate $r(t)$ is chosen in such a way that it will move up and down in step with the rates the bank pays on its liabilities. Thus, if the cost of funds to the bank has gone up or down when the bank funds its loan for a new interest rate period, the interest rate $i(t)$ on the **rollover credit** will rise or fall.

EXAMPLE 12.1

In 1969 Minos Zombanakis of the London merchant bank Manufacturers Hanover Ltd. organized one of the earliest rollover credits in the eurodollar market when he assembled a group of twenty-two banks to make a $200 million loan to the government of Italy. The interest rate was set at .75 percent above six-month **LIBOR,** the **London Interbank Offered Rate** — the rate at which eurobanks in London offer to lend to other banks. In this case, LIBOR was the chosen reference rate. As an interbank offer rate, LIBOR would move up and down in conjunction with bid rates, so LIBOR was tied to a London eurobank's cost of funds. The lending margin was .75 percent. The interest rate on the loan was to be revised every six months. That meant eurobanks could fund themselves with new six-month eurodollar deposits at the beginning of each interest period, and thus lock in a profit of .75 percent plus the spread between bid and asked prices in the interbank market. (This profit was locked in, of course, only if the borrower did not default on the loan. Thus the size of the margin had to be adjusted for default risk.)

Usually, the reference rate used in rollover pricing is one of the **IBORs**, or **Interbank Offered Rates**, the rates at which eurobanks will lend to other eurobanks in the interbank market. Some frequently used reference rates include:

LIBOR	The London Interbank Offered Rate, for one of the fifteen currencies listed in Table 12.1
BIBOR	Bahrain Interbank Offered Rate
BRIBOR	Brussels Interbank Offered Rate
DIBOR	Dublin Interbank Offered Rate
HKIBOR	Hong Kong Interbank Offered Rate
KIBOR	Kuwait Interbank Offered Rate
LUXIBOR	Luxembourg Interbank Offered Rate
MIBOR	Madrid Interbank Offered Rate

SIBOR   Singapore Interbank Offered Rate
JLTP   Japan Long-Term Prime Rate
ECU Interbank Offered Rate
U.S. Prime Rate
U.S. CD Rate
U.S. Banker's Acceptance Rate
Sterling Acceptances Commission
Canadian Prime Rate

Of course, not all these reference rates are eurocurrency interest rates. Domestic reference rates sometime appear in eurocredits because international loans often involve groups of banks, some of which may be lending from domestic sources and others of which may be eurobanks. The final reference rate may represent a compromise between domestic and eurocurrency funding.

LIBOR is also a frequently used reference rate for floating rate notes. In addition, the rate on floating rate notes is sometimes tied to LIMEAN (the mean of the bid and offer rate) or LIBBR (the London Interbank Bid Rate).

The lending margin is the fixed spread borrowers agree to pay above the reference rate. Since the loan rate on a eurocredit is adjusted according to the bank's cost of funds, the lending margin (along with any fees) represents the bank's profit in the event of no default. The bank will set the margin according to credit conditions and the perceived riskiness of the loan. Some times the lending margin is a *floating margin*. An example of a floating margin is a lending margin that is set at .3 percent above six-month LIBOR for the first three years of the loan but 1 percent above six-month LIBOR for the remaining life of the loan.

There are two general types of eurocredits as seen from the point of view of when and how the borrower gets the money involved in the loan: term credits and revolving credits. A term credit has a set time schedule during which the principal in the loan gradually becomes available to the borrower, a period of grace during which the full amount of the loan is available to the borrower, and then a schedule of repayments of the principal. Interest is paid at set time intervals, usually on a rollover basis, but occasionally at a fixed interest rate. In revolving credit the borrower has a certain maximum line of credit that he can use or not use as he wishes. In either a term credit or a revolving credit, interest is paid by the borrower only on the amount of the credit actually in use, but there is a *commitment fee* paid by the borrower on the unused portion. In revolving credit, the amount not used is at the borrower's discretion; in term credit, the amount not used is partly determined by the time schedule.

SIZE AND GROWTH OF EUROBANKING

Since 1963 the Basel-based **Bank for International Settlements (BIS)**, which serves as a clearing house among central banks, has collected data on the eurocurrency market. Another major source of eurocurrency data is Morgan Guaranty Trust Company's *World Financial Markets,* which supplements the BIS data with some additional estimates. Following is Morgan Guaranty's estimated aggregate balance sheet for eurobanks as of December 1984. The data, though stated in U.S. dollar terms, includes all eurocurrencies. Eurodollars constitute about 82 percent of the total liabilities listed.

Eurobanks, December 1984

Assets (billions)		Liabilities (billions)	
Claims on banks	$1668	Liabilities to other banks	$1789
Claims on nonbanks	$ 684	Liabilities to official monetary institutions	$ 97
Conversion into domestic currencies	$ 31	Liabilities to nonbanks	$ 497

We see that most eurobanking business is with other banks. That is, the interbank market, which involves borrowing and lending interbank deposits at a small bid-ask spread, accounts for most eurobank activity. Loans to banks were $1668 billion, while deposits from other banks were $1789 billion. The most important category, from the point of view of its importance to economic activity, is the category "claims on nonbanks," which represents the eurocredits market. As of December 1984, that amount was estimated to be $684 billion. Since eurobank-granted credits of this amount are roughly matched by $594 billion of liabilities to nonbanks and official monetary institutions, the amount of economic resources being funneled from ultimate savers to ultimate borrowers by the eurobanking sector at this time was probably in the neighborhood of $600 to $700 billion. (The residual category "conversion into domestic currencies" is used to describe the matching of eurocurrency liabilities by domestic currency assets.)

How did eurobanks come to be so important in the world economy? In Chapter 1 we saw that eurobanking and the eurocurrency market had grown up as a competitive challenger to noncompetitive domestic financial intermediaries. We traced the origin to the sterling crisis of late 1956 and early 1957. British authorities raised the bank rate (the rate charged by the Bank of England to British discount houses that make markets in government securities and commercial bills) to 7 percent and banned the use of sterling to finance trade between non-sterling countries. British banks began making trade loans in dollars. That is, they created a market for the U.S. dollar outside the geographical and legal boundaries of the U.S. Involved in this were British overseas banks and merchant banks. Overseas banks, including branches of foreign banks, are commercial banks that emphasize international transactions. Merchant banks are either *accepting houses,* which specialize in financing international trade by accepting (guaranteeing) and discounting bills of exchange, or *issuing houses,* which focus on raising investment capital.

Later in the 1960s, bursts of growth occurred in 1966 and 1968–1969 when market interest rates (interest rates on Treasury bills and commercial paper) rose above the maximum rates commercial banks could pay as allowed by the Federal Reserve's Regulation Q. Eurobanks, again, were able to capture deposits by their ability to offer competitive market interest rates, since they were not subject to Federal Reserve restrictions.

With the breakdown of the Bretton Woods system of par values for currencies with respect to the U.S. dollar, the restrictions associated with the Interest Equalization Tax and Foreign Credit Restraint Program were removed. But the euromarket continued to thrive even without the artificial advantage granted by U.S. or other domestic regulatory restrictions. In particular, the euromarkets played an important role in the 1970s in funneling savings from OPEC current account surplus countries to LDC current account deficit countries.

EUROCURRENCY CENTERS

A eurocurrency "center" refers to a place where there is a concentration of eurobanks. A number of factors are associated with the rise of a eurocurrency center. There should be political stability: an absence of coups d'état, the threat of foreign takeover, or fear of radical government policy changes. There should be a favorable political environment in which to conduct international finance: favorable tax treatment of banking conducted in foreign currencies, an absence of exchange and credit controls for such business, and a respect for financial privacy. There may be other advantages such as good telecommunication links with other financial centers or a favorable time zone in terms of the geographic location of the center.

Eurocurrency centers can be categorized into five geographical areas: Western Europe, including London, Zurich, Paris, and the Channel Islands; the Caribbean and Central America, including the Cayman Islands, the Bahamas, and Panama; the Middle East, including Bahrain; Asia, including Singapore, Hong Kong, and Tokyo; and the United States, including various states that have provided for the establishment of International Banking Facilities. A few institutional and historical details will be of interest.

Western Europe

London was historically the first, and is still the foremost, eurocurrency center. No other center approaches the diversity of its business conducted in over a dozen foreign currencies. This preeminence is an outgrowth not only of London's history of continual fixed investment in financial expertise but also of U.K. regulations that have differentiated between banking conducted in sterling and banking conducted in other currencies. The London-based eurocurrency market is dominated not, however, by British banks but by U.S. and Japanese overseas banks. A functional difference in the operation of U.S. and Japanese banks in the London market has emerged in that U.S. banks have specialized by funding in CD liabilities, while Japanese banks have come to dominate in funding their lending through the interbank market. It was a U.S. bank, Citibank, that pioneered London dollar CDs in 1966. In terms of eurocurrency assets, London is the principal center for medium-term eurocredit lending, so that LIBOR is the most widely used reference rate in rollover credits.

Caribbean and Central America

The Cayman Islands is one of the most favored locations for establishing a shell branch for U.S. banks. These shell branches are legally incorporated in the Cayman Islands, but the actual "bank" is a separate set of books in the headquarters office in New York or elsewhere. Operational decisions for the Caribbean eurobank are made by traders in the bank's New York trading office.

It is not difficult for a large international bank to open a branch in the Cayman Islands. The $240,000 minimum capital requirement can be met using the capital of the parent bank. There are no lending, interest, or reserve requirements for eurocurrency operations. The language is English and telecommunication facilities are good. Business hours are the same as those of New York. It is perhaps not surprising that this small group of islands with fewer than 20,000 inhabitants is host to more than 350 banks and trust companies.

Establishment costs for a bank, including a class B, unrestricted license — suitable for eurocurrency business — were, according to one estimate made in the early 1980s [see W. S. Walker, "Cayman Islands," in Brown (1982)]:

1. Legal fees $4000
2. Class B license, unrestricted   8400
3. Registration fees as a foreign
   branch   480
4. Miscellaneous   75
5. Auditor's fees   Negotiable

Annual costs, other than the normal operating expenses for the bank's trading activities, which take place in New York, included as major items:

1. Class B license, unrestricted $8400
2. Foreign branch annual fee   240
3. Miscellaneous   50

The Middle East

Bahrain is the center of the Middle East market for both foreign exchange and eurocurrency trading. This has been partly a function of the war in Lebanon, which diminished Beirut's role as the traditional financial center of the Middle East, and partly a function of Bahrain's close proximity to Saudi Arabia. Bahrain is the center of euro-Saudi riyal trading, and eurocredits have been extended based on BIBOR rates for both the U.S. dollar and the Saudi riyal.

The United States

Eurocurrency operations within the geographic area of the United States were legalized on December 3, 1981, through the creation of **International Banking Facilities (IBFs)**. IBFs are a set of books kept at U.S. banks, or at branches and agencies of foreign banks in the United States or at edge corporations. There are no reserve requirements or interest ceilings on deposits booked at IBFs. However, there is a minimum maturity of two business days for nonbank deposits, and nonbank transactions can be in minimum amounts of $100,000. Loan and deposit customers of IBFs are only allowed to be foreign residents, other IBFs, or the IBFs parent. If an IBF makes loans to its parent, the parent bank is subject to the normal reserve requirement that applies to bank liabilities stemming from eurocurrency borrowing. A number of states have passed laws exempting IBFs from state and local tax. IBFs are, however, subject to federal tax. Finally, and perhaps most importantly, IBFs cannot issue negotiable instruments such as CDs or get FDIC insurance.

The prohibition on issuing negotiable instruments was intended to keep them out of the hands of U.S. residents. If IBFs were allowed to issue CDs, it was reasoned, then — even if IBFs did not issue deposits directly to U.S. residents — it would be difficult to prevent U.S. residents from purchasing the CDs of IBFs on the secondary market. This prohibition on issuing negotiable instruments has tended to diminish the attraction of IBFs for many U.S. banks. Many banks would prefer to open (or keep) a Caribbean shell branch that does not suffer from the no-CD restriction. As a consequence, the biggest enthusiasm for IBFs has thus far been exhibited by U.S.-based Japanese and Italian banks. Domestic legal restrictions had prevented either of these groups of banks from opening shell branches in the Caribbean, but do not prohibit them operating IBFs in the United States.

Asia

Singapore is the center of the eurocurrency ("Asian dollar") market in Asia. Eurobanking began in October 1968 when Bank of America, Singapore, received permission to open an international banking facility (called an Asian Currency Unit). Asian Currency Units were allowed to accept foreign deposits from nonresidents and to make foreign loans outside a restricted area. One of the immediate impetuses for the creation of the market seems to have been large area holdings of dollars acquired as a result of the Vietnam War without a concomitant outlet in a convenient time zone. SIBOR is now the commonly used reference rate for Asian dollar loans.

EURODEPOSITS AND SOVEREIGN RISK

Eurobanks and eurodeposits are subject to all the risks normal to banks and banking deposits generally. In addition, the borrowing and lending of currencies across national boundaries implies the additional risk that might stem from government actions to restrict the movement of capital or to impose controls on foreign currency transactions. For example, in October 1983 the Philippine government imposed controls limiting the transfer of foreign currency funds from Philippine banks. As a result Citibank of New York froze several hundreds of millions of eurodollars deposited in its Manila branch. According to *The Wall Street Journal,* Citibank said "it had no choice but to freeze the deposits when the cash-strapped Philippine government imposed controls banning foreign-exchange outflows" (February 23, 1984). This news was not welcomed by Wells Fargo Asia Ltd., a Singapore-based subsidiary of Wells Fargo Bank of San Francisco. Wells Fargo Asia had placed two $1-million deposits with Citibank, Manila in June 1983, one of which was to mature on December 9 and the other on December 12. Wells Fargo Asia expected the deposits to be repaid upon maturity at Citibank, New York. When repayment did not occur, Wells Fargo Asia sued Citibank, New York in a New York federal court. Japanese banks, with the largest amounts of frozen deposits, were not happy either.

Because of sovereign risks like that illustrated above, eurodeposits generally pay a premium above comparable domestic deposits. This premium is usually in the neighborhood of twenty-five basis points. (Citibank, Manila was in addition reportedly paying seventy-five basis points — .75 percent — above the normal eurodollar rate.) The probability of events like the "thrilla in Manila" may be small but is nonetheless real.

Most U.S. international banking takes place through bank *branches.* Branches differ from *subsidiaries.* In U.S. law, the parent bank is responsible (liable) for deposits placed in branches. A subsidiary, by contrast, is legally independent of the parent, and the depositor has no legal recourse if the subsidiary fails to pay up. (Good business practice, however, would usually dictate that the parent pay up on its subsidiary's deposits also in the event the subsidiary failed.)

Since, for example, Citibank, Manila was a foreign branch, most banks with dollar deposits there expected Citibank, New York to make good on them, regardless of the actions of the Philippine government. Citibank, however, claimed an exemption on the basis that the imposition of exchange controls was an "act of state." The act-of-state doctrine in U.S. law essentially implies that since a foreign branch is under foreign jurisdiction, the parent U.S. bank will not normally be held responsible for the failure of its branch to repay if this failure is due to actions of a sovereign government. This means that, to a depositor, a dollar in Manila is not quite the same as a dollar in New York, even if the headquarters bank is the same.

SYNDICATED EUROCREDITS

BANKING SYNDICATES

About half of all eurocredit lending takes place through large groups of banks, called **syndicates**, that band together to loan amounts of money that are too large for any one particular bank. In this chapter we shall see how syndicates are organized and loans priced. The syndication procedure is widely used in international bank lending, whether the loans come from eurobanks or are financed partly or entirely by domestic banks.

There are several parts to a banking syndicate. The **lead manager** (there may be more than one) is the bank with the primary responsibility for organizing a syndicated loan. The lead manager has the main responsibility for agreeing on the terms and conditions of the loan with the borrower, for arranging for other banks to take up a portion of the loan, and for evaluating market conditions. Other banks who are invited to take part in the lending and accept are known as **participating banks**. A special category among the participating banks is the **managing banks**, usually distinguished from other participating banks in that they have a larger share in the loan and may assist or advise the lead bank. Although various other subcategories among the participating banks may be established (such as **comanagers** and so on), the titles usually don't mean much except that banks who lend more money get a more impressive title. Finally, there will be an **agent bank** appointed to oversee the loan. The agent bank (which is often one of the lead managers) collects payments on the loan from the borrower and disburses the payments to the other banks according to their share in the loan. Table 13.1 lists the top twenty lead managers of syndicated loans for the year 1984. The ranking is made according to the total amount of money lent by syndicates of which a particular bank served as lead manager. Ranking may vary considerably from year to year, as can be seen by comparing the 1984 ranking with that for 1983.

Borrowers usually select a particular lead manager on the basis that they already have a relationship with that bank. Well-known borrowers will neverthe-

TABLE 13.1
Top 20 Lead Managers of Syndicated Euroloans and Euronotes in 1984, Compared to 1983 Ranking

Rank 1984	Bank	Amount* ($ millions)	Rank 1983	Amount* ($ millions)
1	BankAmerica Cap. Mkts. Group	30,847.1	1	8,348.5
2	Chase Manhattan	25,739.8	5	3,184.2
3	Citicorp	15,169.6	3	5,164.7
4	Manufacturers Hanover	9,880.0	9	1,914.5
5	Morgan Guaranty	9,283.2	11	1,634.3
6	Bankers Trust Company	7,336.5	2	6,374.0
7	Credit Suisse First Boston	3,368.3	10	1,814.0
8	Bank of Montreal	2,839.7	6	2,335.1
9	Chemical Bank	2,815.5	12	1,374.8
10	Bank of Tokyo	2,660.7	7	2,240.1
11	Natwest Bank Group	2,643.0	4	3,829.1
12	Lloyds	2,598.6	19	1,075.7
13	First National Bank of Chicago	2,264.6	26	973.3
14	Bank of Nova Scotia	2,263.0	21	1,025.4
15	Merrill Lynch	2,236.7	68	302.6
16	Industrial Bank of Japan	2,197.0	13	1,301.3
17	Hongkong Bank Group	2,154.8	14	1,291.0
18	RBC/Orion Royal Bank	2,148.9	20	1,028.3
19	Midland Bank	1,675.4	49	490.5
20	Banque Paribas	1,575.3	29	885.2

* Dollar amounts represent total syndicated loan amounts, irrespective of amount actually lent by the lead manager. Sole lead managers are credited with the full amount of a syndicated loan in the totals above. Co-lead managers are credited with apportioned amount.
Source: Euromoney, *Annual Financing Report,* 1985.

less shop around, and banks themselves will approach potential customers. If approached by a creditworthy borrower, the lead manager will begin to assemble a small group of managing banks, who — with the lead manager — may supply a large part of the total loan. On the basis of demand for the loan, the lead manager will negotiate with the borrower (or potential borrower) the amount of the loan, the interest rate or rates on the loan, other banking fees, and details concerning how other banks will be invited to participate in the loan.

When there seems to be preliminary agreement on details, the lead manager will prepare a **placement memorandum**. The placement memorandum will describe the borrower, including the borrower's financial condition, and give details about the proposed loan. The lead manager will then invite other banks to participate in the loan. Prospective participating banks are usually invited by telex. Invitation telexes may be sent to several hundred banks, who will also be provided with a copy of the placement memorandum.

If demand by other banks to take part in the loan is good, then the amount of the loan may be increased if the borrower wishes. On the other hand, if there is insufficient demand, the managing banks (with the lead manager) may have to make up the difference. If the managing banks have previously guaranteed to the borrower the full amount of the proposed loan, the credit is said to be "fully underwritten." On the other hand, if the credit is on a "best efforts" basis, the managing banks have only promised to try their best. If there is not sufficient demand in the latter case, the size of the loan may be scaled down or the terms changed.

TABLE 13.2
Top 35 Borrowers in Syndicated Loan Market in 1983

Borrower	Country	Amount ($ millions)
1. Gulf Oil Corporation	U.S.	4275.0
2. Petroleos Mexicanos (PEMEX)	Mexico	4121.6
3. Pennzoil	U.S.	2500.0
4. Kingdom of Sweden	Sweden	2453.7
5. Kingdom of Denmark	Denmark	1727.3
6. Republic of Indonesia	Indonesia	1542.0
7. European Economic Community (EEC)	—	1240.0
8. Placid Oil Company	U.S.	1230.0
9. State Energy Commission of Western Australia (SECWA)	Australia	1206.7
10. State of California	U.S.	1200.0
11. Diamond Shamrock Corporation	U.S.	1000.0
12. Sonatrach	Algeria	950.0
13. Bell Canada Enterprises	Canada	916.7
14. Colorado Interstate Corporation	U.S.	875.0
15. International Bank for Reconstruction and Development (IBRD)	—	845.0
16. Kingdom of Spain	Spain	833.1
17. Banque Exterieure d'Algerie (BEA)	Algeria	800.0
18. Santa Fe International Corp.	U.S.	765.0
19. Quintette Coal Ltd.	Canada	760.0
20. Electricite de France (EdF)	France	759.0
21. Costal Corporation Connection	U.S.	750.0
22. Olympia and York Battery Park Co.	U.S.	728.3
23. Ireland	Ireland	728.2
24. Martin Marietta Corporation	U.S.	720.0
25. Warner Communications Inc.	U.S.	700.0
26. Istituto per la Ricostruzione Industriale	Italy	692.2
27. County of Los Angeles	U.S.	678.8
28. Korea Exchange Bank	Korea	651.0
29. Rockefeller Center Service Corporation	U.S.	650.0
30. Republic of Portugal	Portugal	641.3
31. Ente Nazionale per l'Energia (ENEL)	Italy	634.6
32. Hong Kong Land Co. Ltd.	Hong Kong	605.3
33. Midcon Corporation	U.S.	600.0
34. Export-Import Bank of Korea	Korea	587.5
35. Credit National	France	552.0

Source: Euromoney, *Annual Financing Report,* 1984.

For illustration, Table 13.2 lists the top thirty-five borrowers in the syndicated loan market in 1983. Table 13.3 breaks down amounts borrowed in the eurocredits market over the last several years according to the country of origin of borrowers.

LOAN COSTS

There are several types of costs to the borrower in addition to the obligation to repay the loan principal. These may be divided into *periodic costs* and *up-front costs*. Periodic costs include the interest paid on the amount of the credit actually in use. If the interest agreement was six-month LIBOR plus a 1 percent margin, then the borrower will make periodic interest payments on the amount of the credit drawn (the amount of the loan the borrower has actually received). The

TABLE 13.3
Eurocurrency Bank Credits by Country of Borrower*

	1976	1977	1978	1979	1980	1981	1982	1983	1984
Industrial countries	11255	17206	28950	27248	39100	86022	42571	38752	77111
Developing countries	15017	20976	37302	47964	35054	45264	41519	32937	31555
Latin America	8664	9917	21332	28077	24103	30152	26719	15406	16437
Asia	2830	4277	7921	10551	7142	10288	8403	8828	10185
Middle East and Africa	3523	6782	8049	9336	3809	4824	6397	8703	4933
Centrally planned countries	2503	3394	3767	7325	2809	1791	765	1212	3370
International organizations	74	190	160	275	429	302	160	1321	250
Total	28849	41766	70179	82812	77392	133379	85015	74222	112286

* Expressed in millions of U.S. dollars.
Source: Morgan Guaranty, *World Financial Markets.*

interest rate in this example will be the new six-month LIBOR rate established at the beginning of the current six-month period, plus 1 percent. In addition, there will be a **commitment fee** (probably in the range of .25 percent to .75 percent) to be paid periodically on the unused portion of the credit. In a revolving credit, the unused portion of the credit may be anywhere from 0 percent to 100 percent of the total amount of the credit, depending on the wishes of the borrower. In a term credit, the amount of the undrawn portion of the total amount will depend on the time schedule that has been previously agreed on for drawing down and paying back the principal. During the grace period of a term credit, 100 percent of the credit will be available, so there will be no commitment fee if the total credit line has been drawn down. Finally, there will usually be a small *agent fee* paid to the agent bank for its services. In summary:

Periodic costs = (Amount of total credit drawn) × (Reference rate
+ margin)
+ (Amount of total credit not drawn) × (Commitment fee)
+ Agent fee.

The up-front cost is conceptually a .5-to-2.5 percent one-time fee on the total amount of the credit, which is paid to the lead manager and managing banks for organizing and managing the loan. In practice, the managing banks will pass along a portion of this fee to the participating banks, so that we may divide up-front costs into **management fees** and **participation fees**. The lead manager will usually receive a *praecipium,* which means that the lead bank will get a bigger share in the total management fees than will the other managing banks. On a $100,000,000 credit, a typical division of a 1.5 percent total amount of fees ($1,500,000) might be 25 percent to the lead manager ($375,000), 25 percent to be split among the managing banks ($375,000), and 50 percent to be split among the participating banks ($750,000). If, for example, there are fifty participating banks, each of which loans the same amount of money, each will receive $750,000/50 = $15,000 up front when the syndicated credit is extended.

In recent years, many of the larger banks have specialized in managing loans as middlemen. That is, they manage syndicated loans in order to receive up-front fees for their management services; afterward, they will sell off much of their share in the loan to other smaller banks or thrift institutions. This practice has stemmed not only from the comparative advantage of some banks in providing management services but also from new regulatory guidelines. In the summer of 1983, U.S. regulators ordered the nation's seventeen largest multinational banking organizations to maintain a ratio of primary capital to assets of at least 5 percent. Some of these banks did not subsequently have sufficient capital themselves to provide large amounts of new funds.

The amount of margin added to the reference rate in a syndicated credit is related to relative risks, given the overall ratio of desired borrowing to desired lending. Risk exists whether the lending is to companies or to sovereign borrowers. It is futile to apply the usual fiction, often raised in a domestic context, that lending to governments is default-free. Governments that borrow in terms of foreign currencies do not have the power to create foreign currency by fiat, and they cannot acquire foreign currency by taxing foreign citizens. In addition, an attempt simply to produce more domestic currency and exchange it in the FX market for the required foreign exchange will normally be self-defeating, since the purchasing power of the domestic currency over foreign currency will fall

TABLE 13.4
Spread Over LIBOR Paid by Sovereign Borrowers in the Syndicated Eurocredits Market in 1983

Country	Average weighted spread (%)	Average maturity (Years)	Country	Average weighted spread	Average maturity (Years)
New Zealand	.25	2.00	Portugal	.73	6.48
Finland	.34	7.00	Norway	.76	1.66
Taiwan	.37	9.25	Philippines	.76	8.00
Austria	.38	8.00	Nigeria	.83	8.21
Thailand	.38	8.00	Pakistan	.88	3.30
Republic of Palau	.44	6.95	USSR	.91	1.87
France	.47	7.96	Turkey	.95	5.97
Belgium	.47	7.00	Iraq	.99	5.00
India	.48	7.84	East Germany	1.00	5.00
Indonesia	.49	8.12	Ivory Coast	1.00	0.51
Sweden	.49	7.21	Czechoslovakia	1.13	4.00
Malaysia	.50	9.91	Hungary	1.21	3.60
Jordan	.51	7.00	Nepal	1.25	7.00
Tunisia	.54	8.00	Morocco	1.26	4.18
Abu Dhabi	.56	10.00	Columbia	1.41	6.04
Ireland	.57	7.29	Trinidad & Tobago	1.45	7.00
Denmark	.58	7.00	Jamaica	1.50	10.00
Italy	.59	7.20	Egypt	1.50	10.00
Algeria	.59	7.93	Zambia	1.50	1.00
Sri Lanka	.59	7.82	Cameroons	1.63	6.00
Australia	.59	13.97	Argentina	1.75	3.00
Oman	.59	7.00	Venezuela	1.85	5.86
Iceland	.61	6.47	Congo	1.97	4.97
Greece	.65	6.96	Panama	2.00	7.00
Spain	.69	7.16	Brazil	2.11	5.44
Papua New Guinea	.72	8.00	Paraguay	2.41	8.00
Korea	.72	8.09			
Average, all countries	.76	7.04			

Source: Euromoney, *Annual Financing Report*, 1984.

correspondingly. (The effort may succeed in part, however, to the extent the government is successful in extracting real resources from the domestic economy through domestic inflation. These real resources can be used to generate foreign exchange.) Table 13.4 gives the average spread over LIBOR that governments paid in syndicated eurocredits in 1983. As the different margins indicate, some governments were seen as more risky than others. Latin American countries, in particular, paid high spreads.

LOAN AGREEMENTS AND THE RISKS OF LENDING

Getting a borrower to sign a legal document will never turn a bad credit risk into a good one. Nevertheless, syndicated loan contracts are revealing in other ways. The provisions of typical loan agreements are important for our purposes because they give us an indication of the various economic and other risks lenders take into account before lending money. They define the rules of the game each side expects the other to live up to.

PROVISIONS FOR INTEREST RATE RISK

Recall that the concept of rollover pricing was created so that eurobanks (and other banks in syndicated lending) could avoid the problem of funding long-term loans with short-term liabilities. If, for example, a bank funded a five-year eight-percent fixed-rate loan by issuing six-month time deposits, then if short-term interest rates (the rate on six-month deposits) rose sharply, the bank might end up paying, say, 9 percent on its deposits while it was still receiving only 8 percent on the loan. That is, there is interest risk that arises because the maturity of assets (loans) may differ from the maturity of liabilities (deposits).

To be sure, all financial intermediaries engage in some **maturity transformation:** they issue short-term liabilities which are used to fund long-term assets. Since long-term interest rates (received on loans) are generally higher than short-term interest rates (paid on deposits), the financial intermediary (the bank) will make a profit based on the difference between long-term and short-term interest rates. (This process is called "riding the yield curve.") That is, the bank is rewarded for assuming interest rate risk. But, as syndicated lending grew in the early 1970s, it was felt this risk was too great. Eurobanks were accepting great amounts of 30- and 90-day time deposits but being asked for five- and seven-year loans. So, to reduce the amount of maturity transformation they had to undertake, banks began to do part of their lending on a rollover basis, which reduced the amount of interest-rate risk stemming directly from maturity transformation.

Rollover pricing is accomplished by setting a margin over a reference rate, so loan agreements have to spell out the manner in which this reference rate is calculated. If six-month LIBOR is the reference rate, then, since it is a market interest rate, six-month LIBOR will change from minute to minute, and at any one time will differ from bank to bank. The loan agreement will specify the **reference banks,** the banks whose offered prices in the interbank market are used to determine the "London" interbank offered rate. In addition, the agreement will specify the day and the time of day this determination is to be made. Since interbank deposits are traded at prices that are determined in the market today but are for delivery two days later, the loan agreement will usually specify that LIBOR is to be determined two days prior to the new interest rate period, at, say, 10:30 A.M. London time.

While such provisions shield the bank from interest risk due to maturity transformation, it does not shield the bank from all consequences of interest rate changes. In the early 1980s it became apparent that some banks, by using rollover pricing, had simply *transformed interest rate risk into credit risk.* To see why, consider the situation of the borrower. Suppose a borrower like PEMEX, the Mexican state-owned oil company, has borrowed when LIBOR is 10 percent, paying a 1 percent margin above LIBOR, and LIBOR subsequently rises to 15 percent. If the dollar price of PEMEX's product, Maya or Isthmus crude, does not rise commensurately (when adjusted for demand and cost factors), then the real dollar borrowing rate as seen by PEMEX has risen. Faced with higher real borrowing costs, PEMEX may now be a higher credit risk: there may be a higher probability that PEMEX cannot repay the loan. But the bank may have supposed that the 1 percent margin charged on the loan was sufficient compensation for the credit risk involved, while falsely assuming that rollover pricing eliminated interest rate risk. But, in this case, the bank will not really have eliminated the interest risk due to changes in LIBOR, because changes in LIBOR are correlated with changes in credit risk.

PROVISIONS FOR THE RISK OF GOVERNMENT INTERVENTION

Standard loan agreements signed with company borrowers include various provisions that attempt to ensure that government action will not directly diminish the value of the lending margin. Payments must be made free of withholding taxes or other charges. In practice, this means that if, for example, the borrower's government imposes withholding taxes on the borrower's interest payments, the borrower will have to increase its payments sufficiently to meet the requirement of the loan agreement. If a 20 percent withholding tax is imposed, then the borrower will have to make payments of 10 percent interest in order to pay 8 percent to the lending banks $(.10 - .10 (.20) = .08)$.

These provisions also include actions on the part of the lending bank's government. If the lender's central bank alters reserve or deposit requirements in such a way that it is more costly for the lending bank to fund the loan, the loan agreement usually requires the borrower to pay the additional cost. The borrower may also be required to pay for the lender's increased cost if the government alters tax laws in a way that affects the lender's net income.

Governmental action may also affect the way the bank funds its loans. For example, there may be a disruption of the interbank market or the CD market. In such a case, loan agreements usually allow the lender to substitute a new reference rate, or way of calculating interest rates, that reflects the bank's cost of funds. Otherwise, the borrower usually has the option of prepaying the loan.

PROVISIONS RELATED TO BORROWER CREDIT RISK

Loan agreements will be based on information about the financial state of the borrower at the time the loan is made as well as an understanding about how the borrower will conduct its financial affairs over the life of the loan. Statements made by a eurocredit borrower about its financial state at the time the credit is being sought are referred to as **representations** or **warranties**. Promises the borrower makes about its *future* behavior are referred to as **covenants**. A company, for example, may promise to maintain a certain asset-to-liability ratio over the life of the loan or to limit total debt service and dividends in some stipulated way. A government might promise to adhere to an IMP program, or promise that it will not give new creditors security (liens) without offering the existing creditors the same security. A promise of this latter type, a promise to *not* do something, is referred to as a **negative pledge**.

A *pari passu* covenant, like a negative pledge, is a covenant used to ensure that the lending banks will be treated equally with other creditors in the event a borrower becomes insolvent and is subsequently liquidated. Most international loans are unsecured, and *pari passu* provisions prevent the subordination of the lending banks to other *unsecured* creditors. (Negative pledges prevent the subordination of lending banks to *secured* creditors.) A cross-default clause gives the lending banks the right to accelerate the outstanding balance of the loan in the event the borrower defaults on another indebtedness. This may include any other indebtedness or may only include certain types of indebtedness, such as foreign debt. Cross-default clauses allow the banks to accelerate the loan in the event default on the current loan is anticipated as a result of default on other loans.

RULES OF THE GAME FOR SETTLING DISPUTES

In connection with any loan, events can arise about which there was no prior agreement. Therefore loan agreements usually involve an agreement about the rules for settling disputes, such as: Which country's laws shall govern in the dispute? If the borrower is a government, is sovereign immunity waived? If judgment is rendered in a foreign court in a currency other than the lending currency, is the lender protected against currency fluctuations?

THE SECONDARY MARKET FOR EUROCREDITS

Recently various secondary markets for eurocredits have emerged. While not large, these markets may grow and consequently improve the efficiency of risk-sharing in the eurocredits market. One serious impediment to the growth of the secondary market has been the Glass-Steagall Act in the United States, which prohibits banks from dealing in securities (and hence prevents loans from being traded like securities in a secondary market). Another has been the size of past bank lending to LDCs (Chapter 2), which has made bankers unwilling to allow the true value of their loan portfolios to be revealed by market prices.

Banks that have not taken part in a particular syndicated loan may buy shares in the loan from one of the original participating (or managing) banks. That is, if the agreement with the borrower allows, a bank that has taken part in a syndicated loan may later transfer its obligation — or part of its obligation — to another bank. As mentioned previously, this is especially true in the case of large money-center banks which have a comparative advantage in managing loans (and hence earning management fees) and wish to make room on their balance sheets in order to take part in, and manage, new loans.

For New York banks, New York law allows three ways to dispose of a loan asset — novation, assignment, and subparticipation. A novation is the discharge of one obligation and the creation of an entirely new one. The original bank lender is relieved entirely of its obligations with respect to the original loan. With the borrower's consent, a new bank creditor takes over the old creditor's rights and obligations. An assignment, by contrast, usually involves the transfer to another bank of the right to receive principal and interest from the borrower. The second bank now has a direct claim on the borrower but may not be able to sue the borrower under its own name. A subparticipation is the partial assignment of the right to receive principal or interest to another bank, but the debtor/creditor relationship between the original bank and the borrower remains unchanged. The bank buying the subparticipation typically has no recourse either to the debtor or to the bank from which the subparticipation was purchased. Subparticipations usually bear an interest payment that is $\frac{1}{8}$ to $\frac{1}{4}$ percent lower than the original participation in the eurocredit. So, in effect, the original bank continues to collect interest from the borrower and passes this to the subparticipating bank after extracting a fraction of 1 percent. Various banks, including Citicorp, Chase, and Bankers Trust have set up divisions to sell subparticipations.

Swaps are another type of secondary market activity. Loan or debt swaps between banks may take place for many reasons: differences in the perceived riskiness of the debt of different borrowers; differences in individual bank exposures; differences in disclosure requirements; preferences for public-sector or private-sector debt; preferences for loans with tax receipts; differences in the ability to influence different borrowers; differences in writedowns on loans from a particular borrower; differences in the need for liquidity (if cash is involved in the swap). (See Guttentag and Herring [1985].)

Asset-for-Asset Swaps

This type of swap might entail two creditor banks exchanging loans from different countries. A cash payment is sometimes used to make up the difference if the loans have different values. For example, in 1983 Bankers Trust gave the Brazilian bank Banco Real $100 million of Brazilian loans and $90 million in cash in return for $190 million of Banco Real's loans to Mexico.

In general, the debt of different borrowers may be discounted, so the exchange ratio in a loan swap will not be one-for-one. For example, four dollars of Polish debt may trade for three dollars of Mexican debt. In 1983–1984 the following discounts were applied at one time or another in sovereign loan swaps.

Country	Discount %
Poland	40
Argentina	30
Philippines	25
Brazil	25–28
Venezuela	22
Mexico	16–17

A different type of asset-for-asset swap is the exchange of debt for real property. In 1985, for example, foreigners who wished to invest in Argentina could redeem any holdings of government paper for its full face value. This paper could be acquired in the swap market at 70 to 75 percent of face value. The government's redemption of the paper at its face value could be viewed as a risk premium paid by the government to attract foreign investment. It was not clear, however, why the Argentine government did not repurchase its own debt at the cheaper market price. Did it view the debt as overvalued despite the market discount?

Accounting for a sizable share of restructured-loan swap transactions has been Eurinam International, a New York investment bank, in a joint venture with Singer and Friedlander Ltd., a London merchant bank. Eurinam arranged over 100 swaps in 1984. When Eurinam is involved in arranging a swap, the seller assigns the loan to Eurinam, which in turn assigns it to the buyer through a standard participation agreement.

It is not clear that all swap activity represents optimizing behavior. In 1983 the SEC enacted the requirement that banks with publicly traded stock disclose their holdings of country loans if aggregate exposure for the country exceeded the lesser of 1 percent of total assets or 20 percent of primary capital. Annual reports must list the debtor country, the aggregate exposure, and a breakdown of exposure by public, private, and banking sectors and by maturity. In addition, individual country exposures in excess of .75 percent of assets or 15 percent or primary capital have to be reported (but not broken down). Some banks subsequently engaged in swaps simply to manipulate their reported exposure levels.

Asset-for-Debt Swaps

This transaction typically involves Bank A paying off its debt liability to Bank B by turning over one of its own loan assets to Bank B. Bank B in effect replaces its original loan to Bank A with a different loan that it acquired from Bank A.

Asset Sales for Cash

One regional bank traded $2 million in Brazilian government debt for $1.6 million in cash and $400,000 of notes from Grupo Alfa in Mexico. "'When we get the Alfa, we'll just write if off as worthless,' says an official of that bank, pointing out that the transaction in effect amounts to a 20 percent discount for Brazilian government debt" (*Wall Street Journal,* November 27, 1984).

NOTE ISSUE FACILITIES

The years 1984–1985 saw a shift in the pattern of commercial bank activity from direct eurocredit lending to loan underwriting in the form of note issuance facilities (NIFs). In an NIF a developed country borrower plans to raise funds by issuing floating rate notes. The underwriting commercial banks stand ready for a period of three to ten years to buy the borrower's notes or to otherwise make the borrower a loan if the notes cannot be placed in the market at an interest cost below a set maximum (the interest rate cap at which the banks will finance the borrower). The banks charge an annual fee for this service.

With NIFs the process of "securitization" of eurocredits is complete because floating rates *are* securities and can be bought and sold as such on the secondary market. The advantage to the borrower is that overall borrowing costs are reduced, since money and capital markets are accessed directly. The advantage to banks is that fees in the form of underwriting guarantees can be generated without adding new assets to balance sheets. In finance theory terms, the bank's role is that of a writer of interest rate options. The strike price of an option is the maximum interest rate (the interest cap). If the interest rate is above the cap level, the borrower exercises the option and borrows at the strike price. The annual fee corresponds to the option premium.

PROBLEMS FOR CHAPTER 13

1. A London bank makes a term loan at a margin of 1 percent over six months LIBOR. The credit is for $1 million, of which half is drawn down at the beginning of the first

year, and the remaining half at the beginning of the second year. Principal repayments do not begin until the beginning of the third year. There is a commitment fee of $\frac{1}{4}$ percent per annum. The six-month LIBOR reference rates for the first two years are 10, 10, 11, and 11 percent. Assuming 360-day years, what are the amounts of periodic interest and fees the bank receives during the first two years?

2. In order to obtain a syndicated loan from commercial banks, a country promises to limit its rate of expansion of central bank credit to a maximum of 25 percent per annum. This promise is an example of a [choose one]:

   a. representation;
   b. covenant;
   c. warranty;
   d. praecipium;
   e. cross-default clause.

3. In what way could the secondary market trading of eurocredits prove useful in evaluating political risk?

DEPOSIT DEALING AND THE TERM STRUCTURE OF EUROCURRENCY RATES

THE INTERBANK MARKET

Most eurocurrency trading involves the borrowing or lending of time deposits in transaction amounts varying from one to several million dollars. Deposits will be accepted over the phone from banks or corporations, and loans will be made in the same manner to banks or to corporations according to individually established credit lines. Chapter 1 showed how such transactions look in terms of balance-sheet changes. A eurobank receives a eurodollar deposit in the form of a demand deposit balance at some domestic U.S. bank. Similarly, a eurodeposit in Dutch guilders would be made by turning over to the eurobank a guilder deposit at a bank in the Netherlands. Loans are made in the same manner. A eurobank in London will make a $1,000,000 loan by transferring to the borrowing party a $1,000,000 deposit at a U.S. bank.

Settlement dates for eurocurrency deposit trades were covered in Chapter 4 in connection with forward exchange rates. Most trades made today will be good two business days later. Standard maturities are for one, two, three, six, nine, and twelve months. In addition, there are deposits with a maturity of one day ("spot/next"), one week ("spot week"), and two weeks ("spot fortnight"). Deposits can also be traded that are settled (good) on the same day the trade takes place and mature the following day. These are called **overnight** deposits. A similar type of deposit, called **tomorrow/next,** is settled on the day following the trading day, and matures one day later (on the second day after the trade).

As with foreign exchange, eurocurrencies are traded both through direct dealing and through brokers. Marketmakers will quote two-way prices with a bid/offer spread. The bid rate is the rate the trader will pay on deposits, while the offer rate is the rate that will be charged on loans. The size of this spread is usually .125 percent (12.5 basis points) for eurodollar trades. If a broker is used, the broker will receive a brokerage commission of perhaps .03125 percent (3.125 basis points) from each of the two parties that are matched through the broker.

Since eurocurrency deposits are borrowed and lent in the form of a domestic demand deposit, they are close substitutes for domestic deposits. The substitution is not perfect: we saw in Chapter 12 that the threat of exchange or capital controls is an additional source of risk for eurocurrency deposits. To compete with domestic deposits, eurobanks must pay a higher interest rate to compensate the depositor for this risk. Interest rates on three-month eurodollar deposits usually are at a premium of twenty-five to fifty basis points over interest rates on domestic U.S. negotiable certificates of deposit. (Eurodollar CDs—a much smaller market than that for time deposits—usually trade at an interest rate 12.5 basis points below the rate on eurodollar time deposits.) The interest rate on overnight eurodollar deposits tracks closely the U.S. interest rate on federal funds and repos (**repurchase agreements**—a form of secured lending between banks involving the short-term purchase and resale of U.S. government securities). These differentials are illustrated in Figure 14.1 for some recent years. Similarly, the rate on euroyen deposits closely tracks the gensaki (repo) rate in the Japanese domestic market. For some currencies, such as the French franc, the existence of a complex set of controls ensures that there is no close substitute in the domestic market for the eurocurrency deposit.

FIGURE 14.1

Eurodollar rates compared to federal funds and 90-day certificates of deposit. [*Source:* Board of Governors of the Federal Reserve.]

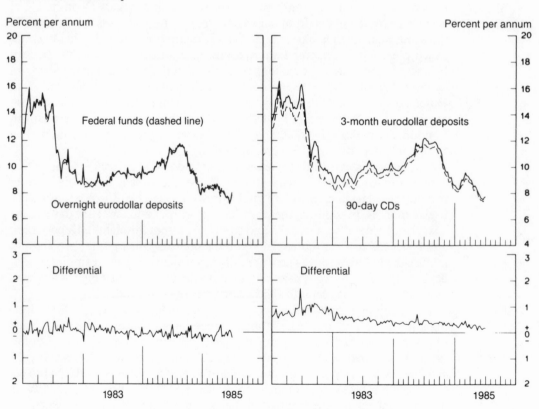

Eurobanks are able to offer higher interest than domestic banks on similar deposits primarily as a result of eurobank specialization in wholesale term lending and borrowing. By specializing in this way, eurobanks have smaller operating costs and can in addition optimize on their holdings of reserves. Domestic banks, by contrast, have set reserve requirements that are always fixed at a level higher than the optimal level from the point of view of the bank. For example, suppose that 5 percent of assets has to be maintained in the form of reserve assets at the central bank and that these assets do not earn interest. If the average interest a bank pays on liabilities is 11 percent, while the average interest it receives from its nonreserve assets is 12 percent, the net interest earning—prior to fixed costs—is $(.95)(12\%) - (11\%) = .4\%$. This compares with a 1 percent net interest earning if no reserves were held. The amount of reserves a bank would normally hold—in the absence of fixed reserve requirements—would depend on the maturity profile of its deposits compared to the maturity of its loans, as well as on the interest rate on reserve assets compared to the interest that could be earned on other assets. The bank would want to hold more reserves the greater its amount of maturity transformation and the higher the return on reserve assets compared to other assets.

The risks faced by eurobanks and eurocurrency dealers can be divided into three types. First, there will be foreign exchange risk if the currency denomination of assets does not match the currency denomination of liabilities. The nature of foreign exchange risk was covered in detail in Part II. Eurobanks will allow some position-taking by their traders but will place overall limits on the amount of currency mismatching that can take place. Some of the currency mismatching arises in connection with the interest parity theorem covered in Chapter 4. Just as eurocurrency deposits can be used to create an artificial forward rate, so spot and forward exchange markets can be used in connection with one eurocurrency to create artificial deposits and loans in another eurocurrency. For example, one may borrow eurodollars, buy Austrian shillings spot, and lend them for three months. Meanwhile, the shillings can be sold forward to cover the exchange risk. Thus one has created a loan of euro-Austrian shillings using the exchange markets in connection with the eurodollar market. Euro-Spanish pesetas are another example where this operation is frequent. (See Problem 1.)

A second type of risk is interest-rate risk to the extent the maturity of assets and liabilities is not matched. Only if maturities are perfectly matched can a bank be sure that a loan at one interest rate is funded by a deposit at a lower interest rate. Eurobanks typically engage in only small amounts of maturity transformation (maturity mismatching) in the interbank market, but a good bit more in the eurocredits market. Interest risk is considered in more detail below in connection with the term structure of interest rate. Traders will have overall position limits on the amount of interest-rate betting they can practice but will be free to take positions within the overall guidelines established by bank management. Finally there is credit risk, which refers to the possibility that someone may not perform on a contract. A loan may not be repaid. This risk is dealt with in the interbank market by establishing limits on the amount of dealing with a bank according to the bank's overall reputation in the market, as well as its geographic location. For retail customers such as companies, credit limits will be established after a careful individual credit evaluation.

THE TERM STRUCTURE

The profitability of lending and borrowing across maturities depends not only on the existence of spreads between bid and asked rates in the interbank market and margins in the eurocredits market, but also on the term structure of interest rates. The term structure of interest rates is a graph of the interest rate (i) seen as a function of the term to maturity (T) of an asset or liability. For example, the current rates on eurodollars may be the following (Chapter 4 explained how eurocurrency rates are quoted in the market).

T (days)	i (per annum)
32	.0987
60	.1000
91	.1013
182	.1038
367	.1065

Here interest rates (measured at an annual rate) are increasing with term to maturity. This is referred to as an "upward-sloping" term structure. If rates decrease with term to maturity, the term structure is "downward-sloping." If interest rates (measured at a common annual rate) are the same across maturities, the term structure is "flat." Other shapes are also possible. For example, rates may rise over earlier maturities, then fall over later ones. The slope of the term structure is not independent of the way in which rates are quoted. Since eurocurrency rates are quoted at an annual rate for a 360-day year, it is better to forgo common interpretations of the slope and instead pay attention to the implied forward rates, which will now be discussed.

For convenience, let us assume there is no bid/asked spread between borrowing and lending rates. (This is done only in order to avoid writing separate bid and ask rates in the equations below.) Consider two deposits at time t, one of which bears an interest rate $i(t,n)$ and matures at time $t + n$ and the other of which bears an interest rate $i(t,T)$ and matures at time $t + T$, with $n < T$. We can conceive of a third interest rate $f(t + n, T - n)$, a *break-even* or **implied forward rate**, such that if the earlier-maturing deposit were reinvested at the interest rate $f(t + n, T - n)$ at time $t + n$ for maturity at time $t + T$, the final yield would be the same as the yield on the deposit of longer maturity:

$$1 + i(t,T)\frac{T}{360} = \left[1 + i(t, n)\frac{n}{360}\right]\left[1 + f(t + n, T - n)\left(\frac{T - n}{360}\right)\right]. \quad (14.1)$$

Solving for $f(t + n, T - n)$, we obtain

$$f(t + n, T - n)\left(\frac{T - n}{360}\right) = \frac{1 + i(t, T)\,(T/360)}{1 + i(t, n)(n/360)} - 1. \quad (14.2)$$

Recognizing that $1/[1 + i(t, T)(T/360)]$ is just the price of a discount bond $B(t, T)$, equation (14.1) may be written in the simple reciprocal form

$$B(t, T) = B(t, n)H(t + n, T - n) \quad (14.3)$$

where

$$H(t + n, T - n) = 1/[1 + f(t + n, T - n)((T - n)/360)]$$

is the implied forward bond price.

EXAMPLE 14.1

Consider interest rates and maturities as follows:

T (days)	i (per annum)	B
182	.1038	.9501
367	.1050	.9033

From equation (14.3), the implied forward bond price $H(t + 182, 185)$ is:

$(.9033) = (.9501) H(t + 182,185)$

or

$H(t + 182, 185) = .9507$.

Alternatively, the implied forward interest rate may be calculated from equation (14.1) as:

$1 + (.1050)(367/360) = [1 + (.1038)(182/360)][1 + f(t + 182, 185)(185/360)]$

or

$f(t + 182, 185) = .1009$.

The implied forward rate is easily interpreted. In Example 14.1, the implied forward rate was .1009, or 10.09 percent. This means that if you invested in 182 day deposits at a rate of 10.38 percent and then reinvested the deposit with interest for another 185 days at the implied forward rate of 10.09 percent, your final return at the end of 367 days would be the same as if you invested at the 367-day rate of 10.50 percent. Alternatively, if you borrowed for 367 days at a rate of 10.50 percent, invested the money for 182 days at a rate of 10.38 percent, and then reinvested again for 185 days at a rate of 10.09 percent, you would break even. This shows that *if you borrow long and lend short, you will break even if the loan is rolled over at the implied forward rate.* The same is true if you borrow short and lend long: *if you borrow short and lend long, you will break even if you refund the loan by borrowing again at the implied forward rate.*

On the other hand, if market interest rates at time $t + n$, for maturity at time $t + T$, were *different* from the implied forward rate, then borrowing short and lending long will earn a profit or a loss. If you were borrowing short and lending long, you would earn a profit if you refunded the loan at a rate below the implied forward rate and a loss if you refund the loan at a rate above the implied forward rate. If you were borrowing long and lending short, you would earn a profit if you rolled over the loan at a rate above the implied forward rate and a loss if you rolled over the loan at a rate below the implied forward rate.

We see that the interest risk associated with maturity transformation is a consequence of the fact that actual short-term market rates may be different from implied forward rates. We can thus characterize maturity transformation in the form of a bet on interest rates. *Borrowing short and lending long represents a bet that actual short-term market rates will turn out to be below the implied forward rate.* Similarly, *borrowing long and lending short represents a bet that actual short-term market rates will turn out to be above the implied forward rate.* The nature of these bets suggests that implied forward interest rates should be related to interest rate expectations.

It is tempting to equate the implied forward rate $f(t + n, T - n)$ with the expected short-term interest rate that will prevail at time $t + n$. That is, if $I(M,t)$ is the market information set at time t, one possibility is that

$$f(t + n, T - n) = E[i(t + n, T - n)|I(M, t)]. \tag{14.4}$$

Equation (14.4) represents the *expectations theory of the term structure.* The expectations theory should be considered a purely empirical proposition, in the same way that the speculative efficiency hypothesis discussed in Chapter 7 is a purely empirical proposition. That is, equation (14.4) is not necessarily a consequence of economic maximization or of rational behavior, for reasons similar to those that allow the forward exchange rate to diverge from the expected spot rate. However, equation (14.4) is a useful reference case for thinking about interest risk in eurobanking. To the extent that maturity transformation can be considered as a pure gamble on interest rates, equation (14.4) defines a condition of zero expected profit.

In certain circumstances, the implied forward rates can be used as a basis for pure arbitrage transactions. If an *actual* forward rate can be locked in in such a way that there is a total net profit on the borrowing or lending transaction, there will be no risk or gamble associated with the unknown market interest rate that will occur in the future. Two ways in which it may be possible to establish a locked-in forward interest rate are through eurodollar futures contracts (discussed below) or through **future rate agreements (FRAs)**. Under a future rate agreement (which is actually a *forward* contract), one bank makes a contract with another bank for a fixed interest rate applying to a future period. For example, it might be an agreement on a three-month interest rate for a three-month period beginning six months from the present and terminating nine months from the present. Such an agreement would be called "three against nine." An interest rate on any FRA available in the market can be compared to the implied forward rate, $f(t + 180, 90)$, for the same period on any contemplated transaction. If the available FRA diverged from the implied forward rate in a favorable direction for the transaction under consideration, a known interest rate profit could be locked in on the transaction. Alternatively, a bank that was asked to quote an interest rate for a FRA deal would look at the implied forward rate as the basic guide to its quotation (see Problems 2 and 3).

EURODOLLAR FUTURES

Eurodollar loans priced on a rollover basis above LIBOR can be hedged for a limited time using eurodollar futures. In addition, banks may find it profitable to arbitrage between the interbank market and the futures market for eurodollars.

To see how this works, we need to first familiarize ourselves with the features of standard eurodollar futures contracts.

Eurodollar futures contracts are traded at the IMM in Chicago, at LIFFE in London, and at the SIMEX in Singapore. (In Singapore, the contract is referred to as an Asian-dollar contract.) Eurodollar futures contracts are like currency and other futures contracts (see Chapter 5) in that the contract, considered by itself in isolation from other assets, is a pure bet. In this case, the bet concerns the direction of movement of the futures price of a eurodollar deposit. As with other futures contracts, there are two sides to the bet. If the price goes up, the *long* side wins and the *short* side loses. The reverse happens if the price goes down.

The eurodollar futures price is based on the interest rate paid on a three-month eurodollar deposit (for future delivery) with a face value of $1,000,000. The interest rate on this (future) three-month eurodollar deposit is, like all eurodollar deposit rates, quoted at an annual rate. The *eurodollar futures price* is then *defined* to be:

100 − (the interest rate, in percentage terms, of a 3-month eurodollar deposit for future delivery).

For example, if the interest rate on the (future) three-month deposit is 10.36 percent, the eurodollar futures price is

100 − 10.36 = 89.64.

Notice what this means. If *interest rates go up,* the eurodollar *futures price goes down,* so the short side of the futures contract makes money. If *interest rates go down,* the eurodollar *futures price goes up,* so the long side of the futures contract makes money. Thus a speculator would go long futures if he was betting that interest rates would fall and short if he was betting that rates would rise. Why use an artificial futures "price" constructed in this way instead of just quoting the interest rate as the price? The answer has to do with consistency with the prices on other futures contracts. Because the eurodollar futures "price" is constructed in the way it is, the *long* side of the futures bet makes money when the "price" goes *up,* just as with DM, soybeans, gold, and greasy wool futures. Traders don't get confused.

Since the face value of the contract is $1,000,000, one basis point (.01 percent) has a value of $100 for a 360-day deposit. For a three-month deposit, the value of one basis point is thus logically $25, and the futures exchanges define a one-basis-point move in the price in terms of a $25 transfer between the long and the short position. For example, if the futures price drops from 88.15 to 88.13, then the short side wins $50 (2 × $25), while the long side loses $50. The futures price is determined in the market minute by minute as the price at which the number of people who want to go long is equal to the number of people who want to go short.

At all three exchanges—the IMM, LIFFE, and the SIMEX—eurodollar futures are traded for delivery in March, June, September, and December. That is, if one were to take delivery on a March eurodollar futures contract, then the three-month period for the deposit would begin counting from the day of delivery in March. Delivery is made on the third Wednesday of the month. The last day of trading is two business days prior to the third Wednesday.

However, there is an important difference between the IMM/SIMEX contract and the LIFFE contract. With the LIFFE contract, those who still have short positions in effect at the close of the final day of trading may have the obligation to turn over a three-month eurodollar deposit in a London bank to those with long positions in the futures contract. The long side of the contract has the option of choosing either actual delivery of a time deposit or settlement in cash (discussed below). If delivery of a time deposit is taken, then on delivery day, the third Wednesday of the delivery month, those with long positions pay $1,000,000 in cash for each futures contract in which they are long. They receive in turn a three-month deposit bearing an interest rate determined by the last day's settlement price. For example, if the last day's settlement price was 90.45, they get a deposit with an annual (360-day) yield of

$$100 - 90.45 = 9.55 \text{ percent.}$$

In truth, the short side can deliver a deposit with an interest rate different from 9.55 percent, but the difference between the yield on the deposit actually delivered and 9.55 percent would be made up in cash.

On the IMM contract, by contrast, delivery is only "in cash." What this means is that no eurodollar deposit is actually delivered. Instead, at the end of the final day of trading on the second business day prior to the third Wednesday there occurs the usual daily cash flow, based on the movement of the futures price. After that nothing happens. The futures contract ceases to exist and no further transfers, of cash or anything else, take place. Similarly at LIFFE, if cash delivery is taken, the final day's cash flow takes place two business days prior to the third Wednesday.

There is a potential problem in that no deposit is actually delivered in the IMM contract. What forces the futures price to be the same as the spot price on the last day of trading? With the LIFFE contract, the answer is simple: arbitrage. On the last day of trading of a LIFFE contract, there will be two equivalent ways of buying a three-month eurodollar deposit. One way is to buy a deposit directly in the interbank market. The other way is to go long on a LIFFE eurodollar futures contract and to take delivery. Hence arbitrage between the two markets would (within a margin of difference allowable because of the bid/asked spread) force the prices in the two markets to be the same. But no such arbitrage is possible with the IMM contract.

The IMM forces the eurodollar futures price to converge to the spot price by the way the exchange determines the settlement price on the final day of trading. The IMM keeps a list of at least twenty London banks that deal in eurodollar deposits. On the last day of trading for a particular contract, they take a sample of twelve of these banks and obtain their quotations for three-month LIBOR. The two highest and two lowest quotations are thrown out, and the other eight quotations are averaged to obtain the three-month deposit rate. This sampling of twelve banks is done twice: once at 3:30 P.M. London time and also at a random time interval in the last ninety minutes of trading. The two samplings yield two values for the three-month deposit rate (each value an average of eight bank quotations). The arithmetic average of these two values is the final settlement price on the final day of trading.

Below are prices on the June 1984 IMM eurodollar futures contract as quoted in *The Wall Street Journal* on March 28, 1984.

	Open	High	Low	Settle	Change	Yield
June	88.78	88.82	88.73	88.81	+.08	11.19

The "open" price of 88.78 was the market-determined price at which a contract traded (someone going long, someone going short) when the market opened at the beginning of the day. Sometime during the day a trade took place at 88.82, and this was the high price of the day. Similarly, the low price at which a trade took place was 88.73. The final settlement price for the day was 88.81, which was eight basis points higher ("change" = .08) than the previous day's settlement price. That is, between the close of the two days, those with long positions had their account balances increased by (credited with) $200 (8 × $25), while those with short positions had their account balances decreased (debited) by $200. The "yield" is an unnecessary column, since the 11.19 percent interest rate on the (future) three-month eurodollar deposit can be obtained as

$$100 - 88.81 = 11.19.$$

HEDGING WITH EURODOLLAR FUTURES

We will consider two examples, one involving a banking hedge and the other involving a borrower of a eurocredit priced at a margin above LIBOR.

EXAMPLE 14.2

On June 12 a bank observes a rate of 10 percent on three-month eurodollar deposits in the interbank market. If a $1,000,000 deposit is borrowed today, the value date will be June 16, and the deposit will mature on September 16, a total of ninety-two days. The bank also observes that it can lend a six-month eurodollar deposit at $10\frac{13}{16}$ percent. If lent today, the value date will be June 16, and the deposit will mature on December 16, a total of 183 days. Meanwhile, September eurodollar futures are trading at 89.23 (10.77 percent). Taken together, these prices imply the bank can lend a six-month deposit, funding this loan by a sequence of two three-month deposits, and be assured of a profit for the six months.

Consider the bank's problem. If it lends for six months, it will receive interest at an annual rate of $10\frac{13}{16}$ percent. But for the first three months it will only pay interest on its borrowed three-month deposit at an annual rate of 10 percent. However, there is the risk that when the three-month deposit is rolled over after three months, the market interest rate on three-month deposits will have risen. Let us first calculate the implied forward rate f, as this is the rate the bank can afford to pay on the second three-month deposit and still break even on the total transaction:

$$1 + (.10\tfrac{13}{16})(183/360) = (1 + .10(92/360))(1 + f(91/360))$$

or

$$f = 11.34\%.$$

Thus, as long as the bank can ensure that it will pay a rate *less* than 11.34 percent for the second three-month period, the bank will make a profit. But September eurodollar futures are at 10.77 percent. So by going *short* one September contract at 89.23 (10.77

percent), the bank will ensure that, if interest rates rise, the bank will have a positive cash flow that will offset the cost of borrowing above 10.77 percent for the second three months. Since the bank will make money at any rate less than 11.34 percent, it will ensure a profit on the six-month loan through the futures hedge.

More realistically, Example 14.2 can be taken as a quasi-arbitrage opportunity in that a bank that deals in the interbank market may assign a trader to arbitrage between the eurodollar deposit market and the eurodollar futures market. The trader will then be continually comparing rates in the interbank market with rates on eurodollar futures and will be looking for opportunities like the one given in Example 14.2.

EXAMPLE 14.3

In this example, the borrower's objective is to insure itself against a *nonanticipated* increase in the interest cost of a loan priced at a margin above LIBOR. It is important that the word "nonanticipated" be stressed, because — as we shall see — the borrower will usually not want to insure against the entire increase. For each $1,000,000 outstanding in the loan, the borrower would go short one eurodollar futures contract. In this way, if LIBOR rates increase so that the borrower will have to pay a higher rate of interest in the new interest-rate period of the loan, there will be a positive cash flow on the futures contract that will offset part of the increased interest cost. (By the same token, of course, if interest rates fall so that borrowing costs fall, there will be a negative cash flow on the short futures position.)

The futures price will converge to the spot price (today's interest rate) at maturity of the eurodollar futures contract. Thus, if the interest rate in the futures contract was already higher than the spot interest rate, the total movement in the futures price will be less than the total movement in the spot price over the period. In that case the cash flow on the futures contract will not completely offset the borrower's increased interest cost if the borrower hedges the principal of the loan dollar for dollar in the futures market. The borrower can, of course, go short futures contracts in an amount larger than the amount of the loan so that the cash flow on the futures price will (more or less) exactly match the increased borrowing cost if interest rates rise. But this is risky. If interest rates fall, the losses on the futures contract will be larger than the reduction in borrowing costs. Most borrowers would not be willing to take this risk.

For simplicity in this example, we will use the same data as in Example 14.2. Consider a loan made at three-months LIBOR plus a 1 percent margin. The loan is rolled over at a new interest rate every three months. The next interest-rate period extends from June 16 to September 16, so LIBOR for the new period will be determined two London business days prior to June 16, which is June 12 in this case. The prices are those in Example 14.2, a three-month eurodollar rate of 10 percent, and eurodollar futures are at 89.23 (10.77 percent). The borrower goes short one eurodollar futures contract for each $1,000,000 principal amount of the loan.

Suppose that interest rates rise and the loan is rolled over on September 14 at a LIBOR of 12 percent. The futures contract will have a price on this date (its expiration date) of 88.00 (12 percent). The profit on each futures contract would be 123 basis points (89.23 − 88.00) or $3075 (123 × $25). The borrower's increased interest cost from September 16 to December 16 would be

$$(91/360) \times (.12 - .10) \times \$1,000,000 = \$5055.55.$$

The increased interest cost of $5055.55 is only offset in part, since the gain on the futures contract is $3075. The $3075 offsets the "unanticipated" change in the interest rate, the difference between 10.77 percent in the original futures price and 12 percent, which was the interest rate that eventually occurred. (The difference between 12 and 10.77 is 123 basis points, and the value of this difference is $3075. The "anticipated" change, the difference between 10 percent and 10.77 percent, was not offset by the futures hedge.)

In general, the dates involved in the interest period on the loan will not match the maturity dates in the futures market. Thus, as explained in Chapter 5, the effectiveness of the hedge will hinge on the degree to which the price movement is one-for-one between movements in LIBOR and movements in the eurodollar futures price.

OPTIONS ON EURODOLLAR FUTURES

Options on eurodollar futures are traded at both the IMM and LIFFE. These options are similar to options on FX futures discussed in Chapter 6. An IMM eurodollar futures call gives the buyer the right to go long an IMM eurodollar futures contract, while a eurodollar futures put gives the buyer the right to go short. The options are American and expire on the last trade date for the futures contract. Premium quotations are in basis points, with each point representing $25. For example, a price of .68 would represent $25 \times 68 = $1700. Strike prices are in intervals of .25 in terms of the IMM index. Thus, one may buy a put on March eurodollar futures with a strike of 89.75, for example. If exercised, it gives the right to go short one IMM eurodollar futures contract at an opening price of 89.75 (see Problems 6–8).

PROBLEMS FOR CHAPTER 14

1. The central bank of Erewhon makes a forward market for Erewhon's currency, the wawa. The current bid/asked quote for 360-day forward wawas is $4.10–4.30/wawa, while the spot wawa is $4.35–4.45/wawa. A trader decides to create a loan of euro-wawas. The trader observes that the current bid/asked quote for eurodollars is $9\frac{1}{2}$–$9\frac{5}{8}$. Given this information — and assuming no default risk on the part of the borrower — the trader will be willing to loan 360-day eurowawas at any interest rate above what level?

2. If 183-day eurodollar deposits bear an interest rate of $10\frac{3}{8}$ percent and 270-day euro-dollar deposits bear an interest rate of $10\frac{1}{2}$ percent, what is the implied forward rate? What is the significance of this implied forward rate for a bank that is borrowing short and lending long in the interbank market?

3. If the bid/asked rate on six-month (183-day) deposits is $10\frac{1}{4}$–$10\frac{3}{8}$ percent, while it is $10\frac{1}{2}$–$10\frac{5}{8}$ percent on nine-month (270-day) deposits, give the profitable ranges of bid or asked prices that the bank could quote its customers for future rate agreements (FRAs) for "three against nine."

4. You buy a June eurodollar LIFFE contract at 89.42 and three weeks later take delivery when the price is 90.12. Explain:
   (a) your cash flow on the futures contract;
   (b) the amount you pay in taking delivery;
   (c) the interest rate you get on your deposit.
   How would your answers differ if your futures contract were at the IMM?

5. A borrower takes out a one-year $10,000,000 loan at a $\frac{2}{8}$-percent margin over six-months LIBOR and sells twenty IMM eurodollar futures contracts at a price of 89.05. The total amount of the loan is drawn down immediately. For the initial period, LIBOR is determined from the reference banks to be $10\frac{1}{2}$ percent. For the second period, LIBOR is determined to be $11\frac{3}{4}$ percent. At that time the borrower closes out his futures contracts at 88.00. What is the borrower's increased borrowing cost minus his futures profit?

6. Explain what happens if the owner of a put option on a June IMM eurodollar contract exercises the option when the futures price is 89.77. (The strike price of the option is 90.00.) If a call option on eurodollar futures is quoted in the *WSJ* with a price of .62, what is the dollar amount you would pay for such an option (ignoring brokerage fees)?

7. A trader has a long eurodollar futures contract and writes a eurodollar futures call option on the same contract. The futures position was opened at 89.73 and the call—with a strike price of 89.75—was written at a price of .32. Later the call is exercised when the futures price is 89.96. What was the net cash flow to the trader, ignoring any fees on the total transaction? What maximum profit would have been possible?

8. In what sense is an IMM futures put a call on the interest rate implied in the futures price? In what sense is an IMM futures call a put on the interest rate implied in the futures price? Explain how puts and calls on eurodollar futures could be used as interest-rate hedging instruments.

MONEY CREATION IN THE EURODOLLAR MARKET

This chapter looks at the economic relationship of eurobanks to domestic banks. In particular, it looks at the connection between eurodollar intermediaries and depository institutions in the U.S. financial system. The eurodollar market is the largest eurocurrency market, and the insights gained from examining it will in general, though not in all details, apply also to other eurocurrency markets.

The main questions we want to answer are these:

What determines the size and growth of the eurodollar market?

Does the eurodollar market size have economic importance?

DO EURODOLLARS MULTIPLY LIKE RABBITS?

When the eurodollar market first came to public attention in the late 1960s and early 1970s, the rumor spread that eurodollars were like rabbits: they hopped around from country to country, and one eurodollar today became ten tomorrow. A succinct expression of this point of view is found in a book called *The Ecospasm Report* by Alvin Toffler:

[Eurodollars] are spectral, almost metaphysical. . . . An American multinational corporation, for example, may shift $10 million from a bank in Chicago to a bank in Milan. The Milanese bank, with the dollars in hand, may now, on the strength of them, lend out $50 million or even more to a hard-pressed company in Manchester or Marseilles. No actual currency need change hands. . . . But $50 million will have slipped into England or France—money over which their central banks have no control.

This quotation illustrates a number of popular misconceptions concerning the eurodollar market. It may be that eurodollars are indeed spectral and almost metaphysical. All information stored in a computer is—whether it is money or the rough draft of a manuscript, a company's record of its accounts receivable or the control software for a spacecraft. But, leaving metaphysics aside, the transactions cited in the quote could never take place. If a eurobank acquires ownership of a $10-million deposit, it can at the very most loan out $10 million (not $50 million). As we saw in Chapter 1, the eurobank will have acquired the $10 million by acquiring ownership of a deposit at a U.S. commercial bank. It will make a loan by loaning out this same deposit. To make the loan it will write a check on the U.S. commercial bank, and—even assuming the eurobank keeps no reserves—could not loan out more than it receives.

Neither is it true that $50 million (or even $10 million) will have "slipped into England or France." The eurobank will make a loan to a company by giving the company a check drawn on a U.S. commercial bank. Ownership of the original $10-million domestic deposit will have changed, but the $10-million deposit itself will remain part of the U.S. domestic commercial banking system.

The Rabbit Theory of eurodollars holds that $10 million can easily mushroom into $50 million—though not in a single transaction, as suggested in Toffler's naive example. Rather, the Rabbit Theory sees one dollar turning into five in the same way that one dollar of high-powered money might turn into five dollars of M1 by a process of redepositing through the U.S. banking system. Is this analogy valid?

In the simple framework typically covered in elementary banking and macroeconomics textbooks, one obtains a "money multiplier" (m) that is a function of the ratio (rd) of reserves that a commercial bank is required to hold against its demand deposits. For a given monetary base H, there is then a money supply M given by the formula:

$$M = mH$$

where

$$m = 1/rd.$$

Some people applied this formula to the eurodollar market, where they let M denote the total size of the eurodollar market, and H denote some type of "eurodollar base." They reasoned: if $rd \rightarrow 0$, $m \rightarrow \infty$. Eurobanks are not regulated. Hence they have no reserve requirements. Thus potentially $rd = 0$. There, potentially, $m = \infty$. Therefore the eurodollar market (M) can grow to an infinite size, based on a very small eurodollar base (H). Some people even claimed to know what this alleged eurodollar base was and used their measure of this base, along with their measure for the eurodollar market, to estimate a multiplier ($m = M/H$). Estimates varied wildly, from $m = 18$ to $m = .2$.

While there may be nothing wrong intrinsically with multiplier analysis, the assumptions used in applying this simple *commercial* bank reserves multiplier directly to the eurodollar market were false. By their nature eurobanks are thrift institutions, not commercial banks, and hence do not make loans by writing checks drawn on themselves as do commercial banks. Moreover, there is no "eurodollar base" apart from the ordinary domestic high-powered monetary base, which is composed of Federal Reserve liabilities. Let us explore each of these concepts in turn.

THRIFT INSTITUTIONS VERSUS COMMERCIAL BANKS

Thrift institutions differ from commercial banks in that they do not give out checking accounts. Traditional examples of thrift institutions in the U.S. banking system include savings and loan associations and mutual savings banks. These two groups of institutions can still be taken as examples of what is meant by "thrift institutions" but, due to changes in U.S. federal regulations in 1980 and 1982, both groups of institutions can now—to a certain degree—offer checking accounts. Thus today a certain percentage of the business of savings and loan associations and mutual savings banks is ordinary commercial banking business. However, in this chapter, the term "thrift institution" will refer to an institution that does not offer checking accounts. Domestic examples of thrifts would thus include savings and loan associations prior to 1980, or the major portion of savings and loan business after 1980.

To see how thrifts differ from commercial banks, let's consider an example of thrift activity. Suppose you loan a friend $100, which he promises to repay in six months with 4 percent interest. To make the loan, you write him a check for $100, drawn on your bank. He deposits the check in his checking account, which may or may not be at the same bank. Once the check has cleared, his checking account has increased by $100, and yours has decreased by $100. The net change in demand deposits is $0. All that has happened is that ownership of a $100 demand deposit has changed from you to your friend. The amount of demand deposits has not altered in the slightest. In fact, you cannot alter the amount of demand deposits in existence by writing checks. You are not a bank. If you were a bank, you could loan your friend $100 by issuing him a checking account, and—subject to reserve availability—alter the amount of demand deposits in existence. But, since you are not allowed to issue checking accounts, you are acting as a thrift institution in making the loan. Because you make a loan by writing a check on a commercial bank and do not issue demand deposits, you do not alter the existing supply of commercial bank demand deposits.

Thus thrift institutions (including eurobanks) are distinguished by the fact that they do not give checking accounts. In fact, they themselves keep checking accounts at commercial banks with which to make loans. In addition, since thrifts must hold some reserves in a form with which they can repay their depositors if necessary, thrifts also hold reserves in the form of deposits at commercial banks. (Thrifts may, in addition, hold reserves in the form of Treasury bills or other types of liquid securities. However, they can use a Treasury bill to repay depositors only after first selling it and receiving in turn a commercial bank demand deposit.)

Thrifts thus form part of a *three-stage banking system.* At the *first stage* is the *central bank,* in this case the **Federal Reserve System.** The liabilities of the Federal Reserve make up the high-powered money base, which is composed of commercial bank checking accounts held at the Fed and printed currency (which is also a Fed liability). The *second stage* is composed of *commercial banks.* Commercial banks hold their reserves in the form of Fed liabilities. They can count as part of their legal reserve requirement any deposits they have at the Fed, and in addition any currency they may have in their vaults. (Currency banks have in their vaults is called, appropriately, "cash in the vault." The other part of currency, which circulates in the pockets of the public, is called "currency in the hands of the public.") The *third stage* is made up of *thrift institutions.* Thrift institutions, including eurobanks, hold their reserves in the form of deposits at domestic commercial banks.

RESERVE STRUCTURE AND DEPOSITORY CHOICE IN THE THREE-STAGE BANKING SYSTEM

We will now examine the structure of this three-stage banking system to analyze the sources of growth of the eurocurrency market. We begin by making some assumptions concerning the *structure (or potential structure) of* reserve requirements. For simplicity we will assume that thrifts—divided into domestic thrift institutions and eurobanks—hold reserves at fixed ratios (*rsl, re*) to their deposit liabilities (*DSL, DE*), either as a legal requirement or a precaution to meet deposit withdrawals (see bottom of Figure 15.1). A "fixed" ratio could be zero as a legal requirement. If there is no legal requirement, the reserve ratio will be set at a precautionary level depending on, among other factors, the degree of maturity transformation typically practiced by the institution. Domestic thrifts and eurobanks hold their depository reserves in the form of deposits at commercial banks.

FIGURE 15.1
Reserve structure in depository intermediaries.

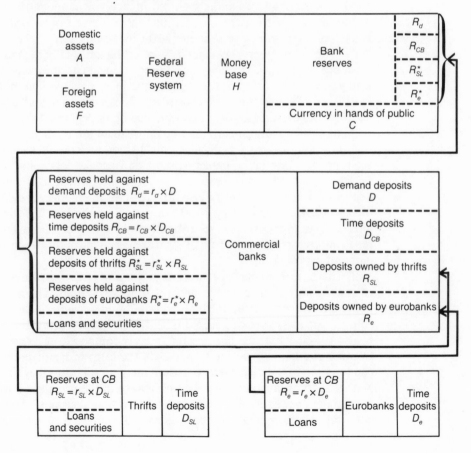

Commercial banks, in their turn, will have four potential types of reserve ratio requirements (re^*, rsl^*, rd, rcb), according to whether their deposit liabilities are owned by eurobanks (RE), by domestic thrifts (RSL), or by other parties in the form either of demand deposits (D) or time deposits (DCB). (The commercial banks' balance sheet is shown in the middle of Figure 15.1.) Commercial banks hold their reserves in the form of Federal Reserve liabilities. Commerical bank reserves plus currency in the hands of the public make up the monetary base (see top of Figure 15.1).

In this framework, the public has the choice of holding dollar assets in the form of time deposits at eurobanks (DE), at domestic thrifts (DSL), or at commercial banks (DCB); in the form of demand deposits at commercial banks (D); or in the form of currency (C) in the hands of the public (remember that currency, if held by the public, is "currency in the hands of the public"; the other part of currency is vault cash and serves as bank reserves). The public may, alternatively, hold nonintermediated dollar assets such as Treasury bills or commercial paper. However, if they buy nonintermediated dollar assets they do so by exchanging a demand deposit for the asset, so that total demand for deposit assets need not be affected by the existence of nondeposit assets.

The menu of asset choices is illustrated in Figure 15.2. The public's choice among these different depository assets will depend on the structure of interest rates, aggregate demand (because of the transactions demand for money), perceptions of risk, and so on. That is, the public's *portfolio allocation* will determine the relative shares of each type of deposit in the total depository portfolio.

Table 15.1 shows how proportional dollar allocations among deposits and currency changed between 1966 and 1978. There was a gradual change in proportions over the period, but it was not erratic. The time trend was fairly smooth, which suggests that for the most part at any point in time during this period there was limited substitutability between different types of depository assets. In the long run, however, there was greater substitutability, as can be seen in the increased eurodollar share from 3 percent to 18 percent over a span of twelve years.

FIGURE 15.2
Potential depository asset choice offered to dollar holders.

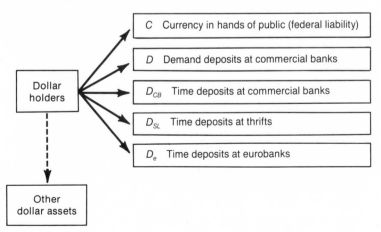

TABLE 15.1
Share Allocation of Dollars Among Deposits and Currency for Selected Years

Year-end	c	d	t	s	e
1966	.08	.26	.30	.33	.03
1967	.07	.25	.31	.33	.04
1968	.07	.25	.32	.32	.04
1969	.07	.25	.30	.33	.06
1970	.07	.23	.31	.32	.07
1971	.06	.22	.32	.32	.08
1972	.06	.20	.32	.33	.09
1973	.06	.19	.33	.32	.11
1974	.05	.18	.34	.30	.13
1975	.05	.16	.33	.31	.14
1976	.05	.15	.32	.32	.15
1977	.05	.14	.31	.33	.17
1978	.05	.14	.31	.32	.18

c: Currency held by the public as a fraction of Z.
d: Demand deposits at commercial banks as a fraction of Z.
t: Time deposits at commercial banks, including certificates of deposit of over \$100,000, as a fraction of Z.
s: Time deposits at savings and loan associations and mutual savings banks as a fraction of Z.
e: Net eurodollar deposits as a fraction of Z.
Z: $C + D + DCB + DSL + DE$ (total deposits plus currency in the hands of the public).
Source: Grabbe (1982).

EURODOLLAR, MONEY, AND OTHER MULTIPLIERS

It is now time to put the pieces together. We will see that three things — the size of the high-powered money base, the structure of reserve requirements, and the depository choice of the public — combine to determine the size of the eurodollar market (DE) as well as the size of the money supply $(C + D)$. ("Money" is used here in its normal economic sense, meaning the medium of exchange. It will thus be measured as currency in the hands of the public plus demand deposits at commercial banks.) At any one time there is a given amount of high-powered money (H), determined by the Federal Reserve System. When the given amount of high-powered money is totally absorbed in the form of reserves, no more deposits can be created. The *rate* at which high-powered money (H) is absorbed depends both on the structure of reserve requirements and on the depository choice of the public.

Define a variable Z, called "total liquidity," to be the sum of all deposit liabilities held by the public:

$$Z = C + D + DCB + DSL + DE. \tag{15.1}$$

Let small letters (c,d,t,s,e) denote, respectively, the proportions of Z made up by each of these types of deposits (C,D,DCB,DSL,DE):

$$Z = (c + d + t + s + e) Z. \tag{15.2}$$

These proportions represent the depository choice of the public among available assets. Next, referring back to Figure 15.1, we see that the high-powered monetary base (H) will be absorbed either in the form of reserves (RD) against commercial bank demand deposits, reserves (RCB) against commercial bank time deposits, reserves (R^*SL) against deposits of thrift institutions at commercial banks, reserves (R^*E) against deposits of eurobanks at commercial banks, or currency in the hands of the public (C). Breaking H into its components and using equations (15.1) and (15.2), we get

$$
\begin{aligned}
H &= RD + RCD + R^*SL + R^*E + C \\
&= (rd)(D) + (rcb)(DCB) + (r^*sl)(RSL) + (r^*e)(RE) + C \\
&= (rd)(D) + (rcb)(DCB) + (r^*sl)(rsl)(DSL) + (r^*e)(re)(DE) + C \\
&= [(rd)(d) + (rcb)(t) + (r^*sl)(rsl)(s) + (r^*e)(re)(e) + c]\,Z.
\end{aligned} \tag{15.3}
$$

Define now a "total liquidity multiplier" (mz) that represents the amount of dollars of Z created from each dollar of H:

$$ Z = (mz)\,H. $$

From (15.3), we get that

$$ mz = 1/[(rd)(d) + (rcb)(t) + (r^*sl)(rsl)(s) + (r^*e)(re)(e) + c]. \tag{15.4} $$

We may also define a "money multiplier" (mm) which represents the total amount of money ($c + D$) which is created from each dollar of H;

$$ mm = (C + D)/H = (c + d)(Z)/H = (c + d)(mz). \tag{15.5} $$

That is, the money multiplier (mm) is just the total liquidity multiplier (mz) multiplied by ($c + d$), which is the fraction of $C + D$ in Z. Finally, we may define a *"eurodollar multiplier" (*me), which represents the amount of eurodollars created from each dollar of high-powered money (*H):

$$ me = (DE)/H = (e)(Z)/H = e\,(mz). \tag{15.6} $$

The eurodollar multiplier (me) is just the total liquidity multiplier (mz) multiplied by e, which is the fraction of eurodollars in total liquidity (Z). *In summary, we have that the size of the eurodollar market* (DE) *is given by*

$$ DE = (me)H = e\,(mz)H. \tag{15.7} $$

SOURCES OF GROWTH OF THE EURODOLLAR MARKET

Equation (15.7) summarizes several sources of growth of the eurodollar market. The first is the monetary base H, which is under the control of the Federal Reserve. As H grows, total deposits of all types—including eurodollars—will increase in quantity.

A second source of growth relates to the portfolio preference of the public. The public's portfolio preference enters in two ways. As seen in equation (15.7), the size of the eurodollar market is a direct function of e, the desired eurodollar portion of Z. In addition, the size of the eurodollar market is a direct function of mz, the total liquidity multiplier, which is in turn a function of the portfolio shares (d,t,s,e,c) (see equation (15.4)).

Total eurodollars will grow over time if the public shifts to a higher percentage of time deposits ($t + s + e$) relative to the share of money ($c + d$), because time deposits absorb proportionately smaller amounts of H than is absorbed by money ($C + D$). Just such a shift out of transactions accounts and into time deposits seems to have taken place during the 1970s (see Table 15.1). This apparently occurred because the 1970s saw a growing interest-rate differential between rates on time deposits and rates on money. By contrast, the 1980s legislation allowing interest-bearing demand deposit accounts in the U.S. has tended to work in the opposite direction, increasing the relative attractiveness of holding money.

The eurodollar market will also grow over time if the share of eurodollars in total time deposits increases relative to other types of time deposits. This relative growth would take place if eurobanks were more efficient than other financial intermediaries, allowing them to offer higher interest rates on deposits and lower interest rates on loans. And historically it is clear that eurobanks have captured a share of the market through greater efficiency. As we have seen, this greater efficiency was due in part to government restrictions on domestic financial intermediaries (recall the Regulation Q ceilings and credit restraints of the 1960s). On the other hand, domestic U.S. financial deregulation in the 1980s has worked in the opposite direction, increasing the efficiency of domestic financial intermediaries relative to eurobanks.

A third source of growth of the eurodollar market, operating in connection with the second source, is the structure of reserve requirements. Because of the reserves-requirement structure, different types of deposits absorb base-money reserves (H) at different rates. Deposits at thrift institutions (DSL) and euro-banks (DE), in particular, absorb few base-money reserves because the fractional reserves of these institutions held at commercial banks (RSL, RE) are in turn subject to only fractional required reserves (R^*SL, R^*E) in terms of deposits at the Federal Reserve or cash in the vault. That is, the absorption of H by eurodol-lar deposits and thrift deposits is only a "fraction of a fraction." For each \$1 of eurodollar deposits (DE), the amount of H absorbed is only $(r^*e)(re)$. For each \$1 of domestic thrift institution deposits, the amount of H absorbed is only $(r^*sl)(rsl)$. Empirical evidence indicates that eurobanks hold a fractional reserve (re) that is less than 1 percent. Hence the size of $(r^*e)(re)$ is essentially zero for all practical purposes.

Notice, however, that the growth of the eurodollar market (DE) is limited even if $(r^*e)(re) = 0$. This results because interest rates and other factors will adjust to bring about equilibrium in the public's portfolio allocation of each \$1 in the proportions (d,t,s,e,c). Since

$$d + t + s + e + c = 1,$$

the denominator of the total liquidity multiplier (mz) in equation (15.4) will not go to zero. Hence (mz) always has a finite value and thus the eurodollar market (DE) is limited in potential size, as can be seen in equation (15.7). For example, suppose as an extreme case that $rd = rcb = rsl = re = 0$. Then $mz = 1/c$. As long as the public holds any amount of Z in the form of currency, c will be positive, so that mz will have a finite value. Even in this extreme case, we have $DE = e$ (mz) $H = e(1/c) H$, so that the size of the eurodollar market (DE) is limited.

Notice that the magnitude of the total liquidity multiplier (mz) depends on the behavior of three separate groups. The Federal Reserve controls the size of rd, rcb, r^*sl, rsl, and r^*e (but not re). The public determines the portfolio shares d, t, s, e, c. Depository institutions as a group influence the allocation of shares d, t, s, e, c through the interest rates they offer, and eurobanks control the size of re.

Commercial banks can increase the proportion of deposits held at eurobank branches by raising interest rates on eurodollar deposits (DE) above the rate on domestic time deposits (DCB) in an amount exceeding the usual risk premium on eurodollar deposits. But they can only do this during periods of excess loan demand when loan rates may be increased; that is, only when domestic-interest ceiling rates or similar restrictions are binding at some point in the system. The shift to the eurodollar market would come to a natural halt when rates on euroloans were high enough that there would be no more excess loan demand and when the higher rate of return on eurodeposits has resulted in public portfolio equilibrium at a new value for e.

During the year 1969, market rates on eurodollar deposits rose 500 basis points above ceiling rates on commercial time deposits. The amount of large-denomination CDs at U.S. banks fell from $24 billion in November 1968 to $11 billion at the end of 1969. This relatively large shift was huge compared to the size of the eurodollar market at the time. The share of e in Z rose from .04 to .06. Since (mz) and H stayed about the same, the size of the eurodollar market ($DE = e\,(mz)\,H$) rose by 50 percent during 1969 as a result of the 50 percent growth in the eurodollar share e. This growth, huge in proportional terms because the eurodollar market was then small, came about because eurobanks were more competitive and not because eurodollars multiplied like rabbits. Eurobanks took away some of the intermediation business of domestic financial institutions. The share of commercial bank time deposits in Z, however, only fell by a small amount, from $t = .32$ to $t = .30$. The size of commercial-bank time deposits was already very large, so the marginal shift to eurodollar deposits was a small percent of the total.

Empirically, the size of the total liquidity multiplier (mz) has risen over time from $mz = 9.01$ in 1966 to $mz = 13.7$ in 1978. That is, in 1966 there were $9.01 of Z created out of each $1 of the monetary base ($H$). In 1978, there were $13.70 of Z created out of each $1 of H. The increase in the size of Z was mostly a result of the growing preference for time deposits ($t + s + e$) as a portion of Z. Since $e = .03$ in 1966 and .18 in 1978, we have that the eurodollar multiplier $me = e\,(mz) = (.03)(9.01) = .27$ in 1966, while $me = e\,(mz) = (.18)\,(13.7) = 2.47$ in 1978. In 1966, each $1 of H created by the Federal Reserve created $.27 of eurodollars, while in 1978 each $1 of H created by the Federal Reserve created $2.47 of eurodollars.

□
SHIFT MULTIPLIERS

The Rabbit Theory of eurodollars had looked at the growth of the eurodollar market as stemming from a "eurodollar base." It had been thought that this base was created when dollars were shifted from domestic deposits to eurodollar deposits. While no such "eurodollar base," apart from the domestic monetary base (H), exists, the question of what happens when a dollar is shifted from a domestic deposit to a eurodollar deposit is an interesting one. Using equations (15.1)–(15.7), we can calculate "shift multipliers" which show what happens to Z when such a marginal shift occurs. The calculation is done in Grabbe (1982). Some estimates of the effects on Z of marginal shifts between two depository asset categories are shown in Table 15.2. The most interesting shift is one from commercial bank time deposits to eurodollar deposits. Table 15.2 shows that $1 shifted from commercial bank time deposits to eurodollar deposits would have increased Z by $.36 in 1966 or $.55 in 1978. The reason such a shift would change

TABLE 15.2
Change in Total Liquidity Z as a Result of Shifts Between Depository Assets*

Shift from asset in first column	Shift to asset in first row				
	C	D .	DCB	DSL	DE
C	0	8.10	8.64	9.01	9.01
	0	12.3	13.1	13.7	13.7
D	−8.10	0	.54	.90	.90
	−12.3	0	.82	1.37	1.37
DCB	−8.67	−.54	0	.36	.36
	−13.1	−.82	0	.55	.55
DSL	−9.01	−.90	−.36	0	0
	−13.7	−1.37	−.55	0	0
DE	−9.01	−.90	−.36	0	0
	−13.7	−1.37	−.55	0	0

* The numbers in the table represent the impact of a shift on the total $C + D + DCB + DSL + DE$.
Two numbers are given for each shift. The first value is for 1966; the second value is for 1978.
   C: Currency in the hands of the public.
   D: Demand deposits at commercial banks.
DCB: Time deposits at commercial banks.
DSL: Time deposits at thrifts.
  DE: Time deposits at eurobanks.
Source: Grabbe (1982).

the size of Z is that the rate of absorption of H through reserve requirements would change. Some types of deposits absorb more base money reserves than others.

Since $DE = eZ$, an increase in Z of $.36 in 1966 would have increased the size of the eurodollar market by $(.03)(\$.36) = \$.01$. In 1978, this same shift would have increased Z by $.55, and hence would have increased the size of the euro-dollar market by $(.18)(\$.55) = \$.10$.

That is, in 1978 an "autonomous" shift of $1 from commercial bank time deposits to eurodollar deposits would have increased the size of the eurodollar market by $1 as a direct result of the shift and by an additional $.10 from the induced effect of an increase in Z. Thus the total increase in eurodollar deposits would be $1 + \$.10 = \$1.10$. On the other hand, commercial bank time deposits would have fallen by $1 as a direct result of the shift, but would have risen by $(.31)(\$.55) = \$.17$ as a consequence of the increase in Z. Thus the total reduction in commercial bank time deposits would be $1 − \$.17 = \$.83$. The net result would be that commercial bank time deposits owned by the public would fall by $.83, while eurodollar deposits would rise by $1.10. (In addition, since Z has increased, the other components of Z—namely, C, D, and DSL—will have changed also.) Eurodollar deposits will have risen from an initial deposit of $1 to $1.10, but most of this $1.10 corresponds to a decrease in commercial bank time deposits (namely, $.83). Thus, not only were the rabbits not very prolific, since they would only add $.10 to the initial $1, but also the arrival of 110 new rabbits in the eurodollar market was accompanied by the departure of 83 bunnies back home. ∎

THE ECONOMIC IMPORTANCE OF THE EURODOLLAR MARKET

In the previous section we saw that the growth of eurodollar intermediation between savers (depositors) and borrowers was mostly a consequence of competitive eurobanks capturing part of the financial intermediation business from less efficient domestic financial institutions. Since many eurobanks are branches of U.S. banks, the growth of eurodollar business represents a transfer of business from a regulated, less efficient environment to a less regulated, more efficient environment. Competition from the eurodollar sector was an important influence toward bringing about financial deregulation in the United States. The eurodollar market's existence limited the scope domestic policymakers had in manipulating financial markets through domestic regulations.

The previous section noted that shifts of deposits to the eurodollar market could affect the aggregate size of Z. As a consequence, there will be an effect on the domestic money supply, because if Z increased by $1, then $C + D$ will increase by $(c + d)(\$1)$. Table 15.3 shows the impact of marginal shifts between the depository aggregates on the domestic money supply $(C + D)$. For example, in 1966 a shift of $1 from commercial bank time deposits to eurodollar deposits would have increased the domestic money supply by $.12, while in 1978 the same shift would have increased the money supply by $.10. These effects are small and are easily allowed for by the Federal Reserve in its alterations of the high-powered monetary base H. It would be difficult to attribute any dollar inflation to the eurodollar market, and not to the Federal Reserve which controls H. In addition, the original incentive for shifting funds from domestic institutions to eurobanks was partly a result of Federal Reserve and other government regulations.

Finally, it should be pointed out that the growth of the eurodollar market is *not* "a consequence of balance of payments deficits." First of all, the balance on international transactions, or balance of payments, is only an accounting record

TABLE 15.3
Change in U.S. Money Supply $(C + D)$ as a Result of Shifts Between Depository Assets*

Shift from asset in first column	Shift to asset in first row				
	C	D	DCB	DSL	DE
C	0	2.67	2.85	2.97	2.97
	0	2.34	2.49	2.60	2.60
D	−2.67	0	.18	.30	.30
	−2.34	0	.16	.26	.26
DCB	−2.85	−.18	0	.12	.12
	−2.49	−.16	0	.10	.10
DSL	−2.97	−.30	−.12	0	0
	−2.60	−.26	−.10	0	0
DE	−2.97	−.30	−.12	0	0
	−2.60	−.26	−.10	0	0

* The numbers in the table represent the impact of a shift in the total $C + D$. Two numbers are given for each shift. The first value is for 1966; the second value is for 1978.
Source: Grabbe (1982).

of what people did over the course of a period of time. It is *not* an explanation of why they did it. So balance of payments totals are never explanations; they are just accounting totals.

Some people, however, have offered the balance of payments explanation, apparently reasoning as follows: "When the United States runs a current account deficit, foreigners earn dollar-denominated financial assets. These foreign-owned dollars form the eurodollar market." If so, this reasoning is false. Foreigners will earn dollar-denominated financial assets if the United States runs a current account deficit, but these assets have the original form of demand deposits at U.S. commerical banks. There is no immediate connection with the eurodollar market. Foreigners may shift out of domestic deposits and into eurodollar deposits, but the motive to do so would depend on economic incentives such as relative returns, relative risks, and other factors. The same economic incentives can lead a U.S. company or citizen to switch from domestic dollar assets to eurodollar assets. Eurodollars can be owned by anyone, not just foreigners. Thus, it is the economic incentive to hold eurodollar assets as opposed to domestic dollar assets that explains why the euromarket may grow relative to the domestic market. The overall market growth depends also on H and (mz), which do not of themselves bear a clear relationship to current account deficits or surpluses.

PROBLEMS FOR CHAPTER 15

1. Why is the public's portfolio choice important in determining the size of the eurodollar market?

2. In 1984 the U.S. current account deficit was estimated at greater than $100 billion. Simultaneously, there was estimated to be no growth in the eurodollar market. Are these facts contradictory?

3. Other things being equal, which of the following can be expected to *decrease* the size of the eurodollar market?
   a. The U.S. monetary base is decreased.
   b. The public has a decreased demand for printed currency.
   c. Interest ceilings are imposed on eurodollar deposits.
   d. Domestic financial intermediaries experience less regulation.
   e. The reserve requirement on commercial bank demand deposits is increased.

4. Assume that the U.S. commercial banking system has a uniform reserve requirement of 8 percent on all types of deposits, demand or time, regardless of ownership. In addition, domestic thrift institutions hold a ratio of 3 percent reserves against their deposits, while eurobanks hold 1 percent reserves against eurobank deposits. Given the current structure of interest rates, the public holds deposits in the ratio of $.10 for each $.40 of demand and $.50 *each* of commercial bank time deposits, domestic thrift institution deposits, and eurodeposits.
   (a) Calculate the money (M1) supply and the amount of eurodollar deposits, assuming the Federal Reserve sets the monetary base at $500 billion.
   (b) Suppose the Fed now sets an interest ceiling on domestic thrift institution deposits. As a result, the public switches to deposit holdings in the ratio of $.10 currency for each $.40 of demand deposits, $.50 *each* of commerical bank time deposits and eurodeposits, and $.40 of domestic thrift deposits. Compare the relative size of the domestic thrift sector to the eurosector before and after this regulation.

INTERNATIONAL BOND MARKETS

CHAPTER

16

INTRODUCTION TO THE INTERNATIONAL BOND MARKETS

There is no unified international bond "market" in the same sense that there is a foreign exchange market or a eurocurrency market. In the case of foreign exchange, common trading of the major convertible currencies against the U.S. dollar takes place in an environment that is sufficiently free of controls and regulatory restrictions, and that has sufficiently small transactions costs, as to create a broad united market. It thus makes sense to speak of a foreign exchange "market," in the singular. The same could be said of the eurocurrency "market": most eurocurrencies, when viewed in the context of spot and forward exchange markets, can be easily interchanged, making it natural in many contexts to treat them as a basket of similar, fairly substitutable items. But trading in international bonds is more usefully considered as taking place in a set of loosely connected individual markets. Each of these individual markets is usually more closely tied to a corresponding domestic bond market than to another one of the international bond markets.

The international bond markets may be divided into two broad groups: foreign bonds and eurobonds. **Foreign bonds** are bonds that are issued by foreign borrowers in a nation's domestic capital market and are denominated in the nation's domestic currency. What makes foreign bonds different from ordinary domestic bonds is that countries typically make legal distinctions between bonds issued by domestic residents and bonds issued by foreigners. These distinctions may include different tax laws, different regulations on the timing or amount of bonds that may be issued, different requirements as to the type or amount of information that the borrower has to disclose prior to the bond issue, different registration requirements, and different restrictions on who can buy the bonds.

The most important foreign bond markets are in Zurich, New York, Tokyo, Frankfurt, London, and Amsterdam. As Table 16.1 shows, in 1984 the value of Swiss franc-denominated foreign bonds issued in Switzerland was $12.6 billion; the value of U.S. dollar-denominated foreign bonds issued in the U.S. was $5.5

TABLE 16.1
New Foreign Bond Issues, by Currency[a,b]

	1976	1977	1978	1979	1980	1981	1982	1983	1984
Swiss franc	5,359	4,970	5,698	9,777	7,617	8,285	11,432	14,299	12,626
U.S. dollar	10,604	7,428	5,795	4,515	3,429	7,552	5,946	4,545	5,487
Japanese yen	226	1,271	3,826	1,833	1,088	2,457	3,418	3,772	4,628
German mark	1,288	2,181	3,779	5,379	4,839	1,310	2,952	2,671	2,243
Dutch guilder	597	211	385	75	259	481	956	1,053	—
British pound	—	—	—	—	168	746	1,214	811	1,292
Total, all currencies	18,190	16,205	20,154	22,264	17,950	21,369	26,397	27,828	27,953

[a] *Note:* New issues with a maturity of three years or more, publicly offered or privately placed in the period.
[b] Expressed in millions of dollars.

billion; the value of Japanese-yen denominated foreign bonds issued in Japan was $4.6 billion; the value of DM-denominated foreign bonds issued in Germany was $2.2 billion; and the value of British pound-denominated foreign bonds issued in Great Britain was $1.3 billion. Some foreign bond markets have common names that are widely used in international finance. For example, foreign bonds issued in the U.S. are referred to as **Yankee bonds,** and the corresponding market is the "Yankee bond market." Foreign bonds issued in Japan are called **Samurai bonds.** Foreign bonds issued in the Netherlands are called **Rembrandt bonds.** And foreign bonds issued in London are **bulldog bonds.**

Foreign bonds can also be taken to include *foreign-currency* denominated domestic bond issues. Examples include **shogun** bonds—foreign-currency bonds issued in Tokyo—and Yankee ECU bonds issued in New York.

Eurobonds differ from foreign bonds in that eurobonds denominated in a particular currency are usually issued simultaneously in the capital markets of several nations. They differ from foreign bonds in that most nations do not have preoffering registration or disclosure requirements for eurobond issues. Neither do they have restrictions on the timing or amount of such issues if the issue is denominated in a foreign currency. Some countries—such as Germany, Japan, and France—will, however, regulate the timing or amount of a eurobond issue if the issue is denominated in the country's domestic currency. The U.S. and Canada, by contrast, do not make any attempt to regulate the issuing of eurobonds denominated in, respectively, the U.S. dollar or the Canadian dollar. The predominant currency used in the eurobond market is the U.S. dollar, but there are also smaller and important markets for eurobonds denominated in the DM, ECU (European Currency Unit), British pound, Canadian dollar, or Dutch guilder. Recent financial deregulation in Japan should make the Japanese-yen eurobond market important in the future. As seen in Table 16.2, in 1984 U.S. dollar-denominated eurobonds had a value of $63.6 billion; DM-denominated eurobonds had a value of $4.6 billion; European composite unit (mostly ECU, but some others) eurobonds had a value of $3.0 billion; and British-pound eurobonds had a value of $4.0 billion.

TABLE 16.2
New Eurobond Issues, by Currency[a,b]

	1976	1977	1978	1979	1980	1981	1982	1983	1984
U.S. dollar	9,276	11,627	7,290	12,565	16,427	26,830	43,959	38,428	63,593
German mark	2,713	4,131	5,251	3,626	3,607	1,277	2,588	3,817	4,604
European composite units	99	28	165	253	65	309	1,980	2,019	3,032
British pound	—	218	234	291	974	501	748	1,947	3,997
Canadian dollar	1,407	655	—	425	279	634	1,201	1,039	—
Total, all currencies	14,479	17,771	14,125	18,726	23,970	31,616	51,645	48,501	79,458

[a] *Note:* New issues with a maturity of three years or more, publicly offered or privately placed in the period.
[b] Expressed in millions of dollars.
Source: Morgan Guaranty, *World Financial Markets.*

FEATURES OF EUROBONDS

Most eurobonds are *bearer* bonds. Your ownership of the bond is evidenced by the fact that you have the bond, just as your ownership of a U.S. dollar bill is evidenced by the fact that you have the dollar bill in your pocket. Bearer bonds contrast with **registered** bonds. Registered bonds have an ownership name assigned to the bond's serial number, and the bond can be transferred to a new owner only through a formal transfer of the registered name. For example, Yankee bonds are registered. The fact that eurobonds are bearer bonds and not registered means that they are attractive investment assets for people who wish to remain anonymous—because they are avoiding taxes or for any other reason.

Interest paid on eurobonds is usually free of all tax. In the event that a nation may impose withholding taxes on the borrower's interest payments, bond convenants specify that the interest payments must be increased enough that, after the tax is applied, the net interest payment is the same as before. For example, if an interest coupon is $100 payable annually, and a 20 percent withholding tax is imposed, the borrower has to pay coupons of $125. Thus the net payment to the bondholder will be

$$\$125 - .2(\$125) = \$100,$$

the same as previously.

Eurobonds differ from eurocredits in that buyers of the bonds do not get involved in the financial affairs of the borrower. In a eurocredit loan agreement, a borrower may commit itself to maintain a certain capital/asset ratio or adhere to an IMF agreement, and if it does not do so, the borrower can be in technical default whether or not the borrower is still making payment on the loan. But with eurobonds, since investors don't have any say about how the borrower conducts its financial affairs, default clauses say default occurs only if there is nonpayment of interest or principal. This means, of course, that investors will not buy the bonds of entities whose financial affairs they worry about. Eurobond issues are thus limited to borrowers who are considered as low credit risks. This simple fact

TABLE 16.3
New International Bond Issues, by Country of Borrower[a,b]

	1976	1977	1978	1979	1980	1981	1982	1983	1984
Industrial	24,183	23,741	24,744	31,716	32,588	40,861	63,062	60,309	91,883
Japan	2,165	1,978	3,467	5,775	5,309	6,928	8,397	13,977	16,978
Canada	9,336	5,276	4,764	4,197	3,797	10,648	11,979	7,487	6,250
U.S.	493	1,354	2,973	6,767	5,587	6,770	14,538	7,328	23,908
France	2,720	1,944	1,286	2,106	2,820	3,156	8,386	6,464	7,520
Sweden	1,111	1,574	876	1,530	3,244	2,050	2,479	3,809	6,291
Developing	1,789	3,533	4,447	3,263	2,629	4,886	5,003	2,535	3,607
Centrally planned	71	248	30	75	65	75	65	75	198
International organizations	6,626	6,454	5,058	5,936	6,638	7,163	9,912	13,410	11,682
Total	32,669	33,976	34,279	40,990	41,920	52,985	78,042	76,329	107,370

[a] *Note:* New issues with a maturity of three years or more, publicly offered or privately placed in the period.
[b] Expressed in millions of dollars.
Source: Morgan Guaranty, *World Financial Markets.*

of life can be seen in Table 16.3, showing international bond issues identified by country of borrower. During the year 1984, for example, borrowers in industrial countries issued $91.9 billion of international bonds (including eurobonds); borrowers in developing countries issued $3.6 billion of international bonds; borrowers in centrally planned (communist) countries issued bonds worth $0.198 billion; and international organizations borrowed $11.7 billion. The country origins of the largest borrowers include Japan with $17.0 billion; Canada with $6.3 billion; the United States with $23.9 billion; France with $7.5 billion; and Sweden with $6.3 billion.

The details of issuing new eurobonds are covered in the next chapter. Briefly, however, there are several stages to the process. The borrower, after negotiation, sells its bonds to a group of managing banks. Managing banks in turn sell the bonds to other banks, who are divided into underwriters and sellers. The underwriting and selling banks in turn sell the bonds to dealers and final investors. Underwriting banks are distinguished from ordinary sellers in that they are committed to buy the bonds at a preagreed minimum price even if the bonds cannot be sold at a higher price on the market. The managing banks themselves also act as underwriters and sellers.

Eurobonds appear in a number of basic guises. Straight bonds pay a fixed interest rate at periodic intervals, usually annually. The choice of annual payments as opposed to the more common interval of six months in domestic issues, is a simple reaction to the higher cost of disbursing interest payments to investors around the world.

EXAMPLE 16.1

The first eurobond issue that was widely recognized as such took place in July 1963. The Italian autostrada issued 60,000 bonds with a face value of $250 each. Each bond paid a fixed coupon of $5\frac{1}{2}$ percent ($13.75) annually on July 15. The issue was managed by London merchant bankers S. G. Warburg & Co., with Banque de Bruxelles SA, Deutsche Bank AG, and Rotterdamsche Bank NV as comanagers. The bond was listed on the London Stock Exchange. This eurobond issue coincided with the proposal (and retroactive imposition) of the Interest Equalization Tax (IET) on Yankee bonds by U.S. President Kennedy on July 18, 1963. The IET was a flat tax of 15 percent of the purchase price of long maturity bonds, which increased the costs to European borrowers coming to New York by about 1 percent. [Background information on the autostrada issue is given in Kerr (1984).]

Floating rate notes (FRNs), by contrast, have more frequent payments — usually every six months. The interest rate on floating rate notes is stated in terms of a spread over some reference rate — usually LIBOR — appropriate for the currency. The rollover pricing feature of floating rate notes is, of course, a reaction to interest rate uncertainty. The more frequently the interest rate is updated, the more the interest payment on the note will reflect current money market rates. The first floating rate notes appeared in 1969 and 1970, during a period of rising interest rates. Most FRNs are dollar-denominated: Japanese yen and German mark FRNs did not appear until 1985.

EXAMPLE 16.2

In February 1984 Sweden made an offering of $500 million of floating rate notes in the U.S. dollar eurobond market. The notes mature in March 2024 and bear semiannual interest of $\frac{1}{8}$ percent over six-month LIBOR. At the time the notes were offered, six-month LIBOR was $10\frac{7}{16}$ percent. So for the first six months Sweden paid an interest at an annual rate of

$$10\frac{7}{16} \% + \frac{1}{8} \% = 10\frac{9}{16} \text{ percent.}$$

Afterward, at the end of each six-month period, the interest rates on the notes are updated to reflect the current six-month LIBOR rate for dollars. The forty-year maturity (1984–2024) was at the time of offering the longest in eurobond history. (Shortly afterward, however, National Westminister Bank issued perpetual floating rate notes. That is, NatWest's FRNs never mature.)

EXAMPLE 16.3

LIBOR is not always the reference rate used. In February 1984 the World Bank offered $250 million of ten-year floating rate notes, which pay quarterly interest at a rate of thirty-five basis points above the money-market yield on certain ninety-one-day U.S. Treasury bills. The World Bank's total interest of about 9.65% for the first three-month period was approximately thirty basis points (.3 percent) *below* three-month LIBOR. The low interest the World Bank was required to pay reflects the fact that the World Bank is considered a very low-risk borrower.

Zero-coupon bonds is the curious name given to bonds that don't pay any coupons. (Treasury bills and commercial paper don't pay coupons either, but are not referred to as "zero-coupon.") These are pure discount securities that are sold at a fraction of their face value but redeemed at face value. The return is the difference between the purchase price and the repayment price. Zero-coupon bonds proved very popular with Japanese investors, because the increase in the bond's price as the bonds matured was treated in Japan as capital gain and was not taxed.

EXAMPLE 16.4

In June 1981, Pepsico Overseas issued three-year zero-coupon eurobonds at an issue price of 67.25 percent of face value. Since the bonds would be repaid in three years at 100 percent of face value, the compounded interest yield was

$(100/67.25)^{\frac{1}{3}} - 1 = 14.14\%.$

Convertible bonds are another fairly frequent type of bond offered in the eurobond markets. Japanese companies in particular issue a great many convertible U.S. dollar eurobonds. A bond is convertible if, in addition to making the usual interest payments, the bond can be exchanged for some other type of asset. The most common type of conversion feature is one that allows the bond to be exchanged at its face value for shares of common stock in the company issuing the bonds. Bonds have also been issued that allow conversion into other assets such as gold or oil or into other bonds with differing payment characteristics (such as bonds paying floating rate interest being convertible, under certain circumstances, into bonds paying fixed rate interest—or vice versa). Some bonds have allowed payments in principal or interest to be received, at the borrower's option, in one of two alternative currencies. That is, the bond has allowed conversion from one currency to another at a preagreed fixed exchange rate. Most conversion features, or whatever type, can be considered as **options**, and their value can be formally established in the same way we value foreign exchange or stock options. Chapter 20 will look further at option features on bonds.

EXAMPLE 16.5

A Canadian company issued 8 percent eurobonds, each with a face value of $1000. The bond principal was convertible at maturity, at the option of the bondholder, into common stock of the parent company at a conversion price per share of Can$ $23\frac{1}{8}$, where each U.S. $1 of face value would be converted to Canadian dollars at a fixed exchange rate of 1.2007 Canadian dollars = 1 U.S. dollar.

EXAMPLE 16.6

In May 1983 CEPME issued £35 million of fixed rate bonds convertible to floating rate notes. Each £1000, twelve-year bond paid a fixed coupon of $11\frac{1}{4}$ percent but was convertible at the bondholder's option into one $1550, twelve-year floating rate note paying semiannual dollar interest equal to six-month LIBOR.

A new and interesting guise in which eurobonds began appearing in 1984 was in the form of *mortgage-backed* eurobonds. Since mostly only borrowers perceived to have low credit risk have thus far been successful in issuing eurobonds, certain institutions, such as regional thrift institutions, would normally be excluded from the eurobond market. Mortgage-backed U.S. dollar eurobonds are a way in which some U.S. thrift institutions have created the equivalent of bonds guaranteed by the U.S. government. The way this is done is that the financial institution puts up as security against the eurobond issue other bonds that are guaranteed by the (U.S.) Government National Mortgage Association (Ginnie Mae).

EXAMPLE 16.7

In March 1984, American Savings & Loan Association issued $125 million of eurobonds through a group of investment banks led by Salomon Brothers. To back the eurobonds, American Savings & Loan placed in escrow $187.5 million in AAA-rated debt of the Government National Mortgage Association. The Ginnie Mae debt, owned by American Savings & Loan, would be used to pay off eurobond holders in the event American Savings & Loan defaulted on its eurobonds. Aside from the mortgage backing, the eurobonds themselves were straight eurodollar bonds paying a fixed coupon of 12 percent.

Dual-currency bonds are bonds that are purchased in terms of one currency and pay coupons in terms of the same currency but repay principal at maturity in terms of a second currency. As explained in Chapter 4, these bonds represent a combination of an ordinary bond combined with a forward contract.

EXAMPLE 16.8

In August 1985 the Federal National Mortgage Association, a U.S. government-sponsored, privately owned corporation, issued a dual-currency yen-denominated eurobond. The bonds were to be purchased in yen, and the 8 percent annual coupon was to be paid in yen. At maturity, however, repayment would be made in U.S. dollars. The yen face amount of the bond would be exchanged for dollars at an exchange rate of ¥ 208/$.

U.S. LEGAL ASPECTS OF EURODOLLAR BOND ISSUES

As we saw in Table 16.2, most eurobonds are dollar-denominated. (Dollar-denominated eurobonds are usually referred to as **eurodollar bonds**. The name is shorthand, and does not imply any association with the eurocurrency market.) It will be worthwhile to look at some of the specific factors that give this important market its character.

First of all, the U.S. authorities make no special attempt to control the issuing of dollar-denominated eurobonds by foreigners. There are, however, a number of U.S. regulations that affect the management and sale of dollar eurobonds. The outdated Glass-Steagall Act prohibits U.S. commercial banks from underwriting securities. Therefore, among U.S. firms only investment banks, or merchant banking subsidiaries of U.S. commercial banks, get involved in dollar eurobond issues. In addition, there are several important legal restrictions that apply to either to the purchase of eurodollar bonds by U.S. citizens, to the issuing of eurobonds by U.S. companies, or to the involvement of U.S. firms in unregistered bond offerings. Three points in particular are important: sales prohibitions, private placement exemption, and withholding tax on bearer bonds.

PROHIBITION ON SALES

The U.S. Securities Act of 1933 requires public issues of new securities in the United States to be registered with the U.S. Securities and Exchange Commission (SEC). Therefore, dollar eurobonds (or other currency eurobonds), or any foreign bonds not registered in the United States, cannot be sold to U.S. citizens at the time of initial distribution. U.S. citizens can only purchase such bonds after the bonds have been seasoned in the secondary market for ninety days.

In addition, the 1933 act would appear to prohibit U.S. investment banks from even taking part in an unregistered eurobond or foreign bond issue, even if the issue were taking place in London and the bonds were being sold to non-U.S. nationals. Nevertheless, U.S. investment banks have lead-managed a great many dollar eurobond issues since the inception of the market in the early 1960s. They are allowed to do so because the SEC granted a release on July 9, 1964, which states that a public offering of securities does not have to be registered with the SEC if it "is made under circumstances reasonably designed to preclude distribution or redistribution of the securities within, or to the nationals of, the United States."

Meeting the requirements of the 1964 release presents investment bankers with a straightforward practical problem: How do you keep bearer bonds out of the hands of U.S. citizens at the time of initial distribution? The way this is typically handled in a new issue is as follows. First, members of the selling group sign an agreement not to sell bonds to U.S. nationals. Second, at the time money is actually paid and credit is received for bonds bought, the individual bonds themselves are not yet distributed. Instead, the borrower issues a global bond, which is a bond certificate representing the total amount of the issue. Those who have bought bonds have ownership shares in the global bond but they do not yet have the individual bearer bonds of $1000 (or so) denomination. After a ninety-day waiting period, individual investors can, if they wish, pick up from the office of a paying agent the bearer bonds they have purchased. At that time, they must present evidence they are not U.S. citizens, and must in addition sign a statement that they were not acting on behalf of U.S. citizens in purchasing the bonds. These procedures are called lock-up procedures and get investment bankers off the hook with respect to the SEC.

PRIVATE PLACEMENT EXEMPTION

If a eurobond offering is structured to fall under the "private placement" exemption of the Securities Act of 1933, then it can be sold to U.S. nationals — such as foreign branches of U.S. banks — during the period of initial distribution, even though the bonds are not registered with the SEC. The private placement exemption applies when the purchasers of the bonds have the following characteristics:

1. They are limited in number;
2. They are "sophisticated";
3. They are able to bear the loss if the bond issuer defaults;
4. They purchase bonds as principals (i.e., not for resale);
5. They have access to information similar to that which would be contained in a registered offering prospectus.

WITHHOLDING TAX AND BEARER BONDS

As a result of U.S. regulatory changes in the summer of 1984, there is currently no U.S. withholding tax on payments to foreigners who hold U.S. government or corporate bonds. In addition, U.S. corporations are allowed to issue bearer bonds directly to non-U.S. residents. These new changes promise to reduce significantly the distinction between domestic bonds in the United States and eurodollar bonds issued by U.S. nationals. Prior to the summer of 1984, many U.S. companies had borrowed in the eurobond market at interest rates lower than the U.S. government's borrowing rate. This will probably no longer be possible, and the net effect of the recent changes will increase corporate borrowing rates relative to that of the U.S. government. The importance of these changes can be seen if we compare the previous regime.

Prior to July 1984, whenever U.S. corporations issued bonds in the U.S. domestic market, the United States imposed a 30 percent withholding tax on interest payments to nonresidents. The same applied when U.S. companies issued eurobonds: under normal circumstances there was a 30 percent withholding tax (since purchasers were normally nonresidents) that was applied to coupon payments. In practice, this meant that U.S. companies who issued eurobonds from the U.S. had to pay a higher rate of interest than other borrowers in the eurodollar bond market, because foreign borrowers who issued dollar eurobonds would not face the same 30 percent U.S. withholding tax. However, there were two ways for U.S. companies to avoid the necessity of withholding the 30 percent tax on interest payments.

1. No withholding tax was required if the bonds were issued by a domestic finance subsidiary that met the "80/20" test of the Internal Revenue Code (section 861). A company's domestic finance subsidiary would meet this test

if it derived less than 20 percent of its gross income from U.S. sources. However, most U.S. parent companies did not have such a domestic finance subsidiary.

2. No withholding tax was required if the bonds were issued by a foreign finance subsidiary. For U.S. companies issuing dollar eurobonds, this foreign finance subsidiary was usually located in the Netherlands Antilles. The reason had to do with a U.S. – Netherlands tax treaty that allowed parent companies to write off on their U.S. taxes most tax payments made in the Netherlands Antilles. That is, a company would not only be exempt from withholding the tax on coupon payments to foreigners but would also be able to write off on its U.S. taxes those taxes it paid in the Netherlands Antilles. In order for a foreign finance subsidiary to meet requirements of the tax code, the subsidiary had to be "independent" (i.e., it could not be a shell company) with its own separate books, and it could not be "thinly capitalized." The meaning of the latter phrase was not clear, but foreign finance subsidiaries with a debt/equity ratio as large as 2.5/1 had made eurobond offerings without stirring up any complaint.

In 1984 the tax treaty with the Netherlands Antilles was not renewed. In addition, the 30 percent U.S. withholding tax was removed and it became permissible for corporations to issue bearer bonds directly to foreigners. These actions removed much, but not all, of the incentive for U.S. corporations to utilize foreign finance subsidiaries. In addition, the changes worked in favor of those investment banking and brokerage firms which specialized in domestic U.S. investment banking, as some of what had previously been eurobond business could now become domestic business. The objective of the U.S. Treasury in sponsoring the changes was to reduce overall borrowing costs for the U.S. government: it was believed the net interest reduction from the increase in the demand for U.S. government debt would more than offset the loss of withholding tax. By the same token, costs to corporate dollar bond issuers in the United States and elsewhere rose, since bond purchasers now found U.S. government securities, without the 30 percent withholding tax, more attractive relative to corporate debt than they had previously.

Differences still remain, however. Congress did not approve the issuing of U.S. government bonds in bearer form. In addition, skepticism remained on the part of some traditional eurobond buyers (such as Swiss banks) whether the tax removal was permanent: what the U.S. government giveth, the U.S. government can take away. As a consequence, domestic and eurobonds had become closer substitutes from a foreign purchaser's point of view, but they were not identical. The long-run effect of the change will result in a closer integration of the eurodollar and domestic dollar bond markets, and will also tend to make the U.S. government borrowing rate a floor level for borrowing rates in the eurodollar bond market.

YANKEE BONDS

For years the Yankee bond market was the largest and most important foreign bond market. In recent years, however, it has been surpassed by the Swiss-franc foreign bond market. The growth of the Yankee bond market was impeded by the U.S. Interest Equalization Tax that was in force during the 1963–1974 period. This tax effectively cut off European borrowers from the Yankee bond market by making them pay higher-than-market interest rates in order to issue bonds in New York. (Other foreign borrowers were, however, exempt from the tax: Canadian borrowers; international organizations, such as the World Bank; and developing countries like Brazil and Mexico.)

Yankee bonds must be registered under the Securities Act of 1933, which involves meeting the disclosure requirements of the U.S. Securities and Exchange Commission. If the bonds are listed (usually on the New York Stock Exchange), they must also be registered under the Securities Exchange Act of 1934. The ordinarily long four-week registration period can be speeded up by *shelf registration*. In shelf registration, the borrower files a prospectus that covers all anticipated borrowings within the coming year. Then at the time of a new issue, the borrower only has to add a prospectus supplement, which takes only a week to clear.

Yankee issues are customarily rated by a bond rating agency such as Standard and Poor's Corporation or Moody's Investors Services, Inc. A rating is necessary if the bonds are to be sold to certain U.S. institutional investors. Use of the Yankee bond market has tended to be restricted to borrowers with AAA credit ratings. There is no withholding tax on coupon payments to foreigners who purchase Yankee bonds. Coupons are usually paid semiannually.

The secondary market for Yankee bonds is more liquid than that for dollar eurobonds and bid-ask spreads are smaller. New issue costs are smaller than for eurobonds (about $\frac{7}{8}$ percent versus 2 percent for eurobonds). The fact of smaller issue costs, combined with more frequent coupon payments, means one should be cautious in comparing interest rates in the Yankee market with rates in the dollar eurobond market. The semiannual coupon payments on Yankee bonds means the annual coupon rate on a Yankee bond is equivalent to a slightly higher coupon on a eurobond. Conversely, the higher up-front fees on eurobonds increases the true borrowing rate on eurobonds proportionately more than the up-front fees on Yankee bonds increase the true Yankee bond borrowing rate.

DM EUROBONDS AND DM FOREIGN BONDS

In Germany there is no separation between investment banking and commercial banking, as there is in the United States, and the international DM bond market is dominated by the major German commercial banks. Prior to October 1984, eurobonds and foreign bonds were legally distinguished from German domestic bonds in that there was a 25 percent coupon tax to nonresidents who purchased German domestic bonds, while the coupon tax did not apply if nonresidents purchased DM eurobonds or DM foreign bonds. This meant foreigners would arbitrage between domestic DM bonds and international DM bonds only if price differences were sufficient to make up the tax differential. For some foreign investors taking advantage of double-taxation agreements there was, however, little tax distinction. German residents are similarly subject to the same tax on interest payments from either type of bond. In effect, this means both bonds are tax-free to German residents, as no coupon tax is withheld; there is no reporting requirement for coupon payments; and domestic bonds are usually issued in bearer form. After the U.S. removed its 30 percent withholding tax to foreigners on U.S. domestic bonds in the summer of 1984, German authorities responded by removing the withholding tax on German domestic bonds.

A DM eurobond is not legally different from a DM foreign bond. If the banking syndicate selling international DM bonds is composed of only German banks, the bonds are classified as DM "foreign" bonds, while if the syndicate includes non-German banks, the bonds are called DM "eurobonds." By an agreement between the Bundesbank and the major German commercial banks, the lead manager in DM eurobond issues was always a German bank prior to 1985. Since DM eurobonds and foreign bonds have no differing economic characteristics, a DM bond will essentially trade at the same price whether it is issued as a foreign bond or a eurobond.

DM eurobonds originated in 1964 when the 25 percent coupon tax was imposed. (Note that a coupon tax is different from the U.S. IET of the time, as the IET was calculated as a percentage of the *purchase price* of a bond.) Foreigners were buying German bonds as a way of speculating against the U.S. dollar (that is, they were anticipating a DM appreciation). The tax was imposed to discourage foreign purchases of DM domestic bonds ("capital inflows"), so international DM bonds were created to avoid the tax.

Prior to 1985, the total volume and the timing of issue of DM eurobonds and foreign bonds was regulated by the Subcommittee for Foreign Issues of the (German) Central Capital Market Committee, which was composed of six German banks and had the central Bundesbank as an observer. These six banks set issue quotas, which they allocated among themselves. The purpose of this cartel arrangement seems to have been an attempt to control the domestic cost of capital by regulating the amount of foreign competition for funds. In 1985 issuing quotas were eliminated, and subsidiaries of foreign underwriters were allowed to lead manage new issues. International DM bonds are issued in cities outside Germany but are listed on German stock exchanges and are cleared through the Effektengiro system, a special clearing system in Frankfurt. (Clearing is explained in Chapter 19.)

Floating rate notes only recently emerged in the DM eurobond market because of Bundesbank opposition. The central bank was attempting to segment the money market and the capital market by prohibiting bond coupon rates being tied to short-term interest rates. Pressure for financial deregulation led to the removal of official opposition in 1985, and German commercial banks reached a consensus on the creation of a FRN reference rate: the Frankfurt Interbank Offered Rate (FIBOR). Twelve banks report their three- and six-months offered rates each day between 11:00 and 11:30 A.M. to Privat-Diskontbank, which eliminates the lowest and highest quotes and publishes an average of the remainder as FIBOR.

SAMURAI BONDS AND YEN EUROBONDS

Japan's domestic bond market is already the second largest in the world, and with its large domestic savings base, Japan easily has the potential to make Tokyo a leading international capital market. For years, however, foreigners have had only limited access to Japan's bond market. The first yen eurobond (by the European Investment Bank) did not appear until 1977, and strict regulations prevented much subsequent growth. The Samurai market began earlier, at the end of 1970, but access was limited mostly to international organizations and foreign governments. The first issue by a foreign corporation (Sears, Roebuck) did not occur until 1979. Restricted access to the bond market extended even to Japanese corporations, who were effectively shut out by the tradition that corporate bond issues had to be fully collateralized with company assets. Most domestic bond issues were made either by government, by one of the long-term credit banks (Nippon Credit Bank, Long Term Credit Bank of Japan, Industrial Bank of Japan), by the trust banks, or by the Bank of Tokyo, which has special status as a commercial bank. (The various banks mentioned here in turn provided working capital and plant and equipment loans to Japanese industry.)

Prior to 1984, the Japanese securities firms, under Ministry of Finance guidelines, allowed only four to six international issues per year, each with a maximum amount of ¥ 15 billion (¥ 20 billion for the World Bank) and a maximum maturity of ten years. Euroyen issues could be made only by supranationals who had previously made at least one Samurai issue, or by government borrowers who had made three previous Samurai issues and who were also rated AAA by a U.S. rating agency. A new bond issue had to be lead managed by one of the Japanese securities houses. As a consequence, over the period 1977–1984 only eleven government and international financial borrowers entered the euroyen market — the most frequent borrowers being the World Bank (IBRD), the Asian Development Bank, and the European Investment Bank.

In the beginning borrowers in the Samurai market had to convert the yen they obtained into foreign currency. Since many Samurai bonds were also purchased by foreigners (at least on the secondary market), in effect yen was just the unit used to denominate the value of the bonds. The amount of a bond issue itself did not necessarily represent net lending by Japanese savers.

To see why this is true, suppose an American company borrows by issuing yen-denominated bonds for a total of ¥2 billion, and suppose the issue is purchased by investors from the United States. Then the net effect is that U.S. investors are lending to U.S. borrowers. The equivalent transaction could have been done in New York. The borrower could have issued bonds worth ¥2 billion in New York, specifying that yen is only the currency of denomination (just like the ECU or SDR). Borrowers would buy the yen bonds by paying dollars, and as coupon payments came due would receive the current dollar value of the yen coupons. For example, if at the time the bonds were offered the exchange rate were ¥200 = $1, then a ¥200,000 bond could be purchased for $1000. If each bond had a 5 percent coupon, paid semiannually, then there would be a payment worth ¥5000 every six months. If the exchange rate were ¥210 = $1 at the time of the first coupon, then the payment in dollars would be $23.81. And so on. The value of such a bond to a U.S. consumer would be equivalent to the value of an ordinary dollar bond, plus the value of a series of forward contracts corresponding to the coupon payment dates and the principal repayment date. The "forward rate" in these contracts would be the spot rate at the time the bond was purchased. Then if, at the time of each coupon payment, the spot rate has changed from its initial value, there will be an opportunity gain or loss, in the same manner that there would be an opportunity gain or loss on a forward contract if the spot rate in the market were different from the forward rate at the time the forward contract matured. If the value of the yen had increased with respect to the dollar, then the nominal dollar value of the bond to the bondholder would have increased. Similarly, the borrower's nominal dollar liability would also have increased. That is, the nominal dollar value of the bond would fluctuate according to the dollar/yen exchange rate, but no direct Japanese lending or borrowing would be involved. (Technically, only 25 percent of a Samurai issue could be purchased by foreign investors at the time of offering, but there was no restriction on purchases on the secondary market. As a consequence, foreign buying of samurai issues was usually higher than the 25 percent figure suggested.)

A similar process took place when Japanese corporations issued eurodollar bonds. Japanese life insurance companies were allowed by the Ministry of Finance a maximum of 10 percent of foreign securities in their portfolios, but dollar bonds issued by Japanese companies were not categorized as foreign. Hence, dollar bonds issued by Japanese companies and purchased by Japanese life insurance firms (Sushi bonds) represented a strictly Japanese savings flow, with the U.S. dollar serving only as the currency of denomination.

In May 1984 the United States and Japan announced, as part of the general agreement on Japanese financial deregulation, a lessening in restrictions on euroyen financing. The euroyen market would be expanded to allow, for the first time, both Japanese and non-Japanese corporations to make public euroyen issues, and foreign banks would be allowed to serve as lead managers. The market was opened to issues by foreign banks in 1985, and dual-currency, zero-coupon, and FRNs were also approved. Although many complex restrictions remained, the consequences of deregulation were immediately apparent, with the amount of yen eurobonds surpassing DM eurobonds in the first half of 1985. Euroyen bonds are usually listed in Luxembourg or London while Samurai bonds are listed on the Tokyo Stock Exchange.

SWISS FRANC INTERNATIONAL BONDS

It may seem surprising that a country as small as Switzerland, with only six million inhabitants, would have the largest foreign bond market in the world. We saw the principle involved, however, in the previous section on Japanese yen bonds. When Swiss-franc denominated bonds are issued in Switzerland, it is not necessarily the domestic savings of Swiss citizens that is being borrowed. More often than not, foreign (to Switzerland) savers are lending to foreign borrowers, with the amount of the debt obligation fixed in terms of Swiss francs. The Swiss franc is chosen as a unit of account with relatively stable purchasing power, while Swiss banks act as international financial intermediaries.

The Swiss National Bank regulated the volume of Swiss franc issues prior to 1984, when the issuing calendar was abandoned. Bonds are usually lead managed by one of the "big three": Swiss Bank Corporation, Union Bank of Switzerland, or Credit Suisse. A certain percentage of the Swiss francs received by the borrower have to be converted to other currencies. While nonresidents are subject to a 35 percent withholding tax on Swiss franc domestic bonds, they are exempt from withholding on Swiss franc foreign bonds. Swiss franc foreign bonds are bearer bonds, have annual coupons, and have a minimum denomination of SF 5000. Foreign bonds are usually listed and traded on one of the Swiss stock exchanges.

After an initial Swiss franc eurobond issue by the city of Copenhagen in 1963, the Swiss franc eurobond market was "closed" from 1963 to 1982. That is, Swiss authorities prohibited the issuing of Swiss franc eurobonds. Legally, of course, there is no way that Switzerland could have stopped foreigners from issuing Swiss franc-denominated eurobonds. But, as a practical matter, there is a heavy cost involved in incurring the displeasure of a major central bank—Swiss franc payments must be channeled through the Swiss commercial banking system—so no one is willing to issue eurobonds without the explicit consent of the authorities in the country whose currency would be used to denominate the bonds.

PROBLEMS FOR CHAPTER 16

1. It has been stated that the Japanese Ministry of Finance opposed development of a euroyen market because, among other reasons,

   . . . competition was not wanted between the Euroyen bond market and the domestic yen (samurai) bond market. Euroyen bonds do not create the politically important capital outflows needed to offset Japanese current account surpluses and thus ease international tensions.

   Criticize this statement. Did it really make a difference, with respect to capital flows, whether bonds were issued in the euroyen market or the samurai market?

2. Explain how a foreign-currency coupon bond issue is, in terms of its cash flow implications for a domestic issuer, equivalent to a domestic-currency coupon bond issue plus a series of forward exchange contracts. How then could a foreign-currency coupon bond issue be completely hedged against foreign exchange risk?

3. Extending your answer in Problem 2, explain how a Japanese company could have issued the equivalent of a euroyen bond even prior to May 1984. [This secret was discovered by Japan Air Lines, Japan Development Bank, All Nippon Airways, and Chubu Electric Power Company.]

NEW ISSUE PROCEDURES IN THE EUROBOND MARKET

Arranging and selling a new eurobond issue has traditionally been a complicated procedure. More recently, competitive pressures have brought about a simplified structure, "the bought deal," which is now standard in the eurobond market. In order to gain a perspective on this evolutionary process, we will first review the more traditional structure as a background to recent changes.

ORGANIZATION OF A TRADITIONAL EUROBOND SYNDICATE

Eurobonds are issued and sold through **underwriting syndicates**. Participants in these syndicates are investment banks, merchant banks, and the merchant banking subsidiaries of commercial banks. The parts of a traditional eurobond syndicate are shown in Figure 17.1. A prospective borrower—a company, a bank, an international organization, or a government—will approach an investment bank and invite it to become the *lead manager* of a eurobond issue on the borrower's behalf. The lead manager may then invite a small additional group of banks to assist it in negotiating terms with the borrower, in assessing the market, and in organizing and managing the new issue. This small group, including the lead manager, is the *managing group*. In addition, two other categories of banks —*underwriters* and the **selling group**—will be invited to participate in bringing the bonds to market. The different syndicate categories reflect the multistage process by which the bonds are sold.

The borrower sells the bonds to the managing group. In turn—depending on the form of syndicate organization—the managing group either sells the bonds directly to both the underwriters and the selling group or else sells the bonds to the underwriters, who in turn sell bonds to the selling group. Members of the selling group, in turn, sell to final investors. Underwriters differ from pure sellers in that underwriters commit themselves ahead of time to buy the bonds at a set minimum price from the managers even if the bonds cannot be resold to sellers or

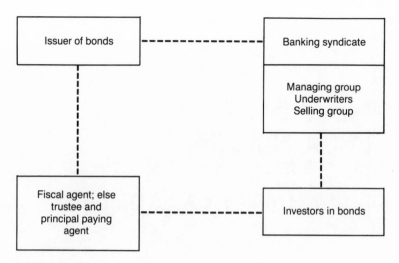

FIGURE 17.1
Role players in a new eurobond issue.

end investors for a price greater than this preagreed minimum. (As will be explained below, the term "underwriter" in the eurobond market differs from its sense as used in a domestic context.) Roles in a eurobond syndicate are nested: managers are also underwriters and sellers, and underwriters are usually also sellers.

The *principal paying agent* in a eurobond issue is the bank that has the responsibility for receiving interest and principal payments from the borrower and disbursing them to end investors. When a *fiscal agent* is used in a new issue, the fiscal agent and the principal paying agent are the same. A fiscal agent is a bank appointed to act on behalf of the borrower, one that takes care of the mechanics of bond authentication and distribution to investors as well as acting as principal paying agent. An alternative to a fiscal agent is a **trustee**. A trustee acts not on behalf of the borrower, as does a fiscal agent, but rather in the interest of investors. A trustee acts as the representative of all bondholders in any legal action stemming from bond covenant defaults. If a trustee is used for a new eurobond issue, then a separate principal paying agent will be appointed to act on behalf of the bond issuer.

Table 17.1 gives the identity of the top lead managers of eurobond issues in 1984, where the ranking is according to the dollar amount of bonds brought to market. The table gives ranking according to overall figures, as well as ranking for two subcategories of eurobonds, namely floating rate notes and bonds with fixed coupons. We see, for example, that in 1984, Credit Suisse First Boston (CSFB) was the top lead manager of eurobond issues overall. It served as lead manager for 11.8 percent of all new issues brought to market, followed by Deutschebank and Morgan Guaranty (7.3 percent each), and Merrill Lynch (6.5 percent). The overall performance of CSFB was aided by its domination of the floating rate note market, with a 21.8 percent share of that segment of the market. In the fixed-rate market, Deutschebank was first with a 12.4 percent share.

TABLE 17.1
Top Lead Managers of Eurobond Issues

	1984 rank	Amount ($ millions)	1983 rank	Amount ($ millions)
Top Eurobond Lead Managers, All Issues				
Credit Suisse First Boston	1	9365.8	1	8003.9
Morgan Guaranty	2	5810.8	4	1840.7
Deutschebank	3	5777.8	2	6093.7
Merrill Lynch	4	5158.2	3	2061.2
Morgan Stanley	5	3615.0	6	1612.6
Salomon Brothers	6	3540.1	9	1061.9
S.G. Warburg	7	2683.9	5	1632.3
Goldman, Sachs	8	2064.2	11	1031.4
Nomura Securities	9	1984.0	13	946.0
Swiss Bank Corporation	10	1924.0	12	1025.0
Union Bank of Switzerland	11	1829.1	18	672.3
Lehman Bros. International	12	1654.7	25	432.5
Dresdner Bank	13	1490.1	8	1278.4
Banque Nationale de Paris	14	1430.8	7	1451.7
Orion Royal Bank	15	1279.2	16	802.6
Top Lead Managers, Floating Rate Notes				
Credit Suisse First Boston	1	6894.4	1	7125.0
Morgan Guaranty	2	4253.9	11	300.0
Merrill Lynch	3	3115.0	2	800.0
Banque Nationale de Paris	4	1450.0	3	600.0
Salomon Brothers	5	1308.6	—	—
Top Lead Managers, Fixed-Rate Eurobonds				
Deutschebank	1	5385.1	1	7183.6
Credit Suisse First Boston	2	4622.3	2	2779.5
Morgan Stanley	3	3854.7	4	1282.9
Salomon Brothers	4	3470.9	10	797.9
Morgan Guaranty	5	1853.8	5	1135.1

Source: Euromoney, *Annual Financing Report*, 1985.

FEE STRUCTURE FOR NEW EUROBOND ISSUES

In the eurobond market, fees are extracted by discounts on the prices at which bonds are provided to syndicate members. Suppose, for example, that $1000 bonds are issued at 100, which means that the issue price for the bonds is 100 percent of face value. (If the bonds are issued at 100 percent of face value, they are said to be issued at "par." An issue price of 99½, by contrast, is "below par." And so on.) The amount the borrower gets is, however, not related to the issue price. For example, the managing group may have agreed to pay the borrower $975 for each $1000 bond. The $25 discount, which is 2½ percent of the $1000 issue price of an individual bond, would be referred to as a "flotation cost" or "investment banking spread" of 2½ percent.

However, syndicate members really receive the full 2½ percent, or $25 per bond, only if the bonds are actually sold to retail customers at the issue price of 100 ($1000). Such may not happen. Once the bonds are in the hands of the underwriters or sellers (after the signing of final terms), there is no enforceable contract to make them sell the bonds in the market at their issue price or better. Consequently, any amount by which the bonds are sold at less than 100 reduces the overall portion of the "spread" that is received by the syndicate and increases the true yield on the bond from the bond-buyer's point of view.

In the U.S. domestic market, by contrast, underwriters are obligated to maintain the market price of the bonds at a level equal to the issue price or higher until the bond syndicate is disbanded. This obligation is enforceable because domestic bonds are registered and hence the identity of parties making particular transactions can be traced. Originally, the term "underwriter" in the eurobond market was intended to have the same meaning as in the domestic market. But legal contracts to maintain the issue price turned out to be nonenforceable, since members who wished to sell unregistered bearer bonds at a lower price could do so through third parties without the transaction being traceable to the original syndicate member. Therefore any or all of a fee may be passed along to the buyer of a bond, depending on the price the bank charges. Also by contrast to the U.S. domestic market, there is considerable price discrimination in sales to final investors. Given that selling members may pass along a part of their fee to the end investor in the form of a discount from the issue price, it follows that different investors may buy bonds at different prices. Institutions with "buying power"—such as insurance companies and banks which administer large trust and fiduciary funds—get considerable discounts.

Here is a typical structure of fees for a eurobond issue with a $2\frac{1}{2}$ percent total investment banking spread, along with terms used to refer to various parts of the fee.

Lead manager pays borrower $975 per $1000 bond.

Lead manager makes bonds available to underwriters at $980.

Lead manager makes bonds available to sellers at $985.

$1000 - \$975 = \$25$	"Flotation cost" or "spread"	(100% of spread)
$1000 - \$985 = \$15$	"Selling concession"	(60% of spread)
$\$~985 - \$980 = \$~5$	"Underwriting allowance"	(20% of spread)
$\$~980 - \$975 = \$~5$	"Management fee"	(20% of spread)

We see that for ordinary sellers, the bonds may be sold for any amount greater than $985, and there will be a marginal profit (before selling expenses are paid). An underwriter is largely just a privileged seller who gets bonds at a lower price than an ordinary member of the selling group. Underwriters who are also sellers get both an underwriting allowance and a selling concession, and managers who are also underwriters and sellers get all three fees.

In this example, total flotation costs of $2\frac{1}{2}$ percent were assumed. For eurobonds, 2 to $2\frac{1}{2}$ percent is the typical spread. Typical spreads for some of the foreign bond markets are these: Yankee bonds, $\frac{1}{2}$ to 1 percent; samurai bonds and DM foreign bonds, 2 percent; Rembrandt bonds, $2\frac{1}{2}$ percent; and Swiss franc foreign bonds, 4 percent. (The unusually large spread for Swiss franc foreign bonds appears to stem from the oligopsony buying power of the three largest Swiss banks, who purchase the greater portion of any Swiss franc foreign bond issue.)

TRADITIONAL TIME SCHEDULE FOR A NEW OFFERING

The key dates in the traditional time schedule for a new dollar eurobond offering are shown in Figure 17.2. Here is a summary of the process. Starting perhaps two weeks before the announcement day shown at the top of Figure 17.2 the lead manager and the borrower will meet for preliminary discussions. They will discuss terms (coupon, amount, offering price) of the bond issue. Except in the case of a bought deal (discussed later), these terms will remain provisional until the formal offering day. A fiscal agent or trustee and principal paying agent will be selected, and if the issue is to be listed on a stock exchange (usually Luxembourg or London), a listing agent as well. Preparation will begin on various legal documents that will be signed between syndicate members and the borrower, and among syndicate members. Work will also begin on the **offering circular** or **prospectus**, which in its preliminary form is called a **red herring**. The prospectus will describe the borrower and its history. For a corporate borrower, audited financial statements will be included in the prospectus, while for a government borrower there will be relevant GNP and central bank data. The prospectus will also include a statement of the preliminary terms of the bond offering.

The lead manager will begin to organize a management group to assist in the administration of the bond issue and will compile a list of potential syndicate members who will be invited to take part either as underwriters or sellers. On the **announcement day** (see top of Figure 17.2) there will be a press release announcing the new issue, and invitation telexes will be sent out inviting other banks to participate in the syndicate. Potential participants will have a week to ten days to respond (the offering period or **subscription period**). Potential underwriters and sellers will be sent a copy of the preliminary offering circular, a timetable of the bond offering, and relevant legal documents that they will sign if they take part in the issue. If the borrower is not well known, the borrower may at this point begin a tour, or "road show," in major financial centers in order to spread information about itself to potential investors.

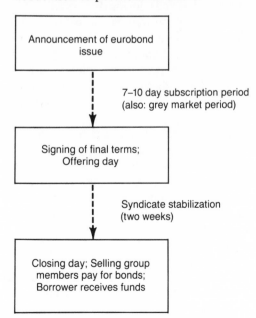

FIGURE 17.2
Time schedule of new eurobond offering.

The lead manager, meanwhile, will keep a *syndicate book* in which a record of the total demand for the bond issue is recorded. As interest in the bond issue is expressed, the lead manager will begin to make preliminary allotments of bonds among syndicate members, while waiting to receive signed underwriting and selling group agreements. Selling group members who cannot sell their entire allotment will later be able to return unsold bonds to the managers, while underwriters will be legally obligated to buy any unsold bonds at a preagreed minimum price. Even though underwriters may face a good deal of risk of a change in market conditions, the underwriting agreement they sign will usually give the managers considerable discretionary control over the issue. The managing group will decide final bond pricing terms with the borrower, and these terms may or may not be subject to an underwriter's approval before the underwriting agreement goes into effect. In addition, the managers will usually have considerable freedom in the number of bonds they decide to allocate to each underwriter and seller, subject to a maximal amount for which an underwriter is liable.

At the end of the subscription period, final bond pricing terms are decided upon between the managing banks and the borrower. Underwriters usually then have a day within which to accept or reject these terms, assuming they have the right of prior approval. Then the bonds are formally offered (the **offering day**) when the borrower and managing banks sign a **subscription agreement** setting out the final terms of the bond issue. At this point, the syndicate has in effect purchased the bonds from the borrower at an agreed price, though the borrower will not actually receive the funds until the closing day. A final offering circular is printed, and the lead manager notifies the underwriters and sellers of their bond allotments. The lead manager may either over- or underallocate the number of available bonds (see Stabilization, below). Sellers then have a number of days, after which they must notify the managers whether their allotments are sold. In the meantime, the newly offered bonds are bought and sold over-the-counter, though no money (or bonds) yet changes hands.

At the end of the stabilization period (**closing day**), syndicate members pay for the bonds they have purchased by depositing money into a bank account opened by the lead manager. Final investors at this point also receive book-entry credit for the bonds they have purchased (although they do not yet receive the individual bearer bonds). The borrower is paid in accordance with the terms of the subscription agreement, and the syndicate disbands. A **tombstone**, or advertisement, of the bond issue will later be published in a financial newspaper or journal.

For those who want them, the individual bearer bonds can usually be picked up from an office of the paying agent after ninety days have passed. In the meantime, there is a **global bond**, a temporary debt certificate representing the entire bond issue. Global bonds are used for U.S. dollar eurobond issues so U.S. investment banks can show that they have exercised due diligence in keeping new bonds out of the hands of U.S. citizens (for reasons explained in Chapter 16).

THE GRAY MARKET

During the subscription period, while potential sellers and underwriters are indicating their willingness to accept an allocation of bonds from the managing banks, there is uncertainty about the final terms of the bond issue, as well about how market conditions may change between the time an allocation of bonds is agreed to and the bonds are sold. If a seller knows he will receive an allocation of bonds from the lead manager (the amount of the allocation not yet certain) and knows that he will get a $1\frac{1}{2}$ percent discount from the issue price of the bonds, he might reason as follows: "I am getting a discount of $1\frac{1}{2}$ percent on a certain number of bonds. If I could sell these immediately for a smaller discount, say a discount of 1 percent, I would lock in a $\frac{1}{2}$ percent profit and could thus avoid the risk that interest rates (and hence bond prices) will change." The bonds themselves, however, are not yet in formal existence: final terms have not been established, and documents pertaining to the issue have not been signed. Nevertheless, there is nothing to prevent a forward market from emerging in which people make contractual commitments to trade these bonds at agreed prices once the bonds officially exist. Such a market in eurobond new issues emerged around 1977. It is referred to as the **gray market** or **premarket**. Gray market trading begins on the announcement day of a new issue. Bonds are traded in the gray market at a percentage discount on the future, as-yet-unknown issue price. A price of "less 1," for example, would mean a price of $98\frac{3}{4}$ if the bonds are issued at $99\frac{3}{4}$. A $1000 bond would then be exchanged between the two parties for $98\frac{3}{4}$ percent of its face value, or for $987.50.

The existence of the gray market raises an interesting practical question. If bonds could be bought on the gray market, say at "less $1\frac{1}{2}$," why would any final investor pay a higher price than this to a member of the selling group? And, if no one would pay higher than gray market prices, then — at the end of the subscription period when the borrower and the lead manager agree on final terms for the bond issue — gray market prices would dictate what final bond terms would be. In fact, there would be no reason to appeal to the lead manager's expertise in canvassing the market to determine the appropriate bond-pricing terms: the bonds would have been de facto priced by the market through gray market trading.

The pricing of new eurobonds issued according to the traditional timetable is, in fact, heavily influenced by gray market prices. As this market continues to develop, the gray market — or forward — price will come to represent the price at which potential demand is brought into equilibrium with potential supply. It is easy to foresee that in the future evolution of the eurobond market the traditional role of the lead manager will continue to be downgraded and new issues will come to be priced by more efficient market techniques. Until recently, however, information has flowed asymmetrically through the bond market. An investment banker named Stanley Ross began putting gray market prices on the Reuters screen in 1978, but access was limited to those members of the **Association of International Bond Dealers (AIBD)** registered as marketmakers. But in 1982 the bond-brokering firm of Guy Butler began making prices more generally available (Anderson, 1982). Such market-oriented approaches will undoubtedly continue, despite the hostility of a number of lead managers.

Sometimes gray market trading in a new bond issue has begun even before the announcement date. That is, not only have final terms not been decided, but even the existence of the prospective bond issue has not yet been announced. Jumping the gun in this fashion has its dangers. In October 1983, based on reports that Canada and the World Bank were to offer $700 million worth of eurobonds, the securities firms of Ross and Partners (Securities) Ltd. and Guy

Butler International Ltd. posted bid and asked prices for these nonexistent bonds and traded them for a day before it was realized that no such issues were in the works.

STABILIZATION

Stabilization refers to efforts by the lead manager to influence the market price of a bond during the time between the offering day and the closing day. The lead manager will put together a small group from the syndicate who will stand ready to buy up bonds to support their price if necessary. The rule of thumb typically followed is that the price of the bond in the market will not be allowed to fall below the amount of the selling concession (which is usually about $1\frac{1}{2}$ percent of the issue price of the bond). The price at which the managing group bids for bonds is referred to as the "syndicate bid." There seems to be several motives for stabilization. One has to do with the prestige of the lead manager. If the price of the bond rises immediately after terms have been signed, it will show that the lead manager didn't do a good job of assessing the market, since the borrower could have borrowed at a lower interest rate. The borrower might be upset and choose a different lead manager the next time around. Conversely, investors who buy bonds at or near their issue price will be upset if the price of the bonds drops immediately in the secondary market.

If interest rates rise over the course of the selling period, bond prices will have a tendency to fall, so the lead manager will be in the position of buying up bonds on the market in order to stabilize their price. If interest rates fall over the course of the selling period, bond prices will have a tendency to rise, so more bonds could be sold without depressing the price. Thus, for example, if the lead manager believes that interest rates will be rising during the stabilization period, the manager may, at the time terms are signed for a new issue, allocate to sellers a total of more bonds than actually exist. This is referred to as a syndicate short. The lead manager will then be obligated to buy back some of these bonds prior to closing, so as to have the required number of bonds available at the time money and bonds actually change hands. The action of the lead manager in buying back bonds on the market will support their price. Alternatively, if interest rates are expected to fall, the lead manager could engage in a syndicate long, which involves underallocating the number of available bonds.

VARIATIONS ON ISSUING PROCEDURE

A number of variations in the traditional procedure for making new eurobond issues exist. These variations represent responses to competitive pressures and interest rate risk. The bought deal is the primary example, as it has become the new standard for eurobond issues. In the bought deal, the lead manager buys the entire bond issue from the borrower at set terms — amount, coupon, issue price — prior to its announcement. Preset prices arise because of competition between individual investment banks to win mandates. They compete by quoting the borrower a package deal up front. The first bought deal is said to be that of CSFB, who bought an entire $100 million issue overnight from General Motors Acceptance Corporation. Only afterward did CSFB arrange a syndication. Such post-syndications result in a diminished role for selling group members and underwriters. Whether a bought deal actually involves more interest rate risk than is involved in the traditional issuing procedure is hard to say. Final terms are set without a subscription period for canvassing demand. However, the total time it takes to bring the issue to market is shortened. Hence some investment bankers use the bought deal to take advantage of windows—a "window" being essentially a stochastic drop in interest rates (or a stochastic rise in bond demand) that is perceived to be of short duration. Given these expectations, an investment banker might view the shorter time frame needed to bring a bought deal to market as implying an overall lower risk in terms of rising interest rates. In any case, the prefixed terms of the offering leads to brisk gray market trading as syndicate members hedge their interest risk by selling forward.

Yield pricing is another way of handling the possible discrepancy between the terms indicated on announcement day and the final terms signed at the end of the subscription period. In yield pricing, no preliminary terms are indicated. Instead, the coupon and the issue price of the bond, and the amount of commissions is fixed toward the end of the subscription period, and prices are set in line with similar issues in the secondary market. Yield pricing is widely used in the U.S. domestic bond market, but has been used in the eurobond market only in recent years.

A different approach is the *auction issue,* in which the borrower announces the maturity and the coupon rate of a new bond issue and invites investors to submit bids. Interested investors—who may be brokerage firms or banks who expect to resell the bonds—submit a bid price as a percentage of par such as 99.3, along with a statement of the amount they are willing to take at this price. The borrower then sells the bonds, starting with the highest bidder and working down until all bonds have been allotted. The auction system is widely used in domestic contexts. U.S. government securities, for example, are sold through an auction system. The auction system eliminates management fees and the costs of syndication and has served well certain widely known borrowers in the eurobond market such as the European Investment Bank. For less well-known borrowers, however, part of the job of an investment banking syndicate is to spread information about the borrower and the borrower's proposed bond issue. Such borrowers will find it necessary to pay the cost of a bond syndicate's marketing expertise.

PROBLEMS FOR CHAPTER 17

1. An investment banking syndicate follows the following table of flotation costs.

Maturity	Management fee (%)	Underwriting allowance (%)	Selling concession (%)	Total (%)
≤5 yrs.	$\frac{3}{8}$	$\frac{3}{8}$	$1\frac{1}{4}$	2
5–8 yrs.	$\frac{3}{8}$	$\frac{3}{8}$	$1\frac{1}{2}$	$2\frac{1}{4}$
>8 yrs.	$\frac{1}{2}$	$\frac{1}{2}$	$1\frac{1}{2}$	$2\frac{1}{2}$

The syndicate launches a $80-million seven-year eurobond issue. The syndicate is composed of a lead manager, who takes half of the management fee, and five co-managers who split the remainder. The issue is underwritten by the six managing banks (who underwrite a total of 30 percent of the issue), fifty major underwriters (who underwrite 50 percent of the issue), and forty minor underwriters who underwrite the rest. The underwriting allowance is split up according to the amount underwritten. The issue is sold by the six managers ($36 million total, divided equally), fifty major underwriters ($20 million total), forty minor underwriters ($12 million total), and 100 additional selling banks ($12 million total). The selling concession is split according to the amount sold. Calculate the dollar amount of total fees going to

(a)   The lead manager;
(b)   Each of the comanagers;
(c)   Each of the major underwriters;
(d)   Each of the minor underwriters; and
(e)   Each of the selling banks, *assuming all bonds are sold at the issue price of 100.*
(f)   In addition, find the dollar amount going to the company.

2.   Assume you were the lead manager for a new eurobond issue. Explain how and under what circumstances the gray market could be helpful to you. Explain how and under what circumstances the gray market could hinder you.

3.   Make the same explanations as in Problem 2, but from the point of view of a life insurance company portfolio manager.

EUROBOND VALUATION IN THE SECONDARY MARKET

Once new eurobonds have been formally offered on offering day, the bonds began to trade in the secondary market. In our discussion of the secondary market, we want to distinguish between trading, which is the buying and selling of bonds at negotiated prices, and clearing, which is the process of transferring ownership of the bonds between parties after the bonds are traded. Trading and clearing are separate functions in the eurobond market.

TRADING

The principal center of eurobond trading is the over-the-counter market in London, although other centers such as Frankfurt, Amsterdam, and Zurich are also important. An over-the-counter market means that traders do not gather together in one physical location to trade bonds—as in a stock exchange or a futures exchange. Rather the market is formed through a telecommunications linkage of U.S. brokerage firms, U.S. multinational banks, and major European and Japanese banks. (DM eurobonds are an exception: most secondary market trading takes place on the German stock exchanges.)

Orders to buy or sell bonds can be placed through market participants, who can be divided into **brokers** and **marketmakers**. Brokers accept orders to buy or sell bonds and try to find a matching party for the other side of the bond transaction. They typically charge a fee of .0625 percent to the party who initiated the transaction. Brokers in the eurobond market may, in addition, buy and sell for their own account. But brokers do not in general stand ready to quote two-way prices. Nor do they typically deal with retail customers. Instead, they act as intermediaries between marketmakers. Marketmakers, by contrast, will quote two-way (bid and offer) prices to retail customers and stand ready to deal in either direction. Marketmakers invest their own capital in a bond inventory and can themselves serve as the matching party in transactions by selling bonds out of their own portfolio or adding bonds to their portfolio.

Except for a brokered transaction, no commissions are charged between participants in the secondary market. A marketmaker's reward for making the market comes through the bid/asked spread between buying and selling prices. Of course, like the marketmakers in the foreign exchange market, discussed in Chapter 3, a marketmaker actually only earns the bid/asked spread to the extent he or she is adept at adjusting prices so that the number of bid orders is matched with the number of asked orders. Bond prices are quoted as a percentage of face value. Thus a bid/ask quotation of $95\frac{1}{2}$–96 would indicate a bid price of $955 and an asked price of $960 for a bond with a face value of $1000. The typical spread on fixed rate bonds is $\frac{1}{2}$ percent ($5 on a bond with a face value of $1000), but there will be a range of spreads depending on market conditions. In the first few days following a new bond issue, when trading is heaviest, spreads may be as low as $\frac{1}{8}$ percent, while at other times thinly traded bonds may have spreads of $1\frac{1}{2}$ percent. The standard-size transaction is 100 bonds (or $100,000 face value), and quoted prices usually are good only for a standard-size transaction. Floating rate notes are more liquid and enjoy a much smaller spread than fixed-rate or convertible issues.

When a trade is made, the price involved in the trade has been established, but money and bonds will not change hands until the **value date**, which is usually set so as to take place one week after the actual trade. Thus if a lot of 100 bonds is traded on Monday, July 23, then the purchaser will actually pay cash, and receive bonds, on Monday, July 30.

Eurobonds are bought or sold in the secondary market "cum coupon." The bond buyer will compensate the bond seller for the amount of interest that has accumulated since the last coupon payment. The amount of accumulated interest for annual coupons is calculated as (coupon payment) $\times$ ($T/360$), where T is the number of days since the last coupon was paid.

EXAMPLE 18.1

A trader buys 100 eurobonds with a face value of $1000 each, bearing a coupon of 12 percent, at a secondary market price of 93. As of the value date for the trade, 221 days will have passed since the last annual coupon. What is the trader's total dollar payment? The payment before the coupon adjustment is:

$100 \times \$1000 \times .93 = \$93,000.$

The coupon adjustment will be:

$100 \times \$1000 \times .12 \times (221/360) = \$7,366.67.$

So the trader's total payment is $93,000 + $7,366.67 = $100,366.67.

CLEARING

The primary goal in clearing procedures is to reduce the costs associated with bond transactions. That means that actual physical bonds should be moved around as little as possible. By analogy, think about how foreign exchange or eurocurrency deposits are traded internationally. Money — a deposit — is simply a number stored in a data bank along with a record of ownership. Thus trading money internationally is very simple. If a $1,000,000 deposit is to be transferred from Party A to Party B, the bank simply removes Party A's name and attaches Party B's name. It costs very little to send electronic signals between New York and London. Imagine what the cost would be, by contrast, if in order to get a $1-million deposit from New York to London a large suitcase had to be stuffed with $20 bills and a courier had to go to Kennedy airport, fly to Heathrow in England, and then cart the suitcase off to the appropriate London bank. This principle applies where bonds are concerned. The costs of clearing will be low only if the bonds are put away in a vault somewhere and ownership of the bonds is simply transferred through bookkeeping entries.

Most eurobonds are clearing through one of two major clearing systems: Euroclear and Cedel. **Euroclear Clearance System Limited** is a clearing system located in Brussels. It is owned by a group of banks but continues to be operated by Morgan Guaranty, which founded the system in 1968. Cedel S.A. is a clearing system located in Luxemborg. It was founded in 1971 by a group of European banks. Euroclear handles about two-thirds of the volume of bonds cleared through the two systems, Cedel one-third. Annual turnover through the clearing systems is over $1 trillion. Each of the systems has a group of depository or custodian banks in which physical bonds are stored. Members of a clearing system will maintain bond and cash accounts with the system. When bonds are purchased or sold, book entry settlements will be made, transferring the ownership of bonds or cash between the two members. The bonds themselves are seldom, if ever, moved. Both Euroclear and Cedel have an approved list of securities that can be cleared through their operations. (In the U.S a similar system exists for clearing U.S. government securities, which are also traded over the counter. Government bonds are stored in Federal Reserve vaults, and traders in government securities make title and money transfers via FedWire. Treasury bills are even simpler: they exist *only* in the form of accounting entries, hence storage costs are minimal.)

Euroclear and Cedel can also be used to distribute new eurobonds from the borrower issuing the bonds to syndicate members and final investors who have purchased bonds. The printed bond certificates are delivered in bulk to the clearing system. The clearing system then collects the subscription payments, gives book-entry credits to the new owners of the bonds, and remits the funds to the eurobond underwriting syndicate. Similarly, a clearing system can be used to distribute coupon payments from a borrower. The borrower pays funds into the clearing system and the clearing system makes the appropriate payments into the accounts of members credited with the ownership of the borrower's bonds.

While most eurobonds are cleared through Euroclear or Cedel, DM eruobonds are an exception. German banks are large dealers in DM eurobonds, and they usually prefer to store bonds in a domestic group of depository banks, the Kassenverein, and to clear bonds through the associated securities clearing system, the Effectengiro system.

The large reduction in transactions costs that comes about from the use of a clearing system can be seen in the following list of Euroclear transactions fees that was in effect in the summer of 1982. Transactions are distinguished according to whether they are simple book entry settlements between Euroclear members or transactions with another clearing system (Cedel or the Frankfurter

Kassenverein), or whether they involve physical movement of the securities. A "transaction" is a single order to transfer bonds, independent of the number of bonds.

**Schedule of Euroclear transactions fees,
Summer 1982**

Transfer of securities between Euroclear participants	$1.00
Transfer of securities against payment between Euroclear participants	$1.50
Bridge clearing of securities against payment with Cedel	$4.00
Transfer of securities via Frankfurter Kassenverein	$8.00
Deposit of securities into Euroclear system	Free
Removal of securities from Euroclear system	$12.50
Removal of securities against payment from Euroclear system	$15.00

In addition to transactions fees, there are custody fees for keeping the securities in the vault. These fees are charged according to the volume of bond turnover in a participant's account and are zero for high turnover.

Thus we can see that, except for transactions involving physical removal of securities, clearing costs are trivially small. For 100 bonds priced at 80 which are cleared against payment between participants, the charge of $1.50 for $80,000 of bonds is .001875 percent of the value of the bonds.

INTEREST RATES AND COUPON BOND PRICES

Coupon bonds can be priced by reference to pure discount (zero-coupon) bonds. Let the current year be t and consider a coupon bond $D(t,T)$ that has coupon payments at times $t + 1$, $t + 2$, . . . , $t + T$, in dollar (or other currency) amounts of $C(t,1)$, $C(t,2)$, . . . , $C(t,T)$. If the coupon payments are all the same, then $C(t,n) = C$, for all n. (For example, $C(t,n) = \$100$ for a 10-percent coupon on a $1000 face-value bond.) The bond also repays the principal $P(t,T)$ at time $t + T$.

Suppose that the coupons are stripped from the bond and each of the coupons and the principal repayment are sold separately. (This is a common practice with U.S. Treasury securities. For example, CATS — certificates of accrual on Treasury securities — are composed of stripped coupons or principal for a particular maturity date.) Since a coupon $C(t,n)$ involves no cash flows prior to time $t + n$, the current value of the coupon is $B(t,n)C(t,n)$, where $B(t,n)$ is the current price of a discount bond that pays $1 (or one unit of other currency) at time $t + n$. Because the coupon will involve a payment of $C(t,n)$ dollars, it has a value of $C(t,n)$ of these $1 discount bonds, or a value of $B(t,n)C(t,n)$.

The value of the entire coupon bond $D(t,T)$ is therefore

$$D(t,T) = B(t,1)C(t,1) + B(t,2)C(t,2) + \ \ldots \ + B(t,T)C(t,T)$$
$$+ B(t,T)P(t,T) \tag{18.1}$$

Equation (18.1) relates the value of the coupon bond $D(t,T)$ to discount bonds of equal or shorter maturity, $B(t,1)$, . . . , $B(t,T)$. If all coupon payments $C(t,n)$ have the same value, $C(t,n) = C$, for all n, equation (18.1) simplifies to

$$D(t,T) = C[B(t,1) + B(t,2) + \ \ldots \ + B(t,T)] + B(t,T)P(t,T). \tag{18.2}$$

There are several ways to refer to an interest rate in connection with the price of a coupon bond. One way is the **coupon yield**, which is the ratio of the coupon to the principal repayment:

$$\text{Coupon yield} = C/P(t,T). \tag{18.3}$$

Another rate is the **current yield**, which is the ratio of the coupon to the current bond price:

$$\text{Current yield} = C/D(t,T). \tag{18.4}$$

For example, if a 10 percent coupon bond with a $1000 face value is currently selling for $975, the current yield is $100/$975 = 10.26 percent.

Finally, there is the **yield to maturity**, which applies a uniform discount rate to each future time period. To calculate yield to maturity, let B be a fictional bond price such that, when it is raised to powers $1, 2, \ldots , T$:

$$D(t,T) = C[B + B^2 + \ldots + B^T] + B^T P(t,T). \tag{18.5}$$

Then the yield to maturity (measured as a fraction) is defined as

$$\text{Yield to maturity} = (1/B) - 1. \tag{18.6}$$

For example, if a 10-percent annual coupon bond with a face value of $1000 and with five years remaining to maturity has a yield to maturity of 11.11 percent (i.e., $B = 1/1.1111 = .9$), the current price $D(t,5)$ is:

$$\begin{aligned}
D(t,5) &= \$100\ [.9 + .9^2 + .9^3 + .9^4 + .9^5] + .9^5(\$1000) \\
&= \$100\ [3.6856] + .59\ (\$1000) \\
&= \$368.56 + \$590.00 = \$958.56.
\end{aligned}$$

The yield to maturity of 11.11 percent is higher than the current yield of $100/$958.56 = 10.43 percent.

Any one of these rates has a clear economic interpretation only in special circumstances. The coupon rate only indicates the size of the coupon payments, though it usually also represents the market interest rate on bonds in the present bond's risk class at the time the bond was first issued, assuming the bond was issued at par. The current yield would represent the return on a bond if it were bought at its present market value now and sold at the same price a year later, following a single coupon payment. The yield to maturity is relevant to individuals or institutions who apply uniform discount rates to the future, since in that case a bond with a higher yield to maturity is a more attractive asset than one with a lower yield to maturity. For an individual or institution that applies nonuniform discount rates to the future, the yield to maturity is a misleading method of ranking bond investments.

It is therefore best to ignore any of the above associated interest rates as applied to bonds and to focus on the relationship given in equation (18.1). Equation (18.1) gives an arbitrage relationship between coupon bonds and discount (zero-coupon) bonds. In practice, arbitrage is not feasible if it involves several transactions, because purchase or sale of any of the individual discount bonds $B(t,n)$, as well as the coupon bond $D(t,n)$ itself, will involve bid-offer spreads and other transactions costs. Some eurobond investment or speculative strategies are considered in the next section.

EUROBOND VALUATION

Eurobonds are intermediate to long-term assets, and their valuation depends upon the relation between short-term interest rates and bond coupon rates. Interest rates in today's market, combined with a market participant's expectations of future interest rates, give rise to a number of different trading strategies whose execution influences bond prices. Here are some examples.

Arbitrage

As bonds mature, there may be straightforward profit opportunities based on borrowing or lending short-term and buying or selling bonds. If a profit can be locked in with certainty, then this is a form of arbitrage. (If the bonds are denominated in a foreign currency, then there must also be an exchange rate transaction in order to fix with certainty the domestic currency value of the entire operation.) The process of arbitrage will bring about price adjustments so that arbitrage opportunities are eliminated. The absence of arbitrage opportunities will thus define a relation between bond prices and short-term interest rates.

EXAMPLE 18.2

A trader in the over-the-counter market in London observes a DM 1000 eurobond with a 4 percent coupon and with one year to maturity quoted with a bid/ask prices of $95\frac{1}{2}$–96. He has access to the interbank market, and observes that one-year eurodollar deposits are available at $10\frac{1}{2}$–$10\frac{5}{8}$ percent, that spot rates are quoted at DM 2.4783–2.4798/\$, while one-year forward rates are DM 2.3954–2.3981/\$. If he buys any number of bonds, clearing charges through Euroclear will be \$1.50. Given these prices, will the trader buy the DM eurobond?

In one year the DM bond will pay DM 1000 principal plus a coupon of DM 40. The DM return on the bond is 1040/960 = 1.0833 or 8.33 percent. DM can be purchased spot for DM 2.4783/\$ and sold forward for DM 2.3981/\$, so the dollar return is

$$(1.0833)(2.4783/2.3981) = 1.1195$$

or 11.95 percent. This is greater than the trader's borrowing rate of $10\frac{5}{8}$ percent, so the trader will buy the bond. [For a lot of 100 bonds, the trader will need to pay DM 96,000. This implies that he must borrow

$$\$38,736 = (DM\ 96,000)/(DM\ 2.4783/\$)$$

and pay back in one year

$$\$42,851.70 = (\$38,736)(1.10625).$$

If he sells forward today the DM he will receive in one year, he will sell forward DM 104,000 for

$$\$43,368 = (DM\ 104,000)/(DM\ 2.3981/\$\overline{X}).$$

The profit at the end of one year will be \$516.30, from which should be substracted the Euroclear fee of \$1.50 plus about \$.16 in interest, the interest being the opportunity cost of paying the \$1.50 fee one year in advance. Alternatively, the value of the profit discounted to the present time when the transaction is made would be:

$$\$516.30/1.10625 - \$1.50 = \$465.21.]$$

Of course, in practice the procedure in the example would be simplified. Exchange exposure, if it existed, would be dealt with in the context of the total bond portfolio, not on the basis of individual transactions. An arbitrager would buy the bond if the total return, calculated in terms of DM, were greater than the arbitrager's DM borrowing rate.

Riding the Yield Curve

If the term structure of interest rates is upward-sloping — that is, if short-term interest rates are lower than long-term interest rates — then this strategy involves borrowing at short term in order to finance a bond portfolio. If the level of coupon payments on the bonds is greater than the level of interest payments on the borrowing by an amount sufficient to cover management expenses, this strategy will yield a profit. The risk is, of course, that short-term rates may rise above long-term rates. If the yield curve becomes inverted in this fashion, the cost of financing the portfolio will exceed the income from coupon payments and principal repayments on the bonds in the portfolio. Moreover, the bond portfolio could not in that case easily be liquidated without incurring a large capital loss, since bond prices will have fallen with the rise in short-term interest rates. If a eurobond futures market existed, this risk of capital loss could be more easily managed. Unfortunately, no such futures market currently exists (see, however, Eurobond Futures, below).

Most eurobond dealers finance their bond portfolios by borrowing through the clearing systems — Euroclear and Cedel. A clearing system will loan a dealer up to 90 percent of the value of bonds the dealer has deposited within the clearing system, so that only a small portion of the bond portfolio must be financed using the dealer's own capital.

Speculation on Capital Gains and Losses

As short-term interest rates rise and fall, bond prices fall and rise (refer back to equation (18.1)). Bond investors discount future coupon payments according to current and expected future short-term interest rates. A change in current short-term interest rates usually entails also a change in expected future interest rates. As a result, when the new present and expected future interest rates are used to discount the future coupon and principal payments on a bond, the bond's value — and market price — will change.

The speculator's strategy in this case is to sell bonds short if the speculator expects interest rates to rise since — if the expectations prove accurate — the price of a bond when it is sold will be greater than the price of a bond when it is repurchased. If the speculator expects interest rates to fall, the strategy is to be long bonds now, with an anticipation of selling bonds after interest rates have fallen and bond prices risen. The execution of these strategies is made easier by recent institutional innovatons. The two clearing systems have bond borrowing and lending facilities. This makes possible short-selling, since bonds may be borrowed from the system at a preagreed interest rate for a preagreed period of time and sold.

EUROBOND FUTURES

Bond dealers in the U.S. government securities market regularly manage the risk on their bond portfolios using the U.S Treasury bond futures contract traded at the Chicago Board of Trade. The contract is based on a $100,000 U.S. Treasury bond with twenty years to maturity bearing an 8 percent coupon yield, for delivery in March, June, September, and December. The price is quoted as a fraction of face value, expressed in percent and $\frac{1}{32}$ percent. A price of 61 '07, for example, would denote $61\frac{7}{32}$ percent of par. If the price moved from 61 '07 to 61 '08, the long side of the T-bond futures contract would make

$$\tfrac{1}{32} \times .01 \times \$100,000 = \$31.25,$$

while the short side would lose $31.25. If the price went from 61 '07 to 60 '31, the long side would lose

$$\tfrac{8}{32} \times .01 \times \$100,000 = \$250$$

on each contract, while the short side would gain $250 on each contract.

Dealers in the U.S. government securities market can hedge the risk of capital losses on their bond portfolios that would result from rising interest rates by going short T-bond futures. If interest rates rise, the price of T-bond futures will fall, and any profit on the futures position will offset capital loss on the portfolio. A short bond futures position can be hedged by going long T-bond futures. The precision of this hedge will depend on the change in value of the T-bond futures contract compared with the change in value of an equal dollar position in government securities. If the two value changes are not exactly the same, the hedge will not be perfect. Nevertheless, such valuation changes are sufficiently predictable that T-bond futures prove in practice to be a useful way to hedge. (Review futures hedging in Chapter 5.)

EXAMPLE 18.3

A dealer has a government bond portfolio with a current market value of $850,000. The current price of T-bond futures is 65 '16, for an underlying contract value of

$$65\tfrac{16}{32} \times \$100,000 = \$65,500.$$

Hence, if the change in value of the futures contract is expected to match the change in value of $65,500 in government bonds, the dealer will hedge by going short $850,000/ $65,500 = 13 T-bond futures contracts.

Dealers in eurobonds can, of course, use T-bond futures as a way of hedging. However, a change in the value of a T-bond future contract and the value of an equal dollar position in eurobonds will not generally be one-for-one, so a delta hedge is appropriate. Hence, letting x be the change in the value of each dollar in the eurobond portfolio, while y is the change in the value of $1 in T-bond futures, one establishes a delta hedge in the manner described in Chapter 5. Fitting the equation $y = \hat{b} x$, the rule is to go short $1/\hat{b}$ dollars in futures value for each dollar one is long in eurobonds. The amount of risk reduction, as shown in Chapter 5, would depend on how well the equation fitted — on the variance of the error term.

EXAMPLE 18.4

A eurobond trader has a short position of $1,500,000 in eurobonds, which — based on her expectations — the trader decides to hedge completely on a temporary basis. The trader estimates that the change in value of a T-bond futures contract for a particular delivery date will be $1.25 for each $1 change in the value of the portfolio. Thus, in the trader's calculation $b = 1.25$, implying a long position of $1/1.25 = .8$ dollars in futures for each dollar she is short in eurobonds. For a current T-bond futures price of 71 '00, she would thus go long ($1,500,000/$71,000) (.8) = 17 futures contracts.

One study on hedging corporate debt with U.S. Treasury bond futures has concluded that

1. Hedging with Treasury bond futures offers substantial protection from unexpected changes in corporate bond prices;
2. Hedging with Treasury bond futures is more effective if higher-quality corporate debt (which would include eurobonds) is being hedged;
3. In choosing among the available T-bond contracts as hedge instruments, the futures contracts for nearby delivery are superior to the contracts for more distant delivery (Kuberek and Pefley, 1983).

The amount of risk reduction that can be obtained from hedging a eurobond portfolio using T-bond futures is less than would be possible if there existed a eurobond futures contract based on a standardized eurobond. Eurobond futures contracts are being considered at some futures exchanges. In the meantime, some market participants have created the equivalent to a eurobond futures contract through private forward contracting.

In October 1983 Weyerhaeuser Capital Corporation issued $60 million in seven-year eurobonds bearing a coupon of $11\frac{1}{2}$ percent. At the same time, it took out a side bet with the investment banking firm of Morgan Stanley concerning the direction of movement of interest rates over the next seven months. If eurobond interest rates fell within the next seven months, Morgan Stanley was to pay Weyerhaeuser a cash amount such that Weyerhaeuser's borrowing cost would be reduced to the equivalent of borrowing the $60 million at the reduced interest rate. Conversely, if eurobond interest rates rose, Weyerhaeuser was to pay Morgan Stanley a cash amount such that Weyerhaeuser's borrowing cost would be increased to the equivalent of borrowing the $60 million at the increased interest rate.

The way to view this deal between Weyerhaeuser and Morgan Stanley is as a eurobond forward contract, with Morgan Stanley on one side of the contract going short, while Weyerhaeuser was on the other side going long. If interest rates fell, the value of the long side of the eurobond forward contract would rise, and the short side of the contract would pay the long side. The converse transaction would occur if interest rates rose.

It was reported at the time (*Business Week,* November 28, 1983) that Morgan Stanley simultaneously offset its risk on the contract with Weyerhaeuser by taking a position in T-bond futures. If so, it would be logical for Morgan Stanley, which was short a eurobond forward contract, to have gone long T-bond futures. Then if interest rates fell, the gain on the T-bond futures would be used to offset the loss on the eurobond forward contract, while if interest rates rose, the loss on T-bond futures would be offset by the gain on the eurobond forward contract with Weyerhaeuser. Of course Morgan Stanley would still face the risk that the gain or loss on the T-bond futures contract might not match the gain or loss on the forward contract. That would depend on the effectiveness of its delta hedge.

PROBLEMS FOR CHAPTER 18

1. A trader buys 100 eurobonds in the secondary market at a price of 84, each bond with a face value of $1000 and bearing an annual coupon of 12 percent. As of the value date for the trade, 112 days will have passed since the last coupon. What is the trader's total dollar payment for the bonds?

2. A French franc bond with a market price of FF 8765 and a face value of FF 10,000 pays annual coupons of FF 700 and matures in one year. Calculate the coupon yield, the current yield, and the yield to maturity. Interpret each number.

3. A eurobond with a face value of $1000 and an annual coupon of $115 is purchased when the current yield is 10 percent. A year later the bond is sold for $995. What is the capital gain or loss on the purchase/resale?

4. During the subscription period of a eurodollar bond issue, a member of the managing group sells short 100 T-bond futures at the CBOT at an average price of 70'12. Later the futures position is closed out at an average price of 71'01. What was the net gain or loss on the futures position?

5. A marketmaker with a long position of $346,500 in eurobonds at a current price of 99 goes short three CBOT T-bond futures contracts at 71'16. Rising interest rates cause the price of the eurobonds to fall to 97½, while the price of T-bond futures falls to 69'04. What is the change in the total value of the marketmaker's position?

INTEREST RATE
AND CURRENCY
SWAPS

The subject of this chapter should not be confused with that of Chapter 4. In Chapter 4 we saw that in the FX interbank market, a swap contract involved a spot sale or purchase of currency combined with a forward purchase or sale of the same currency. In this chapter, the term "swap" will have a somewhat different meaning. A **currency swap** is simply an exchange of debt or assets denominated in one currency for debt or assets denominated in another currency. An **interest rate swap** is the exchange of fixed-interest rate debt or assets for floating-interest rate debt or assets (or floating for fixed). If a swap involves the exchange of fixed-rate debt or assets in one currency for floating-rate debt or assets in another currency, it is both an interest rate swap and a currency swap.

Swaps represent an important new institutional development in the international financial markets. One should, however, be careful to read between the lines in accounts of swap activity reported in the news media. Many of these reports have a "free lunch" flavor: they imply that one gets something for nothing, that a swap involves no tradeoffs.

Most currency and interest rate swaps can be economically interpreted in one of three ways: risk-sharing, arbitrage, or as market completions. Many currency and interest-rate swaps represent simple risk-sharing. A company (or other party) has unmatched cash flows in terms of foreign currencies, or in terms of the proportion of variable-rate assets matched by variable-rate liabilities. The company finds a second party with a complementary mismatch and arranges a swap in such a way that its foreign-currency cash flows are now more closely matched (currency swap), or that its variable-interest-rate assets and liabilities are now more closely matched (interest rate swap). In some cases, however, currency or interest-rate swaps can be interpreted either as arbitrage or as market completions. Swaps may take place because arbitrage opportunities exist. These arbitrage opportunities may arise from exchange or capital controls, tax regulations, or simple inconsistencies in market pricing of fixed- versus floating-rate assets or assets of different currencies. Finally, swaps could be termed "market completions" if they represent the emergence of new markets for risk-sharing, giving rise to beneficial transactions that were not economically possible given the previously available markets and the associated costs of transacting in those markets.

The fact that some currency and interest-rate swaps involve arbitrage is obvious. Suppose a Japanese company wanted debt denominated in Japanese yen. There are at least two (or more) ways to get yen debt:

1. Issue yen debt.
2. Issue dollar debt and swap it for yen debt.

Why might a company take the second route of issuing dollar debt? Answer: Issuing dollar debt and swapping may be a cheaper way of getting yen debt than would a direct issue of yen debt. If so, then the Japanese company is taking advantage of an arbitrage opportunity. A few Japanese companies have, through swaps, borrowed at yen interest rates lower than the concurrent borrowing rate paid by the Japanese government.

In the same way, it may in some circumstances be cheaper to get fixed-rate debt by issuing floating-rate debt first and then swapping it for fixed-rate debt. For example, the market might be pricing the fixed-rate debt of one company relative to the fixed-rate debt of another company at a ratio that is inconsistent with the ratio at which the market is pricing the floating-rate debt of each company. If so, then both companies can arrange a debt swap that will exploit the inconsistencies in current market pricing. If these inconsistencies are large enough to pay a bank to put the two companies in touch with each other so that the bank also makes a profit, then a debt swap can take place.

Swaps in some cases represent market completions. A company that wishes to issue French franc debt may not have access to the French market. As a result, it may make a deal with a second company that has French franc debt and assume the second company's obligation to pay coupons and principal denominated in French francs in return for the second company's taking on of the obligation to pay coupons and principal of a different currency. Often the two companies will not be known to each other. A banking intermediary may arrange the deal, and may guarantee both sides of the swap transaction.

TYPES OF CURRENCY SWAPS

The term "swap" is currently used in a fairly broad sense to denote a trade of one sort or another. The following types of transactions are generally considered examples of currency swaps.

LONG-TERM FORWARD CONTRACTS

These contracts are not any different from the FX forward contracts in the interbank market. However, in the interbank market, forward contracts for certain less-traded currencies are not available, and even for widely traded currencies forward contract maturities are fairly short. There is a market failure for forward trade in certain currencies and certain maturities. A long-term forward contract is thus essentially a barter transaction. A company or institution seeks out a counterparty with which it arranges a contract to exchange two currencies at some time in the future, the exchange to take place at a price that is agreed to today. The market failure in this case may be only one of degree. Commercial or investment banks may act as brokers who find a matching party on behalf of a company. They will keep careful (and carefully guarded) lists of particular institutions who are potential matching parties for particular transactions. There is a sense in which this collective set of institutions constitutes a market through the broker's intermediation.

STRAIGHT CURRENCY SWAPS

A "straight" currency swap is the exchange of two currencies at the current exchange rate with an agreement to reverse the trade—at the same exchange rate—at some set date in the future. One of the parties will pay the other annual interest payments. These interest payments are usually agreed to on the basis of the interest parity relation. If interest rates on assets denominated in currency A are higher than in currency B, then the party who receives currency A in exchange for currency B will pay the interest differential to the other party. For example, if $1,000,000 is swapped for ¥240,000,000 and dollars pay 5 percent higher interest than yen, then the party getting dollars might pay the other party annual interest in the amount of $50,000.

BACK-TO-BACK AND PARALLEL LOANS

Back-to-back loans are loans between two companies in different countries, each of which makes the other a loan in its respective currency. Parallel loans involve two companies in different countries, each of which has a subsidiary in the other's country. Each company makes a loan to the other company's subsidiary. For example, a U.S. company might loan dollars to a Brazilian company's U.S. subsidiary, while the Brazilian company would loan cruzeiros to the U.S. company's subsidiary in Brazil. Parallel loans got started for the same reason the eurodollar market got started: Bank of England regulations. At one time, if U.K. companies went through the London FX market, they had to pay a premium over the market rate for U.S. dollars in order to finance their foreign subsidiaries. To avoid this tax on dollar purchases, they arranged for their foreign subsidiaries to get dollar loans from U.S. companies, while the U.K. companies in turn loaned sterling to the subsidiaries of the U.S. companies in the United Kingdom.

The periodic payments of interest on each loan in a parallel loan transaction, and the repayment of principal, are usually timed to coincide in the two countries, and each company has the right to deduct payments not received in one country from payments due in the other country. Often the loan agreement includes a futures contract: if one currency depreciates in value relative to the other currency, the lender of the depreciated currency has to increase its loan to offset the changes in the loan's value due to exchange-rate changes. The typical futures contract in this case, however, does not involve a cash flow for every small change in the exchange rate. Rather, it is a step function: only if the exchange rate moves beyond certain limit points (for example, above $1.60/£ or below $1.40/£) will additional lending or repayment take place.

SWAP OF DEBT PAYMENTS

In this type of currency swap, each company (or other party) issues fixed-rate debt in a currency that is available to it, then the two companies swap the proceeds of the debt issue and also assume each other's obligation to make interest and principal payments. One company may issue debt in the amount of $10,000,000, while the other issues debt in the amount of French franc 80,000,000. The two companies then swap currencies and in addition assume each other's obligation to make interest payments and principal repayments. The dollar-issuing company will make periodic French franc coupon payments, while the French franc issuing company will make periodic dollar payments. The coupon payment dates are set so that they coincide. The payments may be made directly between the two companies, or the payments may be made to a commercial or investment banking intermediary that passes the payment to the other company. The intermediary may, or may not, guarantee one or both sides of the transaction and may, or may not, skim off part of a payment before passing it along. When the French franc issuing company receives the coupon payments from the other company, it then passes these along to its debtholders. Similarly, when the dollar-issuing company receives dollar coupon payments from its counterparty, it then pays the owners of the dollar debt. The debtholders of either company are not usually aware of the currency swap arrangement.

One example of a swap of debt payments in different currencies was the one that took place between IBM and the World Bank in August 1981, with Salomon Brothers as the intermediary. In previous years IBM had borrowed in the capital markets of West Germany and Switzerland, acquiring fixed-interest rate debt in DM and in Swiss francs. When the dollar appreciated sharply against these two currencies during 1981, IBM enjoyed a capital gain from the reduced dollar value of its foreign debt liabilities. The DM, for example, fell in value from DM 1.93/$ in March 1980 to DM 2.52/$ in August 1981. Thus a coupon payment of DM 100 had fallen in dollar cost from $51.81 to $36.68. By swapping its foreign-interest payment obligations for dollar obligations, IBM could realize this capital gain immediately. This is similar to closing out an FX forward contract after a profit has accumulated. IBM chose to get out of the bet regarding the direction of exchange rate movements. The way this took place is that the World Bank issued two dollar eurobonds, one that matched the maturity of IBM's DM debt and one that matched the maturity of IBM's Swiss franc debt. The World Bank agreed to pay all future interest and principal payments on IBM's DM and Swiss franc debt, while IBM in turn agreed to pay future interest and principal payments on the World Bank's dollar debt.

INTEREST RATE SWAPS

In an interest rate swap, one party issues fixed-rate debt while another issues floating-rate debt, and the two parties swap their interest payment obligations. For example, a bank might want floating-rate dollar debt while a company wants fixed-rate dollar debt. Assume the bank can borrow at $11\frac{1}{2}$ percent fixed or at LIBOR. The company can borrow at 14 percent fixed or at 1 percent above LIBOR. The bank and the company enter into an interest-rate swap agreement that involves the following provisions. The bank issues $50,000,000 of fixed-rate debt at $11\frac{1}{2}$ percent while the company issues $50,000,000 of floating-rate debt at 1 percent above LIBOR. The company subsequently makes coupon payments to the bank in the amount of 12 percent, while the bank makes LIBOR payments to the company. The company's net interest cost on its debt is

$$(\text{LIBOR} + 1\%) + (12\%) - (\text{LIBOR}) = 13 \text{ percent}.$$

The bank's net interest cost is

$$(11\tfrac{1}{2}\%) - (12\%) + (LIBOR) = (LIBOR - \tfrac{1}{2}\%).$$

Each party has reduced its borrowing cost: the bank gets floating-rate funds at $(LIBOR - \tfrac{1}{2}\%)$ instead of LIBOR; the company gets fixed-rate funds at 13% instead of 14 percent.

However . . . ! There may be no magic in the above transaction. The bank, for example, is in a riskier position than if it just borrowed at LIBOR, because if the company were to default on its payments (in which case the bank would also halt interest payments to the company), the bank would be left with $11\tfrac{1}{2}\%$ fixed-rate debt. In that case, the bank would not have the floating-rate debt it had wanted. Thus, the *reduction in the bank's cost of funds from LIBOR to* $(LIBOR - \tfrac{1}{2}\%)$ *may only compensate it for the greater funding risk.* Only if the $\tfrac{1}{2}$ percent reduction in funding cost were greater than the amount sufficient to compensate it for the greater risk involved would the bank be unambiguously better off. That is, for the transaction to be an arbitrage transaction, it would have to be the case that the risk premium on the company's fixed-rate debt (relative to the bank's debt) was not consistent with the risk premium on the company's floating-rate debt.

In Chapter 18 we saw that changes in interest rates and interest-rate expectations could bring about capital gains and losses on assets such as long-term bonds. The same is true from the point of view of a debt-issuer: if interest rates rise, the market value of a company's debt falls. Hence the company can realize a capital gain by getting rid of its current debt obligation at current market prices. One way to do this is for the company to buy up its own debt in the secondary market. Another way is to swap its coupon and principal obligations to another party.

A special type of interest-rate swap is the *cross-currency interest-rate swap.* This involves the swap of floating-rate debt denominated in one currency for fixed-rate debt denominated in another currency. One such swap took place between Renault, the French automotive company, and Yamaichi, the Japanese securities firm. Renault wanted to issue fixed-rate yen debt, but faced regulatory barriers that prevented it from issuing fixed-rate yen debt directly. A swap arranged by Bankers Trust Company had the following components. Yamaichi *purchased* dollar floating-rate notes, and passed the dollar payments (interest and principal) on the notes to Renault via Bankers Trust. Renault used the dollar payments to make payments on its own floating-rate dollar debt. In return for the floating-rate payments, Renault made yen fixed-rate interest and principal payments to Yamaichi via Bankers Trust. Thus Renault had turned its floating-rate dollar payment obligations into fixed-rate yen obligations. Yamaichi had acquired dollar assets but had subsequently hedged its exchange risk, as it now received payments in yen from Renault.

Interest-rate swaps are documented in a manner similar to syndicated loans. The documentation of an interest-rate swap is not nearly so elaborate, since the risk involved is only related to the interest payments and not to the principal. But many of the issues are the same. There has to be agreement on the manner in which the floating rate is calculated, the circumstances under which another reference rate can be substituted, when and how interest payments are to be made, and the governing law to be used in the event disputes arise.

PRICING OPTION FEATURES IN INTERNATIONAL BONDS

Bond covenants in international bond issues often contain creative contingency provisions that distinguish them from ordinary bonds. Many of these contractural features can be identified as options. Since most types of options can be given explicit values in terms of other market assets, it follows that such contingency features in a bond convenant can be given an explicit value. Thus the total value of the bond will not be determined in the usual way. The value of a coupon bond with an option feature, for example, is no longer given by the arbitrage relation of equation (18.1) in Chapter 18. Equation (18.1) expresses the current value of a coupon bond in terms of the discounted value of its future coupon and principal payments (where the market price of pure discount bonds for maturity at the coupon payment dates acts as the discount factor). But if the bond covenant has option features in addition to coupon and principal payments, the option features have to be treated explicitly. Options may also be found in domestic bond contracts, but historically they have been more prevalent in international bonds.

In this chapter we will look at some examples in which a bond can be priced in two parts as the sum of (1) the value of an ordinary bond with cash flow features, and (2) the value of one or more options. That is, many bonds with option features can split into two distinct pieces. One part is just an ordinary bond X. The other part is an option (or options) Y. Each of these is priced separately. Since the bond covenant includes both parts, the value W of the bond is the sum of the values of its two parts:

$$W = X + Y.$$

(Not all bonds can be valued this simply. In some cases, the ordinary cash flows are contingent on whether the option is exercised. In such a case, the value of the bond W is not a simple sum of two independent parts but has a more complex structure

$$W = W(X,Y),$$

where $W(X,Y)$ denotes a general function of X and Y.)

IDENTIFYING OPTION FEATURES IN BONDS

Before attempting actually to price a bond with an option feature, we will first acquire some practice in identifying exactly what the option feature is. After the option feature has been identified, valuing the option feature is made easy through the use of standard formulas.

Attached Options

The most obvious case of an option feature on a bond is one explicitly labeled "option [warrant] attached." **Warrant** is the name given to an option contract issued by a company. Below are two examples of stock options, the second of which involves a foreign exchange factor (but not a foreign exchange option) from the point of view of the option buyer.

EXAMPLE 20.1

In November 1983 Prudential Overseas Funding Corporation NV issued $150 million worth of U.S. dollar bonds. Each $10\frac{1}{8}$ percent ten-year note had attached to it seven warrants. These warrants gave the holder the right to purchase ten shares of the (reorganized) American Telephone & Telegraph Company, plus one share each of the seven new regional U.S. telephone companies. The strike price at which the warrants could be exercised was fixed at a premium over the market price of the stock at the time the bonds were issued.

The fair value of one bond thus depended on (1) the fair value of the ten-year stream of $10\frac{1}{8}$ percent coupon payments and principal repayment, plus (2) the fair value of the seven warrants. Each of the warrants represented an American call option on stock. They were *call* options because they gave the right to *purchase* stock at a prefixed strike price. They were *American* call options because they could be exercised at any time.

EXAMPLE 20.2

On February 19, 1982, BASF Overzee NV issued $165 million worth of six-year 11-percent coupon bonds at par, each with three warrants (which could be detached and traded separately as of April 19) to subscribe to, respectively, one, nine, and ten bearer shares of BASF at DM 136 per share.

The fair value of each $1000 bond was the sum of (1) the value of an ordinary $1000, six-year 11-percent coupon bond issued at par, plus (2) the value of the three warrants. Each of the three warrants had a value that was different from the others. It is easy to see that the warrant on nine shares of stock had a value that was nine times the value of the warrant on one share, while the warrant on ten shares of stock had a value that was ten times the value of the warrant on one share.

Consider the value of the warrant to purchase one share of BASF for DM 136. Seen from the point of view of a German consumer, this is just the current DM value of an American call option on one share of BASF with a strike price of DM 136. This can be priced by means of an option formula for stock options. Denote this value by $V(t)$. The same option, seen from the point of view of a consumer in the United States, who — not being a member of the jet set — is interested only in U.S. dollar consumption, has the current value $S(t)V(t)$, where $S(t)$ is the spot U.S. dollar price of 1 DM. For example, if

$V(t) = DM\ 5$ and $S(t) = \$.42/DM$,

then

$S(t)V(t) = (\$.42/DM)(DM\ 5) = \$2.10$.

Then, on the same assumption, the value of the warrant to buy nine shares would be

$(9)(\$2.10) = \$18.90$,

while the value of the warrant to buy ten shares would be

$(10)(\$2.10) = \$21.00$.

Bonds with Options on the Principal Repayment

We now look at some bonds which have the characteristic that the principal repayment can, at the choice of the bondholder, be valued in one of two ways. The bondholder, in choosing one value, will be giving up the other. Thus the choice of two alternative methods of valuation represents a European call option. The choice is a call option, because it gives the right to "purchase" one value of the bond by "paying" (giving up) the other value. It represents a *European* call option, because the exchange — if it occurs — only takes place at the maturity of the bond. (The same valuation feature could also be represented as a put option, but we will not pursue that representation here.)

EXAMPLE 20.3

In 1980, at a time when Nelson Bunker Hunt had bid up the market price of silver, a happy company called Sunshine Mining issued fifteen-year $8\frac{1}{2}$ percent bonds. Each $1000 bond was to be redeemed at maturity (1995) at par or at the market price of 50 ounces of silver, whichever was higher.

The option to receive the market price of silver (and forgo $1000) was equivalent to a European call option on 50 ounces of silver, with an exercise price $X = \$1000$. The option will end up "in the money" in 1995 if the market value of the silver at that time is greater than $20 per ounce, because in that case the value of 50 ounces would be greater than (50 ounces)($20/ounces) = $1000. The maturity T of this European option is $T = 15$ years, because the option cannot be used prior to the time the bond is redeemed.

Thus the value of one of Sunshine Mining's bonds was the value of an ordinary fifteen-year $8\frac{1}{2}$ percent bond in the same risk class as Sunshine Mining, plus the value of a European call option on 50 ounces of silver with a strike price of $X = \$1000$ and a maturity of $T = 15$ years.

EXAMPLE 20.4

A Japanese company issues $1000 bonds at par in the eurobond market. The coupon rate is 12 percent payable annually in U.S. dollars, and the bonds mature in May 1990. At maturity the bonds may be redeemed, at the owner's discretion, for dollars or for yen at an exchange rate of ¥200/$. What value would one place on this bond?

Assuming the bondowner is interested in U.S. dollar consumption, she would clearly opt for repayment of principal in yen if the number of yen per dollar were less than ¥200 in May 1990. For example, if the exchange rate were ¥166.67/$, she could redeem her bond for

($1000)(¥200/$) = ¥200,000,

and then sell the yen for

(¥200,000)/(¥166.67/$) = $1200.

Thus the value of this eurobond can be viewed as the sum of (1) the value of an ordinary $1000 bond with a 12 percent coupon, and (2) the value of a European call option on ¥200,000, with an exercise price $X = 1000, and with an expiration date in May 1990. If, in May 1990, the number of yen per dollar is 200 or greater, the option is worthless, so it will not be exercised. The bondholder will simply take the $1000. But if the number of yen per dollar is less than 200, the owner will exercise the option by giving up the right to receive $1000 and instead take payment of ¥200,000.

EXAMPLE 20.5

A company issues $1000 8 percent bonds, the principal of which is convertible into common stock of the parent company at maturity at a fixed exchange rate of Can$ 1.2007/$. The conversion price per share is Can$ 23⅛. How should the bond be valued?

The first thing to note is that the combination of a fixed conversion price and a fixed exchange rate to be used for the conversion implies that the bond is exchangeable for a fixed number of shares. Namely, the bond is convertible into

($1000)(Can$ 1.2007/$)/(Can$ 23⅛) = 51.92 shares.

Suppose, for example, that at maturity the market price of the shares were Can$25 per share, and the market exchange rate were $.80/Can$. Then the Canadian dollar value of the shares would be

(Can$25)(51.92) = Can$1298.05.

The U.S. dollar value of the shares (the conversion value) would in that case be

($.80/Can$)(Can$1298.05) = $1038.44.

Hence, for that share price and exchange rate it would be to the bondholder's advantage to convert the bond into shares rather than to simply take repayment of the $1000 principal. For that share price and exchange rate, the conversion option would expire in the money.

In general, the bond has as its value the sum of (1) an ordinary 8 percent bond, plus (2) a European call option on the U.S. dollar value of 51.92 shares of stock in the parent company. The exercise price of the option is $1000, and the expiration date of the option corresponds to the maturity date of the bond.

Coupon Options

In the following example, payment of coupons as well as principal can be taken in a choice of two alternative currencies, where the conversion of one currency into another is made at a prefixed exchange rate. As a result, there is a European FX option feature associated with each coupon payment as well as the principal repayment. Since the coupon payments all take place at different times, the expiration dates of the associated options differ in each case.

EXAMPLE 20.6

A British company issues five-year $1000 bonds with 10 percent annual coupons. The holder of a bond has the right to receive payment of coupons or principal in either dollars or pounds. If the option to take pounds is chosen, the dollar payment will be converted to pounds at a fixed exchange rate of $1.50/£. How is the bond to be valued?

Each annual coupon payment of $100 can be converted to pounds at a fixed exchange rate of $1.50/£, which implies that the bondholder can take payment of

$$(\$100)/(\$1.50/\pounds) = \pounds 66\tfrac{2}{3}$$

in place of $100. At maturity, the bondholder has the option to take repayment of principal in the amount of

$$(\$1000)/(\$1.50/\pounds) = \pounds 666\tfrac{2}{3}$$

in place of $1000. Thus we can value the conversion feature as the value of six FX options:

	Exercise Price	Time to Maturity	No. of £s
Option 1	$ 100	1 year	$66\tfrac{2}{3}$
Option 2	$ 100	2 years	$66\tfrac{2}{3}$
Option 3	$ 100	3 years	$66\tfrac{2}{3}$
Option 4	$ 100	4 years	$66\tfrac{2}{3}$
Option 5	$ 100	5 years	$66\tfrac{2}{3}$
Option 6	$1000	5 years	$666\tfrac{2}{3}$

The total value of the bond is thus the sum of an ordinary bond without the privilege to convert to pounds, plus the value of the six FX options. Notice that each of the options may be valued separately from the others, because the decision to exercise any one of the options does not affect the decision to exercise (or not exercise) any of the remaining options with a later maturity. On the other hand, since Options 5 and 6 have the same maturity—and since Option 5 will be exercised if and only if Option 6 is exercised—they could be considered as a single option. If Option 5 and Option 6 are combined this way, then the exercise price of the combined option is

$$\$100 + \$1000 = \$1100.$$

The number of £s on which the combined option is written would be

$$\pounds 66\tfrac{2}{3} + \pounds 666\tfrac{2}{3} = \pounds 733\tfrac{1}{3}.$$

The value of the combined option would have a value identical to the sum of the values of Option 5 and Option 6.

PRICING BONDS WITH OPTION FEATURES—NUMERICAL EXAMPLES

Up to this point we have practiced dividing up bonds into their ordinary cash flow features and their option features, but we have not yet formally priced any option features themselves. The following numerical examples will show how this is done. One example involves European FX options and the other involves European stock options. An explanation will be given on how to convert the FX European option formula into a formula for European stock options.

EXAMPLE 20.7

A British company offers five year $1000 bonds with an annual coupon rate of 8 percent. It also offers bondholders the option to take payment of coupons or the principal repayment in £s or dollars at a fixed exchange rate of $1.60/£. The current spot exchange rate is $1.55/£ and the forward rates for years one through five are $1.6275/£, $1.6926/£, $1.7434/£, $1.7782/£, and $1.7960/£. Over the past five years, the yearly average instantaneous standard deviation rate of the logarithm of the forward exchange rate (v) has been $v = .15$, and there is no reason to expect the next five years to be different. The term structure of dollar interest rates on pure discount securities is flat at nine percent per annum for years one through five. What is the fair value of each $1000 bond?

Each coupon and the principal repayment can be priced separately as a European FX option (compare Example 20.6). Coupon payments are either $80 or £50, and the principal repayment is either $1000 or £625. The pricing formula for a European FX option was given in equation (6.22) of Chapter 6. The pricing formula for a European call option on one unit of foreign exchange (here one British pound) uses as inputs X, $F(t,T)$, $B(t,T)$, T, and v. Applying this formula to the data in the present problem we obtain:

X	$F(t,T)$	$B(t,T)$	T	v	No. of £s	Value of call on 1 £	Total call value
$1.60	$1.6275/£	$1/(1.09)$	1	.15	50	$.1017	$ 5.09
$1.60	$1.6926/£	$1/(1.09)^2$	2	.15	50	$.1601	$ 8.01
$1.60	$1.7434/£	$1/(1.09)^3$	3	.15	50	$.1960	$ 9.80
$1.60	$1.7782/£	$1/(1.09)^4$	4	.15	50	$.2145	$ 10.73
$1.60	$1.7960/£	$1/(1.09)^5$	5	.15	675	$.2193	$148.03
Total option value							$181.66

The value of the options in the bond contract is $181.66. To this we must add the value of the ordinary cash flows. Discounting by the discount bond prices $B(t,T)$ given in the table above, we get that the present value of the coupons is

Year	1	2	3	4	5
Cash flow	$80	$80	$80	$80	$1080
Present value	$73.39	$67.33	$61.77	$56.67	$701.93
Total present value of cash flows: $961.08.					

Therefore the value of a $1000 8 percent coupon bond with the FX option features is

$961.08 + $181.66 = $1142.74.

Example 20.7 valued a bond with the coupon rate fixed at 8 percent. In practice, most companies would wish to choose a coupon so that the bond would sell at par at the time the bond is issued. In the previous example, this would require an adjustment of one or more of the contractural features of the bond. For example, the exercise price of the FX option could be changed, or the coupon rate could be changed. The following example shows how to adjust the coupon — leaving the other features unchanged — so that the fair value of the bond in Example 20.7 would be the par value of $1000.

EXAMPLE 20.8

In Example 20.7, what is the appropriate coupon rate such that the bond will sell at par? Let the unknown coupon payments by $Q. The present value of the cash flows on the bond is then

Year	1	2	3	4	5
Cash flow	$Q	$Q	$Q	$Q	$Q + $1000
Present value	$Q/(1.09)	$Q/(1.09)^2	$Q/(1.09)^3	$Q/(1.09)^4	($Q + $1000)/(1.09)^5

The value of the FX call options can be calculated as:

No. of £s	Value of call on 1 £	Total call value
£Q/1.6	$.1017	$.1017(Q/1.6)
£Q/1.6	$.1601	$.1601(Q/1.6)
£Q/1.6	$.1960	$.1960(Q/1.6)
£Q/1.6	$.2145	$.2145(Q/1.6)
£(Q + 1000)/1.6	$.2193	$.2193(Q + 1000)/1.6)

The value of the bond is the sum of the cash flow value and the value of the five call options. We want this total bond value to equal $1000, so that the bond will sell at par. Thus *we set the sum of the above amounts equal to $1000, and solve for the unknown Q.*

$$1000 = $Q[(1/1.09) + (1/1.09)^2 + (1/1.09)^3 + (1/1.09)^4 + (1/1.09)^5$$
$$+ $1000(1/1.09)^5] + ($Q/1.6)(.1017 + .1601 + .1960 + .2145 + .2193)$$
$$+ ($1000/1.6)(.2193)$$

Solving for Q, we obtain $Q = $47.90. Coupon payments of $47.90 correspond to a coupon rate of 4.79 percent. Hence the coupon on the bond should be lowered to 4.79

percent for the bond to sell at par. If this coupon seems too low, an alternative adjustment so that the bond is fairly priced at par is to change the exercise price of the option.

The final example will involve an option on stock. To convert the European
FX option-pricing formula given in equation (6.22) to a European stock option-
pricing formula, we need to change our interpretation slightly. The symbol $S(t)$
will now be used to denote the price of one share of stock in domestic currency
terms. For example, $S(t) = \$40/\text{share}$. If the stock is that of a foreign company,
then the foreign currency price will need to be converted to domestic currency
terms using the spot exchange rate. $B^*(t,T)$ will no longer represent the price of a
foreign bond. Rather, interpret $B^*(t,T)$ as the current price of a bond that pays $1
at maturity, and *whose average yield is the same as the average dividend yield on
the stock.* For example, if a \$40 stock pays an annual dividend of \$2, the dividend
yield is $\$2/\$40 = .05$. This corresponds to a value for $B^*(t,1)$ of

$$B^*(t,1) = 1/(1.05) = .95238.$$

The same annual dividend yield corresponds to a value for $B^*(t,2)$ of

$$B^*(t,2) = 1/(1.05)^2 = .90703.$$

And so on. The other variables are the same. X is the exercise price, v is the
average instantaneous standard deviation of log $F(t,T)$ [where

$$F(t,T) = S(t)B^*(t,T)/B(t,T),$$

as reinterpreted], and $B(t,T)$ is the market price of a discount bond that pays one
unit of domestic currency at maturity.

EXAMPLE 20.9

A Canadian company issues seven-year 6 percent annual coupon \$1000 bonds, the
principal of which is convertible into common stock of the parent company at maturity
at a fixed exchange rate of Can\$1.2007/\$. The conversion price per share is Can\$23$\frac{1}{8}$.
The current spot rate is \$.80/Can\$, and the current market price of the stock is Can\$18.
The current annual yield on discount dollar bonds is 8 percent for years one to seven.
No dividends are paid on the stock. What is the fair value of one of these bonds, if the
yearly standard deviation rate for the *U.S. dollar value of the shares* is $v = .25/\text{year}$?
(Note that the value of v calculated from changes in the U.S. dollar value of the stock
would be different from the value of v calculated from the Canadian dollar value of the
stock because the volatility in U.S. dollar terms includes the volatility of the Can\$/U.S.\$
exchange rate.)

The bond is convertible into

$$\$1000(\text{Can}\$1.2007/\$)/(\text{Can}\$23\tfrac{1}{8}) = 51.92 \text{ shares of stock.}$$

The current dollar value of 51.92 shares of stock is

$$S(t) = (51.92)(\text{Can}\$18)(\$.80/\text{Can}\$) = \$747.648.$$

The value for $B^*(t,T) = 1.00$, as the stock pays no dividends. The exercise price of the
option to buy 51.92 shares is $X = \$1000$, the face value of the bond. The maturity $T = 7$

years, while $v = .25$/year. Thus the price of a call is:

$c(t) = S(t)B^*(t,T)N(d1) - X B(t,T)N(d2)$
$= (\$747.648)(1.00)N(d1) - (\$1000)(1/(1.08)^7)N(d2)$.
$= (\$747.648)N(d1) - (\$583.49)N(d2)$.

Solving for $d1$ and $d2$, we get

$d1 = .70552$ and $d2 = .04408$.

Thus

$N(d1) = .75974$ and $N(d2) = .51759$.

Hence

$c(t) = (\$747.648)(.75974) - (\$583.49)(.51759)$
$= \$266.01$.

The value of the cash flows is

Year	1	2	3	4	5	6	7
Cash flow	$60	$60	$60	$60	$60	$60	$1070
Present value	$55.56	$51.44	$47.63	$44.10	$40.83	$37.81	$618.50

The total present value of the cash flows is $895.87. Thus the bond has a value of

$895.87 + $266.01 = $1161.88.

The bond is selling above par because the option is currently "in the money."

PROBLEMS FOR CHAPTER 20

1. PEMEX issues $1000 bonds, with the bondholder having the right to take repayment of principal at maturity either as a payment of $1000 *or* forty barrels of Maya crude *or* the dollar value (at market exchange rates) of sixty-five cases of Dos Equis. Then the option feature on these bonds can be described as [choose one]:
   a. Forty European call options, each on one barrel of Maya crude, each with a strike price of $25 a barrel;
   b. One European call option on sixty-five cases of Dos Equis, each with a strike price of $1000;
   c. Forty European call options, each on 1.625 cases of Dos Equis, each with a strike price of one barrel of crude;
   d. Sixty-five European call options, each on one case of Dos Equis, each with a strike price of $15.3846 a case;
   e. Forty European call options, each on the maximum of the value of one barrel of Maya crude or 1.625 cases of Dos Equis, each with a strike price of $25.

2. A Japanese company, Toshiba Corp., issued fifteen-year eurodollar bonds, each bond convertible into shares of common stock at ¥198 per share, at a fixed exchange rate of ¥226.45/$. That is, each $1000 (face value) bond was convertible into ($1000)(226.45/198) = 1143+ shares of stock. Explain how this conversion feature is an option whose value depends both on the yen value of the stock and the yen/dollar exchange rate. [*Hint:* As an example, do the following calculations. Suppose the market exchange rate were ¥245/$. What would the yen share price have to be for the

option to be "at the money" if the market price of the bond is $1000? For what range of share prices would the option then be "in the money"? Alternatively, suppose the share price were ¥270/share. What would the exchange rate have to be for the option to be "at the money" if the market price of the bond is $1000? For what range of exchange rates would the option then be "in the money"?]

3. Available are European call and put options on the British pound, each with a strike price of $1.20/£, and with a maturity of one year. Then if I wish to purchase the equivalent of the current dollar value of a one-year discount (zero-coupon) British pound bond, I can do so by [choose one]:
   a. buying the put, writing the call, and buying 1.2 dollar discount bonds;
   b. buying the call, writing the put, and buying 1.2 dollar discount bonds;
   c. buying the put, buying the call, and buying 1.2 dollar discount bonds;
   d. writing the put, writing the call, and issuing 1.2 dollar discount bonds;
   e. buying the put, writing the call, and buying 1.2 dollar discount bonds.

4. A one-year zero-coupon bond with a face value of $1000 is issued at a price of $97\frac{1}{2}$. Bondholders have the option of taking repayment of principal in the form of $1000 or £800. The yield-to-maturity on similar zeros without option features is 10 percent. Assuming the zero with the option is fairly priced at the time of issue, what is the fair value of a one-year European call option on one British pound with a strike price of $1.25/£?

5. A company is issuing a two-year $1000 eurobond with options to take payment of the annual coupons and principal in either of two currencies at a prefixed exchange rate. Zero-coupon bonds for one- and two-year maturity are yielding 10 percent and 11 percent, respectively. The value of the option on the first coupon is determined to be $5, while the value of the option on the second coupon and principal is determined to be worth $27. It is desired that the bond sell at par when issued. Given current market interest rates, at what value should the coupon on the bond be set?

6. A company issues dollar-denominated zero-coupon bonds at an interest rate of 11 percent, which corresponds to the current market rate on dollar instruments. The bonds mature in 360 days. At expiration, a bondholder may redeem each bond for either $1000 or SF 2500. The current spot rate is $.40/SF and the 360-day Swiss interest rate is 6 percent. If a potential bond buyer assumes a yearly standard deviation rate of .12 (for a 365-day year) for the logarithm of the $/SF forward exchange rate, what would be the value of each bond?

GLOSSARY

Agent Bank A bank appointed in a syndicated credit to oversee the loan.

AIBD (Association of International Bond Dealers) A private organization founded in Zurich, Switzerland, in April 1969 to establish uniform issuing and trading procedures in the international bond markets.

Allotment The number or amount of bonds in a new bond issue set aside by the lead manager for sale by a member of the issuing syndicate.

Announcement Day The day on which a new issue of bonds is publicly announced, with invitation telexes sent out to prospective underwriters and sellers.

Appreciation An increase in the market value of a currency with respect to a second currency or a real asset. The term is used in reference to a *market* price as opposed to an official price or par value.

Arbitrage The simultaneous purchase and sale or lending and borrowing of two assets or two groups of equivalent assets in order to profit from a price disparity.

Asked Price The price at which a marketmaker in an asset will sell the asset; the price sought by any prospective seller.

Assignment The transfer from one bank to another of the right to receive loan principal and interest from a borrower.

At the Money A term used to refer to a call option or a put option whose strike price is equal (or virtually equal) to the current price of the asset on which the option is written.

Backwardation A relationship in which spot or cash prices are higher than futures (or forward) prices.

Balance of Payments An accounting record of all officially recorded economic transactions between residents of one country and residents of other countries over a stated period of time. Sources of funds (such as exports, sales of assets, and foreign borrowing) are recorded with a plus sign, while uses of funds (such as imports, purchases of foreign assets, and foreign lending) are recorded with a minus sign. Transactions are recorded in the form of double-entry book-keeping so that plus and minus items always match (the total balance is zero). A positive or negative balance can only be obtained by restricting attention to a subset of total transactions (such as the current account, the capital account, or the reserves account).

Barter An exchange of goods or services directly between two parties without the use of financial instruments such as currency or credit.

Basis The cash or spot price minus the futures price.

Basis Point One-hundredth of a percentage point (.0001).

Bearer Bonds Bonds on which the coupon and

principal is payable to whoever has possession of the bond certificate.

Bid Price The price at which a marketmaker in an asset will buy the asset; the price sought by any prospective buyer.

BIS (Bank for International Settlements) An international bank located in Basel, Switzerland, which serves as a forum for monetary cooperation among the major central banks of Europe, the United States, and Japan. It monitors and collects data on international banking activity and serves as a clearing agent for the European Monetary System. The bank was originally founded in 1930 to handle the payment of German reparations after World War I.

Black Market Any private market that operates in contravention of government restrictions. For example, such a market may involve the exchange of currencies or goods at prices that are outside government-mandated levels, the trading of prohibited goods, or trading between individuals and/or institutions that are not approved by the government.

Bond A security issued by a corporation or official borrower which promises to pay a fixed terminal or redemption amount at maturity, and which usually also promises to pay fixed or variable amounts of interest at stated times prior to maturity.

Bought Deal A procedure for a new bond issue whereby the lead manager or managers buy the entire issue from the borrower on previously agreed fixed terms, including coupon level and issue price.

Bretton Woods Agreement Agreement signed by 44 nations at Bretton Woods, New Hampshire, in July 1944; basis of the post-World War II monetary system. Each participating nation declared a par value for its currency and agreed to intervene in foreign exchange markets to maintain the exchange rate with respect to the U.S. dollar within plus or minus 1 percent of the par value. The United States agreed to the obligation to convert dollars to gold at $35 per ounce.

Broker An individual who matches buy and sell orders in return for a commission. A broker, by contrast to a marketmaker, does not buy or sell for his or her own account and hence does not ordinarily risk the firm's capital in order to stand behind a price quotation.

Bulldog Bonds British pound sterling-denominated foreign bonds issued in London.

Call Option A contract giving the purchaser the right, but not the obligation, to buy an asset at a stated strike price on or before a stated date.

Capital Account Those items in the balance of payments showing net changes in the domestic private sector's holdings of foreign financial assets or in foreign holdings of domestic financial assets.

Capital Controls Governmental restrictions (such as prohibitions, taxes, quotas) on the acquisition of foreign assets or foreign liabilities by domestic citizens, or the acquisition of domestic assets or domestic liabilities by foreigners.

CBOE Chicago Board Options Exchange. An options exchange where European foreign currency options on spot exchange are traded.

Cedel One of two main clearing systems in the eurobond market. Cedel S.A. is based in Luxembourg and began operations in January 1971.

Certificates of Deposit (CDs) Negotiable instruments issued by a bank and payable to the bearer. CDs pay a stated amount of interest and mature on a stated date, but may be bought and sold daily in a secondary market.

CFTC (Commodities Futures Trading Commission) A U.S. regulatory body that regulates all exchange-based futures trading in the United States. Established by the Commodity Futures Trading Commission Act of 1974.

Clearing Corporation A clearing house that exists as an independent corporation rather than as a subdivision of an exchange.

Clearing House A department of an exchange or an independent corporation through which all trades must be confirmed, matched, and settled daily until offset.

Clearing Member A firm qualified to clear trades through a clearing house or clearing corporation.

Clearing System An institutional arrangement for transferring securities and payment between sellers and buyers subsequent to the establishment of a trading price.

CME (Chicago Mercantile Exchange) Futures exchange where foreign currency options on futures are traded.

Closing Day The day in which new bonds from the borrower are delivered against payment by members of a bond issuing syndicate.

Comanager A bank ranking just below that of lead manager in a syndicated eurocredit or an international bond issue. The status of comanager usually indicates a larger share in the loan or a larger bond allotment, and a larger share in the fees, than banks of lower rank. Comanagers may also assist the lead managers in assessing the market or deciding borrower terms.

Commercial Paper A short-term, unsecured debt instrument issued by a corporation and sold at a discount from its maturity value.

Commitment Fee A fee paid on the unused portion of a credit line.

Common Market See EEC.

Contango A relationship in which spot or cash prices are lower than futures (or forward) prices.

Convertibility Freedom to exchange a currency, under certain circumstances, without government restrictions or controls. "Current account" convertibility connotes the freedom to buy and sell foreign exchange in relation to trade in goods and services. "Capital account" convertibility connotes a similar freedom in relation to direct investment or trade in financial assets.

Coupon The periodic interest payment on a bond. Many bond certificates come with literally detachable coupons which must be removed and presented for payment usually annually or semiannually.

Coupon Yield The interest yield on a bond when calculated as the annual amount of money paid on coupons, divided by the face value of the bond.

Covenant Agreement in a syndicated loan or bond contract concerning the borrower's future conduct. Such a covenant may involve, for example, the agreement to maintain a given balance sheet ratio in the future, or the agreement to adhere to an IMF program.

Cross-default Term used to describe a clause in a syndicated loan or bond contract which gives the lender the right to accelerate repayment of the loan if the borrower defaults on another loan.

Cross-hedging The hedging of an asset with a futures contract of a different asset.

Cross Rate An exchange rate between two currencies neither of which is the U.S. dollar. A cross rate is usually constructed from the individual exchange rates of the two currencies with respect to the U.S. dollar.

Currency Swap A contractual obligation entered into by two parties to deliver a sum of money in one currency against a sum of money in another currency at stated intervals (or a stated interval) or according to stated circumstances. In the interbank FX market, see *Swap*.

Current Account Those items in the balance of payments involving imports and exports of goods and services as well as unilateral transfers (gifts).

Current Yield The interest yield on a bond when calculated as the annual amount of money paid on coupons, divided by the current market price of the bond.

Depreciation A decrease in the market value of a currency with respect to a second currency or a real asset. The term is used in reference to a *market* price as opposed to an official price or par value.

Delivery The offset of an obligation to buy or sell an asset by the actual transfer of title to the asset at a preagreed price. In the futures market, the transfer or receipt of a cash instrument against a short or long futures contract.

Delivery Month In the futures market, the calendar month during which delivery can be made or taken on a futures contract.

Delta Option Delta The ratio of a change in the option price to a small change in the price of the asset on which the option is written. The partial derivative of the option price with respect to the price of the underlying asset. Futures Delta is the ratio of a change in the futures price to a small change in the spot price.

Devaluation A decrease in the official value of a currency with respect to a second currency or a real asset. The term is used in reference to an *official* price, such as a fixed exchange rate or a declared par value, as opposed to a market price.

Disintermediation A process in which savers withdraw deposits from financial intermediaries (like commercial banks and thrift institutions) and lend directly to investors and consumers by purchasing debt instruments such as commercial paper, bonds, and Treasury bills.

Divergence Indicator System One aspect of the European Monetary System that measures the departure of a country's economic policies from the European Economic Community "average." The measure of divergence is based exclusively on the movement of a country's exchange rate with respect to the ECU, which represents the community average exchange rate. In the event of excessive divergence (see Chapter 2), the country is expected to alter economic policy to conform with the EEC average.

Dual Trader A floor broker on a futures exchange who trades for his or her own account in addition to executing customer orders.

ECU (European Currency Unit) A portfolio currency used in the European Monetary System as a community "average" exchange rate, and used in the private market as a means of payment and as a currency of denomination of lending, borrowing, and trade. Since September 1984 the ECU has been defined as the sum of .719 German marks, 1.31 French francs, .0878 British pounds, .256 Dutch guilders, 140 Italian lira, 3.71 Belgian francs, .14 Luxembourg francs, .219 Danish krone, .00871 Irish punts, and 1.15 Greek drachma.

Edge Corporations Specialized banking institutions, chartered by the Federal Reserve Board in the United States, which are allowed to engage in transactions that have a foreign or international character, and which are not subject to any restrictions on interstate banking. U.S. banks chartered outside New York, for example, may conduct foreign exchange trading in New York City through an edge corporation.

EEC (European Economic Community) An economic association of European countries founded by the Treaty of Rome in 1957. The goals of the EEC were the removal of trade barriers among member countries, the formation of a common commercial policy toward non-EEC countries, and the removal of barriers restricting competition and the free mobility of factors of production. Original members were West Germany, France, Belgium, Lexembourg, the Netherlands, and Italy. The United Kingdom, Ireland, and Denmark joined the EEC in 1973, and Greece was added in 1981. Spain and Portugal are scheduled to become members in 1986.

Elasticity The percentage change in an option price that results from a 1-percent change in the price of the asset on which the option is written.

Eurobank A bank which regularly accepts foreign-currency denominated deposits and makes foreign-currency loans.

Eurobonds Bonds that are issued simultaneously in the capital markets of several nations and which are issued outside the normal regulatory restrictions which apply to domestic issues in each of those capital markets.

Euroclear One of two main clearing systems in the eurobond market. Euroclear Clearance System Limited began operations in December 1968. It is located in Brussels and managed by Morgan Guaranty.

Eurocredits Intermediate-term loans of eurocurrencies made by banking syndicates to corporate and government borrowers.

Eurocurrency Market The money market for borrowing and lending currencies that are held in the form of deposits in banks located outside the countries in which those currencies are issued as legal tender.

Eurodollar A dollar-denominated deposit in a bank outside the United States or at International Banking Facilities (IBFs) in the United States.

Eurodollar Bonds Eurobonds denominated in U.S. dollars.

European Monetary System An exchange arrangement formed on March 13, 1979, that involves the currencies of EEC member countries. Included in the arrangement are a parity grid and a divergence indicator system.

Exchange Controls Governmental restrictions (such as prohibitions, taxes, quotas, or government-set prices) on the purchase of foreign currencies by domestic citizens or on the purchase of the local domestic currency by foreigners.

Exercise The use of the right given by an option: purchase (if a call) or sale (if a put) of an asset at the strike price stated in the option contract.

Exercise Price See *Strike Price.*

Expiration Date The last day on which an option may be exercised.

Face Value The monetary amount paid on a bond at redemption (excluding any terminal coupon payment). The face value is printed on the bond certificate.

Federal Funds Market Federal funds are deposits held by commercial banks at the Federal Reserve System. The federal funds market is the interbank market for borrowing and lending these deposits. Since reserve requirements of commercial banks are satisfied by federal funds, banks with deposits in excess of required reserves will lend the excess deposits to banks with a reserve shortage at a market-determined interest rate, the federal funds rate.

Federal Reserve System The central bank of the United States, created by the Federal Reserve Act of 1913, consisting of a board of governors in Washington, D.C., and twelve regional Federal Reserve banks. The Federal Reserve has monopoly control over the monetary base and has the power to set reserve requirements, to conduct open market operations, and to lend directly to commercial banks.

Floating Exchange Rate An exchange rate whose value is not constrained by central bank intervention to remain within a fixed range.

Floating Rate Notes Bonds that pay interest at an agreed margin above a market reference rate. The interest rate varies according to variations in the market reference rate.

Floor Broker In the futures market, an exchange member who executes orders on the floor of the exchange for the account of one or more clearing members and is licensed by the CFTC.

Floor Trader In the futures market, an exchange member who is qualified to trade on the exchange floor and who primarily trades for his or her own account or for accounts he or she controls.

Foreign Bonds Bonds issued by nonresidents in a country's domestic capital market. Such bonds are subject to domestic regulations and are underwritten primarily by banks registered in the country where the issue is made.

Foreign Exchange Market The market in which the currencies of different nations are bought and sold (in the form of bank deposits) with respect to each other. Most trading takes place with respect to the U.S. dollar.

(At a) Forward Discount Phrase used to describe a currency whose forward price is cheaper than its spot price.

Forward Exchange Foreign currency traded for settlement beyond two working or business days from today.

Forward Option A forward exchange contract (as opposed to an option contract) that differs from an ordinary forward contract only in that it has a variable, instead of a fixed, maturity date. The buyer of a forward option may, for example, be entitled to take delivery of a currency at any time during a given month, as opposed to a specific day.

(At a) Forward Premium Phrase used to describe a currency whose forward price is more expensive than its spot price.

Fundamental Forecasting Forecasting that is primarily based on processing information about ultimate supply and demand factors.

Fungible Securities Securities that are not individually designated by serial number as belonging to a particular owner. Instead, a clearing system or depository institution credits owners with a given number of a particular bond issue (or other security issue). The owner has title to, say, fifty bonds, but not to fifty specific bonds with designated serial numbers.

Future Rate Agreement (FRA) A forward contract for borrowing or lending at a stated interest rate over a stated time interval that begins at some time in the future.

Futures Commission Merchant (FCM) A firm that is registered with the CFTC and legally authorized to solicit or accept orders from the public for the purchase or sale of futures contracts. Acts as an intermediary between a public customer and a floor broker.

Futures Contract An obligation incurred pursuant to the rules of a futures exchange that results in daily cash flows that occur with changes in the futures price. If held until expiration, the futures contract may involve accepting (if long) or delivering (if short) the asset on which the futures price is based.

Gambler's Ruin Problem A problem in probability theory which shows that, for players with limited capital, the odds of winning or losing a repeated series of similar bets are different from the odds of winning or losing any one of the individual bets.

Gamma The ratio of a change in the option delta to a small change in the price of the asset on which the option is written. The second partial derivative of the option price with respect to the price of the underlying asset.

Global Bond A temporary debt certificate issued

by a eurobond borrower, representing the borrower's total indebtedness. The global bond will subsequently be replaced by the individual bearer bonds.

Gray Market A forward market for newly issued bonds that takes the form of forward contracting between market participants during the period between the announcement day of a new issue and the day final terms of the bond issue are signed. Bonds are traded at prices stated at a discount or premium to the (now unknown) issue price.

Hedging The process of reducing the variation in the value (from price fluctuations) of a total portfolio. Hedging is accomplished by adding to an original portfolio items such as spot assets or liabilities, forward contracts, futures contracts, or options contracts in such a way that the total variation of the new portfolio is smaller than that of the original portfolio.

High-powered Money See *Monetary Base.*

IBF (International Banking Facility) An IBF is a division of an existing U.S. banking operation that is allowed to conduct eurocurrency business but is (unlike a Caribbean eurobank branch) prohibited from issuing negotiable certificates of deposit. IBFs were allowed by the Federal Reserve Board beginning December 1981, and have since become popular with U.S.-based Japanese and Italian banks.

IBOR (Interbank Offered Rate) The rate at which banks will lend to other banks for a particular currency at a particular location. Examples include BIBOR, BRIBOR, DIBOR, HKIBOR, KIBOR, LIBOR, LUXIBOR, MIBOR, and SIBOR, defined in Chapter 12.

IBRD (International Bank for Reconstruction and Development) See *World Bank.*

IMF (International Monetary Fund) Organization founded at Bretton Woods in July 1944, and located in Washington, D.C., with the goal of overseeing exchange arrangements and lending foreign currency reserves to members. Members were pledged to eliminate exchange controls; they agreed not to alter the exchange values of their currencies without IMF approval, except once by an amount not greater than 10 percent; members could borrow reserves from the IMF, subject to conditions imposed by the IMF; the IMF obtained funds

to lend through member subscriptions usually paid 25 percent in gold and U.S. dollars and 75 percent in the member's own currency.

IMM (The International Money Market of the Chicago Mercantile Exchange) The IMM is the world's largest market for foreign currency and eurodollar futures trading.

Implied Forward Rate The rate of interest at which a borrowing or a lending transaction of a shorter maturity may be rolled over to yield an equivalent interest rate with a borrowing or a lending transaction of longer maturity.

Interest Parity An equilibrium condition under which a borrower (lender) is indifferent between borrowing (lending) in the domestic currency or in the foreign currency, taking into account the need to convert currency now through the spot market, with exchange risk covered by a reverse transaction through the forward market. A restatement of the interest parity condition yields the forward exchange rate as a function of the spot rate and the interest rates on the two currencies.

Interest Rate Swap A contractual obligation entered into by two parties to deliver a fixed sum of money against a variable sum of money at periodic intervals. Typically involves an exchange of payments on fixed and floating-rate debt. If the sums involved are in different currencies, the swap is simultaneously an interest rate swap and a currency swap.

International Bonds Collective term referring to both eurobonds and foreign bonds.

In the Money A term used to refer to a call option whose strike price is below, or to a put option whose strike price is above, the current price of the asset on which the option is written.

Initial Margin The minimum deposit a futures exchange requires from customers for each futures contract in which a customer has a net long or short position.

Interest Equalization Tax (IET) A measure proposed in July 1963 by U.S. President John Kennedy which levied a 15 percent tax on the purchase price of foreign bonds issued by European and Asian borrowers in New York. The tax was extended to certain bank loans in early 1964 and was repealed as of the beginning of 1974.

Issue Price The price, stated as a percentage of face value, at which a new eurobond is announced. It is used as a basis for calculating investment banking fees, but does not necessarily represent the actual price paid by any investor.

Lambda The ratio of a change in the option price to a small change in the option volatility. The partial derivative of the option price with respect to the option volatility.

Last Trading Day The final day on a futures or options exchange when trading may occur in a given futures contract month or in a given option series. Futures contracts that are still open at the end of the last trading day must be settled by making (if short) or taking (if long) delivery of the underlying asset (e.g., foreign currency futures), except for cash-settled contracts (e.g., eurodollar futures).

Lead Manager The commercial or investment bank with the primary responsibility for organizing a syndicated bank credit or bond issue. This includes the recruitment of additional lending or underwriting banks, the negotiation of terms with the borrower, and the assessment of market conditions.

Lending Margin The fixed percentage above the reference rate paid by a borrower in a rollover credit or on a floating rate note.

LIBOR (London Interbank Offered Rate) The rate at which banks in London will lend eurocurrencies in the interbank market.

LIFFE (The London International Financial Futures Exchange) A London exchange where foreign currency and eurodollar futures are traded as well as futures-style foreign currency options on spot exchange.

Limit Order An order given to an exchange, bank, or other agency to make a transaction at a given price or better. A purchase order is not to be executed above, and a sale order is not to be executed below, the stated price.

Listing The formal process required in order to have the price of a bond or other security regularly quoted on a stock exchange. Eurobonds are usually listed so that they can be purchased by those institutional investors who are constrained to invest in listed securities.

Lock-up Term used to refer to procedures following in a eurobond issue to prevent the sale of securities to U.S. investors during the period of initial distribution.

Long A term used to describe a position which involves an excess of foreign currency purchases over sales, an excess of foreign currency assets over liabilities, or an excess of purchases of a particular futures contract over sales of the same contract.

M1 A measure of the money supply that is composed of demand deposits at commercial banks and currency in circulation.

Maintenance Margin The minimum equity a futures exchange requires in a customer's account for each futures contract subsequent to deposit of the initial margin. If equity drops below the maintenance level, funds must be added to the account to bring the equity up to the initial level.

Management Fee The portion of total investment banking fees accruing to the managing banks in a bond issue. In a syndicated credit, the fee paid to the managing bank or banks for organizing the loan.

Margin The amount of money and/or securities that must be posted as a security bond to ensure performance on a contract. In the futures market, both short and long positions post margin. This ensures that the side with a daily cash flow loss will meet its payment obligation. See also *Initial Margin* and *Maintenance Margin.*

Mark to Market The revaluation of a futures contract or a security to reflect the most recently available market price.

Marketmaker An individual who quotes both buying and selling prices and who stands ready to commit the firm's capital in order to complete buying or selling transactions at the prices quoted.

Market Order An order that is to be executed immediately at the best available price in the market.

Marshall Plan The European Recovery Program proposed by U.S. Secretary of State George C. Marshall in June 1947. The program was intended to rebuild the economies of Europe in order to create political stability and to inhibit the spread of communism. Led to an accumulation of foreign exchange (U.S. dollar) reserves on the part of European countries. The absence of such reserves had been used as an excuse to prohibit free trading in foreign exchange throughout post-World War II Europe.

Martingale A price series forms a martingale with drift k if, conditional on today's information, the expected price for next period is equal to $1 + k$ times the current price.

Maturity Transformation Long-term lending financed by short-term borrowing in such a way that interest costs on borrowings will be updated to reflect market rates more frequently than will interest earnings from loans.

Maxidevaluation (Maxi) A large, unscheduled devaluation of a currency that normally follows a minidevaluation schedule.

Minidevaluation (Mini) A small devaluation of a currency that takes place at scheduled intervals. The amount of the devaluation may be equal to a fixed number or may vary according to a known set of indicators.

Monetary Base The amount of central bank liabilities that will potentially serve to satisfy the required reserves of the commercial banking system. In the United States, the monetary base consists of deposits at the Federal Reserve and currency in circulation.

Money Multiplier The number of units of the money supply (M1) that will be created by the banking system from one unit of the monetary base. The size of the money multiplier depends on reserve requirements and the public's portfolio choice among different depository assets.

Negative Pledge A contractual promise by a borrower in a syndicated loan or a bond issue not to undertake some future action. One typical negative pledge is that future new creditors will not be given rights which existing creditors do not have.

Novation The discharge of one obligation in a debtor/creditor relationship and the creation of an entirely new one.

OECD (Organization for Economic Cooperation and Development) Founded in 1961 as a successor organization to the Organization for European Economic Cooperation (OEEC). The OEEC had been set up in 1948 to administer Marshall Plan aid. The goals of the successor OECD were to stimulate world trade, economic growth, and economic development. Members included Austria, Belgium, Canada, Denmark, Finland, France, the Federal Republic of Germany (West Germany), Greece, Iceland, Ireland, Italy, Japan, Luxembourg, the Netherlands, Norway, Portugal, Spain, Sweden, Switzerland, Turkey, the United Kingdom, and the United States.

Offer Price See *Asked Price.*

Offering Circular A document giving a description of a new securities issue, as well as a description of the firm or entity making the issue.

Offering Day The day on which final terms of a bond issue are signed between the managing banks and the borrower.

OPEC Organization of the Petroleum Exporting Countries, a federation of country oil exporters formed in 1960 as a response to the unilateral reduction in posted oil prices by major oil companies the previous year. OPEC resolved to restore oil prices to previous levels and to unify petroleum policies for member countries. Founding members were Iran, Iraq, Kuwait, Saudia Arabia, and Venezuela. Subsequently admitted were Qatar (1961), Libya and Indonesia (1962), Abu Dhabi (1967), Algeria (1969), Nigeria (1971), Ecuador (1973), and Gabon (1975).

Open Interest The total number of futures contracts for a particular asset that have not been liquidated by an offsetting trade or that have not been fulfilled by delivery.

Open Market Operations Purchases or sales of securities or other assets by the central bank. Such actions change the monetary base. Usually the term is restricted to purchases and sales of domestic assets (such as government bonds), while purchases and sales of foreign exchange are called "foreign exchange intervention." Either activity changes the monetary base in a similar way.

Open Position A net long or short foreign currency or futures position whose value will change with a change in the foreign exchange rate or futures price.

Option An exchange-traded contract giving the purchaser the right, but not the obligation, to buy (call option) or to sell (put option) an asset at a stated price (strike or exercise price) on a stated date (European option) or at any time before a stated date (American option). Any nonexchange traded contract with similar economic characteristics to an exchange-traded option.

Options Clearing Corporation (OCC) A Delaware corporation that is owned equally by the Chicago Board Options Exchange, the American Stock Exchange, the Philadelphia Stock Exchange, the Pacific Stock Exchange, and the Midwest Stock Exchange. The OCC clears all options, including foreign currency options, traded at a U.S. securities exchange.

Overnight In the foreign exchange market, term used to describe a swap transaction for value today with the reverse transaction taking place the next business day. In the eurocurrency market, term used to describe a loan or deposit for value today with maturity on the next business day.

Out of the Money A term used to refer to a call option whose strike price is above, or to a put option whose strike price is below, the current price of the asset on which the option is written.

Parity Grid The system of fixed bilateral par values in the European Monetary System. The central banks of both countries whose currencies are involved in an exchange rate are supposed to intervene in the foreign exchange market to maintain market rates within a range defined by an upper and a lower band around the par value. The upper (lower) band is obtained by multiplying (dividing) the par value by 1.022753 except for par values involving the Italian lira, where the multiplier (divisor) is 1.061798.

Participation The act of taking part in a syndicated credit or a bond issue. In a syndicated credit, participation may involve membership in the original group of lending banks, or may involve lending later via a participation certificate. In a eurobond issue, a participation refers to the size of the underwriting commitment.

Participation Fees The portion of total fees in a syndicated credit that go to the participating banks.

Paying Agent One or a syndicate of banks responsible for paying the interest and principal of a bond issue to bondholders on behalf of the bond issuer.

PHLX (Philadelphia Stock Exchange) A securities exchange where American foreign currency options on spot exchange are traded.

Placement Memorandum A document in a syndicated eurocredit that sets out details of the proposed loan and that gives information about the borrower.

Point The last decimal place of a foreign currency price quotation.

Premarket See *Gray Market.*

Premium The price of an option agreed upon between the buyer and writer or their agents in a transaction on the floor of an exchange.

Prospectus See *Offering Circular.*

Purchasing Power (of a currency) The value of a currency expressed in terms of its exchange value against a basket of goods and services.

Purchasing Power Parity (PPP) The notion that in equilibrium the market exchange rate for any two currencies will exactly reflect the relative purchasing powers of the two currencies.

Put Option A contract giving the purchaser the right, but not the obligation, to sell a particular asset at a stated strike price on or before a stated date.

Rating A letter grade given to a bond by a rating agency (such as Moody's or Standard & Poor's) signifying the amount of credit risk on the bond.

Real Interest Rate The market interest rate as commonly quoted (nominal interest rate) minus the rate of inflation of the price level. The ex ante real rate is calculated by subtracting expected inflation, while the ex post real rate is calculated by subtracting actual inflation.

Redemption Discharge of a bond obligation by the issuer by payment of the bond's face value to the bondholder. Redemption may occur at bond maturity or earlier, under conditions stated in the bond contract.

Red Herring A preliminary prospectus (offering circular) giving the expected, but not final, details of a forthcoming securities offering.

Reference Banks The group of banks surveyed in order to determine a reference rate.

Reference Rate A market interest rate that is periodically monitored in connection with a rollover credit or a floating rate note in order to determine the subsequent interest payment by the borrower.

Registered Term used to refer to bonds which are recorded in the bond issuer's books in the name of the bondowner. Ownership of such bonds can only be transferred by a formal transfer of the ownership name in the issuer's books.

Rembrandt Bonds Dutch guilder-denominated foreign bonds issued in Amsterdam.

REPO (Repurchase Agreement) An agreement by one party to sell a security with an agreement to buy it back at a specified price on a specified date. The seller gets immediate cash, for the use of which he will in return pay the difference between the repurchase price and the sale price. If the buyer takes possession of the security in the meantime, a repo represents a form of secured lending from the buyer's standpoint, since if the seller defaults on the repurchase, the buyer still has the security.

Representations Statements made by a borrower in a syndicated credit or bond issue describing the borrower's current state of affairs, such as the borrower's financial condition.

Reserve Account Those items in the balance of payments measuring changes in the central bank's holdings of foreign assets (such as gold, convertible currencies, or SDRs).

Reserve Currency A foreign currency held by a central bank (or exchange authority) for the purposes of exchange intervention and the settlement of intergovernmental claims.

Reserve Requirements Obligations imposed on commercial banks to maintain a certain percentage of deposits with the central bank or in the form of central-bank liabilities.

Revolving Credit A line of bank credit that may be used or not used at the borrower's discretion. Interest is paid on the amount of credit actually in use, while a commitment fee is paid on the unused portion.

Risk-averse Term used to describe any decision-maker who would prefer a known amount of wealth to a fair bet (a bet with the same amount of wealth as its expected value).

Rollover Credit A bank loan whose interest rate is periodically updated to reflect market interest rates. The interest rate in the loan for each subperiod is specified as the sum of a reference rate and a lending margin.

Samurai Bonds Yen-denominated foreign bonds issued in Tokyo.

SDR (Special Drawing Right) An artificial reserve asset created and held on the books of the IMF. At the time of first issue on January 1, 1970, the SDR was defined as having a value equal to $\frac{1}{35}$ ounce of gold. The definition was altered in 1974 to specify the value in terms of a portfolio of sixteen currencies. Since 1981 the SDR has been defined as the sum of .54 U.S. dollars, plus .46 West German marks, plus .74 French francs, plus 34 Japanese yen, plus .071 British pounds.

Seasoned Securities Securities which have traded in the secondary market for more than ninety days.

SEC (Securities and Exchange Commission) A U.S. regulatory agency established in 1934 to regulate the issuing and trading of securities.

Secondary Market A market in which securities, such as bonds, are traded following the time of their original issue.

Selling Concession The share of total investment banking fees accruing to the selling group.

Selling Group All banks involved in selling or marketing a new issue of bonds. Sometimes the term is used in reference to dealers acting only as sellers, and is intended to exclude reference to underwriters or managers.

Selling Period A period following the signing of terms of a new bond issue during which bonds are bought and sold (in the form of price agreements) prior to actual payment for, and distribution of, the bonds themselves.

Settlement Day The day in which the actual transfer of two currencies, or the transfer of money for an asset, takes place at a previously arranged price.

Settlement Price The official daily closing price for any futures or option contract. This price is established and used by a clearing house or clearing corporation to determine each clearing firm's settlement variation.

Settlement Variation The sum of all changes in dollar (or local currency) amount for each of a firm's futures or options positions as calculated from each day's settlement price. This amount is paid to, or received from, the clearing house or clearing corporation each day based on the previous day's trading.

Shogun Bonds Foreign bonds issued in Tokyo and denominated in currencies other than the Japanese yen. The usual denomination is the U.S. dollar.

Short A term used to describe a position which involves an excess of foreign currency sales over purchases, an excess of foreign currency liabilities over assets, or an excess of sales of a particular futures contract over purchases of the same contract.

Smithsonian Agreement A revision to the Bretton Woods system that was signed at the

Smithsonian Institution in Washington, D.C., in December 1971. Included were a new set of par values, widened bands to plus or minus $2\frac{1}{4}\%$ around par, and an increase in the official value of gold to \$38/ounce.

Speculative Efficiency Hypothesis (SEH) The empirical proposition that forward or futures prices represent expected spot prices.

Speculator An individual or firm who attempts to anticipate price movements and attempts to profit from them by taking appropriate long or short positions on market-traded assets.

Spot Exchange Foreign currency traded for settlement generally two business or working days from the trade date.

Spot Month The futures contract month that is also the current calendar month.

Spot /Next In the foreign exchange market, term used to describe a swap transaction for value on the spot date with the reverse transaction taking place the next working day after the spot date. In the eurocurrency market, term used to describe a loan or deposit for value on the spot date with maturity on the next working day after the spot date.

Spread The difference between the buying and selling rates of a foreign currency or a bond, or the difference between borrowing and lending rates on eurocurrency deposits.

Stabilization The efforts by a lead manager in a bond issue to regulate the price at which bonds trade in the secondary market during the period while the bond syndicate is still in existence.

Sterilization Intervention in the foreign exchange market by a central bank where the change in the monetary base caused by the foreign exchange intervention is offset by open market operations involving domestic assets.

Straight Bonds Bonds with fixed coupon payments and without any option features (such as provisions for conversion into equity, other bonds, or other currencies).

Strike Price The price at which an option buyer may purchase (if a call option) or sell (if a put option) the asset upon which the option is written.

Subparticipation The partial assignment by one bank of the right to receive monetary sums from a borrower to another bank.

Subscription Agreement An agreement between a bond issuer and the managing banks which describes the terms and conditions of the issue and the obligation of the parties to the agreement.

Subscription Period The time period between the day on which a new bond issue is announced and the day on which the terms of the issue are signed and the bonds are formally offered for sale.

Sushi Bonds Dollar-denominated eurobonds issued by Japanese companies, which are managed by Japanese banks, and which are purchased primarily by Japanese investors. Such bonds were not subject to the Japanese Ministry of Finance prohibition of more than 10% foreign securities in the portfolios of life insurance companies.

Syndicate A group of banks that acts jointly, on a temporary basis, to loan money in a bank credit (syndicated credit) or to underwrite a new issue of bonds (bond issuing syndicate).

Swap In the interbank foreign exchange market, the simultaneous purchase and sale of identical amounts of a currency for different value dates. (The currency will be priced in terms of a second currency whose amounts will differ, depending on the relationship between the purchase price and the sale price of the first currency.) More generally, a swap is a contractual obligation entered into by two parties to deliver one sum of money against another sum of money at stated intervals. See also *Currency Swap* and *Interest Rate Swap.*

Technical Forecasting Forecasting that is primarily based on processing price information, as opposed to the ultimate supply and demand factors that lead to a price series.

Term Credit A bank loan which is made according to a time schedule. In the initial period, increasing portions of the total loan amount become available to the borrower. In the final period the loan is repaid at scheduled intervals.

Term Structure The level of interest rates on debt instruments of a particular type viewed as a function of term to maturity. The interest rate level may rise or fall with increasing maturity.

Theta The ratio of a change in the option price to a small change in the option term-to-maturity. The partial derivative of the option price with respect to the option term-to-maturity.

Tombstone Advertisement placed in a newspaper or magazine by banks in a syndicated credit to record their participation in the loan, or in a bond issue to record their role in managing, underwriting, or placing the bonds.

Tomorrow/Next In the foreign exchange market: term used to describe a swap transaction for value tomorrow with the reverse transaction taking place the next working day after tomorrow. In the eurocurrency market: term used to describe a loan or deposit for value tomorrow with maturity on the next working day after tomorrow.

Treasury Bills U.S. government debt instruments that are auctioned by the Federal Reserve, and which have a maturity of three, six, or twelve months. The bills are sold at a discount from their par or face value, and repay the face value at maturity. The return on the bills is determined solely by the difference between the purchase price and the face value. Three- and six-month bills are auctioned each Monday, and twelve-month bills are auctioned once every month.

Trustee An institution or group appointed in a bond issue to look after investor interests.

Underwriting Syndicate The banks, in a new bond issue, which agree to pay a minimum price to the borrower even if the bonds cannot be sold on the market at a higher price.

Underwriting Allowance The share of total investment banking fees accruing to the underwriting group.

Unilateral Transfers Items in the current account of the balance of payments which correspond to gifts to or from foreigners. A gift of military goods to a foreign country would, for example, be recorded under exports as a plus item, but there would be no corresponding minus item in the capital account as no payment was received in turn. Hence a special category, unilateral transfers, is created. The same gift of military goods would be recorded as a minus item under unilateral transfers.

Value Date In the foreign exchange market, same as settlement date.

Volatility The standard deviation of changes in the logarithm of an asset price, expressed at a yearly rate. The volatility is a variable which appears in option formulas. The units of this variable are such that the square of the volatility multiplied by the option term-to-maturity is a pure number (is unit-free).

Warrant An option issued by a company. A warrant differs from an exchange-traded option in that that exchange-traded options are issued typically by individuals and performance on an exchange-traded option contract is guaranteed by a clearing house or clearing corporation.

Withholding Tax A tax deducted at source, such as a deduction prior to the payment of coupon interest or dividends.

World Bank (International Bank for Reconstruction and Development) A creation of the Bretton Woods negotiations in July 1944, the bank began operations in June 1946. The original intent of the bank was to make postwar reconstruction loans, a role soon supplanted by the Marshall Plan. The bank consequently shifted its attention to development lending. Funds for lending are obtained from the paid-in capital subscriptions of member nations, from borrowings in the world's capital markets, and from net earnings.

Writer An individual who issues an option and consequently has the obligation to sell the asset (if the option is a call) or to buy the asset (if the option is a put) on which the option is written if the option buyer exercises the option.

Yankee Bond A dollar-denominated foreign bond issued in New York.

Yield Curve See *Term Structure.*

Yield to Maturity The rate of interest on a bond when calculated as that rate of interest which, if applied uniformly to future time periods, sets the discounted value of future bond coupon and principal payments equal to the current market price of the bond.

Zero-coupon Bond A bond which pays no interest but which is redeemed at its face value at maturity. Such bonds are sold at a discount from their face value, and the return to the bond depends solely on the relation between the purchase price and the face value.

SELECTED BIBLIOGRAPHY

Adler, Michael and Bernard Dumas, International Portfolio Choice and Corporation Finance: A Synthesis, *Journal of Finance,* 38 (June 1983), 925–984.

Adler, Michael and B. Lehmann, Deviations in PPP in the Long Run: A Random Walk?, Columbia University Working Paper, 1982.

Aliber, Robert Z., The Interest Parity Theorem: a Reinterpretation, *Journal of Political Economy,* 81 (November 1973), 1451–1459.

Anderson, Tim, Stop. You're Broking My Bonds, *Euromoney,* December 1982.

Andrews, Michael D., Recent Trends in the U.S. Foreign Exchange Market, *Quarterly Review,* Federal Reserve Bank of New York, Summer 1984.

Antl, Boris, ed., *Swap Financing Techniques,* Euromoney Publications, London, 1983.

Antl, Boris and Richard Ensor, ed., *The Management of Foreign Exchange Risk,* Euromoney Publications, London, 1982.

Bahmani-Oskooee, Mohsen and Satya P. Das, Transactions Costs and the Interest Parity Theorem, *Journal of Political Economy* 93 (August 1985), 793–799.

Bank of England, The London Gold Market, *Quarterly Bulletin,* March 1964.

Bank of England, Intervention Arrangements in the European Monetary System," *Quarterly Bulletin,* June 1979.

Bank of England, The Effects of Exchange Control Abolition on Capital Flows, *Quarterly Bulletin,* September 1981.

Bank for International Settlements, *Payments Systems in Eleven Developed Countries,* Bank Administration Institute, May 1985.

Bank for International Settlements, *Annual Report,* Basel, various years.

Barnett, Richard J., *The Alliance—American, Europe, Japan,* Simon and Schuster, New York, 1983.

Bilson, John F. O., The "Speculative Efficiency" Hypothesis, *Journal of Business,* 54 (July 1981), 435–451.

Black, Fischer and Myron Scholes, The Pricing of Options and Corporate Liabilities, *Journal of Political Economy,* 81 (May 1973), 637–659.

Board of Governors of the Federal Reserve System, Commodities Futures Trading Commission, Securities and Exchange Commission, *A Study of the Effects on the Economy of Trading in Futures [and] Options,* December 1984.

Bodner, David E., "The Major Foreign Exchange Markets," in William H. Baughn and Donald R. Mandich, *The International Banking Handbook,* Dow-Jones-Irwin, Homewood, Ill., 1983.

Bodurtha, Jr., James N. and Georges R. Courtadon, Empirical Tests of the Philadelphia Stock Exchange Foreign Currency Options Market, The Ohio State University, August 1984.

Brennen, Michael J. and Eduardo S. Schwartz, The Valuation of American Put Options, *Journal of Finance,* 32 (May 1977), 449–462.

Brown, Bowman, ed., *International Banking Centers,* Euromoney Publications, London, 1982.

Bunge, Frederica M., ed., *Japan: a Country Study,* 4th ed., U.S. Government Printing Office, Washington, D.C., 1983.

Chicago Mercantile Exchange, *Clearing House Manual,* mimeographed, 1985.

Coninx, Raymond G. F., *Foreign Exchange Dealer's Handbook,* Woodhead-Faulkner, Cambridge, 1982.

Cornell, Bradford and J. K. Dietrich, The Efficiency of the Market for Foreign Exchange Under Floating Exchange Rates, *Review of Economics and Statistics,* 60 (February 1978), 111–120.

Cornell, Bradford and Marc R. Reinganum, Forward and Futures Prices: Evidence from the Foreign Exchange Markets, *The Journal of Finance,* 36 (December 1981), 1035–1045.

Cox, J. C., J. E. Ingersoll, and S. A. Ross, The Relationship Between Forward and Futures Prices, *Journal of Financial Economics,* 9 (December 1981), 321–346.

Cox, J. C., Stephen A. Ross, and Mark Rubinstein, Option Pricing: A Simplified Approach, *Journal of Financial Economics,* 7 (September 1979), 229–263.

Culbertson, W. P., The Welfare Costs of Exchange Control Systems, *Southern Economic Journal* (April 1977).

Cumby, R. E. and M. Obstfeld, A Note on Exchange Rate Expectations and Nominal Interest Differentials: A Test of the Fisher Hypothesis, *Journal of Finance,* 36 (June 1981), 697–704.

Darby, M. R., Does Purchasing Power Parity Work?, *Proceedings of Fifth West Coast Academic/Federal Reserve Economic Research Seminar,* Federal Reserve Bank of San Francisco, 1982.

Deardorff, Alan V., One-Way Arbitrage and Its Implications for the Foreign Exchange Market, *Journal of Political Economy,* 87 (April 1979), 351–364.

Dooley, M. P. and P. Isard, Capital Controls, Political Risk, and Deviations from Interest Rate Parity, *Journal of Political Economy,* 88 (April 1980), 370–384.

Dornbusch, Rudiger, *Open Economy Macroeconomics,* Basic Books, New York, 1980a.

Dornbusch, Rudiger, Exchange Rate Economics: Where Do We Stand?, *Brookings Papers on Economic Activity,* 1980:I, 143–185.

Dornbusch, Rudiger, Exchange Rate Risk and the Macroeconomics of Exchange Rate Determination, *Research in International Business and Finance,* 3 (1983), 3–27.

Einsig, Paul, *The Theory of Forward Exchange,* Macmillian, London, 1937.

Einsig, Paul, *The Euro-dollar System,* 4th ed., Macmillan, New York, 1970.

Fama, E. and A. Farber, Money, Bonds, and Foreign Exchange, *American Economic Review,* 69 (September 1979), 639–649.

Federal Reserve, Intervention in Foreign Exchange Markets: A Summary of Ten Staff Studies, *Federal Reserve Bulletin,* November 1983.

Feller, William, *An Introduction to Probability Theory and Its Applications,* Vol. I, 3rd ed., John Wiley & Sons, New York, 1968.

Fisher, Frederick G. III, *International Bonds,* Euromoney Publications, London, 1981.

Fitzgerald, M. Desmond, *Financial Futures,* Euromoney Publications, London, 1983.

Frankel, Jeffrey A., The Dazzling Dollar, *Brookings Papers on Economic Activity,* I (1985), 199–217.

Frenkel, J. A. and R. M. Levich, Covered Interest Arbitrage: Unexploited Profits?, *Journal of Political Economy,* 83 (April 1975), 325–338.

Frenkel, J. A. and R. M. Levich, Transaction Costs and Interest Arbitrage: Tranquil Versus Turbulent Periods, *Journal of Political Economy,* 85 (November 1977), 1209–1226.

Friedman, Milton, The Case for Flexible Exchange Rates, *Essays in Positive Economics,* University of Chicago Press, Chicago, 1953.

Garman, Mark B. and Steven W. Kohlhagen, Foreign Currency Option Values, *Journal of International Money and Finance,* 2 (December 1983), 231–237.

George, Abraham and Ian Giddy, ed., *International Finance Handbook,* 2 vols, John Wiley & Sons, New York, 1983.

Geske, R. and H. Johnson, The American Put Valued Analytically, *Journal of Finance,* 39 (December 1984), 1511–1524.

Giddy, I. H., Measuring the World Foreign Exchange Market, *Columbia Journal of World Business,* Winter 1979.

Goodman, Stephen, Evaluating the Performance of the Technical Analysts, in Antl and Ensor, above.

Grabbe, J. Orlin, Liquidity Creation and Maturity Transformation in the Eurodollar Market, *Journal of Monetary Economics,* 9 (July 1982), 39–72.

Grabbe, J. Orlin, The Pricing of Call and Put Options on Foreign Exchange, *Journal of International Money and Finance,* 2 (December 1983), 239–253.

Grabbe, J. Orlin, The Pricing of First-Passage and Perpetual American Options, Department of Finance, The Wharton School, January 1985.

Green, Timothy, *The New World of Gold,* Walker and Company, New York, 1981.

Grossman, S. and J. Stiglitz, On the Impossibility of Informationally Efficient Markets, *American Economic Review,* 70 (June 1980), 393–408.

Guttentag, Jack M. and Richard J. Herring, Financial Innovations to Stimulate Credit Flows to Developing Countries, Wharton Program in International Banking and Finance, Working Paper, April 1985.

Guttentag, Jack M. and Richard J. Herring, The Current Crisis in International Lending, in *Studies in International Economics,* The Brookings Institute, January 1985.

Hansen, L. P. and R. J. Hodrick, Forward Exchange Rates as Optimal Predictors of Future Spot Rates: An Econometric Analysis, *Journal of Political Economy,* 88 (October 1980), 829–853.

Hansen, L. P. and R. J. Hodrick, Risk Averse Speculation in the Foreign Exchange Market: An Econometric Analysis, in J. Frenkel, ed., *Exchange Rates and International Macroeconomics,* University of Chicago Press, Chicago, 1983.

Herring, R. J. and R. C. Marston, The Forward Market and Interest Rates in the Eurocurrency and National Money Markets, in Carl H. Stein, John H. Makin, and Dennis E. Logue, eds., *Eurocurrencies and the International Monetary System,* American Enterprise Institute, Washington, 1976.

Hilley, J. R., C. R. Beidleman, and J. A. Greenleaf, Why There Is No Long Forward Market in Foreign Exchange, *Euromoney,* January 1981.

Hodrick, Robert J. and Sanjay Srivastava, An Investigation of Risk and Return in Forward Foreign Exchange, *Journal of International Money and Finance,* 3 (April 1984), 5–30.

Houthakker, Hendrik, The Breakdown of Bretton Woods, in Werner Sichel, ed., *Economic Advice and Executive Policy,* Praeger Special Studies, New York, 1978.

Huang, Roger D., Some Alternative Tests of Forward Exchange Rates as Predictors of Future Spot Rates, *Journal of International Money and Finance,* 3 (August 1984), 153–167.

Hudson, Nigel R. L., *Money and Exchange Dealing in International Banking,* John Wiley & Sons, New York, 1979.

International Monetary Fund, *Annual Report,* various issues.

International Monetary Fund, *World Economic Outlook,* various issues.

Isard, P., How Far Can We Push the Law of One Price?, *American Economic Review,* 67 (December 1977), 942–948.

Joint Economic Committee, *The European Monetary System,* U.S. Government Printing Office, Washington, D.C., 1979.

Kerr, Ian M., *A History of the Eurobond Market: The First 21 Years,* Euromoney Publications, London, 1984.

Keynes, John Maynard, *The Economic Consequences of the Peace,* 1919.

Keynes, John Maynard, *A Tract on Monetary Reform,* 1923.

Keynes, John Maynard, *General Theory of Employment, Interest, and Money,* Harcourt, Brace, and World, New York, 1936.

Korajczyk, Robert A., The Pricing of Forward Contracts for Foreign Exchange, *Journal of Political Economy,* 93 (April 1985), 346–368.

Kravis, I. B. and R. E. Lipsey, Price Behavior in the Light of Balance of Payments Theory, *Journal of International Economics,* 8 (May 1978), 193–246.

Krueger, A. O., Some Economic Costs of Exchange Controls: The Turkish Case, *Journal of Political Economy,* October 1966.

Kuberek, Robert C. and Norman G. Pefley, Hedging Corporate Debt with U.S. Treasury Bond Futures, *The Journal of Futures Markets,* 3 (1983), 345–353.

LeRoy, Stephen F. Expectations Models of Asset Prices: A Survey of Theory, *Journal of Finance,* 37 (March 1982), 185–217.

Lessard, Donald, Principles of International Portfolio Diversification, in George and Giddy.

Levich, Richard, Evaluating the Performance of the Forecasters, in Antl and Ensor.

Levy, M. D., Taxation and "Abnormal" International Capital Flows, *Journal of Political Economy,* 85 (1977), 635–646.

Arthur D. Little, Inc., *Report on the Payments System* to the Association of Reserve City Bankers, April 1982.

Longworth, D., Testing the Efficiency of the Canadian-U.S. Exchange Market Under the Assumption of No Risk Premium, *Journal of Finance,* 36 (March 1981), 43–49.

Maddala, G. S., *Econometrics,* McGraw-Hill, New York, 1977.

Mandelbrot, B., The Variation of Certain Speculative Prices, *Journal of Business,* 36 (October 1963), 394–419.

McCulloch, J. Huston, The Value of Options with Log-Stable Uncertainty, The Ohio State University, November 1984.

McFarland, James W., Richardson Pettit, and Sam K. Sung, The Distribution of Foreign Exchange Price Changes: Trading Day Effects and Risk Measurement, *Journal of Finance,* 37 (June 1982), 693–715.

McKinnon, Ronald I., *Money in International Exchange,* Oxford University Press, Oxford, 1979.

Meese, R. A. and K. Rogoff, Empirical Exchange Rate Models in the Seventies: Do They Fit Out of Sample?, *Journal of International Economics,* 14 (February 1983), 3–24.

Merton, Robert C., Theory of Rational Option Pricing, *Bell Journal of Economics and Management Science,* 4 (Spring 1973), 141–183.

Monnet, Jean, *Memoirs,* Doubleday, Garden City, New York, 1978.

Morgan Guaranty, *World Financial Markets,* various issues.

Mussa, M., Empirical Regularities in the Behavior of Exchange Rates and Theories of the Foreign Exchange Markets, *Carnegie-Rochester Conference Series on Public Policy,* 11 (Autumn 1979), 9–57.

Muth, John F., Rational Expectations and the Theory of Price Movements, *Econometrica,* 29 (July 1961), 315–335.

Neumann, Manfred J. M., Intervention in the Mark/Dollar Market: The Authorities' Reaction Function, *Journal of International Money and Finance,* 3 (August 1984), 223–240.

Parkinson, Michael, Option Pricing: The American Put, *Journal of Business,* 50 (January 1977), 21–36.

Protopapadakis, Aris and H. R. Stoll, Spot and Futures Prices and the Law of One Price, Federal Reserve Bank of Philadelphia Working Paper No. 82–4, April 1982.

Revey, P., Evolution and Growth of the U.S. Foreign Exchange Market, *Quarterly Review,* Federal Reserve Bank of New York, Autumn 1981.

Richardson, J. D., Some Empirical Evidence on Commodity Arbitrage and the Law of One Price, *Journal of International Economics,* 8 (May 1978), 341–352.

Riley, David H., "Foreign Exchange and International Money Broking," in William H. Baughn and Donald R. Mandich, eds., *The International Banking Handbook,* Dow-Jones-Irwin, Homewood, Ill., 1983.

Rogalski, R. J. and J. D. Vinso, Price Level Variations as Predictors of Flexible Exchange Rates, *Journal of International Business Studies,* 8 (Summer 1977), 71–81.

Roll, Richard, "Violations of Purchasing Power Parity and Their Implications for Efficient International Commodity Markets," in M. Sarnat and G. P. Szego, ed., *International Finance and Trade,* Vol. I, Ballinger Publishing Co., Cambridge, 1979.

Roll, Richard, A Simple Implicit Measure of the Effective Bid-Ask Spread in an Efficient Market, *Journal of Finance,* 39 (September 1984), 1127–1139.

Ross, Stephen A., Options and Efficiency, *Quarterly Journal of Economics,* 90 (February 1976), 75–89.

Sachs, Jeffrey D., The Dollar and the Policy Mix: 1985, *Brookings Papers on Economic Activity* I (1985), 117–185.

Samuelson, P. A., Proof That Properly Anticipated Prices Fluctuate Randomly, in *Collected Scientific Papers of Paul A. Samuelson,* Vol. 3, MIT Press, Cambridge, 1972, 782–790.

Schulze-Gaevernitz, Gerhard von, *Volkswirtschaftliche Studien aus Russland,* Duncker und Humblot, Leipzig, 1899.

Seidel, Andrew D. and Philip M. Ginsburg., *Commodities Trading: Foundations, Analysis, and Operations,* Prentice-Hall, Englewood Cliffs, N.J., 1983.

Sercu, P., A Generalization of the International Asset Pricing Model, *Revue de l'Association Française de Finance,* 1 (June 1980), 91–135.

Shapiro, Alan C., What Does Purchasing Power Parity Mean?, *Journal of International Money and Finance,* 2 (December 1983), 295–318.

Shastri, Kuldeep and Kishore Tandon, Valuation of American Options on Foreign Currency, Graduate School of Business Working Paper #579, University of Pittsburgh, February 1985.

Sheffrin, Steven M., *Rational Expectations,* Cambridge University Press, Cambridge, 1983.

Silber, William L., Marketmaker Behavior in an Auction Market: An Analysis of Scalpers in Futures Markets, *Journal of Finance,* 39 (September 1984), 937–953.

So, Yuk-Chow (Jacky), The Stable Paretian Distribution of Foreign Exchange Rate Movement, Nonstationarity and Martingale: An Empirical Analysis, Ph.D. dissertation, Ohio State University, 1982.

Solomon, Robert, *The International Monetary System, 1945–1981,* Harper & Row, New York, 1982.

Solnik, Bruno, *European Capital Markets: Toward a General Theory of International Investment,* Lexington Books, Lexington, Mass., 1973.

Solnik, Bruno, Why Not Diversify Internationally Rather than Domestically, *Financial Analysis Journal* 30 (July 1974), 48–54.

Stein, Jerome L., Mark Rzepczynski, and Robert Selvaggio, A Theoretical Explanation of the Empirical Studies of Futures Markets in Foreign Exchange and Financial Instruments, *Financial Review,* 18 (February 1983), 1–32.

Stigler, George, The Economics of Information, *Journal of Political Economy,* 68 (June 1961), 213–235.

Stulz, Rene, A Model of International Asset Pricing, *Journal of Financial Economics,* 9 (December 1981), 383–406.

Taylor, Dean, Official Intervention in the Foreign Exchange Market, or Bet Against the Central Bank, *Journal of Political Economy,* April 1982.

Tobin, James and William C. Brainard, Financial Intermediaries and the Effectiveness of Monetary Controls, *American Economic Review,* 53 (July 1963), 383–400.

Tousey, Mark J., Secondary Markets for Restructured Debt, Advanced Study Project, The Wharton School, April 1985.

Van Dormael, Armand, *Bretton Woods: Birth of a Monetary System,* Holmes & Meier, New York, 1978.

Walmsley, Julian, *The Foreign Exchange Handbook: A User's Guide,* John Wiley & Sons, New York, 1983.

Westerfield, Janice Moulton, An Examination of Foreign Exchange Risk Under Fixed and Floating Rate Regimes, *Journal of International Economics,* 7 (May 1977), 181–200.

Yeager, Leland, *International Monetary Relations: Theory, History, and Policy,* 2nd ed., Harper & Row, New York, 1976.

Uchino, Tatsuro, *Sengo Nihon keizaishi,* 1978. Translated by Mark A. Harbison as *Japan's Postwar Economy,* Kodansha International Ltd., Tokyo, 1983.

Wriston, Walter, The Information Standard, *Euromoney,* October 1984.

U.S., *Economic Report of the President,* various years.

INDEX